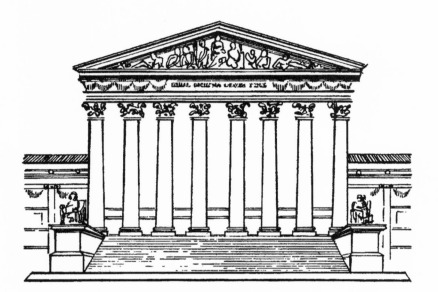

200

The

"Judges as persons, or courts as institutions, are entitled to
no greater immunity from criticism than other persons
or institutions . . . [J]udges must be kept mindful of their limitations and
of their ultimate public responsibility by a vigorous
stream of criticism expressed with candor however blunt."
—*Felix Frankfurter*

". . . while it is proper that people should find fault when
their judges fail, it is only reasonable that they should recognize the
difficulties. . . . Let them be severely brought to book,
when they go wrong, but by those who will take the trouble
to understand them."
—*Learned Hand*

THE LAW SCHOOL
THE UNIVERSITY OF CHICAGO

Supreme Court Review

EDITED BY
DENNIS J. HUTCHINSON
DAVID A. STRAUSS
AND GEOFFREY R. STONE

 THE UNIVERSITY OF CHICAGO PRESS
CHICAGO AND LONDON

INTERNATIONAL STANDARD BOOK NUMBER: 0-226-36250-7

LIBRARY OF CONGRESS CATALOG CARD NUMBER: 60-14353

THE UNIVERSITY OF CHICAGO PRESS, CHICAGO 60637

THE UNIVERSITY OF CHICAGO PRESS, LTD., LONDON

© 2002 BY THE UNIVERSITY OF CHICAGO, ALL RIGHTS RESERVED, PUBLISHED 2002

PRINTED IN THE UNITED STATES OF AMERICA

The paper used in this publication meets the minimum requirements of American National Standard for Information Sciences–Permanence of Paper for Printed Library Materials, ANSI Z39.48-1984. ∞

T O

B E R N A R D   D .   M E L T Z E R

Who has marshaled his strengths
in an unsparing search for excellence,
not just for himself, but also for others
and for the institutions he has inhabited

CONTENTS

CASS R. SUNSTEIN

REGULATING RISKS AFTER *ATA*

The last two decades have seen recurring conflicts between two strands in the law of risk regulation. The first strand, captured in what we might call "1970s environmentalism," places a high premium on immediate responses to evident hazards, rejects claims for quantification of likely benefits, and avoids or downplays consideration of cost. These tendencies play a role in prominent legislation[1] and also in the courts.[2] The second strand, captured in enthusiasm for what we might call "the cost-benefit state," urges a highly quantitative approach to risk control, based on careful specification of both costs and benefits, and on close attention to relevant trade-offs, including the risks sometimes introduced by regulation. These tendencies can be seen in prominent executive orders,[3] in legislation,[4] and in courts as well.[5]

Some of the most noteworthy conflicts between the two strands have involved efforts by courts to authorize agencies to make cost-benefit comparisons under statutes not explicitly calling for those comparisons.[6] Recent presidents and courts have gone so far as to

Cass R. Sunstein is Karl N. Llewellyn Distinguished Service Professor of Jurisprudence, University of Chicago, Law School and Department of Political Science.

AUTHOR'S NOTE: I am grateful to Richard A. Posner and Adrian Vermeule for helpful comments on a previous draft, and to Crista Leahy for valuable research assistance.

[1] See, for example, Clean Air Act, 42 USC § 7409(b) (1994), as interpreted in *Whitman v American Trucking Associations, Inc.*, 121 S Ct 903, 908–12 (2001).

[2] See *Lead Industries Association, Inc. v EPA*, 647 F2d 1130, 1148–56 (DC Cir 1980); *Ethyl Corp. v EPA*, 541 F2d 1, 11–33 (DC Cir 1976).

[3] See, for example, Exec Order No 12291, 3 CFR 127 (1981); Exec Order No 12498, 3 CFR 323 (1985); Exec Order No 12866, 3 CFR 638 (1993).

[4] See, for example, Safe Drinking Water Act, 42 USC § 300j et seq (1994).

[5] See *Corrosion Proof Fittings v EPA*, 947 F2d 1201, 1217 (5th Cir 1991).

[6] See *Michigan v EPA*, 213 F3d 663, 678–79 (DC Cir 2000) (per curiam).

create a series of cost-benefit default rules, allowing agencies to disregard trivial risks, requiring agencies to show significant benefits from regulation, allowing agencies to consider the substitute risks introduced by regulation, and authorizing agencies to take costs into account when statutes are not explicit on the point.[7]

Within the judiciary, the recent conflicts have pressed two questions in particular: When must agencies, including the Environmental Protection Agency (EPA), consider costs?[8] When, if ever, will Congress be required to legislate with particularity?[9] The latter question is not often thought to be especially interesting, because courts have not invoked the nondelegation doctrine to invalidate a federal statute since 1935.[10] But a number of commentators have suggested that it is past time to revive the doctrine, partly in order to ensure legislative attention to trade-offs rather than pleasant homilies.[11] And in the last decade or so, some courts, concerned about the grant of open-ended discretion to the executive, have shown an unmistakable interest in doing exactly that.[12]

Because it promised to help answer both of these questions, *Whitman v American Trucking Associations, Inc.*[13] was the most eagerly anticipated case in administrative law in many years. In some circles, a dramatic decision was anticipated, raising the possibility of significant new directions in the law of environmental protection and risk regulation. On the central issues, however, the Court's unanimous, steady, lawyerly, even formalistic opinion amounted to a return to the status quo—and to an understated but unmistakable rebuke to the court of appeals for the District

---

[7] See Cass R. Sunstein, *Cost-Benefit Default Principles*, 99 Mich L Rev 1651, 1654 (2001).

[8] See, for example, *National Resources Defense Council, Inc. v EPA*, 824 F2d 1146, 1154–66 (DC Cir 1987); *George Warren Corp. v EPA*, 159 F3d 616, 623–24 (DC Cir 1998).

[9] See, for example, *Michigan v EPA*, 213 F3d 663, 670–71 (DC Cir 2000) (per curiam).

[10] *Panama Refining Co. v Ryan*, 293 US 388, 432 (1935); *ALA Schechter Poultry Corp. v United States*, 295 US 495, 541–42 (1935).

[11] See David Schoenbrod, *Power Without Responsibility: How Congress Abuses the People Through Delegation* 155 (Yale, 1993); John Hart Ely, *Democracy and Distrust: A Theory of Judicial Review* 131–34 (Harvard, 1980).

[12] See *American Trucking Associations, Inc. v EPA*, 175 F3d 1027, 1034 (DC Cir 1999) (per curiam), reversed in part as *Whitman v American Trucking Associations, Inc.*, 121 S Ct 903 (2001); *International Union, UAW v OSHA*, 938 F2d 1310, 1316–21 (DC Cir 1991); *South Dakota v Department of Interior*, 69 F3d 878, 881–82 (8th Cir 1995); *Massieu v Reno*, 915 F Supp 681, 707–11 (D NJ 1996).

[13] 121 S Ct 903 (2001).

of Columbia Circuit. In its principal ruling, the Supreme Court reaffirmed long-settled law to the effect that in setting national ambient air quality standards, the EPA is not permitted to consider costs.[14] The Court also rejected a constitutional attack on the Clean Air Act, reestablishing long-settled law allowing Congress to delegate broad discretionary authority to regulatory agencies.[15] And through this return to the status quo, the current Court treated the court of appeals for the District of Columbia Circuit in the same way that the 1970s Supreme Court treated that court of appeals—attacking new judicial innovations and calling for at least a form of "hands off."[16]

The Supreme Court ruled quite broadly on both of the key issues in *ATA*, but it also reasoned in an extremely unambitious way, invoking statutory language and precedent while saying little about the meaning of the key statutory provisions and offering astonishingly little in the way of theoretical ground for its reluctance to invoke the nondelegation doctrine. If we consider the importance of the case, the opinion seems a bit of an anticlimax, potentially even a judicial return to 1970s environmentalism. We know that the relevant provisions of the Clean Air Act do not allow costs to be considered, but we know little about what those provisions actually mean. We know that the Court is not much interested in reviving the nondelegation doctrine, but we do not know why it lacks that interest.

In evaluating the Court's approach, I will argue that the Court reached an entirely sound result, and in the process disapproved of a court of appeals initiative that fully deserved disapproval. But at the same time, the Court's formalistic opinion was exceedingly unhelpful on the central questions, in a way that leaves open many issues for the future. In the end, it will not be possible to avoid some of the conflicts between 1970s environmentalism and the cost-benefit state, and I will suggest that the conflicts should generally be resolved in favor of the latter. In making that suggestion,

---

[14] For the initial part of the long settlement, see *Lead Industries*, 647 F2d at 1148–56.

[15] See, for example, *Touby v United States*, 500 US 160, 164–67 (1991).

[16] The leading case here is *Vermont Yankee Nuclear Power Corp. v National Resources Defense Council, Inc.*, 435 US 519, 558 (1978). See Antonin Scalia, *Vermont Yankee: The APA, the D.C. Circuit, and the Supreme Court*, 1978 Supreme Court Review 345, 359–75. Professor Scalia's general (not unqualified) approval of the Supreme Court's rejection of policy initiatives by the D.C. Circuit finds a kind of echo in his majority opinion in *ATA*.

I will argue on behalf of a large role, even after *ATA*, for the cost-benefit default principles, suggesting that they deserve a continuing place in the lower courts. I will also urge that serious nonconstitutional challenges to ambient air quality standards remain viable after *ATA*. The two standards in the case involve ozone and particulates; I will urge that the ozone standard is more vulnerable than the particulates standard, simply because, for low levels of ozone, the evidence of adverse public health effects is so much weaker.

Two particularly interesting sets of issues lie beneath the dry surface of the *ATA* opinion. The first involves the state of the nondelegation doctrine. To be sure, the Court has signaled its lack of enthusiasm for the doctrine—indeed, it has given its clearest signal yet on that point. At the same time, the Court's rejection of the approach of the court of appeals produces new questions about the nondelegation doctrine in some important domains of risk regulation, above all involving the Occupational Safety and Health Act (OSHA).[17] As we shall see, *ATA* raises anew a serious constitutional question about a key provision of OSHA.

The second and more pressing set of issues stems from the Court's remarkably thin and unhelpful discussion of the meaning of the Clean Air Act (CAA). The court of appeals' decision was prompted by evident uncertainty about what the key provisions actually asked the EPA to do, and the Supreme Court did precious little to resolve that uncertainty. As we shall see, the same concerns that led the court of appeals to invoke the nondelegation doctrine might well reemerge on remand in *ATA*—and in many other contexts involving risk regulation. Above all, the court of appeals sought to require the EPA to attempt to *quantify* the risks that it was seeking to control, so as to ensure that the agency was attacking large problems rather than small ones.[18] After *ATA*, this goal might be achieved through other, more modest routes, not involving the Constitution at all. While the *ATA* Court spoke largely in the terms of 1970s environmentalism, it did so in the context of an Article I challenge and a highly adventurous effort to inject cost considerations into an apparently cost-blind statutory provision. As I will urge, the decision should not be seen as an attack on more modest judicial innovations, nonconstitutional in

---

[17] 29 USC § 651 et seq (1994).

[18] See *American Trucking*, 175 F3d at 1039–40.

nature, that attempt to increase the sense and rationality of risk regulation.

In a period in which the Court is often criticized for allowing its own political convictions to overwhelm its duty of fidelity to the law, the quiet, lawyer-like analysis in *ATA* deserves respect, however many questions remain unresolved. In the process of exploring those questions, I investigate one of the most interesting features of *ATA:* the sharply conflicting approaches of the Court's two specialists in administrative law. Justice Scalia's opinion for the Court is lawyerly, formalistic, textualist, and apparently indifferent to the matter of consequences. Justice Breyer's concurring opinion is highly pragmatic, going well beyond the legal materials to try to make sense of the regulatory regime that Congress created. With respect to the law of risk regulation, I believe that Justice Breyer's opinion, an unambiguous rejection of 1970s environmentalism, is the harbinger of the future, and potentially the most important opinion in the case. Invoking Justice Breyer's concerns, I suggest that a number of challenges remain available to national ambient air quality standards—and that the most plausible of these challenges, connected directly with Justice Breyer's opinion, promise to increase the sense and rationality of national environmental policy.

This article comes in four parts. Part I describes the background. Part II discusses the Court's opinion and offers an evaluation. Part III briefly explores the three concurring opinions in the case, with particular reference to Justice Breyer's emphasis on recurring issues in risk regulation. Part IV discusses the future. I pay special attention here to the problems not resolved in *ATA*, including the place of cost-benefit default principles, the constitutional status of OSHA, and the possibility of nonconstitutional challenges to the EPA's particulates and ozone regulations, and indeed to ambient air quality regulations in general.

I. The Setting

To understand *ATA*, it is necessary to know something about what happened in the EPA and the court of appeals. For many years, the EPA had refused to issue a new national standard for particulates, notwithstanding scientific evidence apparently indicating grounds for action. Eventually the EPA was spurred to act by a decision of a district court, with an exceedingly rapid time-table for action.[19]

So spurred, the EPA issued a new standard for small particulates in 1997;[20] at the same time, the EPA issued a standard for ozone.[21] In both cases, the scientific issues are extremely complex, and reasonable people might well argue about whether the evidence adequately supported the EPA's decisions. But a general reading of the evidence suggests an important distinction, one that is relevant both to *ATA* and to the future of risk regulation. Under the EPA's own data, the particulates standard promises significant health gains, both in terms of mortalities averted and in terms of morbidity.[22] Thus, for example, the EPA estimates that the particulates standard would save over 300 lives annually and prevent 6,800 cases of chronic bronchitis. But EPA data suggest a much more mixed picture for ground-level ozone. (Some data on both proposed regulations are set forth in the appendix to this article.) The evidence is more mixed for two reasons. First, the mortality and health gains from the new standard appear much more modest; it is possible that the ozone standard would save no additional lives per year. Indeed, tighter regulation of particulates, going well beyond the EPA's rule, would appear to do a great deal more to protect health than would the new regulation of ozone. Second, the evidence for ozone is more mixed because ground-level ozone provides protection against cataracts and skin cancer.[23] To be sure, cataracts and skin cancer are not the most serious of health problems, in light of the very high cure rate for skin cancer. But if the protective effects are taken into account, it is not entirely clear that the new regulation of ozone will actually produce a big improvement in terms of health.

---

[19] See *American Lung Association v Browner*, 884 F Supp 345, 348–49 (D Ariz 1994).

[20] National Ambient Air Quality Standards for Particulate Matter, 62 Fed Reg 38652 (1997).

[21] National Ambient Air Quality Standards for Ozone, 62 Fed Reg 38856 (1997).

[22] The clearest evidence comes from United States EPA, Innovative Strategies & Economics Group, Office of Air Quality Planning and Standards, Regulatory Impact Analyses for the Particulate Matter and Ozone National Ambient Air Quality Standards and Proposed Regional Haze Rule 12–43 (1997). For an overview, see the appendix.

[23] See Randall Lutter and C. Wolz, *UV-B Screening by Tropospheric Ozone: Implications for the National Ambient Air Quality Standard*, 31 Envir Science & Tech 142A (1997); Randall Lutter and Howard Gruenspecht, *Assessing Benefits of Ground-Level Ozone: What Role for Science in Setting National Ambient Air Quality Standards?* (unpublished manuscript, 2001).

ture (but no reference to the legislative history), it held that standard setting must indeed be cost-blind.[38] The Court said that the key statutory term, "public health," requires an analysis of the effects of the pollutant, and that costs are irrelevant. At first glance, this does indeed seem correct: If a provision asked an agency to do what is "requisite" to protect the "public health," the more natural (though not inevitable) reading is that the agency is to concentrate on benefits, not on balancing benefits against costs. But the American Trucking Associations and their allies pressed some good questions from common sense: Can the EPA possibly issue national standards on the basis of an inquiry into public health only? If the costs of compliance are extremely high, won't the EPA inevitably impose more lenient regulations than it would if the costs are extremely low? Isn't it obviously worthwhile to achieve some small improvement in air quality, if the costs of compliance are (say) $500,000, and obviously less worthwhile to do so if the costs of compliance are (say) $10 billion? These questions seem especially powerful in light of the fact, acknowledged by the EPA, that there is no "safe threshold" for many pollutants, including those involved in *ATA* itself. If there is no safe threshold, a cost-blind analysis would seem to require the EPA to eliminate pollutants from the ambient air—a result that would ban automobiles, coal-fired power plants, and much more. Consideration of costs would appear necessary to avert this ludicrous conclusion. And the argument seemed to draw further strength from the apparent fact, urged by credible observers, that the EPA had in fact considered costs, although tacitly and without public supervision.[39]

In fact, it makes most sense to interpret the "requisite to protect the public health" language to require the EPA to make a showing of significant risk, a point that goes some (not all) of the way toward answering these objections.[40] If the remaining risks are trivial, additional regulation should not be seen as "requisite to protect the public health." But the Supreme Court's major answer to these points was simple: Tell it to Congress.[41] For the Court, the only

---

[38] *Whitman*, 121 S Ct at 911.

[39] See Marc K. Landy, Mark J. Roberts, and Stephen R. Thomas, *The Environmental Protection Agency: Asking the Wrong Questions* (1994).

[40] Justice Breyer emphasized this point. See *Whitman*, 121 S Ct at 923–24 (Breyer concurring in part and concurring in judgment).

[41] Id at 908–11 (Scalia).

real question was whether "public health" could be understood to be a reference not only to environmental effects, but also to the adverse effects introduced by regulation. Invoking the dictionary as its principal authority,[42] the Court suggested (not so helpfully) that the ordinary meaning of "public health" is "the health of the public," that this is the "most natural of readings," and that the natural reading is inconsistent with the claim that costs are relevant to the EPA's decision.[43]

To be sure, the cross-petitioners did not rely on policy arguments alone. They also urged (and the Court acknowledged, also with the dictionary's aid) that "public health" is a not an unambiguous phrase. In their view, "many more factors than air pollution affect public health," and "a very stringent standard might produce health losses sufficient to offset the health gains achieved in cleaning the air—for example, by closing down whole industries and thereby impoverishing the workers and consumers dependent upon those industries."[44] There is evidence to support this claim. Expensive regulation does appear to produce health risks.[45]

The Court did not reject the empirical claim, but it held that arguments of this kind could not defeat the more "natural" interpretation of the Act. Indeed, the Court analyzed the statutory structure to give further support to that interpretation. Unlike the apparently cost-blind provision governing national ambient air quality standards, other provisions of the Clean Air Act explicitly permitted cost to be taken into account. For example, a key provision of the Act asks the EPA to consider costs in selecting the "best system" for emissions reductions from new pollution sources.[46] The fact that some statutes expressly referred to cost seemed to support the view that the provision at issue in *ATA*, most naturally read as cost-blind, did in fact have this meaning. To this the Court added that Congress was "unquestionably aware" of the potentially adverse effects of expensive regulation, and hence

---

[42] Use of the dictionary has become a common textualist theme. See Note, *Looking It Up: Dictionaries and Statutory Interpretation*, 107 Harv L Rev 1437, 1438–40 (1995); William N. Eskridge, Jr., *The New Textualism*, 37 UCLA L Rev 621, 655 (1990).

[43] *Whitman*, 121 S Ct at 908–09.

[44] Id at 909.

[45] See Robert W. Hahn, Randall W. Lutter, and W. Kipp Viscusi, *Do Federal Regulations Reduce Mortality?* 12–22 (AEI-Brookings Joint Center for Regulatory Studies, 2000).

[46] 42 USC § 7411(a)(1) (1994).

allowed the EPA to waive the compliance deadline for stationary sources upon a showing, inter alia, that " 'the continued operation of such sources is essential . . . to the public health or welfare.' "[47]

All this was enough to suggest that the basic provision of the Act banned consideration of cost. Because that basic provision is "the engine that drives nearly all"[48] of the subsequent provisions of the Act, Congress would not lightly be taken to have required cost consideration in such subsequent provisions.[49] Congress "does not alter the fundamental details of a regulatory scheme in vague terms or ancillary provisions—it does not, one might say, hide elephants in mouseholes."[50] Hence the statute's terms "adequate margin" and "requisite" should not be taken to allow consideration of cost, because it is "implausible that Congress would give to the EPA through these modest words the power to determinate whether implementation costs should moderate national air quality standards."[51] To be sure, a number of provisions of the Act expressly require the EPA to generate information about compliance costs.[52] But in the Court's view, these provisions are designed to allow the EPA to assist the states in finding low-cost strategies for attainment.[53] They do not suggest that the EPA is allowed to consider costs on its own. All of these considerations converged on a single conclusion: Ambient standards must be based on considerations of health, and cost simply does not matter.

B. DELEGATION?

If the EPA's task is to assess public health alone, is the statute an unconstitutional delegation of power? Common sense might suggest that there is a serious problem here. The question of what level is "requisite to protect the public health" seems unaccompa-

---

[47] *Whitman*, 121 S Ct at 909, quoting the Clean Air Act Amendments of 1970, § 111(f)(1), 84 Stat 1683 (codified as amended at 42 USC § 7411 (1994)).

[48] Id.

[49] This is a considerable overstatement, to the point of inaccuracy. A number of provisions of the CAA are affected by the national ambient air quality standards, but most of the (countless) provisions are not affected by national standards.

[50] Id at 910.

[51] Id.

[52] 42 USC § 7408(b)(l) (1994); 42 USC § 7409(d)(2)(C)(iv) (1994).

[53] *Whitman*, 121 S Ct at 911.

nied by statutory standards. If there are no safe thresholds, perhaps the EPA could (or must) require some pollutants to be eliminated entirely from the ambient air. But even in the absence of safe thresholds, perhaps the EPA could decide that certain risks are to be treated as residual or ordinary—the stuff of everyday life. If the statute does not tell the agency what it must do, perhaps its range of discretion is unacceptable. Note in this regard that many people do not believe that certain imaginable steps are "requisite" to protect their own health: They walk at night in dangerous neighborhoods; they eat peanut butter; they fail to exercise; they gain weight; they drive cars, sometimes (believe it or not) above the speed limit; they use cell phones, sometimes while driving; they own large dogs. In all of these cases, the risks may well be nontrivial as a statistical matter, and perhaps the EPA could build on such practices in deciding what level of regulation is "requisite." But without statutory guidance, perhaps the Act gives the EPA excessive discretion—the discretion essentially to choose the level of risk regulation that it wants, with essentially no legislative guidance.

A statute requiring cost-benefit balancing might, on this line of reasoning, raise similar nondelegation issues, at least in the absence of legislative guidance on how to assess both costs and benefits. Without such guidance, is an agency permitted to say that a statistical life is worth $1 million? $10 million? $50 million? Can an agency discount lives saved in the future? By 1 percent? By 7 percent? If the statute allows agencies to value statistical lives as they choose, there might seem to be an unacceptably high level of discretion. Thus a constitutional attack on the "requisite to protect the public health" language would raise doubts about many other provisions, including those that give costs a role to play in regulatory choices.[54]

Troubled by the wide range of discretion apparently enjoyed by the EPA, the court of appeals held that the Constitution required the agency to come up with clear standards by which to explain why it would exercise its discretion to regulate to one "point" rather than another. But as a constitutional matter, the Supreme Court found the lower court's approach quite implausible. "In a

---

[54] For a discussion of costs in regulatory choices, see Sunstein, 98 Mich L Rev at 324–30 (cited in note 34); Sunstein, *The Arithmetic of Arsenic* (cited in note 34).

that phrase, as "requisite" is a function of cost, not merely benefit. A reasonable court might well be drawn to this interpretation, at least if it were seen as the only way of making sense, rather than nonsense, of the statute as a whole. Such an opinion would not have been beyond the pale.

Nor would this approach entirely lack precedential support. In the Benzene Case,[67] the Court interpreted the Occupational Safety and Health Act in a way that would ensure against regulatory absolutism—not by requiring cost-benefit balancing, but by saying, without textual support, that the agency could not regulate a risk not shown to be "significant." In dissent, Justice Marshall, sounding very much like Justice Scalia in *ATA*, contended that conventional legal tools could not justify imposing a "significant risk" requirement, which, in Justice Marshall's view, was a judicial fabrication.[68] In defending its conclusion, and its somewhat irreverent approach to the statutory text, the *Benzene* plurality emphasized that the government's approach "would give OSHA power to impose enormous costs that might produce, little, if any, discernible benefit."[69] It would not have been a gigantic stretch from this line of reasoning to a holding, in *ATA*, that the EPA should be permitted to consider whether an enormous outlay of expenditures can be justified by the benefits received. In any case, a number of lower court decisions have not stayed close to the statutory text where common sense seemed to require a measure of regulatory flexibility.[70]

Nonetheless, the path that the Court chose was unquestionably the easier one, because it fit so much more naturally with the statutory language. The Court was right to say that "requisite to protect the public health" is more naturally read to focus on benefits alone. To this I might add three further points. First, the pressure on the Court was greatly relieved by the fact that in the implementation process, costs could indeed be considered, and at multiple stages. This point sharply distinguished the CAA from OSHA,

---

[67] *Industrial Union Department, AFL-CIO v American Petroleum Institute*, 448 US 607 (1980).

[68] Id at 689–90 (Marshall dissenting).

[69] Id at 645 (plurality).

[70] See, for example, *Michigan v EPA*, 213 F3d 663, 678–79 (DC Cir 2000); *American Water Works v EPA*, 40 F3d 1266, 1271 (DC Cir 1994). Many such cases are discussed in Sunstein, 99 Mich L Rev 1651 (cited in note 7).

which lacks any comparable implementation stage.[71] If Justice Scalia's majority opinion in *ATA* is close to Justice Marshall's dissenting one in the Benzene Case, it might be partly because the consequences of a cost-blind approach to EPA standard setting are not quite what they seem—as Justice Scalia was undoubtedly aware. Second, the "requisite to protect the public health" language might well be regarded as imposing a significant-risk requirement. The Court said little on this issue, a gap to which I will turn in due course; but even on the Court's view, the CAA does not require the EPA to remove all risks, regardless of their magnitude. If a regulation leaves small risks, it can be argued, reasonably enough, that more stringent controls would not be "requisite." For this reason the EPA's position in *ATA* was far more cautious and modest than OSHA's more extreme position in the Benzene Case. Third, textualism might be regarded as a kind of "penalty default," imposing a burden on Congress, and on relevant interest groups, to provide a corrective for any problems introduced by a cost-blind approach. There is room for reasonable debate about whether Congress is sufficiently responsive to penalty defaults of this kind. But some comfort can come from the fact that a legislative corrective is certainly possible, and has in fact been provided in a somewhat analogous context.[72]

2. *Delegation.* On the nondelegation issue, the Court's opinion is also entirely plausible, indeed correct, but even less satisfying. At least at first glance, the Court appears to have delivered a death blow to those who have sought to revive the nondelegation doctrine. It appears to have delivered such a blow less by its holding than by its evident lack of interest in preserving much future space for the doctrine. Why, exactly, did the Court do this? The Court's opinion is quite wooden on the point. The Court said little about

---

[71] This is because the Clean Air Act requires states to produce implementation plans to bring about compliance with federal standards, whereas OSHA regulations are directly binding on the private sector.

[72] See 21 USC § 376(b)(5)(B) (1994) ("Delaney Clause"), as discussed in *Public Citizen v Young,* 831 F2d 1108, 1111–18 (DC Cir 1987). In 1996, Congress amended the Delaney Clause in various ways, softening its absolutist character by replacing the flat ban with a requirement of a "reasonable certainty of no harm," defined in the legislative history to reflect a policy of reducing cancer risks in the exposed population to no more than one in 1 million additional lifetime risk. 21 USC § 346a(b)(2)(A)(ii) (1994 & Supp 1999). For discussion, see Robert V. Percival et al, *Environmental Regulation: Law, Science, and Policy* 496–97 (3d ed 2000).

the nondelegation doctrine in principle—about what values it serves, about why courts should or should not be reluctant to invoke it. The Court's analysis consisted mostly of a lawyer-like (law clerk-like?) effort to show that the delegation in the CAA was no different from those delegations found acceptable in many other cases. This was an example of the dullest and the most unambitious form of analogical reasoning—the sort of thing recently associated with Chief Justice Rehnquist, or even former Chief Justice Burger, and very different from what usually emerges from Justice Scalia's pen.

Most strikingly, the Court made no effort to explain exactly why it was so willing to allow Congress to grant considerable discretionary authority to the EPA. Nor did the Court explain why it was uninterested in reviving the nondelegation doctrine in general. With respect to analogies, the Court basically skimmed the surface, arguing, plausibly if not entirely convincingly, that the delegation here was not evidently greater than the delegation in other cases. The Court offered exceedingly little in the way of detail. To be sure, the "requisite to protect the public health" language does not seem, in the abstract, to be as open-ended as other statutory language, such as the "public interest" standard in the Federal Communications Act. But recall here the central concern of the lower court in *ATA:* What limits does the Clean Air Act impose on the EPA's exercise of discretion? If this question turns out to be hard to answer, it would not be terribly difficult to distinguish most of the prior cases. The EPA, for example, is authorized to cover a much larger portion of the American economy than was involved in the precedents, and it would be at least plausible to say that its discretion was broader as well. To know whether this latter argument is convincing, it would be necessary to say much more about the meaning of the relevant provision of the Clean Air Act. But here the Court's efforts were thin to the point of being comical. The repetition of statutory terms—"requisite to protect the public health"—was not much aided by the Court's (repeated) explanation that these terms meant "not lower or higher" than necessary to protect the health of the public.[73]

We might say that with respect to the nondelegation doctrine,

---

[73] *Whitman*, 121 S Ct at 914.

the Court's opinion is remarkably shallow, in the sense that it lacks any theoretical ambition, but also remarkably wide, in the sense that it appears to dispose of a wide range of imaginable nondelegation challenges.[74] The Court has made it clear that the nondelegation doctrine will be used, if at all, only in the most extreme cases. But it has given little indication of why it is taking this approach. Is it possible to say what lies beneath the surface here?

Some clues come from Justice Scalia's separate writing on the topic.[75] Justice Scalia has objected to the nondelegation doctrine on the ground, not that it lacks constitutional roots, but that it is not subject to principled judicial enforcement. The line between permissible and prohibited delegations is inevitably one of degree: How much discretion is too much discretion? Judicial efforts to answer that question are not susceptible to rule-bound judgments, and hence particular rulings would inevitably have the appearance, and perhaps the reality, of judicial partisanship. In these circumstances a judicially enforced nondelegation doctrine might even be said to violate that very doctrine's aspiration to rule-bound law. A judge who aspires to reduce judicial discretion will inevitably be skeptical about the nondelegation doctrine.

I believe that these concerns help explain the Court's surface-skimming in *ATA*—and also that the concerns are well founded, in general and in the particular case. These institutional problems are best combined with a point about the nature of the regulatory state. There is no good evidence that a large-scale revival of the nondelegation doctrine would make constitutional government work better, from any point of view. In this light the case for reviving the doctrine seems weak indeed.[76] In fact, the purposes underlying the doctrine can better be achieved through other routes, including substantive reform, the hard look doctrine, and narrowly targeted "nondelegation canons."[77] In *ATA* itself, it is reasonable to think that the relevant provisions were not so open-ended as to run afoul of a sensible nondelegation doctrine. Indeed, it would

---

[74] For a discussion of shallowness/depth and narrowness/width, see Cass R. Sunstein, *One Case at a Time: Judicial Minimalism on the Supreme Court* 10–23, 244–58 (Harvard, 1999).

[75] See *Mistretta v United States*, 488 US 361, 413 (1989) (Scalia dissenting).

[76] See Sunstein, *Is the Clean Air Act Unconstitutional?* 225–27 (cited in note 34).

[77] See Cass R. Sunstein, *Nondelegation Canons*, 67 U Chi L Rev (2000).

be possible to say that those provisions are valid even if the doctrine should be used in the extreme cases.

But all this leaves a nagging question: What does the Act mean? Here the Court's answer is embarrassingly thin. The respondents urged that the statutory standard—"requisite to protect the public health"—could mean anything at all. To respond to their complaint, it would be necessary to explain how the standard creates ceilings and floors on agency action. I will return to the question in Part IV.

III. Fundamentalism, Semantics, and Pragmatism

ATA produced three separate opinions of considerable interest. Justice Thomas's concurring opinion is noteworthy because of his brief remarks on the nondelegation doctrine. Justice Stevens's far longer concurrence is noteworthy because of the caveat he seeks to add to the majority's view. Justice Breyer's opinion is the most important of all, because of its effort to make sense of the regulatory scheme, and because of its attempt to provide some guidance for the future of risk regulation.

A. FUNDAMENTALISM

Justice Thomas agreed that the CAA provided "no less an 'intelligible principle' than a host of other directives that we have approved."[78] But he objected that the parties had provided "barely a nod to the text of the Constitution," which does not speak of "'intelligible principles.'"[79] Instead, he urged, "it speaks in much simpler terms: 'All legislative powers herein granted shall be vested in a Congress.'"[80] In Justice Thomas's view, some statutes might contain "intelligible principles" but still involve a delegated decision whose significance "is simply too great . . . to be called anything other than 'legislative.'"[81] For this reason, Justice Thomas indicated his willingness "to address the question whether our delegation jurisprudence has strayed too far from our Founders' understanding of separation of powers."[82]

---

[78] *Whitman*, 121 S Ct at 919 (Thomas concurring).

[79] Id at 919–20.

[80] Id at 920.

[81] Id.

[82] Id.

At first glance, Justice Thomas's reasoning seems mysterious, perhaps even ridiculous. The requirement of an "intelligible principle" is many decades old.[83] It would be truly astonishing if the Court were to abandon the requirement as an understanding of the nondelegation principle. In any case, the idea that "all legislative power" is vested in a Congress is hardly self-interpreting; the question is what this provision means. It would even be possible to read the constitutional background to suggest that Congress can delegate such legislative power as it wishes. If this conclusion is overdrawn—as I believe that it is[84]—then the question becomes when some amount of executive discretion becomes "legislative" in nature. The requirement of an intelligible principle is simply a means of answering that question.

But underneath the implausible formalist veneer, Justice Thomas might well have a point. His key sentence is this: "I believe that there are cases in which the principle is intelligible and yet the significance of the delegated decision is simply too great for the decision to be called anything other than 'legislative.'"[85] Perhaps Justice Thomas is suggesting that an otherwise acceptable delegation would be objectionable if the area or context—the "significance"—suggested that an intelligible principle is not enough. So understood, Justice Thomas's view is fully consistent with the majority's suggestion "that the degree of agency discretion that is acceptable varies according to the scope of the power congressionally conferred."[86] On this view, the nondelegation doctrine is not entirely without life. Where an agency is given the power to regulate much of the American economy, the statutory principle must be more intelligible than it must otherwise be. All statutory principles must be intelligible, but some must be more intelligible than others. This is a perfectly reasonable suggestion.

B. SEMANTICS

In an opinion joined by Justice Souter, Justice Stevens urged that the Court should admit that agency rulemaking authority

---

[83] See *J. W. Hampton, Jr. & Co. v United States*, 276 US 394, 409 (1928).

[84] For a discussion, see Sunstein, *Is the Clean Air Act Unconstitutional?* at 335–39 (cited in note 34).

[85] *Whitman*, 121 S Ct at 920 (Thomas concurring).

[86] Id at 913 (Scalia).

His overall suggestion was that as construed, the statute would, at pertinent phases, allow consideration of costs after all, and that the EPA would be permitted to construe the statute reasonably, by making it less draconian than it appeared. To this end he offered four points, each of considerable interest:

1. As part of its cost-blindness, the statute was designed not to take pollution control technology as a given, but to force technological innovation. This was, and is, an entirely realistic hope.[93] In fact, the catalytic converter was developed as a result of a seemingly draconian statutory mandate. And because the statute was expressly designed to force technological innovation, regulatory efforts to calculate the costs of compliance were "both less important and more difficult"[94]—because the relevant calculations would be based on speculation about the cost of unknown future technologies. These calculations "can breed time-consuming and potentially unresolvable arguments about the accuracy and significance of cost estimates."[95] In these circumstances, cost-benefit analysis might itself fail cost-benefit analysis.

2. Even as interpreted by the Court, the Act allows cost and feasibility to be considered.[96] These factors are relevant, for example, to states deciding on the mix of control devices used to achieve compliance; and those facing economic hardship can seek an exemption from state requirements. The EPA is also permitted to consider costs, not in setting standards, but in setting deadlines for attainment. Congress is also available to extend deadlines if necessary.[97] In fact, noncompliance with national standards has been a persistent pattern under the Act, in part because compliance can be so costly. The relevant provision of the CAA might be cost-blind; but this is not at all true for the statute as a whole.

3. The EPA is not required to "eliminate every health risk, however slight, at any economic cost, however great."[98] Standards "'requisite to protect the public health'" need not produce "a world that is free of all risk—an impossible and undesirable objec-

---

[93] Id at 922.

[94] Id at 923.

[95] Id.

[96] Id.

[97] Id.

[98] Id.

tive."[99] In fact, the terms "requisite" and "public health" should be understood in their context. It is relevant for the EPA to consider "the public's ordinary tolerance of the particular health risk in the particular context at issue."[100] Hence the EPA is allowed to produce a kind of common law of "acceptable" risks, rather than eliminating all risks as such. In deciding what is "requisite to protect the public health," the EPA is allowed "to consider the severity of a pollutant's adverse health effects, the number of those likely to be affected, the distribution of the adverse effects, and the uncertainties surrounding each estimate."[101] On this count, Justice Breyer is saying something more cautious than, but something not terribly far from, what was said by the court of appeals. In his own way, Justice Breyer was urging the EPA to develop standards for separating acceptable from unacceptable risks.

4. The EPA is allowed to "consider whether a proposed rule promotes safety overall."[102] If a rule causes "more harm to health than it prevents," it is unlawful.[103] In this way Justice Breyer endorsed the lower court's conclusion that the EPA is required to consider the health benefits of ground-level ozone, not just the health risks.

What is most important about Justice Breyer's opinion is the effort not merely to read the statutory terms, but also to make sense out of them—to show that the statutory framework is not as silly, or absurd, as it might seem to be in the abstract. There is a noteworthy contrast here between Justice Scalia's approach, for the majority, and the approach favored by Justice Breyer.[104] And because it pays such attention to the pragmatic issues, Justice Breyer's opinion might well prove to be the more important for the future. Each of the four points just mentioned has significant

---

[99] Id at 923–24.

[100] Id at 924.

[101] Id.

[102] Id.

[103] Id.

[104] I will not discuss here the more general jurisprudential issues raised by formalism and pragmatism in statutory interpretation. A large issue is empirical—whether one or another approach can be defended on pragmatic grounds. If judges are undistinguished, formalism starts to look a lot better; hence the best defenses of formalism are pragmatic in character. For the best discussion of this point, see Adrian Vermeule, *Interpretive Choice*, 75 NYU L Rev 74 (2000); in the same spirit, see Cass R. Sunstein, *Must Formalism Be Defended Empirically?* 66 U Chi L Rev 636 (1999).

implications for EPA decisions and indeed for regulation more generally, as we shall shortly see.

IV. IMPLICATIONS — AND THE FUTURE

ATA leaves many issues open. For the future, the three crucial questions involve (*a*) the place of the cost-benefit default principles, which have played a large role in the last two decades of federal administrative law; (*b*) the status of the nondelegation doctrine; and (*c*) the legal standards governing ambient air quality standards, including the very standards involved in *ATA*.

A. COST-BENEFIT DEFAULT PRINCIPLES

The Court was well aware that a number of lower court decisions have established a new interpretive principle: Where statutes are ambiguous, agencies are allowed to consider costs.[105] What is the status of this principle after *ATA?* While things are not entirely clear, the best answer is that the principle is unaffected. In fact, Justice Breyer went out of his way to endorse the basic idea.[106] Justice Breyer was careful to say that courts "should read silences or ambiguities in the language of regulatory statutes" to permit consideration of "all of a proposed regulation's adverse effects," at least where those effects would "clearly threaten serious and disproportionate public harm."[107] For its part, the majority specifically referred to the cases establishing the principle and worked to distinguish them from the case at hand: "None of the sections of the CAA in which the District of Columbia Circuit has found authority for the EPA to consider costs shares [this provision's] prominence in the overall statutory scheme."[108] Thus the Court was at pains to cite, with apparent approval, the key cases creating the basic principle, and appeared to be saying that the EPA might well be permitted to consider costs if the statute did not expressly forbid it from doing so.

On the other hand, Justice Breyer was clearly concerned that

---

[105] See, for example, *Michigan v EPA*, 213 F3d 663, 678–79 (DC Cir 2000).

[106] *Whitman*, 121 S Ct at 921 (Breyer concurring in part and concurring in judgment).

[107] Id.

[108] Id at 910 n 1 (Scalia).

the Court's approach would override the cost-benefit default principle.[109] Remember his words: "[i]n order better to achieve regulatory goals . . . regulators must often take account of all of a proposed regulation's adverse effects, at least where those adverse effects clearly threaten serious and disproportionate public harm. Hence, I believe that, other things being equal, we should read silences or ambiguities in the language of regulatory statutes as permitting, not forbidding, this type of rational regulation."[110] This point was meant as a rejoinder to the majority, which Justice Breyer took to be saying that to allow costs to be considered, Congress was required to be "clear." But at first glance, Justice Breyer's concern seems baseless. The Court was saying only that in view of the clarity of the main provision of the Clean Air Act, judges would be reluctant to find permission to consider costs elsewhere, since Congress "does not alter the fundamental details of a regulatory scheme in vague terms or ancillary provisions—it does not, one might say, hide elephants in mouseholes."[111] This is a standard approach to statutory interpretation. It does not suggest that where a statute's "fundamental details" are vague, they will be interpreted to forbid consideration of cost.

But it would not be impossible to read the Court's opinion a bit more broadly. Recall that in concluding that the EPA need not consider costs in issuing national standards, the Court emphasized that some provisions of the CAA explicitly refer to costs, and explicitly require them to be taken into account. Here the Court was using the canon of construction "expressio unius est exclusio alterius": the expression of one thing is the exclusion of another. In the particular context of environmental statutes, the "expressio unius" canon could have explosive implications. When Congress does not explicitly refer to costs, agencies may not consider them, and for one simple reason: Congress often does explicitly refer to costs. If the canon is to govern the future, the cost-benefit default principles are in some trouble.

There is a further point. The Court seems to suggest that a statute should not be taken to confer broad discretionary authority on agencies: "[W]e find it implausible that Congress would give

---

[109] Id at 921 (Breyer concurring in part and concurring in judgment).

[110] Id.

[111] Id at 910 (Scalia).

to the EPA through these modest words the power to determine
whether implementation costs should moderate national air quality
standards."[112] To support the view that *ATA* is best taken to disal-
low agencies to interpret ambiguous statutes to allow consideration
of costs, it would be necessary to make a simple, two-step argument. First: Statutes should be construed so as to give agencies
less rather than more in the way of discretion. Second: A construction of a statute that would allow agencies to decide whether to
consider costs significantly increases agency discretion. Now the
claim here is not that a statute requiring cost-benefit analysis is
itself disfavored on delegation grounds. The claim is instead that
an interpretation should be disfavored if the consequence of the
interpretation would be to authorize the agency to decide whether
to engage in cost-benefit balancing. If this claim is accepted, then
the default rule in favor of allowing agencies to consider costs
stands as repudiated.

But it is most unlikely that the Court would accept these lines
of argument. The "expressio unius" canon can be a useful guide
to statutory construction, and the more natural, cost-blind reading
of "public health" is certainly supported by the fact that some provisions of the CAA make explicit reference to costs. But here as
elsewhere, the "expressio unius" idea should be taken with many
grains of salt. If Congress has not, in some ambiguous statutory
term, referred to costs, it will often be because Congress, as an
institution, has not self-consciously resolved the question whether
costs should be considered. The fact that Congress explicitly refers
to costs under other provisions is not a good indication that, under
an ambiguous text, costs are statutorily irrelevant. This would be
an extravagant and therefore implausible inference. The use of the
"expressio unius" approach in *ATA* is best taken as a sensible way
of fortifying the most natural interpretation, and not at all as a
way of urging that explicit references to cost, in some provisions,
mean that costs may not be considered under ambiguous provisions. And if Congress has not resolved the issue either way, the
agency is entitled, under standard principles of administrative law,
to consider costs if it chooses.[113]

What about concerns about agency discretion? Agencies are typ-

---

[112] Id.

[113] See *Chevron, USA, Inc. v National Resources Defense Council, Inc.*, 467 US 837 (1984).

ically allowed to interpret statutory ambiguities,[114] and in countless cases in which that principle is invoked, the agency exercises a great deal of discretion over basic issues of policy and principle.[115] To allow an agency to decide to consider costs is not to allow it to exercise more discretion than it does in numerous cases. Where the statute is unclear, agencies should be authorized to seek rational regulation; and nothing in *ATA* suggests otherwise. This is especially so in light of the fact, emphasized by both the Court[116] and Justice Breyer,[117] that the Clean Air Act allows the EPA to consider costs at numerous stages in the implementation process. I conclude that *ATA* is best taken not to question the cost-benefit default principle, and indeed that the most reasonable reading of the opinion is that the Court has explicitly embraced that principle.

B. NONDELEGATION AGAIN? NONDELEGATION EVER?

At first glance, the Court's nondelegation ruling seems to be a kind of return to the status quo—as an effort to place the doctrine where it has been since 1935: in the constitutional coffin. This is a reasonable reading of the opinion, with the proviso that the doctrine remains available, now as before, for the extreme cases. What makes a case extreme? Apparently an extreme case would be one in which the agency has far more discretion than does the EPA under the "requisite to protect the public health" language. Cases of that sort are, by the logic of the Court's opinion, very few and far between. *Schechter Poultry*[118] remains good law, and the Court was careful to say that when the area of agency authority is very broad, the statutory principle will certainly have to be intelligible. But the Court's basic message was that its own precedents suggest that almost all nondelegation challenges will be unavailing—and indeed that a mere repetition of any statutory standard will be a sufficient response.

---

[114] See id.

[115] See, for example, id at 855–56; *Babbitt v Sweet Home Chapter of Communities for Greater Oregon*, 515 US 687, 708 (1995); *Young v Community Nutrition Institute*, 476 US 974, 981 (1986).

[116] *Whitman*, 121 S Ct at 910–11.

[117] Id at 923 (Breyer concurring in part and concurring in judgment).

[118] *ALA Schechter Poultry Corp. v United States*, 295 US 495 (1935).

1. *An unusual line of cases.* In one sense, however, the Court's nondelegation ruling was no mere return to the status quo, and for a simple reason: It places some long-standing doctrine in disarray. In a series of cases, of which *ATA* was the culmination, the court of appeals for the District of Columbia circuit has held that a narrowing construction by an agency will be a sufficient and necessary condition for saving an otherwise objectionable delegation of authority.[119] The doctrine originated in a challenge to the statute granting the President the authority to fix prices and wages.[120] The relevant provisions appeared not to limit the President's discretion—to allow the President to set prices and wages however he chose. In upholding the statute against constitutional attack, the court said not only that Congress had set out an intelligible principle, but also that the executive was obliged to come up with "subsidiary" principles to cabin its own discretion.[121] This part of the Court's opinion owed its origins to some imaginative writing from Kenneth Culp Davis.[122] The requirement of "subsidiary" principles seemed important to the decision, but it need not be seen as indispensable to it. It would be possible to read the relevant statute, in its context, as sharply limiting executive discretion, and thus to uphold it without relying at all on the need for a narrowing construction by the agency.[123]

But the basic idea was significantly extended in an important case involving the Occupational Safety and Health Act.[124] The relevant provision authorized the agency to set standards "reasonably necessary or appropriate" to provide safe and healthful places of employment.[125] But what does this mean? Is this an open-ended

---

[119] *Amalgamated Meat Cutters v Connally*, 337 F Supp 737, 746–47 (D DC 1971); *International Union, UAW v OSHA*, 938 F2d 1310, 1318–21 (DC Cir 1991); *International Union, UAW v OSHA*, 37 F3d 665, 669 (DC Cir 1994).

[120] *Amalgamated Meat Cutters*, 337 F Supp 737 (D DC 1971).

[121] Id at 759.

[122] See Kenneth Culp Davis, *A New Approach to Delegation*, 36 U Chi L Rev 713, 725–30 (1969).

[123] In brief: The wage and price freeze was a response to the perception that the nation was in the midst of "cost-push" inflation. That was the statutory background. If that is what the statute was about, then the President could not play favorites, or reward his friends and punish his enemies. I say a bit more on this issue below. (See text accompanying notes 130–31.)

[124] *International Union*, 928 F2d at 1316–21.

[125] 29 USC § 652(8) (1994).

delegation of authority? Would it be sufficient to say that the statute told the agency to do no more, and no less, than was "reasonably necessary or appropriate"? The court of appeals did not think
that that would be sufficient. It was concerned that the statutory
terms could mean any number of things. They could mean, for
example, that OSHA should engage in cost-benefit analysis; perhaps a standard is not "reasonably necessary or appropriate" unless
the benefits justified the costs. Or they could mean that OSHA
was supposed to regulate all "significant risks" to a maximally protective point, subject perhaps to a constraint that the regulation
be "feasible" for industry.[126] Or they could mean something else.
Because of the statutory terms' apparent plasticity, the court was
obviously tempted to strike down the statute on nondelegation
grounds. But instead of doing so, the court remanded the case to
OSHA, concluding that the agency could save the statute with a
narrowing construction. On remand, the agency generated what
the court found—barely—to be a sufficient response.[127] According
to the agency, the statute required it to regulate only "significant
risks," and only to the point of "feasib[ility]," and within those
constraints the agency was required to select the standard that
would be most protective of workers.[128] The court said that this
was enough to satisfy the constitutional concern.

Notwithstanding the Supreme Court's ruling in *ATA*, the approach of the court of appeals is not impossible to understand. If
we are concerned about an absence of accountability, and also
about values associated with the rule of law, a narrowing construction at the agency level can be important. Such a construction can
expose the agency's standard to public oversight and review; it increases transparency and to that extent accountability. And by ensuring that agency action will be undertaken pursuant to a clear
standard, a narrow construction can go a long way toward alleviat-
ing the concern of arbitrary, unpredictable agency action, treating
the similarly situated differently. But we should be careful not to
say that the purposes of the nondelegation doctrine are the doctrine itself, or to dissociate the doctrine from Article I, its legal
source. At most, a narrowing construction can be helpful when the

---

[126] *International Union*, 37 F3d at 668.

[127] Id.

[128] Id.

Court is otherwise in equipoise. The nondelegation concern is not eliminated by such a construction.

This is basically the Court's response in *ATA*.[129] And it is evident that after *ATA*, the court of appeals' approach is entirely unacceptable. The Supreme Court has made clear that a narrowing interpretation by the agency cannot save an otherwise objectionable delegation. And in the end the Court's reasoning does seem to make sense. If the problem is that Congress has failed to lay down standards for agencies to follow, how can the agency's own standards resolve that problem? The question seems all the harder to answer in light of the fact that the source of the nondelegation doctrine is Article I, section 1, which vests legislative power in a "Congress of the United States." The purpose of the nondelegation doctrine, it would seem, is to require Congress to legislate. With respect to that requirement, agency narrowing is neither here nor there.

2. *The line revisited—and OSHA's fate.* How, then, should the now-rejected court of appeals decisions be understood? Might the Court have (inadvertently?) given a small boost to the nondelegation doctrine by suggesting that a narrowing construction cannot be helpful? These questions are not simple to answer.

The case of freezing wages and prices is the easier to handle. To be sure, Congress did not give clear standards in the text of the statute. But statutory terms receive meaning from context, and the context behind the Act suggested a desire to protect the nation from a certain kind of inflationary pressure, captured in the notion of "cost-push inflation," in accordance of which unions and employers create a kind of psychological spiral, one that needs to be broken through law.[130] To be sure, the statute itself did not refer to this theory, and perhaps a committed textualist would want to strike down the statute because of its open-ended terms. But it is clear, from context, that Congress did not seek to give the President the authority to freeze prices and wages in a way that involved political favoritism. If the statute should be interpreted so as to avoid the constitutional difficulty, it would not be an intolerable stretch to say that any executive action should be reviewed with

---

[129] See *Whitman*, 121 S Ct at 912.

[130] See Stephen G. Breyer and Richard B. Stewart, *Administrative Law and Regulatory Policy* 80–83 (Little, Brown, 2d ed 1985).

the particular context in mind—and hence that statutory purpose sharply limited presidential discretion. Perhaps it will be responded that Congress should be required to say all this clearly in the statutory text itself. But would much be gained by requiring this step? This is far from obvious. Thus the lower court's decision in the case of wage-price freezes probably remains good law, on the grounds that: (1) the statute should be construed so as to be constitutional rather than the opposite, and (2) the key provisions, read in their context, do not allow the President to play favorites, but on the contrary require him to act in accordance with the statutory purpose as understood in the context that motivated it. Note that the point here is not that courts are supplying, on their own, an intelligible principle to discipline agency discretion. Instead I am urging that the statute, taken in its context, supplies that principle.

The contested provision of OSHA is much harder. The phrase "reasonably necessary or appropriate" seems, on its face, to leave everything open. To be sure, the phrase might also appear similar to the standard that the Court found sufficient in *ATA*. But there is a big difference. In *ATA*, the Court held, immediately before upholding the statute against nondelegation attack, that the statute required a "health only" determination, and that it did not allow consideration of costs.[131] The *ATA* Court held the statute constitutional in part because (in its view) Congress was clear on this point; Congress itself decided that costs would not count, and hence the agency was not permitted to create the legal standard out of thin air. It seems to follow that if a statute itself requires consideration of costs, and hence a form of cost-benefit balancing, it would also be constitutional, notwithstanding the high levels of residual discretion that would remain. Indeed, no one seems to argue that there is a nondelegation problem with a statute that calls for cost-benefit balancing, even though significant discretion is left with the agency.

What makes the relevant provision of OSHA much harder is that it seems to give the agency discretion to decide whether the statute does or does not allow consideration of costs—and thus to decide what the statutory standard is. This was Chief Justice

---

[131] *Whitman*, 121 S Ct at 909–12.

Rehnquist's objection to another provision of OSHA[132]—an objection that was rejected on the ground that that provision could be authoritatively construed sharply to discipline the agency's discretion.[133] Nothing in *ATA*, in short, resolves the question whether a court should uphold a statute that leaves the agency the authority to construct its most fundamental meaning, by deciding, for example, whether the statute requires the agency to show that benefits justify costs, that a significant risk has been shown, or something else. It would therefore be possible to conclude that the "reasonably necessary or appropriate" language is too open-ended, because it allows the agency to decide, without any real limits, on the substance of the statute that it is implementing.

It is important to be careful with this point. As we have seen, lower courts have created an interpretive principle authorizing agencies to consider costs if they see fit, and *ATA* seems to approve of this principle. It would be implausible to suggest that a statute is unconstitutional if it allows an agency to decide whether or not to consider costs; this kind of decision has been found acceptable in many contexts, and *ATA* cannot be taken to say that the underlying statutes are now unconstitutional. After *ATA*, the appropriate answer to the constitutional question is this: Statutes that allow agencies to decide whether to consider costs admittedly confer considerable discretion. But after *ATA*, this is the furthest thing from fatal. The key provisions of the relevant statutes typically contain sufficient limits on agency discretion, and typically these provisions govern a small domain of the economy,[134] a relevant factor under *ATA*. Even if agencies are allowed to decide whether or not to consider costs, they do not, under those statutes, have anything like a blank check.

But OSHA's "reasonably necessary or appropriate" language seems quite different on these counts. OSHA's authority involves no small domain, and in the abstract, the "reasonably necessary or appropriate" language allows the agency to choose the statutory

---

[132] See *Industrial Union Department, AFL-CIO v American Petroleum Institute*, 448 US 607, 671 (1980) (Rehnquist concurring in judgment) (objecting on nondelegation grounds to 29 USC § 655(b)(5)).

[133] See id at 639–46 (Stevens) (plurality) (interpreting provision in a way that implicitly rejects the nondelegation challenge); see also *Whitman*, 121 S Ct at 912–13 (interpreting the Benzene Case as rejecting nondelegation challenge).

[134] See *Michigan v EPA*, 213 F3d 663, 675 (DC Cir 2000).

standard. The significance of *ATA* is that if this conclusion is to be avoided, it cannot be for the reason invoked by the court of appeals. It must be because the statute is best construed to cabin agency discretion to some degree. We know, for example, that the statute bars measures that are unreasonable, or inappropriate, as means of achieving safe workplaces. In this way the statute can be taken to require cost effectiveness, and also to require the agency to pursue the end of worker safety. But is this enough? The end of worker safety can be pursued in multiple ways. To be sure, the constitutional doubt would be removed, under *ATA*, if the statute were construed to require cost-benefit balancing.[135] We can easily imagine a judicial opinion that would so construe the statute; perhaps a step is "reasonably necessary or appropriate" if and only if it survives balancing, all things considered. But the court of appeals was probably right to say that this interpretation, while possible, is not ordained by the statutory text. And it is because the interpretation is not ordained that the court remanded the case to the EPA for an authoritative construction. The problem, after *ATA*, is that such a construction is, with respect to the nondelegation issue, neither here nor there.

In these circumstances, future courts have only three options. The first would be a version of the route taken in *ATA:* to point to other statutes giving agencies broad discretion (such as the "public interest, convenience, and necessity" standard of the Federal Communications Commission) and to urge that the disputed provision is not much different. The difficulty with this approach is that it would be somewhat irresponsible to invoke the analogies, without making some effort to show how the agency is not permitted to do whatever it chooses. The second option would be to generate an interpretation of the provision that adequately cabins agency discretion. This would certainly be possible, but the strategy in *ATA*—merely repeating the statutory language, with the added words "no less and no more"—would not be helpful. Certainly an interpretation that requires cost-benefit balancing would be adequate. The third option would be to strike down the statute on

---

[135] I have suggested above that a cost-benefit standard by itself leaves agencies a great deal of discretion, especially in the valuation of benefits. But under *ATA*, this degree of discretion, which is in fact quite standard, cannot possibly be taken to raise a serious constitutional problem.

nondelegation grounds. It is ironic but true that this route may have been made more rather than less likely as a result of the Supreme Court's rejection of the approach of the court of appeals.

Should the court take this step? In general, I think that the *ATA* Court was entirely correct to suggest that the nondelegation doctrine deserves little place in modern constitutional law. For this reason, some combination of the first and second routes would probably be best: an effort to construe the statute to impose some limitations, perhaps by calling for cost-benefit balancing, alongside a recognition that a great deal of discretion is constitutionally legitimate. But if the nondelegation doctrine deserves any place at all, the "reasonably necessary or appropriate" language, in context, would not be the worst imaginable place for judicial invalidation.

C. THE FUTURE OF NATIONAL STANDARDS (WITH SPECIAL REFERENCE TO PARTICULATES AND OZONE)

After *ATA*, a major question is how a plaintiff might be able to challenge a national standard, if costs cannot be considered and if the constitutional route is unavailable. With its unhelpful "not lower or higher" language, *ATA* offers only a little guidance here.[136] If the regulation is less stringent than is "requisite to protect the public health," with an "adequate margin of safety," it will be unlawful. If the regulation is more stringent than is "requisite," it will also be unlawful. In the easy cases, at least, the lessons are clear. A regulation will be subject to challenge, as insufficiently stringent, if it allows significant adverse health effects. If we accept the EPA's evidence (see Appendix, Table A1), it would therefore be reasonable to argue that the EPA was required, and not merely permitted, to produce a new and perhaps even more stringent regulation for particulates. A regulation will also be subject to challenge if significant adverse effects cannot be expected at levels that the EPA forbids. On a reasonable reading of the evidence governing ozone (see Appendix, Table A2), the new EPA regulation might be unlawful for that reason.

In the end I will urge that the particulates rule should probably be upheld, but that the ozone standard should probably be remanded, so that the EPA can give a better, more quantitative ex-

---

[136] *Whitman*, 121 S Ct at 914.

planation of why it chose the particular regulatory "points" that it selected. This judgment is tentative and highly dependent on the details. What is more important than the conclusion is an appreciation of the three possible ways in which any national ambient air quality standard, including the particulates and ozone standards, might be analyzed in court.

1. *A soft look.* The court might say that there is substantial scientific evidence to support the view that both pollutants produce significant adverse health effects at currently permitted levels—and hence the new controls are, in the administrator's reasonable judgment, "requisite to protect the public health." The statutory requirement of an "adequate margin of safety" might well be taken to support this view. As I have emphasized, the evidence supporting regulation of ozone seems a good deal weaker than the evidence supporting regulation of particulates, especially if we take into account the fact that ground-level ozone seems to have nontrivial health benefits. But perhaps a court should say that there is much scientific uncertainty here, and that the EPA should be allowed to resolve the doubts as it sees fit. If the court took this route, it would be following the direction established in the *Lead Industries* case, in which the EPA was given a great deal of room to maneuver.[137]

There are several advantages to this approach, especially if we consider the institutional role of the courts. A serious problem with intense judicial review of agency action is that it creates delay—and hence ensures a bias in favor of the status quo.[138] In light of the inevitable scientific uncertainties, it should be exceptionally easy for a skillful litigant to challenge a national standard as either too high or too low.[139] On the basis of the EPA's own data, an environmental group would have had a quite plausible argument that the regulation of particulates was insufficiently stringent under the statute.[140] In order to allow agencies room to maneuver in the face of scientific uncertainty, it would be reasonable to say that

---

[137] See *Lead Industries Association v EPA*, 647 F2d 1130, 1160–61 (DC Cir 1980).

[138] See Jerry L. Mashaw and David L. Harfst, *The Struggle for Auto Safety* 95–103, 245–47 (Harvard, 1990).

[139] See the discussion of arsenic in Sunstein, *The Arithmetic of Arsenic* (cited in note 34).

[140] This is because a more stringent standard would, on the EPA's own numbers, produce substantial health benefits. See Table A3 in the appendix.

on the basis of minimally plausible evidence, courts should simply uphold the relevant decisions. A special virtue of this approach is that the Bush Administration would be permitted to come to a different conclusion from the Clinton Administration, and vice-versa, because different judgments of value could lead to different conclusions about how to proceed in the face of ambiguous science.

2. *Evidentiary review.* A second possibility, hinted at above, would be to invalidate the ozone regulation while upholding the regulation of particulates. The simple claim here would be that on the evidence given, the new particulates standard was shown to be requisite to protect the public health—but the new ozone standard was not, especially if we take into account the health benefits of ground-level ozone.[141] We have seen the possibility that, all things considered, the regulation would increase rather than reduce health problems.

Justice Breyer's opinion rightly suggests that under the "requisite to protect the public health" language, the EPA is not supposed to remove all risks from the air, or to make the air "risk-free."[142] The EPA should take account of context to compare the risk at hand to risks that people face in ordinary life. The statistical risks from low levels of ozone do appear smaller than the statistical risks that people find acceptable in multiple domains (see Appendix, Table A2). Particulates are very different on this count. Here the existing hazards do seem high, on a plausible reading of the evidence. By upholding the particulates standard, and asking the EPA to explain itself more thoroughly with respect to ozone, the court would be contributing to the development of a kind of common law of acceptable risks, of the sort that Justice Breyer seemed to be encouraging.

The approach I am suggesting—upholding the particulates standard as requisite, while invalidating the ozone standard as not shown to be requisite—would certainly be reasonable. The principal objection would be institutional; it would involve the special

---

[141] I am not attempting here to reach definitive conclusions about the scientific data. I am simply suggesting how a reviewing court might reasonably respond to the data that the EPA has compiled.

[142] *Whitman*, 121 S Ct at 924 (Breyer concurring in part and concurring in judgment), quoting the Benzene Case, 448 US at 642.

limitations of judicial review. The evidence shows the possibility of nontrivial health gains from the ozone regulation, and in the face of scientific uncertainty, the agency should be permitted to make whatever (reasonable) policy choices it likes. Especially in view of the risk of status quo bias, perhaps the court should refuse to invalidate a judgment like that in the ozone case, even if the judgment seems wrong.

There is a further set of questions. Suppose that the new particulates standard should be, and is, upheld. At that stage, the EPA will have to decide what, exactly, to regulate, and to do this it will have to decide what fine particulates consist of. This is not a simple question. Currently the EPA is focusing on nitrogen oxides and sulfur oxides, but ignoring mobile sources, even though mobile sources appear to be emerging as the principal source of fine particulates. Ideally, the EPA should be able to create a trading system for the precursors for fine particulates, just as it has for ozone, and just as the Clinton Administration proposed for control of global warming.[143] But the EPA has refused to attempt this step, and for one simple reason: It does not know what the precursors are, or at least how they relate to one another. There are many complexities here. Ideally, an agency that is sensitive to the need for high benefits and low costs will try to design a system that promotes regulatory goals at the lowest possible expense. But in view of the technical complexities, it is not clear how much a court can do to require such an approach here.

3. *Requiring a clear standard.* A third possibility would be to invalidate both regulations as arbitrary or as inadequately justified, not because the risks are too low, but because the EPA did not explain on what grounds it chose these particular regulations, rather than regulations that would be somewhat more strict or somewhat more lenient. This would be the administrative law analogue of what the District of Columbia Circuit took to be a constitutional requirement in *ATA*.[144] The Supreme Court's holding that the nondelegation doctrine does not require this form of specificity says nothing about whether such specificity might be required as

---

[143] On the advantages of economic incentives and trading systems, see Cass R. Sunstein, *Risk and Reason*, chap 10 (forthcoming, Cambridge, 2002).

[144] See text accompanying notes 25–31.

a matter of administrative law. If the EPA cannot explain, in concrete terms, why it chose the particular levels it chose, how can courts know that the agency's decision was not arbitrary?

In doctrinal terms, judicial invalidation on these grounds might take one of two routes. First, the court might invoke the statutory language and say that it cannot know whether the particular level chosen is "requisite to protect the public health" unless it has a clear sense of why the EPA reached that conclusion. Without numbers and criteria, it is impossible to obtain any such sense. Second, the court might put the statutory language to one side and say that it cannot tell whether the agency's action is arbitrary or capricious, within the meaning of the Administrative Procedure Act,[145] unless the EPA has given a more detailed explanation of its choice. Either of these conclusions would be relatively conventional, and neither would mark a huge departure from current law.

But there would be a genuine innovation here. Thus far, courts have not required anything like a quantitative basis for health and safety regulation. Sometimes they have required agencies to show that the costs are not grossly disproportionate to the benefits;[146] sometimes they have prohibited agencies from acting when it seems as if there are not benefits at all.[147] But the relevant decisions have been more qualitative than quantitative, and when they have been quantitative, the overall judgment has seemed overwhelmingly clear.[148] It would be a significant step from these decisions to a holding that agencies must quantify the effects of pollutants at various levels, so as to explain, in specific terms, why one level was chosen rather than another.

Would the step be worthwhile? While I cannot discuss the issue in detail, I believe that it would be, at least for the ozone rule, where the evidence of harm is relatively thin. Such a ruling would not impose an unacceptable informational burden on the EPA. In fact, the EPA routinely gathers enough information to provide the necessary explanation. At the same time, such a requirement would provide a useful spur to the agency, one that would also produce

---

[145] 5 USC § 706 (1994).

[146] See *Corrosion Proof Fittings v EPA*, 947 F2d 1201, 1216–17 (5th Cir 1991).

[147] See *Chemical Manufacturers Association v EPA*, 217 F3d 861, 865–67 (DC Cir 2000).

[148] See *Corrosion Proof Fittings*, 947 F2d at 1222–23.

a higher degree of rationality and coherence. The result would be to show when, and why, environmental groups or industry would be able to mount a successful challenge to an ambient air quality standard.

In sum: On remand, the court should probably uphold the particulates standard, on the ground that on a reasonable view of the evidence, the agency had sufficient basis to conclude that that standard was "requisite to protect the public health," even without an attempt to quantify. At the same time, the court should probably remand the ozone rule, on the ground that the EPA has not given an adequate explanation of why that rule is "requisite." The court should encourage the EPA to be as quantitative as possible. And on remand, the EPA should take up the invitation, attempting in the process to give a clear sense, for the first time, of why it has chosen one regulatory "point" rather than another. But my principal goal has not been to urge any particular result, which will obviously turn on close engagement with the record. I have attempted instead to give a sense of the arguments that are available, post-*ATA*, and a general sense of the grounds on which one might choose among them.

V. Conclusion

The Court's principal rulings in *ATA* represented a return to the status quo—a rejection of some imaginative suggestions about how to read both the Clean Air Act and the Constitution. The Court established, quite correctly under existing law, that national standards should be set without regard to cost, and that the nondelegation doctrine has a small place in constitutional doctrine—or perhaps no place at all.

At the same time, the Court's unambitious opinion offered an almost comically vague interpretation of the key provisions of the Act—an interpretation that will greatly frustrate those who seek to know what, exactly, the EPA is supposed to do. Indeed, the Court left a large number of questions unresolved. There is some ambiguity in the opinion, but it is best taken not to question, but on the contrary to endorse, the cost-benefit default principles developed by lower courts. And while the Court showed no interest in the nondelegation doctrine, its rejection of the approach of the lower court now makes it impossible to invoke an agency's narrowing construction to support an otherwise objectionable delegation. For that reason, the nondelegation doctrine is not quite dead. I have attempted to show that the little life that remains in the nondelegation doctrine might support a plausible constitutional attack on a central provision of the Occupational Safety and Health Act.

ATA also leaves open a number of challenges to national ambient air quality standards, including the very standards at issue in the case. The principal challenges would involve the language of the relevant provision of the CAA ("requisite") and the arbitrary or capricious standard of the APA. On the basis of the evidence before the agency, it would make sense for a court to uphold the particulates standard as having been reasonably judged "requisite" while also invalidating the ozone standard as not shown to qualify as such. For the EPA itself, it would certainly make sense to move in the direction of greater quantification, in which national standards are issued only after an effort to specify the expected benefits, to compare them with the expected benefits of alternatives, and in that way to produce clear standards for choosing appropriate levels of ambient air quality. This is essentially an administrative task, not one for the courts. But it would be entirely appropriate for courts to spur regulatory agencies in this direction. Justice Breyer wrote only for himself, and his pragmatic, consequence-centered concurring opinion attracted no additional justices; but I believe that it will exert an enduring influence on the law of risk regulation. If so, the *ATA* decision will stand not only as a responsible resolution of the principal questions in the case, but also as a modest step toward a more sensible system of environmental protection.

APPENDIX

This appendix offers the EPA's own findings about the effects of its proposed particulates and arsenic regulations, and of alternative approaches. The tables are taken verbatim from Innovative Strategies and Economics Group, Regulatory Impact Analysis for Particulates and Ozone Regulations (1998).

TABLE A1

Particulates Standard National Annual Health Incidence Reductions

Endpoint	Partial Attainment Scenario
Annual PM$_{2.5}$ (g/m^3)	50
Daily PM$_{2.5}$ (g/m^3)	150
1. Mortality: short-term exposure	360
long-term exposure	340
2. Chronic bronchitis	6,800
Hospital admissions:	
3. All respiratory (all ages)	190
All resp. (ages 65+)	470
Pneumonia (ages 65+)	170
COPD (ages 65+)	140
4. Congestive heart failure	130
5. Ischemic heart disease	140
6. Acute bronchitis	1,100
7. Lower respiratory symptoms	10,400
8. Upper respiratory symptoms	5,300
Shortness of breath	18,300
Asthma attacks	8,800
9. Work loss days	106,000
10. Minor restricted activity days (MRADs)	879,000

TABLE A2

Ozone Standard

Endpoint	0.08 4th Max Low- to High-End Estimate
Ozone health:	
1. Mortality	0–80
Hospital admissions:	
2. All respiratory (all ages)	300–300
All resp. (ages 65+)	2,300–2,330
Pneumonia (ages 65+)	870–870
COPD (ages 65+)	260–260
Emer. dept. visits for asthma	130–130
3. Acute respiratory symptoms (any of 19)	29,840–29,840
Asthma attacks	60–60
MRADs	650–650
4. Mortality from air toxics	1–1
Ancillary PM health:	
1. Mortality: short-term exposure	0–80
long-term exposure	0–250
2. Chronic bronchitis	0–530

TABLE A2

CONTINUED

ENDPOINT	0.08 4TH MAX Low- TO HIGH-END ESTIMATE
Hospital admissions:	
3. All respiratory (all ages)	0–90
All resp. (ages 65+)	0–60
Pneumonia (ages 65+)	0–20
COPD (ages 65+)	0–20
4. Congestive heart failure	0–20
5. Ischemic heart disease	0–20
6. Acute bronchitis	0–400
7. Lower respiratory symptoms	0–4,670
8. Upper respiratory symptoms	0–430
Shortness of breath	0–1,220
Asthma attacks	0–5,510
9. Work loss days	0–50,440
10. Minor restricted activity days (MRADs)	0–420,300

TABLE A3

COMPARISON OF ANNUAL BENEFITS AND COSTS OF PM ALTERNATIVES IN 2010[a,b]

PM$_{2.5}$ ALTERNATIVE (g/m³)	ANNUAL BENEFITS OF PARTIAL ATTAINMENT[c] (BILLION $) (A)	ANNUAL COSTS OF PARTIAL ATTAINMENT (BILLION $) (B)	NET BENEFITS OF PARTIAL ATTAINMENT (BILLION $) (A–B)	NUMBER OF RESIDUAL NONATTAINMENT COUNTIES
16/65 (high-end estimate)	90	5.5	85	19
15/65 (low-end estimate) (high-end estimate)	19–104	8.6	10–95	30
15/50 (high-end estimate)	108	9.4	98	41

[a] All estimates are measured incremental to partial attainment of the current PM$_{10}$ standard (PM$_{10}$ 50/150, 1 expected exceedance per year).

[b] The results for 16/65 and 15/50 are only for the high-end assumptions range. The low-end estimates were not calculated for these alternatives.

[c] Partial attainment benefits based upon postcontrol air quality as defined in the control cost analysis.

TABLE A4

Comparison of Annual Benefits and Costs of Ozone Alternatives 2010[a,b] (1990$)

Ozone Alternative (ppm)	Annual Benefits of Partial Attainment[c] (billion $) (A)	Annual Costs of Partial Attainment (billion $) (B)	Net Benefits of Partial Attainment (billion $) (A–B)	Number of Residual Nonattainment Counties
0.08 5th Max (high-end estimate)	1.6	0.9	0.7	12
0.08 4th Max (low-end estimate) (high-end estimate)	0.4–2.1	1.1	(0.7)–1.0	17
0.08 3rd Max (high-end estimate)	2.9	1.4	1.5	27

[a] All estimates are measured incremental to partial attainment of the baseline current ozone standard (0.12 ppm, 1 expected exceedance per year).

[b] The results for .08, 5th and .08, 3rd max. are only for the high-end assumptions. The low-end estimates were not calculated for these alternatives.

[c] Partial attainment benefits based upon postcontrol air quality estimates as defined in the control cost analysis.

DAVID A. MARTIN

GRADUATED APPLICATION
OF CONSTITUTIONAL PROTECTIONS
FOR ALIENS: THE REAL MEANING
OF ZADVYDAS v DAVIS

May deportable aliens with criminal records be detained indefinitely when their countries of nationality refuse their return? A
narrow majority of the Supreme Court said no in *Zadvydas v
Davis*.[1] The decision rests importantly on observations about the
constitutional rights of such aliens, although the Court delivered
the final blow to extended detention in the name of statutory construction. The ruling strongly suggests important protection under
the Due Process Clause for what is, in the end, a narrow and distinctive class of persons facing a particularly harsh fate, even while
the Court indicates that not all aliens could claim such rights. But

David A. Martin is Henry L. and Grace Doherty Charitable Foundation Professor of
Law and F. Palmer Weber Research Professor of Civil Liberties and Human Rights, University of Virginia.

AUTHOR'S NOTE: I would like to express my appreciation for comments received from
and discussions with Alex Aleinikoff, Linda Bosniak, Brad Glassman, Amy Meyer, Hiroshi
Motomura, and Margaret Taylor, who approach these issues from many different directions,
all a bit different from my own, but whose questions and challenges have made this a better
paper. I also benefited considerably from the interchange during a faculty workshop at the
University of Virginia, and from the comments of many colleagues there. Thanks for able
research assistance go to Yvonne Lamoureux and Grace Hyun Im, and to the staff of the
reference desk of the University of Virginia Law Library. I should also note that I served
as General Counsel of the Immigration and Naturalization Service from 1995 until the
beginning of 1998, during which time the key legislation and regulations discussed here
were debated and enacted.

[1] 121 S Ct 2491 (2001).

the decision's subtle implications for other aliens' rights controversies, including some controversies sharpened by the September 11 terrorist attacks, may be even more significant.

I have two main objectives in this article. I want first to explore in detail just what the various justices in *Zadvydas* mean by their evaluations of aliens' rights in this specific detention context. Justice Breyer's opinion for the Court, in particular, seems deliberately obscure (or completely unconvincing) on why these aliens, ruled deportable in orders that had long since become final and were no longer contested, could claim constitutional protection when other aliens cannot. Developing a better justification for the majority's result brings us to wider insights that the Court should employ in other cases raising aliens' rights questions. Before we get to that point, however, this initial inquiry requires a rather lengthy review, in Part I, of the background of relevant constitutional rulings and the oft-changing immigration statutes and administrative practice against which the Court measured (or could have measured) the specific claims presented to it in *Zadvydas*. Part II begins to unpack the opinions and assess their impact, and I return in Part III, especially Sections D and E, to the task of filling in more of the rationale and making sense of the exact contours of the majority ruling.

My second objective, a more important one, occupies the remainder of the article. *Zadvydas* exemplifies a graduated categorical approach to noncitizens' rights that the Court has long taken, but without complete clarity about its dimensions. Certain categories of aliens enjoy a strong measure of constitutional protection, while others have reduced protection, and on some issues, it appears, no protection. Although some observers object to virtually any differentiation between citizens and noncitizens in the observance and enforcement of constitutional rights, some such differentiation corresponds to an appropriate understanding of the meaning of national community, as reflected in the Court's own jurisprudence and in long-standing practice. To be sure, it is a proud part of our constitutional tradition that aliens are emphatically included among constitutional rights holders for most purposes—that is, they are not wholly outside the bounds of membership in some form of community in which reciprocal obligations are owing. But that tradition need not mean, and has not meant, that the extent of protection is unaffected by considerations of status or level of membership. Though the Court often enforces such gradations, it has not been entirely revealing or convincing about the differences, and certainly has failed to make clear just what dividing lines count for various categorical distinctions. My second objective is to sketch more justifiable and better-anchored dividing lines.

Perhaps one important barrier to the development of usable gradations for constitutional purposes has been confusion caused by the complexities of immigration law. Those complexities surely exist, compounded by frequent amendment and the use of technical jargon, but they have been allowed to obscure certain consistent features—broad categorical continuities that have held stable since this country's immigration control framework matured in the 1920s. The description here is in part meant as a roadmap for the nonspecialist to those immigration categories, offered in the hope that it might at least help frame and focus future debates over aliens' rights, even for those readers who ultimately reach different conclusions about the precise significance we should accord these categorical differences for constitutional purposes.

The one categorical line that usually receives the most attention, in scholarly commentary and in court decisions (importantly including *Zadvydas*), is the division between excludable and deportable aliens, which I examine in Part I. But this line should be understood as holding far less significance than that between lawful permanent residents (LPRs), who are expressly invited by the polity to settle here and sink roots, and all other aliens present temporarily or illegally. For many purposes, I will argue, LPRs should enjoy constitutional protections on a par with citizens. I outline the reasons for this claim, which can help make better sense of much of the Court's doctrine on questions involving aliens and the Constitution.[2] But I do not maintain that that line tells the whole story. I therefore try, in Part IIIC, to sort out more systematically than the Court ever has five distinct categories of noncitizens that could and should be used in the future to establish greater clarity in distinguishing rights gradations among aliens. My claim is not that the categories are always determinative—that depends on the precise right at issue—nor that those in the lower-ranking categories deserve no protections. In fact, a Court that

---

[2] I focus here on due process questions, but I hope in later writings to elaborate on how this analytical approach can advance understanding of the nature of First Amendment and certain other constitutional protections for aliens as well.

candidly accepts this graduated framework and then carefully applies it might well enforce more protection under the Constitution, measured but real, for those on the lower rungs of the categorical ladder, who sometimes seem to be rightless under reigning understandings of the exclusion-deportation line. Finally, in Part IIIF, I illustrate the usefulness of such a graduated approach by applying it to a long-vexing due process issue that has become more urgent with the country's expanded battle against terrorism: the use of secret evidence in immigration proceedings.

I. The Statutory, Administrative, and Constitutional Framework for Detention of Aliens

The issues the Court confronted in *Zadvydas* arose from a change in the governing law in 1996, one of many restrictive provisions adopted that year in the Antiterrorism and Effective Death Penalty Act (AEDPA) and the Illegal Immigration Reform and Immigrant Responsibility Act (IIRIRA).[3] To appreciate those changes, and the constitutional context in which they occurred, it is useful to survey the rules governing detention as they existed before 1996, as well as the key court cases interpreting and applying them.

A. BACKGROUND

Indefinite detention is not part of the mission of the Immigration and Naturalization Service (INS) nor an objective of the immigration laws.[4] Even if a person is detained throughout his re-

---

[3] Antiterrorism and Effective Death Penalty Act of 1996 (AEDPA), Pub L No 104-132, 110 Stat 1214; Illegal Immigration Reform and Immigrant Responsibility Act of 1996 (IIRIRA), Pub L No 104-208, Div C, 110 Stat 3009-546. See generally Margaret H. Taylor, *The 1996 Immigration Act: Detention and Related Issues*, 74 Interpreter Releases 209 (1997).

[4] The special detention measure for aliens certified by the Attorney General as dangerous to national security, enacted as part of the USA PATRIOT Act of 2001, is not necessarily an exception to this statement. Uniting and Strengthening America by Providing Appropriate Tools Required to Intercept and Obstruct Terrorism Act of 2001, § 412, Pub L No 107-56, 115 Stat 272, adding a new § 236A to the Immigration and Nationality Act (INA). Although the text lends itself to a broader reading, the Department of Justice has indicated that the new power is meant to provide for assured detention only during immigration proceedings. It will apparently result in extended detention thereafter only if the country of nationality refuses return or if the Convention Against Torture forbids return. For example, in response to a question about this section during a hearing before the Senate Committee on the Judiciary, Sept 25, 2001, Secretary Ashcroft commented: "During the pendancy [*sic*] of adjudication of being deported on other grounds, that person can be held in custody

moval proceedings in immigration court—a detention practice solidly approved in the case law, at least when release requests are adjudged on a case-by-case basis[5]—that detention has a finite end point. Should he prevail in his defense, immigration detention will end. If the government prevails, once all appeals are over the removal order will be enforceable, and the government has every incentive to execute it promptly. Detention is expensive, running from $50 to $200 a day per detainee, and INS district directors are sensitive to the limits on their detention budgets, even with the major increases in funding that INS has received over the last decade. The vast majority of INS detainees are deported within a matter of days or weeks after the removal order becomes final.

For some detainees it does not work out this way, however. The country of nationality refuses to accept return, either because of a broad policy of noncooperation with the United States or because of disagreements about whether a particular deportee is a national. Cuba, Vietnam, and Cambodia have been persistent noncooperators, although diplomatic advances with Vietnam in recent years have opened prospects for returns in the foreseeable future. In the latter category, some countries, including Jamaica and Guyana, have often been exquisitely demanding of proof of nationality, particularly if the returnee has a criminal record. But of course any country may legitimately question whether the person presented by INS is actually its national. If return is refused, or even badly delayed, INS still has substantial incentives to let the individual await the outcome while on some form of release, if the governing law permits it.[6] Not only are the costs substantial, but authorities on prisons agree that the absence of any prospect for release complicates the process of maintaining order in a detention facility. The balance of administrative incentives may swing in the

---

and that's the nature of this provision." Reported on the Newshour with Jim Lehrer, transcript at <http://www.pbs.org/newshour/bb/terrorism/july-dec01/war_9-25.html>.

[5] *Carlson v Landon*, 342 US 524, 538 (1952); *Reno v Flores*, 507 US 292, 294–95 (1993).

[6] Statistics quoted in Justice Kennedy's dissent in *Zadvydas* bear out this view. From February 1999 to mid-November 2000, 6,200 unremovable aliens were provided custody reviews as the statute's ninety-day "removal period" came to an end. Of these, 3,380 were released. 65 Fed Reg 80285 (2000). The statute also fully recognizes that release is a significant possibility in case the country of nationality fails to cooperate in repatriation. It permits work authorization for aliens who "cannot be removed due to the refusal of all countries . . . to receive the alien," even though it denies such permission to other persons with orders of removal. Immigration and Nationality Act (INA) § 241(a)(7), 8 USC § 1251(a)(7) (2000).

other direction, however, when release poses security concerns—
either the high-politics version we tend to label "national security"
or the more mundane but nonetheless immediately understandable
form that derives from a returnee's serious or persistent criminal
record.

1. *The exclusion-deportation line.* From the 1950s to the late
1980s, the legal structure governing these situations was relatively
stable and well understood (which does not mean uncontroversial,
particularly in academic commentary). That structure was
grounded on the distinction between exclusion and deportation
proceedings, a distinction that was fundamental to the architecture
of U.S. immigration laws until Congress engaged in significant re-
design in 1996. In brief, it was understood that excludable aliens
could be detained indefinitely, after the order was final, if repatriation was delayed, whereas deportable aliens could be held only for
six months, a period prescribed by statute but possibly of constitutional significance. Thereafter they had to be released but could
be subjected to certain requirements of supervision and reporting.

Because the exclusion-deportation line (or perhaps some close
analogue) played an important role in *Zadvydas*, it is important to
understand its contours. Before 1996, an alien was placed in exclusion proceedings if INS questioned his right to be in the United
States during an encounter at the border, whether at a port of
entry or through interception before he could accomplish entry
away from the inspection station. In contrast, those who had made
an entry, either by means of inspection and admission at a port
of entry or by crossing the border surreptitiously, were placed in
deportation proceedings whenever their entitlement to remain was
put at issue. Importantly, this distinction placed entrants without
inspection (EWIs) on the more favorable side of the line.[7]

The Immigration and Nationality Act of 1952 (INA), building
on prior law, provided separate statutory provisions for aliens in
these two different circumstances, governing both substantive
grounds and procedures for the hearing and eventual removal. Exclusion procedures could be more summary, and the statute provided fewer grounds for contesting excludability or seeking relief
that might otherwise override formal removability (such as a claim

---

[7] See Thomas A. Aleinikoff, David A. Martin, and Hiroshi Motomura, *Immigration: Process
and Policy* 474–76 (3d ed 1995).

that persecution awaited at home). Over time, regulatory development ments eroded the procedural and substantive distinctions in practice, and most exclusion hearings before immigration judges looked a lot like deportation hearings before the same officials, and with most of the same important defenses available. But a few points of distinctiveness lingered in the regulatory details, set against a backdrop of sharply different understandings of the constitutional rights of aliens in the two settings.

2. *The detention rules for excludable aliens.* Since the late nineteenth century, the Supreme Court has announced doctrine that is extremely deferential to the political branches whenever an alien challenges *substantive* provisions of the immigration laws and regulations.[8] This is the famous "plenary power doctrine," and it remains stubbornly alive despite a steady barrage of academic criticism.[9] But not long after the Court launched this doctrine, it announced in the 1903 decision of *Yamataya v Fisher* a rather specific exception under which courts might take a closer independent look at constitutionality. It held that the procedures used to make immigration decisions are subject to the Due Process Clause and

---

[8] See, e.g., *Chinese Exclusion Case* (*Chae Chan Ping v United States*), 130 US 581 (1889); *Nishimura Ekiu v United States*, 142 US 651 (1892); *Fong Yue Ting v United States*, 149 US 698 (1893); *Harisiades v Shaughnessy*, 342 US 580 (1952); *Galvan v Press*, 347 US 522 (1954); *Kleindienst v Mandel*, 408 US 753 (1972); *Fiallo v Bell*, 430 US 787 (1977).

[9] For a sampling of the abundant academic critique of the plenary power doctrine, see Gerald L. Neuman, *Strangers to the Constitution: Immigrants, Borders, and Fundamental Law* 119–38 and passim (1996); Victor C. Romero, *The Congruence Principle Applied: Rethinking Equal Protection Review of Federal Alienage Classifications after Adarand Constructors, Inc. v Pena*, 76 Or L Rev 425 (1997); Frank H. Wu, *The Limits of Borders: A Moderate Proposal for Immigration Reform*, 7 Stan L & Policy Rev 35 (1996); Linda Kelly, *Preserving the Fundamental Right to Family Unity: Championing Notions of Social Contract and Community Ties in the Battle of Plenary Power versus Aliens' Rights*, 41 Vill L Rev 725 (1996); Margaret H. Taylor, *Detained Aliens Challenging Conditions of Confinement and the Porous Border of the Plenary Power Doctrine*, 22 Hastings Const L Q 1087 (1995); Michael Scaperlanda, *Polishing the Tarnished Golden Door*, 1993 Wis L Rev 965 (1993); T. Alexander Aleinikoff, *Federal Regulation of Aliens and the Constitution*, 83 Am J Intl L 862 (1989); Louis Henkin, *The Constitution and United States Sovereignty: A Century of Chinese Exclusion and Its Progeny*, 100 Harv L Rev 853 (1987); Stephen H. Legomsky, *Immigration Law and the Principle of Plenary Congressional Power*, 1984 Supreme Court Review 255 (1985). For a more skeptical view of the distinctiveness of the plenary power doctrine, see Gabriel J. Chin, *Is There a Plenary Power Doctrine? A Tentative Apology and Prediction for Our Strange but Unexceptional Constitutional Immigration Law*, 14 Georgetown Immig L J 257 (2000). For broad reviews of the evolution of the doctrine, see Hiroshi Motomura, *The Curious Evolution of Immigration Law: Procedural Surrogates for Substantive Constitutional Rights*, 92 Colum L Rev 1625 (1992); Hiroshi Motomura, *Immigration Law after a Century of Plenary Power: Phantom Constitutional Norms and Statutory Interpretation*, 100 Yale L J 545 (1990); Peter Schuck, *The Transformation of Immigration Law*, 84 Colum L Rev 1 (1984).

signaled that they would be independently evaluated by the courts.[10]

Yamataya turned out to offer this procedural due process protection only to deportable aliens. In the 1950 *Knauff* case, the Supreme Court essentially ruled that excludable aliens had no right to a judicial audit, applying independent constitutional standards, of the procedures used in exclusion proceedings: "Whatever the procedure authorized by Congress is, it is due process as far as an alien denied entry is concerned."[11] This was a severe ruling, especially in the context of that case. Ellen Knauff was no tourist simply denied a right to visit New York museums; she was a war bride coming to join her U.S. serviceman husband under the highly favorable terms of the War Brides Act. She was ruled excludable based on confidential information never shared with her, a procedure established, not by statute, but by administrative regulations adopted as World War II was beginning. In the view of the Justice Department, the confidential information demonstrated that she posed a national security threat. Her court challenge had focused on the procedural unfairness of exclusion based on secret evidence, not on questions of detention (for there was no barrier to her return to Europe once her case was final). In enacting the 1952 Immigration and Nationality Act (INA) two years later, Congress took *Knauff* to heart and enacted specific statutory authority for exclusion orders based on confidential national security information—a provision that has survived with little change into today's law.[12]

---

[10] *Yamataya v Fisher*, 189 US 86 (1903). Yamataya still lost the case, despite procedures that look woefully deficient to the modern eye. Hence the procedural due process review was still deferential, but the promise of independent judicial evaluation of the adequacy of the procedures nonetheless marked a significantly different approach from the cases that rejected challenges to substantive immigration law.

[11] *United States ex rel Knauff v Shaughnessy*, 338 US 537, 544 (1950). The Court inserted an unelaborated "cf." cite to *Yamataya*. Professor Hart, in his famous dialogue on federal jurisdiction, was especially critical of the Court's meager acknowledgment that a different rule applied in deportation proceedings, and its failure to give any serious account of why exclusion cases merit such different treatment. Henry Hart, *The Power of Congress to Limit the Jurisdiction of the Federal Courts: An Exercise in Dialectic*, 66 Harv L Rev 1362, 1390–96 (1953).

[12] INA § 235(c), 8 USC § 1225(c) (2000). Ellen Knauff and her supporters kept her cause alive after the Supreme Court ruling. Eventually she was admitted after a hearing in which the once secret information was made available, and she wrote a book about her treatment. Ellen Knauff, *The Ellen Knauff Story* (1952).

That the Court's *Knauff* doctrine had at least some application to detention questions (which could be seen as implicating a mix of substantive and procedural rights) became apparent a few years later. Ignatz Mezei was also deemed excludable on national security grounds, under the same secret-evidence procedures the government had applied to Ellen Knauff. But Mezei could not simply return to Europe. Because he had been born in Gibraltar of Hungarian or Rumanian parents, his nationality was disputed, and no country had agreed to accept him despite several attempts to send him away. Throughout this time, a period of roughly three years, he remained in detention on Ellis Island. The Court first ruled that he would be treated as an excludable alien, even though, unlike Knauff, he had lived in the United States as a lawful permanent resident for twenty-five years before the travel at issue. Because he had been away nineteen months, whatever claims he might have had as a lawful resident had evaporated. He could be treated as "an entrant alien or 'assimilated to [that] status' for constitutional purposes."[13] Entrant aliens, under *Knauff*, clearly could be subjected to secret-evidence procedures—although another case decided about a month before *Mezei, Kwong Hai Chew v Colding*, strongly suggested that deportable aliens and those whose status was "assimilated" thereto could not constitutionally be denied access to the crucial evidence.[14]

Mezei is less important for placing a returning resident on the disfavored side of the line—indeed, that part of the holding has eroded[15]—than for its ruling allowing indefinite detention of excludable aliens, even when the exclusion order rested on secret procedures:

---

[13] *Shaughnessy v United States ex rel Mezei*, 345 US 206, 214 (1953).

[14] *Kwong Hai Chew v Colding*, 344 US 590 (1953). Kwong was a lawful permanent resident who was also at the border, but he had been gone only six weeks while serving on a U.S. merchant ship following full security screening. Technically the Court's decision in *Kwong* involved statutory construction in the shadow of constitutional doubt, but later cases treated it as firmly establishing the constitutional right of deportable aliens to procedural due process protection. *Rosenberg v Fleuti*, 374 US 449, 460 (1963); *Landon v Plasencia*, 459 US 21, 32–33 (1982).

[15] *Landon v Plasencia*, 459 US 21 (1982), ruled that a lawful permanent resident who had been gone for two days could be placed in statutory exclusion proceedings but retained the full measure of constitutional due process protection she would have enjoyed had she not traveled. The Court suggested that the eleven-hour notice she was given before her hearing did not afford her sufficient time to prepare, but it remanded for the lower court to give full consideration to her procedural due process claim.

That exclusion by the United States plus other nations' inhospitality results in present hardship cannot be ignored. Congress may well have felt that other countries ought not shift the onus to us; that an alien in respondent's position is no more ours than theirs. Whatever our individual estimate of that policy and the fears on which it rests, respondent's right to enter the United States depends on the congressional will, and courts cannot substitute their judgment for the legislative mandate.[16]

Because the government did not often have occasion to detain unremovable excludable aliens, over the next twenty-five years few cases arose to test the limits or the continued viability of the *Mezei* doctrine. That quiescence ended in dramatic fashion in 1980, when the Cuban government found a shrewd way of diverting attention from an embarrassing episode of diplomatic asylum in the Peruvian embassy in Havana. It announced that the northern port of Mariel was open for American citizens or residents to come and pick up their family members. The ensuing boatlift brought 125,000 Cubans to U.S. shores over the space of four months. Encountered upon arrival, the Marielitos were excludable aliens. But the political will did not exist to repatriate them en masse, particularly once the boat flow was brought under control several weeks after it began, and in any event each Marielito could have been expected to pursue an asylum claim if pressed to return. From the earliest days, the vast majority of Marielitos were released to family members or community supporters after brief initial INS interviews and screening. Most never had to attend an exclusion hearing because most eventually obtained permanent resident status under special legislation.

The Cuban government, however, had not allowed the U.S. boats that came to Mariel to depart only with the family members the owner or charterer was desperate to pick up. In an effort to tar the image of all Marielitos, it emptied several jails and prisons and placed the inmates aboard the waiting boats. Alert to this practice, U.S. authorities detained those Marielitos believed to have criminal records, in the hopes that they might be repatriated once the frenzy of the boatlift subsided. When those hopes faded, over

---

[16] 345 US at 216. Mezei was eventually released on parole after several additional years of congressional and media pressure. See Charles Weisselberg, *The Exclusion and Detention of Aliens: Lessons from the Lives of Ellen Knauff and Ignatz Mezei*, 143 U Pa L Rev 933 (1995).

time virtually all of even these Marielitos were released, but on immigration parole.[17]

Parole is another key element in the architecture of U.S. immigration law. Classically, it permitted an excludable alien to be released at large into the United States, but—crucially—parole is not regarded as admission into the country. In the eyes of the law, a parolee remains at the border, with only whatever statutory or constitutional rights an excludable alien might hold, even though in reality a parolee may travel farther into the United States and for a longer period than a clandestine entrant. Parole gives rise to what the trade calls the "entry fiction"—the view that a parolee has never entered the country, and so has not graduated into the more favored category reserved under pre-1996 law for those who were deportable. Practices vary depending on the purpose of the parole, but INS typically grants parole for a limited period (one year is common), which is renewable. The INS may, but often does not, prescribe other conditions, such as reporting requirements or limitations on travel. Parole is revocable at the instance of the government.[18]

Several thousand among the paroled Marielitos committed criminal offenses after release.[19] When they had served their criminal sentences, most were redetained by INS and placed into exclusion proceedings. The objective was to obtain a final and enforceable order and thereby to position these individuals for involuntary removal once negotiations enabled repatriation to Cuba.[20] As Cu-

---

[17] See Thomas A. Aleinikoff, David A. Martin, and Hiroshi Motomura, *Immigration and Citizenship: Process and Policy* 914–16 (4th ed 1998); Gilburt Loescher and John Scanlan, *Calculated Kindness: Refugees and America's Half-Open Door, 1945 to the Present* 179–87 (1986).

[18] INA § 212(d)(5), 8 USC § 1182(d)(5) (2000). See Aleinikoff, Martin, and Motomura, *Immigration and Citizenship* at 507–10 (cited in note 17).

[19] This group included not only individuals initially held by INS because of suspicion of a criminal background, but also some from the group initially released after minimum border screening. All Marielitos who were not detained were technically immigration parolees at first, until the special legislation, enacted in 1984, enabled most Marielitos to gain lawful permanent resident status. Immigration Reform and Control Act of 1986, § 202, Pub L No 99-603, 100 Stat 3359, 3404. Parolees with serious criminal records were not eligible for that status, and INS went ahead to obtain exclusion orders against them, if it had not already done so.

[20] Many of these Marielitos lodged asylum claims, but their criminal convictions either made them ineligible for such protection or justified a discretionary denial of asylum. A few hundred Marielitos with criminal records were returned in 1984 pursuant to a short-lived agreement with the Cuban government. Aleinikoff, Martin, and Motomura, *Immigration and Citizenship* at 914 (cited in note 17).

ba's intransigence deepened, however, INS developed what it called the Cuban Review Plan to allow for selective releases. These systematic procedures provided for at least annual review of the individual's case, to determine whether he had shown sufficient progress on rehabilitation or other factors that would merit an end to custody (still pending agreement on return to Cuba).[21] The INS often put conditions on release under this program, perhaps requiring residence at a halfway house or periodic reporting to INS.

Marielitos denied release—which meant Marielitos with criminal records—faced detention that appeared to be of indefinite duration. Not surprisingly, from the earliest days, they began to challenge this confinement through habeas corpus, pointing out that they had served their criminal sentences and that they were not responsible for the Cuban government's resistance to return. Although the detainees gained favorable constitutional rulings in certain district courts and from some panels in the courts of appeals, eventually every circuit court that reached the constitutional question (sometimes through en banc reconsideration) found that the detention was legally justified. The Supreme Court declined several opportunities to consider the question.[22]

Mezei featured importantly in the conclusions of the courts of appeals, but nearly every decision also gave prominent mention to the existence of a systematic plan for regular review of the individ-

---

[21] 8 CFR § 212.12 (2000).

[22] The cases upholding indefinite detention of excludable aliens (a few of the petitioners were not Marielitos) include: *Guzman v Tippy*, 130 F3d 64 (2d Cir 1997) (per curiam); *Chi Thon Ngo v INS*, 192 F3d 390 (3d Cir 1999); *Palma v Verdeyen*, 676 F2d 100 (4th Cir 1982); *Gisbert v U.S. Att'y Gen.*, 988 F2d 1437, amended, 997 F2d 1122 (5th Cir 1993); *Carballo v Luttrell*, 2001 WL 1194699 (6th Cir, Oct 11, 2001), rehearing en banc granted and opinion vacated (Nov 23, 2001); *Carrera-Valdez v Perryman*, 211 F3d 1046 (7th Cir 2000); *Barrera-Echavarria v Rison*, 44 F3d 1441 (9th Cir 1995) (en banc), cert denied, 516 US 976 (1995); *Alvarez-Mendez v Stock*, 941 F2d 956 (9th Cir 1991), cert denied, 506 US 842 (1992); *Ho v Greene*, 204 F3d 1045 (10th Cir 2000), overruled in part (as applied to deportable alien) by *Zadvydas v Davis*, 121 S Ct 2491 (2001); *Sierra v INS*, 258 F3d 1213 (10th Cir 2001); *Garcia-Mir v Meese*, 788 F2d 1446 (11th Cir 1986), cert denied, 479 US 889 (1986); *Fernandez-Roque v Smith*, 734 F2d 576 (11th Cir 1984). The Sixth Circuit deviated from this pattern in *Rosales-Garcia v Holland*, 238 F3d 704 (6th Cir 2001), vacated and remanded for reconsideration in light of *Zadvydas* as *Thomas v Rosales-Garcia*, 122 S Ct 662 (2001), but a few months later, before the Supreme Court had acted on the government's certiorari petition, another Sixth Circuit panel held that the *Zadvydas* decision had essentially overruled the earlier *Rosales-Garcia* ruling. *Carballo v Luttrell*, supra. The Tenth Circuit also ruled shortly after the Mariel boatlift that indefinite detention was not permitted as a matter of statutory construction. *Rodriguez-Fernandez v Wilkinson*, 654 F2d 1382 (10th Cir 1981). In *Ho v Greene*, supra, however, the court held that *Rodriguez-Fernandez* had been superseded by later statutory amendments.

ual's releasability. Some courts appeared to condition their approval of detention on the continuation of the annual reviews, and a few signaled that they would provide ongoing scrutiny to assure procedural fairness in the reviews.[23] That program, along with the promised ongoing interest of the State Department in negotiating repatriation, enabled the judges to couch their holdings as something other than an approval of permanent and hopeless lifetime detention. As of 1996, then, when Congress passed major amendments to the INA, the indefinite detention question seemed reasonably settled insofar as excludable aliens were concerned.

3. *The detention rules for deportable aliens.* Throughout most of this same period, up to 1988, the rules governing post-order detention of deportable aliens could be much more easily described because of a clear statutory provision that governed. The statute was passed in response to a rash of refusals of return in the late 1940s, mostly on the part of Communist countries. Congress was specifically concerned by restrictive court rulings in such cases, applying an earlier, ambiguously worded statute.[24] Some courts read the former statute to impose onerous procedures on INS as it searched for a country willing to take a deportable alien, and most had imposed close temporal limits on immigration detention. Some had even ordered release before all efforts to repatriate were completed. Congress therefore enacted a new statute in 1950 meant to define clearly the authority of the Attorney General when the country of nationality refused return. Although the House bill had proposed indefinite detention for many categories of unremovable deportable aliens (including all those who had entered less than ten years before the deportation order was issued),[25] the Senate Judiciary Committee thought that such a measure "presents a constitutional question."[26] In its stead the Senate proposed, and Congress ultimately enacted, a section clearly authorizing detention for up to six months while INS made arrangements for removal. Thereafter the bill provided for supervised release, and it author-

---

[23] The clearest such holding is *Chi Thon Ngo v INS*, 192 F3d at 397–99 (3d Cir 1999), discussing other cases that appear to take the same approach.

[24] See HR Rep No 1192, 81st Cong, 1st Sess 4–5 (1949).

[25] Id at 3. Representatives Celler and Gorski appended a minority report strenuously attacking the constitutionality of these detention provisions. Id at 17–20.

[26] Sen Rep No 2239, 81st Cong, 2d Sess 8 (1950).

ized several specific terms that could be imposed in the supervisory order, including periodic appearances at a specified INS office, an obligation to provide requested information, and "reasonable written restrictions" on the individual's conduct.[27] Individuals who disobeyed these terms, or who failed to cooperate in attempting to get travel documents or in completing other necessary steps incident to removal, could be prosecuted and, if proven guilty, fined and imprisoned for not more than one year.

Essentially the same provision was incorporated into the comprehensive recodification of immigration laws in 1952, the Immigration and Nationality Act (INA).[28] The INS understood this provision to set a six-month limit, counting from when the deportation order became final, on its efforts to secure return permission from the destination country. Thereafter the person had to be released.[29] Hence there was no occasion for a court ruling on indefinite detention of *deportable* aliens because the statute did not give rise to such a practice. Terms of supervision could be fairly restrictive, although the Supreme Court at one point read some of the supervisory powers narrowly in order to avoid constitutional problems.[30] But INS did not believe it had the authority simply to redetain if the person violated the conditions. Instead, it would have to prosecute for the violation, as the statute permitted. Further detention would then be in prison, not in INS custody, on the basis of a specific sentence imposed after granting the full protections of the criminal justice system.

---

[27] Internal Security Act of 1950, § 23, Pub L No 831, 64 Stat 987, 1010.

[28] INA § 242(c), Pub L No 414, 66 Stat 163, 210 (1952).

[29] Several cases found an equitable exception suspending the running of the six-month period if the alien "hampered" the process of securing travel documents. Most such delays were based on collateral litigation by the alien that had resulted in stays or injunctions preventing the execution of the removal order, even though it remained technically final. See, e.g., *Dor v District Director*, 891 F2d 997, 1002–03 (2d Cir 1989). *Bartholomeu v District Director*, 487 F Supp 315, 319–20 (D Md 1980). But at least two cases extended the six-month period when the alien had been otherwise uncooperative with the process, such as by refusing to provide information to the foreign consulate to be used in its issuance of travel documents. *Balogun v INS*, 9 F3d 347, 351 (5th Cir 1993); *Riley v Greene*, 149 F Supp 2d 1256, 1262 (D Colo 2001). These rulings do not at bottom question the soundness of the six-month rule. The statute now contains an explicit provision extending the detention and removal period if the alien is uncooperative. INA § 241(a)(1)(C), 8 USC § 1251(a)(1)(C) (2000).

[30] *United States v Witkovich*, 353 US 194, 195, 202 (1957) (construing the provision in INA § 242(d) allowing the Attorney General to require supply of any information he "may deem fit and proper" as limited to questions "reasonably calculated to keep the Attorney General advised regarding the continued availability for departure of aliens whose deportation is overdue").

That six-month provision remained on the books until enactment of IIRIRA in 1996. But the statutory picture did become
more complicated beginning with the 1988 Anti–Drug Abuse Act,
which began to carve out special provisions mandating the detention of any alien who had been convicted of an offense that the
INA designated as an aggravated felony.[31] The initial definition of
"aggravated felony," a new concept added to the INA by that 1988
law,[32] was lean—murder, drug trafficking, and firearms trafficking—but Congress could not resist adding to the definition relent-
lessly in several waves over succeeding years.[33] The earliest court
challenges to this detention mandate focused on detention in the
period before the immigration court ruled ("preorder detention,"
which is of finite duration). They were brought by respondents
who had been lawfully admitted, most of them as permanent residents. Most of the district courts that considered the question under that law held that such aliens were constitutionally entitled to
individualized consideration of release, although a few reached the
opposite result.[34] Before that question could be considered by the
courts of appeals, Congress chose to change the law in 1990 to
permit release of lawful permanent residents after an individualized
inquiry.[35] A further amendment in 1991 expanded the category
entitled to individual review to include any alien who had been
lawfully admitted (whether temporarily or permanently). It also
clearly put the burden of proof on the alien to show that he or
she "is not a threat to the community and . . . is likely to appear
before any scheduled hearings."[36] These amendments, though they

---

[31] Anti-Drug Abuse Act of 1988, § 7343, Pub L No 100-690, 102 Stat 4181, 4470, adding
a new INA § 242(a)(2) providing that the Attorney General must take into custody aliens
convicted of an aggravated felony upon completion of the sentence and "shall not release
such felon from custody."

[32] Id § 7342.

[33] The current version appears at INA § 101(a)(43), 8 USC § 1101(a)(43) (2000).

[34] Cases holding that individualized consideration was required included *Kellman v District
Director*, 750 F Supp 625 (SDNY 1990); *Probert v INS*, 750 F Supp 252 (ED Mich 1990);
Paxton v INS, 745 F Supp 1261 (ED Mich 1990); *Leader v Blackman*, 744 F Supp 500
(SDNY 1990); *Agunobi v Thornburgh*, 745 F Supp 533 (ND Ill 1990). Holdings to the
contrary appeared in *Davis v Weiss*, 749 F Supp 47 (D Conn 1990); *Morrobel v Thornburgh*,
744 F Supp 725 (ED Va 1990).

[35] Immigration Act of 1990, § 504(a), Pub L No 101-649, 104 Stat 4978, 5049.

[36] Former INA § 242(a)(2)(B), 8 USC § 1252(a)(2)(B) (1994), as amended by the Miscella-
neous and Technical Immigration and Naturalization Amendments of 1991, § 306(a)(4),
Pub L No 102-232, 105 Stat 1733, 1751.

still left entrants without inspection (EWIs) subject to the mandate, mooted the then-pending challenges to preorder detention.

Nonetheless, the amended statute still permitted (and in some cases mandated) post-order detention, no longer limited by a six-month deadline, of aggravated felons who could not be removed. Of the few decisions that considered this issue in cases filed by lawfully admitted aliens, most sustained the detention, laying some emphasis on the fact that the individual's appeal for release had been given individualized consideration.[37] By statute, those who were not lawfully admitted, however—that is, EWIs—had no such right to try to demonstrate qualification for release. The only reported case to consider such confinement of an EWI found a constitutional violation, but not because of indefinite detention per se. The constitutional flaw lay in the lack of an opportunity for individualized review of dangerousness and flight risk in a release hearing.[38]

Those early 1990s cases might seem to mark a near-convergence in the rules governing post-order detention of excludable and deportable aliens, suggesting that indefinite detention is allowed, provided there is an opportunity for regular review of releasability. But far fewer cases had addressed the constitutional issue in the setting of deportable aliens, all of them district courts, and the very fact that Congress kept changing the rules governing detention of deportable aliens seemed to signal doubts about whether departure from the long-standing six-month detention limit was truly justified. Furthermore, it was hardly settled that individualized review of the detention of excludable aliens was constitutionally required. *Mezei* certainly suggested the contrary, and the lower court rulings that seemed to rely on such review all arose in the context of administrative action that had provided such review voluntarily, on the agency's own initiative.

B. THE 1996 AMENDMENTS

Cracking down on illegal immigration featured as a prominent theme in the election year of 1996, and a seeming competition

---

[37] See, e.g., *Hernandez-Ebank v Caplinger*, 951 F Supp 99 (ED La 1996); *Tran v Caplinger*, 847 F Supp 469 (WD La 1993).

[38] *Caballero v Caplinger*, 914 F Supp 1374 (ED La 1996).

erupted in Congress to see who could be toughest on criminal aliens. Few members were willing to raise public questions about any measure a colleague proposed, lest they be attacked by opposing candidates in the upcoming elections for being too soft on a doubly unpopular group. As a result, Congress packed together a host of measures directed at criminal aliens, without careful thought about what the net effect of the mass might be. The first batch of changes was enacted in a hastily assembled title on immigration that was included in the Antiterrorism and Effective Death Penalty Act (AEDPA), passed in April.[39] As a first step, Congress repealed the 1991 proviso that had allowed release of aggravated felons who had been lawfully admitted, thereby returning to the unrelenting detention mandate, without time limit, that Congress had originally enacted in 1988.[40] At the same time, the AEDPA continued a trend that had already seen the definition of "aggravated felony" expand from its initial coverage, in 1988, of three categories of offenses into a definition with seventeen subparagraphs. The 1996 law added four more.[41] It also made nearly all deportable aliens with criminal offenses ineligible for a relief provision, INA § 212(c), that had previously allowed seven-year lawful permanent residents who committed crimes to seek discretionary relief from deportation from an immigration judge by showing rehabilitation, family or community ties, and other favorable factors.[42]

The AEDPA detention mandate had no time limit. Thus if an aggravated felon could not be removed because no country would accept him, INS was statutorily bound to detain him. These post-order detainees came to be called "lifers" under the AEDPA regime.

---

[39] AEDPA §§ 401–443 (cited in note 3).

[40] AEDPA § 440(c), amending INA § 242(a)(2), 8 USC § 1252(a)(2) (1994).

[41] AEDPA § 440(e), amending INA § 101(a)(43), 8 USC § 1101(a)(43) (1994). IIRIRA, passed in September 1996, applied the concept of aggravated felony to a still wider range of offenses, by lowering certain thresholds that had to be exceeded before several of the most widely applicable parts of the definition would apply. For example, before 1996, theft offenses and crimes of violence would count as aggravated felonies only if the offender received a sentence of five years or more. Fraud offenses had to involve a loss of at least $200,000. IIRIRA reduced the former to a one-year threshold and the latter to $10,000. IIRIRA § 321(a)(3) (cited in note 3). Thus the definition now includes some offenses that are neither felonies nor, in any reasonable view of the matter, truly aggravated.

[42] AEDPA § 440(d), amending INA § 212(c), 8 USC § 1182(c) (1994). See *Matter of Marin*, 16 I & N Dec 581 (BIA 1978).

The Clinton administration placed a high priority on changing this AEDPA detention mandate, both pre- and post-order, as it attempted to influence the shape of the full immigration reform bill that was expected to pass that year before Congress adjourned. Key officials in the Department of Justice were keenly aware of the potential impact of mandated detention on individuals—knowing that the "criminal alien" slogan, for all its power on the campaign trail, embraces a vast spectrum of human character and behavior. Some such criminals are truly dangerous, but a large fraction of this class made single mistakes or had shown genuine rehabilitation and remorse. In the view of those officials, most such deportable aliens should at least be eligible for consideration of release during proceedings and for a discretionary waiver of deportation altogether, as had earlier been possible under INA § 212(c). The INS also wanted at least the discretionary authority to release unremovable aliens—lifers. The administration was eager to amend the detention provisions for an additional reason: detention mandates can gobble up detention space in unpredictable ways that hamper the strategic use of detention resources to support all parts of the enforcement mission. This is bad enough with inflexible pre-order detention mandates, but the lifer category would permanently occupy an ever-growing number of detention beds, utterly foreclosing their use for other purposes. In the ugly climate of the 1996 election, the latter theme, enforcement, received the most prominent public mention in the effort to ease the detention mandates. Sympathy or understanding for criminal aliens—or even honest acknowledgment of human variety within the category— found little resonance in Congress or the electorate that year.

The immigration reform bill, the IIRIRA, gained passage shortly before Congress adjourned to campaign in 1996.[43] To understand the changes it made with regard to detention, one needs to appreciate the broad changes it enacted in the overall architecture of our immigration laws, particularly its revamping of the exclusion-deportation line. Congress acted on a frequent observation that the old rules ironically privileged entrants without inspection (EWIs) who knowingly evaded all border inspection, by placing them in the more favorable category of deportable aliens, in con-

---

[43] IIRIRA (cited in note 3).

trast with those who did what they were supposed to do and presented themselves for inspection at the port of entry. The latter
group would find themselves in the less favorable setting of an
exclusion proceeding if their right to enter were questioned. In
the IIRIRA, Congress accordingly changed the key dividing line
from entry into the United States, which, whether lawful or sur-
reptitious, previously marked the difference between excludables
and deportables. The new dividing line is based on admission following inspection.[44]

Those who have been admitted are subject to the grounds of
deportability and have somewhat better access to defenses and
waivers; those who have not, including EWIs, are in the less-
favored category of "inadmissible" aliens. Whether Congress
thought this change might affect the constitutional status of EWIs
is less clear. But Congress did not rest content with retention of a
simple two-category system whose dividing line was simply moved.
Apparently in order to avoid jeopardizing the enforcement advantages that could derive from *Knauff* and *Mezei*, Congress chose to
subdivide the inadmissible alien category still further, distinguishing "arriving aliens" (basically those formerly called excludables)
from other inadmissibles (basically EWIs).[45] It then reserved the
most restrictive possible measures for arriving aliens. For example,
arriving aliens—and not EWIs—can be subjected to the broadest
form of secret-evidence procedures, the section that is the direct
descendant, little changed, from the 1952 provision that codified
Ellen Knauff's treatment.[46] For ease of exposition here, I will often
continue to use the terminology of "excludable aliens" to refer as
well to the category now known as arriving aliens. "Deportable
aliens" remains a part of today's lingo, now describing only per-

---

[44] See INA § 101(a)(13) (definition of "admission," which replaces the former statutory
definition of "entry"), and the opening clauses to §§ 212(a) (grounds of inadmissibility)
and 237(a) (grounds of deportability). 8 USC §§ 1101(a)(13), 1182(a), 1227(a) (2000). This
change necessitated adding a new ground of inadmissibility based on entry without inspection. INA § 212(a)(6)(A)(i), 8 USC § 1182(a)(6)(A)(i) (2000).

[45] See Aleinikoff, Martin, and Motomura, *Immigration and Citizenship* at 425–26 (cited in
note 17).

[46] INA § 235(c)(1), 8 USC § 1225(c)(1) (2000). Congress also applied new summary border procedures, known as expedited removal, to all arriving aliens removable for fraud or
lack of documents as a matter of course, while providing discretionary authority to the
Attorney General to apply these measures to EWIs, but only if the EWI has been present
for less than two years. INA § 235(b)(1), 8 USC § 1225(b)(1) (2000). This discretionary
authority has not yet been invoked.

sons who have been admitted, and thus excluding EWIs. I will try to make clear the groups I mean to cover when I use that term.

In IIRIRA, Congress did respond in measured fashion to the Clinton administration's request to ease mandatory detention, particularly as applied to lifers.[47] The IIRIRA enacted a new section of the law, INA § 241(a), that comprehensively governs post-order detention, whatever the ground of excludability or deportability and irrespective of criminal record.[48] It mandates the detention of all removable aliens for a ninety-day "removal period" beginning when the order becomes final, and it directs INS to secure their departure within that time. It then provides for release on supervision (with terms very much like the pre-1996 law) if removal has not been achieved during that period. If this section said nothing further, the law would have been the analogue of the six-month period for deportable aliens under prior law, with two changes that seem to look in contradictory directions. Detention is absolutely required during the period while INS makes initial travel arrangements,[49] but the period is shortened to ninety days.

The law does say something further, however. In the key provision at issue in *Zadvydas*, INA § 241(a)(6), the law provides:

---

[47] Besides the new provision for post-order detention described in the text, Congress also responded to the Administration's request for greater flexibility by permitting the Attorney General to invoke for two years what the statute called the Transition Period Custody Rules. IIRIRA § 303(b) (cited in note 3). Those rules allowed pre-order release of lawfully admitted aliens (a return to provisions very much like that in place after the 1991 amendment) and also allowed post-order release of any other alien who could not be removed. In both cases the aliens were required to satisfy the INS before release that they were neither dangerous nor likely to flee. *Matter of Noble*, 21 I & N Dec 672 (1997).

[48] 8 USC § 1231(a)(6) (2000).

[49] This statutory provision may make it sound as though all aliens ordered deportable are taken into custody when the immigration judge rules against them. In practice, the impact is far more limited. Because the detention mandate of INA § 241(a) does not begin until the order is final, there is no detention requirement during the thirty-day period allowed after an immigration judge's ruling for filing an administrative appeal, and thereafter, during the pendency of administrative and judicial review. Further, a high percentage of removal cases are resolved with what is called an "alternate order." It permits the individual a specified period (up to 120 days) in which to depart voluntarily from the United States. If she does so, she will not be considered to have been deported. If she is still present at the end of the voluntary departure period, however, the order issued by the immigration judge turns into an enforceable deportation order without the need for any further appearances or proceedings. Typically the appeal time has run by then, so that the removal period, with its detention mandate, commences. But aliens who do not honor their voluntary departure pledge are not easy to find by this time; INS successfully locates and detains a relatively small percentage. Persons not detained during the many months or years awaiting an appeal also have plenty of time to move and leave a cold trail.

An alien ordered removed who is inadmissible . . . , removable under [specified sections covering criminal convictions and violations of the terms of a nonimmigrant admission], . . . or who has been determined by the Attorney General to be a risk to the community or unlikely to comply with the order of removal, may be detained beyond the removal period and, if released, shall be subject to the [specified] terms of supervision . . . .[50]

Note that detention after the ninety-day removal period is not mandated for anyone, a striking change from the AEDPA. Instead, it is made permissible for specified categories, and a single unified post-order detention regime covers both inadmissible aliens and some deportable aliens. The categories tied to immigration status include those formerly deemed excludable aliens as well as deportable criminals; the extended post-order detention of these specific categories had been either mandated or authorized in at least some versions of prior law. But it was a 1996 innovation to add two new groups to this list: those who violate the terms of a nonimmigrant admission and also those who entered without inspection. All these status-related categories together embrace 97 percent of aliens who are placed in removal proceedings.[51] But as if that coverage were not broad enough, the final descriptive clause permits extended detention of anyone else, if there is a finding of the classic criteria used to deny release: dangerousness *or* flight risk.

Implementation has nonetheless tracked earlier practice very closely, and those held by INS for lengthy detention have been persons with serious criminal convictions. Their release has been decided upon by the relevant officials under standards that call for an evaluation of flight risk and dangerousness.[52]

As challenges to lengthy detention under § 241(a)(6) began to reach the courts, INS and the Civil Division of the Department of Justice, mindful of the usefulness of the Cuban Review Plan to the Department's success in sustaining detention of excludable

---

[50] INA § 241(a)(6), 8 USC §1231(a)(6) (2000).

[51] Percentage derived from Tables 60, 61, and 66 (exclusion and deportation data covering the period 1981–95) of Department of Justice, *1995 Statistical Yearbook of the Immigration and Naturalization Service* at 166, 170.

[52] See *INS Clarifies Its Interpretation of Detention and Release of Aliens with Final Orders of Removal*, 77 Interpreter Releases 631 (2000).

Marielitos, moved to implement a similar systematic review procedure under the new framework. Initially adopted in the form of a lengthy memorandum to the field from the head of INS Field Operations, the procedures were eventually enshrined in regulations, which took full effect, after notice and comment rulemaking, before the Supreme Court heard oral argument in the *Zadvydas* case.[53] The regulations provide for initial consideration of releasability at the end of the ninety-day removal period, and for at least annual review thereafter, by a specialized unit in INS headquarters. The alien can submit whatever material he or she wishes for consideration by the district director or the review panel and will be personally interviewed on each of these occasions if release is not ordered on the basis of the paper record alone. Any decision to deny release must be accompanied by a statement of reasons, and certain other procedural protections are provided.

In this institutional setting, against the backdrop of the history sketched above, the Supreme Court granted certiorari to resolve questions surrounding the use of indefinite detention.

II. The Zadvydas and Ma Decisions

A. THE RULINGS BELOW

Zadvydas v Davis combined two cases that had led to opposite results in the courts of appeals. Both involved aliens who had enjoyed the status of lawful permanent resident (LPR) after immigrating as children.

Kestutis Zadvydas immigrated to the United States with his family at the age of eight in 1956. He compiled a lengthy criminal history, including drug distribution, armed robbery, and attempted burglary, and he had also absconded for lengthy periods, both while on bail for one of his criminal charges and during immigration proceedings initially launched in the 1980s. He was ruled deportable in 1994 and pursued no further challenges to that ruling. But he was apparently stateless, and INS proved unable to remove him. Neither Germany, where he was born in a displaced persons camp in the confused aftermath of World War II, nor Lithuania,

---

[53] 65 Fed Reg 80281 (2001), primarily codified in 8 CFR § 241.4. The earlier provisions are described, and the memorandum reproduced, in *INS Issues New Policy Memo on Release Authority for Aliens Held Beyond Removal Period*, 76 Interpreter Releases 422 (1999).

the apparent country of nationality of his parents, would accept him, although certain further procedures that might secure such permission were not entirely foreclosed. The INS held him in detention in view of his record, and he had been unable to carry his burden of satisfying INS that he was releasable. The Fifth Circuit found that for detention purposes there was no meaningful distinction between deportable aliens with final orders of removal and an excludable alien like Mezei.[54] At least so long as INS provided a procedure for periodic review of releasability, coupled with good faith efforts to effectuate deportation, ongoing detention did not violate the Constitution.[55]

Kim Ho Ma left Cambodia with his family at age two and came to the United States in 1985 after five years in refugee camps. He became a lawful permanent resident in 1987. In 1996 he was convicted of first-degree manslaughter deriving from a gang-related shooting, committed when he was seventeen years old. Sentenced to thirty-eight months in prison, he served twenty-six before release. The INS thereupon assumed custody, placed him in proceedings, and obtained a removal order. Ma appealed unsuccessfully to the Board of Immigration Appeals but did not pursue judicial review, and his removal order became final in late 1998. Cambodia has been generally unwilling to accept return of its nationals from the United States, and no exception was made for Ma. The INS reviewed his detention according to the administrative review procedures, but when he was denied release, he challenged his continuing confinement in court. For the Ninth Circuit, unlike the Fifth, the distinction between excludable and deportable aliens marked a significant constitutional divide. Distinguishing Ninth Circuit precedents that had relied on *Mezei* to sustain indefinite detention of Marielitos, and unpersuaded by the Fifth Cir-

---

[54] In some circles this approach became known as the "exit fiction," in ironic parallel to the entry fiction that has permitted courts to treat parolees as though they had never entered, even after years of presence inside the country. Under the exit fiction, the court treats the alien as though he had already departed, as the removal order legally decreed, and therefore held no greater rights than an alien who had never entered. See Maria V. Morris, *The Exit Fiction: Unconstitutional Indefinite Detention of Deportable Aliens*, 23 Houston J Intl L 255, 278–80 (2001).

[55] *Zadvydas v Underdown*, 185 F3d 279, 283–84, 294–97 (5th Cir 1999), rev'd as *Zadvydas v Davis*, 121 S Ct 2491 (2001). The Tenth Circuit adopted most of the reasoning of the Fifth Circuit's *Zadvydas* decision and sustained indefinite detention in *Ho v Greene*, 204 F3d 1045 (10th Cir 2000).

cuit's reasoning, the court held that indefinite confinement of a deportable alien raised substantial constitutional problems. Therefore it construed INA § 241(a)(6) to allow confinement only for a reasonable period after the ninety-day removal period, and it ordered Ma's release.[56]

The Supreme Court had three basic stances it could have taken toward indefinite detention in immigration proceedings involving such aliens when it considered the combined cases: (1) place a reasonably firm limit on the length of detention, as the pre-1988 statute covering deportable aliens had done; (2) leave the matter entirely to the political branches, without even any judicially supervised requirement for periodic review of release, as *Mezei* had done; or (3) permit extended detention, but provide ongoing judicial scrutiny of the procedures and standards used to decide on releasability, as the lower court in *Zadvydas*, as well as several of the Marielito decisions, had done. The Court split in precisely these ways.

B. THE MAJORITY DECISION

Justice Breyer, writing for the five-Justice majority, adopted the first outcome, framing his conclusions as statutory construction meant to avoid substantial constitutional doubts that would arise if the law were construed to permit indefinite detention. The tone of his opinion was set in an important early passage: "Freedom from imprisonment," he opened, "lies at the heart of the liberty that [the Due Process] Clause protects."[57] Although some detention is an inescapable part of immigration removal, indefinite detention must find an especially strong justification. When actual removal is "a remote possibility at best," flight risk could not justify continued INS detention.[58] Although public safety, the other ground the government asserted for the confinement, has sometimes justified detention even without a criminal conviction, Justice Breyer found those other precedents readily distinguishable. *United States v Salerno*[59] approved preventive detention under the

---

[56] *Ma v Reno*, 208 F3d 815, 819–20, 823–27 (9th Cir 2000), remanded as *Zadvydas v Davis*, 121 S Ct 2491 (2001).

[57] 121 S Ct at 2498.

[58] Id at 2499.

[59] 481 US 739 (1987).

Bail Reform Act, but that statute provided for strict time limitations and highly protective procedures administered by a judicial officer, both lacking here. In other cases, detention of potentially indefinite duration has been allowed only when "the dangerousness rationale [is] accompanied by some other special circumstance, such as mental illness, that helps to create the danger."[60]

The government also argued that alien status itself could justify indefinite detention, relying on *Mezei*. But *Mezei*, Breyer held, "differs from the present cases in a critical respect." Mezei was treated as if stopped at the border, and that basic territorial distinction "made all the difference. The distinction between an alien who has effected an entry into the United States and one who has never entered runs throughout immigration law."[61] As apparent illustration of the latter group, the majority opinion then immediately cited two cases involving long-time parolees, thus rather clearly endorsing the entry fiction and keeping parolees on the disfavored side of the line.[62] It continued:

> But once an alien enters the country, the legal circumstance changes, for the Due Process Clause applies to all "persons" within the United States, including aliens, whether their presence here is lawful, unlawful, temporary, or permanent. Indeed, this Court has held that the Due Process Clause protects an alien subject to a final order of deportation, though the nature of that protection may vary depending upon status and circumstance.[63]

Justice Breyer also found unavailing the government's express appeal to plenary power. That power too, Breyer held, is subject to constitutional limitations.[64] In focusing on those limitations in

---

[60] 121 S Ct at 2499, citing *Kansas v Hendricks*, 521 US 346, 358, 368 (1997) (sustaining Kansas procedure for detention of dangerous sexual predators), and also discussing *Foucha v Louisiana*, 504 US 71, 81–83 (1992) (striking down insanity-related detention scheme because it placed the burden on the individual to prove that he was not dangerous).

[61] 121 S Ct at 2500.

[62] *Kaplan v Tod*, 267 US 228, 230 (1925) (a parolee who had over seven years' presence "was still in theory of law at the boundary line and had gained no foothold in the United States"); *Leng May Ma v Barber*, 357 US 185, 188–90 (1958) (parolee with eighteen months' presence did not qualify for an asylum provision the Court found applicable only to deportable aliens).

[63] 121 S Ct at 2500–01 (citations omitted).

[64] Id at 2501. In emphasizing that even plenary power "is subject to important constitutional limitations," Justice Breyer cited *INS v Chadha*, 462 US 919, 941–42 (1983) (Congress must choose "a constitutionally permissible means of implementing" that power); and *The Chinese Exclusion Case*, 130 US 581, 604 (1889) (congressional authority limited "by the Constitution itself and considerations of public policy and justice which control, more

this decision, the Court was not denying the government's power to control entry, nor "to remove aliens, to subject them to supervision with conditions when released from detention, or to incarcerate them where appropriate for violations of those conditions."[65] These ongoing governmental powers meant that the Court was leaving no "unprotected spot in the Nation's armor."[66] Justice Breyer also suggested that there might be room for greater governmental authority in cases involving "terrorism or other special circumstances" involving national security.[67] No such factors had been claimed here. Therefore, the only relevant question was whether the aliens who could not be removed "are to be *condemned* to an indefinite term of *imprisonment* within the United States."[68] The words I have italicized reveal that the dominant perspective for the majority was that of the alien facing the bleak prospect of indefinite confinement.

With these serious constitutional doubts hovering over indefinite detention, Justice Breyer found ambiguity in the statutory language of INA § 241(a)(6), primarily in the words "may be detained." Accordingly, he construed the statute to place an outer limit on such detention, described as "a period reasonably necessary to secure removal."[69] The dissenting judges found this conclusion utterly out of keeping with any possible reading of congressional intent, which plainly meant in their view to bestow a broader

---

or less, the conduct of all civilized nations"). In both instances these are Justice Breyer's parentheticals. Using the latter case to suggest constitutional limitations on the traditional plenary power has to be a startling citation for most who follow the immigration law literature, because *The Chinese Exclusion Case* is generally condemned as the very fountainhead of the plenary power doctrine and the case that first gave the political branches unchecked authority over immigration. See, e.g., Henkin, 100 Harv L Rev at 853, 862 (cited in note 9). The critics focus not on the passage that Justice Breyer quotes, but on later passages ruling that the government's determination of how and when to exercise the power "is conclusive upon the judiciary." 130 US at 606. For the critics the crucial issue is not whether the Constitution controls, but whether the courts would play any role in holding the executive and Congress to such limitations. *The Chinese Exclusion Case* strongly signals that they would not, and recent cases continue the message, although couched in language that speaks only of greatly enhanced deference to the political branches' decisions, not complete disavowal of review. See, e.g., *INS v Aguirre-Aguirre*, 526 US 415, 425 (1999), and *Fiallo v Bell*, 430 US 787, 793–94 (1977).

[65] 121 S Ct at 2501–02.

[66] Id at 2502, quoting from *Kwong Hai Chew v Colding*, 344 US 590, 602 (1953).

[67] 121 S Ct at 2502.

[68] Id (emphasis added).

[69] Id at 2504.

authority on the Attorney General.[70] Breyer was unmoved by that critique. Although acknowledging that a court applying the constitutional doubt canon would have to yield if Congress had been totally clear,[71] in the introductory section of the opinion he was surprisingly blunt about what the majority was doing. Because of the constitutional doubt, he stated, "*we read* an implicit limitation *into* the statute."[72]

The majority also proved unwilling simply to remand these cases (and others held pending this decision) to let the lower courts work out the contours of a "reasonable period." In a move not much seen since Warren Court days, it laid down precise numerical guidance for habeas courts. Six months, counting from the time the order becomes final, is declared a "presumptively reasonable period of detention."[73] This time period was expressly borrowed from the long-standing pre-1996 statutory framework for deportable aliens. The Court neatly deflected back to Congress most of the responsibility for this mixed statutory and constitutional guideline. It found in the legislative history of the 1950 statute that established that pattern, recounted above, "reason to believe . . . that Congress previously doubted the constitutionality of de-

---

[70] Id at 2505 (Scalia, J, dissenting); 2507 (Kennedy, J, dissenting).

[71] Id at 2502.

[72] Id at 2498 (emphasis added). This blunt phrasing goes beyond what the constitutional doubt doctrine normally countenances, as Justice Kennedy emphasizes in dissent. The rule normally is said to apply only to the choice between two constructions, each of which is "fairly plausible." Id at 2508 (Kennedy, J, dissenting), quoting *Crowell v Benson*, 285 US 22, 62 (1932). The constitutional doubt doctrine played a comparable, and equally contested role in another major immigration decision decided during the October 2000 term, *INS v St. Cyr*, 121 S Ct 2271 (2001). There the question was whether the 1996 amendments to the immigration laws foreclosed habeas corpus review in the district court for aliens with criminal convictions, who, the Court held in a related case, had clearly been statutorily barred from the normal avenue of review in the courts of appeals. *Calcano-Martinez v INS*, 121 S Ct 2268 (2001). The Court found sufficient ambiguity in a provision foreclosing "review" "[n]otwithstanding any other provision of law" to construe the statute so as to leave untouched habeas corpus petitions under 28 USC § 2241. In this way it avoided substantial constitutional questions that would be presented were access to the courts blocked altogether. 121 S Ct at 2279, 2285–86. On behalf of the four dissenters, Justice Scalia furiously disputed the existence of sufficient ambiguity to trigger the constitutional doubt rule. Id at 2294–99.

It is noteworthy that the constitutional doubt doctrine plays a role in the immigration arena in any event—a field often thought to be a constitutional wasteland because of the plenary power doctrine. See note 9. For an insightful argument that this anomaly reveals significant soft spots in the plenary power doctrine, see Motomura, 100 Yale L J at 545, 560–64, 573–74 (cited in note 9).

[73] 121 S Ct at 2504.

tention for more than six months."[74] After six months, "once the alien provides good reason to believe that there is no significant likelihood of removal in the reasonably foreseeable future, the Government must respond with evidence sufficient to rebut that showing."[75] Absent a showing of foreseeable removal, release is required.

In the end, at least absent terrorism charges (or equivalent "special circumstances"), reasonably foreseeable removal is the only relevant fact the majority countenanced that might justify detention beyond six months.[76] But on a somewhat inharmonious note,

---

[74] Id at 2505. A close reading of the Senate report to which reference is made suggests that this overreads the Senate's comment, but Reps. Celler and Gorski did provide a strong statement of constitutional objections in their dissenting views appended to the House report on the same legislation. HR Rep No 1192, 81st Cong, 1st Sess 17–20 (1949). See notes 24–26.

[75] 121 S Ct at 2505.

[76] Id. Justice Kennedy, in dissent, also recognizes this feature: "The rule the majority creates permits consideration of nothing more than the reasonable foreseeability of removal." Id at 2512.

In this connection, Attorney General Ashcroft's initial response to the *Zadvydas* decision must be seen as ill-advised (and also disappointing). The INS's budgetary and operational incentives to release "lifers" had always been balanced against district directors' concerns over personal blame in the media if a released alien committed later crimes. Mr. Ashcroft could have accepted the Court's decision as a welcome shouldering of responsibility by the politically insulated judicial branch for any such consequences. He could have noted quietly that the decision merely reinstated a release mandate that the nation had accommodated, without disastrous consequences, through 1988, and that the full range of other criminal law deterrents and penalties still applied. Instead, he gave an alarmist speech at a "Safe Neighborhoods Event," declaring that the *Zadvydas* decision had created "an emergency situation." Attorney General's Prepared Remarks, Long-Term INS Detainees/Colorado, July 19, 2001.

His specific guidance to INS contained both problematic steps and promising ones. For example, the Attorney General misread the Court's reservation of the possibility for continued detention in "special circumstances"—treating the exception as though it could cover any "especially dangerous individuals," rather than only those linked somehow to national security risks. 66 Fed Reg 38433–34 (2001). The guidance also suggested that any aliens who violate the terms of their supervision would be redetained through administrative decision, rather than via prosecution under INA § 243(a), 8 USC § 1233(a) (2000). Justice Breyer's opinion, in contrast, although not wholly clear on this point, always links its comments about redetention to a reference to § 243. If redetention for such a violation is not thus linked, serious new problems could arise. Surely the principle of *Zadvydas* is not satisfied if a person were detained indefinitely for missing a single reporting date with INS while on supervised release. The pre-1988 system solved this problem by assuring that the length and terms of redetention for various types of defaults would be established through a prosecution under the predecessor to § 243, resulting in a criminal sentence of identified length. On the other hand, the Ashcroft guidance did outline several useful and quite legitimate steps in response to the decision. It signaled a renewed determination by the Department of Justice to press for diplomatic efforts to get recalcitrant countries to accept their nationals—recent activity suggests that the State Department has gotten the message—and to press the individuals involved to live up to their statutorily imposed duties, on pain of criminal punishment, to cooperate in obtaining travel documents.

the opinion does spend a few paragraphs telling habeas courts to "take appropriate account" of the expertise of the executive branch in making this prediction and to "listen with care" to foreign policy judgments about the status of repatriation negotiations.[77] The quoted phrases seem chosen with close attention. Perhaps the price of the crucial fifth vote was a reiteration of these familiar themes—expertise and foreign policy links—from immigration cases. But the themes are phrased in a more standoffish manner than is customary. These verbs may hint of deference, but they do not require it.

C. THE DISSENTS

Justice Scalia's dissent, joined by Justice Thomas, adopted the second of the two outcomes mentioned in Part IIA: The post-order detention question is to be left entirely to the political branches, without even any constitutional requirement that executive officials periodically review dangerousness or flight risk. In Justice Scalia's view, there are no situations in which the courts can order release of an alien whose removal order has become final but who cannot be removed because no country will take him.[78]

Scalia urged that analysis begin with a " 'careful description' of the substantive right claimed."[79] Taking dead aim at Breyer's starting premise, Scalia noted that the right can be "repackaged" as

---

As it happens, the interim final regulations ultimately issued in response to the Ashcroft directive seem acutely aware of the problems mentioned here. 66 Fed Reg 56967 (2001) (adding new §§ 241.13 and 241.14 to 8 CFR). They provide for prolonged detention under the "special circumstances" exception only in four defined circumstances: highly contagious diseases, serious adverse foreign policy consequences, security or terrorism concerns, and "aliens determined to be specially dangerous." 8 CFR § 241.14(b)–(f). The last category seems at first glance to provide for ongoing detention of those guilty of particularly severe crimes (which the initial Ashcroft announcement seemed to prefer, but which would be inconsistent with *Zadvydas*). But on closer examination, that category applies only to persons with both a serious criminal conviction *and* a mental condition or personality disorder, as found in a special proceeding before an immigration judge. That additional requirement is plainly meant to conform to Supreme Court doctrine governing preventive detention of the mentally ill. See, e.g., *Kansas v Hendricks*, 521 US 346, 358, 368 (1997). The regulations do allow for administrative redetention without prosecution when the individual violates a term of the supervised release, but they limit the new detention in such cases to six months, no matter what the violation. 8 CFR § 241.13(i); see 66 Fed Reg 56971. They also sharpen the requirements that the alien cooperate in obtaining travel documents. 8 CFR § 241.13(d)(2), (e)(2).

[77] 121 S Ct at 2504.

[78] Id at 2505 (Scalia, J, dissenting).

[79] Id, quoting from *Reno v Flores*, 507 US 292, 302 (1993).

freedom from physical restraint or from indefinite detention. But in reality it should be understood as "a claimed right of release into this country by an individual who *concededly* has no legal right to be here. There is no such constitutional right."[80] In a deft flanking maneuver, he invoked the dissenters from the passionately contested 5–4 *Mezei* decision in support of his conclusion. They dissented, he points out, because they thought Mezei was entitled to better procedural protections before being left to his fate: expulsion or, if no country would receive him, indefinite detention. None asserted that Mezei had a substantive constitutional right to release into the country.[81] This is a fully correct reading. Justice Jackson's powerfully written and moving dissent in *Mezei* targets only procedures. In addressing substantive due process, it expressly lumps excludables and deportables together when it avers that, in a procedurally proper case, neither has "the right to remain against the national will."[82]

Justice Breyer's angle of vision proceeded from the eyes of the individual "condemned" to an "imprisonment" that appears to have no end. Scalia's view plainly starts from the opposite pole, that of the nation. Once the removal order is final, he asserts, the national will is identical with regard to both excludable and deportable aliens, and *Mezei* therefore provides the applicable constitutional doctrine. There is thus no constitutional doubt to avoid. In any event, Justice Scalia fully agreed with that part of Justice Kennedy's dissent finding that no ambiguity exists in the statute. Congress clearly meant to allow extended detention, wholly at the discretion of the Attorney General.

On the constitutional issue, however, Justice Kennedy and Justice Scalia took sharply different positions. Kennedy, joined by the Chief Justice, staked out the third position identified in Part IIA: Lengthy confinement of unremovable aliens does demand constitutional scrutiny from the courts, but it can be justified if the procedures for deciding on release are adequate. Kennedy began by

---

[80] 121 S Ct at 2505 (emphasis in original). Justice Breyer's response was to suggest that Scalia is the one who distorts the nature of the alien's claim. He asks not for a "right of release into this country"—what the government's brief had characterized as "living at large." He asks instead to be moved from "imprisonment [to] supervision under release conditions that may not be violated." Id at 2502.

[81] Id at 2506.

[82] 345 US 206, 222–23 (Jackson, J, dissenting) (cited in note 13).

noting that extended detention does pose a substantive liberty issue under the Due Process Clause, giving the courts a reviewing role to assure against "detention that is arbitrary or capricious." But it is "neither arbitrary nor capricious to detain the aliens [situated like Zadvydas and Ma] when necessary to avoid the risk of flight or danger to the community."[83] Why? "The reason detention is permitted at all is that a removable alien does not have the same liberty interest as a citizen does. The Court cannot bring itself to acknowledge this established proposition."[84] The due process question therefore turns on "whether there are adequate procedures to review their cases, allowing persons once subject to detention to show that through rehabilitation, new appreciation of their responsibilities, or under other standards, they no longer present special risks or danger if put at large."[85]

The current INS regulations met this test, in Kennedy's view, assuring review at least annually, with what is, in general, an adequate opportunity for the individual to make his case, both on paper and through personal interview. Perhaps in future litigation particular elements of the regulations, such as the provision placing the burden of proof regarding nondangerousness on the alien, could be challenged, but no such focused procedural complaint had been made here.[86] Moreover, Kennedy left open the possibility that a habeas court might be called upon to review more than procedures—such as the substantive decision on dangerousness or

---

[83] 121 S Ct at 2515 (Kennedy, J, dissenting). Justice Kennedy argues that this possible substantive test for judicial review, focusing on flight risk and dangerousness, is far more appropriate and judicially manageable than the majority's, which "would have the Judiciary review the status of repatriation negotiations," perhaps to the point of calling high State Department officials to testify on them. Id at 2517. He even suggests elsewhere, id at 2511, that the majority's general six-month release requirement will "undercut the position of the Executive in repatriation negotiations." These scenarios are far-fetched. Negotiations on individual returns are almost never conducted at such high levels; they typically involve an INS deportation officer and a member of the other government's consular corps. (Travel documents are also frequently obtained even though there is no repatriation agreement with the home country; the misunderstanding that formal repatriation agreements are required also infected the Ninth Circuit's decision in Ma, 208 F3d at 828.) With countries that have been resolutely resistant to all returns, a new general agreement or framework, involving higher-level negotiators, may be relevant. But the majority probably contemplated that its test, because it leans so strongly toward release, would discourage the U.S. government from claiming reasonable foreseeability of return until a public announcement about such agreement has been cleared.

[84] 121 S Ct at 2513.

[85] Id at 2515.

[86] Id at 2516.

flight risk. Kennedy even suggested that, "[g]iven the undeniable deprivation of liberty caused by the detention, there might be substantial questions concerning the severity necessary for there to be a community risk."[87] But these matters did not require decision in *Zadvydas*.

One other element in the Kennedy dissent is striking. He and Justice Rehnquist would not let the substantive liberty question turn on the exclusion-deportation line. "[B]oth removable and inadmissible aliens," as he phrases the distinction, "are entitled to be free from detention that is arbitrary or capricious."[88] Plainly this stance does not implicate the same test as would be applied to detention of citizens. But it does indicate that excludable aliens like the Marielitos are also constitutionally entitled to procedurally adequate ongoing review, subject to judicial monitoring, of dangerousness and flight risk. It follows that Kennedy and Rehnquist would have dissented from *Mezei*'s holding countenancing indefinite detention without further qualification, and presumably would overrule that part of the decision today.

Whether they would overrule the procedural part of *Mezei*, which allows secret evidence, is far less clear. Justice Kennedy's opinion offers up a meandering passage reflecting on the majority's use of *Mezei* and on various questions that case raises, including a description of Mezei's later release through executive action seventeen months after the Court's ruling. This account might possibly be taken as critical of the overall holding and of using the exclusion-deportation line even on the procedural question.[89] But at the bottom line, Justice Kennedy appears to accept that different procedural entitlements apply in the two settings, a difference that lasts only up to the point that the removal order is final: "Removable and excludable aliens are situated differently before an order of removal is entered; the removable alien, by virtue of his continued presence here, possesses an interest in remaining, while the excludable alien seeks only the privilege of entry."[90]

---

[87] Id at 2517.

[88] Id at 2515.

[89] Id at 2514–15.

[90] Id at 2515.

III. The Significance of Zadvydas

What might account for the differences in due process protections that the Supreme Court's decision reinforces, between aliens like Zadvydas and Ma on the one hand, and Mezei[91] and the Marielitos on the other? I will examine critically several possible factors that are candidates for helping to explain the outcome, and then go beyond that analysis to suggest a better way to understand the difference and to sketch a more satisfying way to explain different levels of constitutional protection for various categories of aliens. I wish to defend Justice Breyer's ultimate conclusion as applied to the particular individuals before the Court in *Zadvydas*, as well as the basic idea that the Due Process Clause may implement different levels of protection for different categories along the alienage-citizenship spectrum. But in the end there should be more than two rungs on the ladder of due process protection for aliens, and even the bottom rung deserves some level of judicial enforcement, rather than the complete surrender to Congress that *Mezei* seemed to decree.

In the analysis that follows, I adopt the following methodology: I assume that the majority's discussion of due process truly represents its views of what the Constitution requires, not simply the existence of constitutional doubts, and that the majority intends to sustain in some form the *Mezei* exception, denying to certain categories of aliens the protections it finds for these two individuals. The tone of the opinion lends credence to that reading of the majority's views, although one must acknowledge that the Court

---

[91] Mezei in reality was a former lawful permanent resident, returning after nineteen months abroad. Permanent residents, I will argue, deserve a far higher measure of protection, even when returning from foreign travel. But I accept the abstract principle at work in *Mezei:* that a sufficient, willful absence constitutes abandonment of residence and can extinguish a one-time LPR's claims to heightened protection. I will therefore in text treat Mezei as the Court did, on a par with an applicant alien appearing at the border for the first time. A footnote should at least observe, however, that the basic principle seems badly misapplied on the facts of *Mezei* itself. According to the facts as he pled them, he tried mightily to return after a brief absence, but was prevented by factors beyond his control. This account is bolstered by the fact that his wife and children remained behind in Buffalo, their home for twenty-five years. See *Mezei*, 345 US at 220 (Jackson, J, dissenting) (observing that the Court should treat the facts as he pled them for present purposes, since he had never had a factual hearing); Weisselberg, 143 U Pa L Rev at 964–84 (cited in note 16) (describing Mezei's situation). Cf. *Landon v Plasencia*, 459 US 21, 29 (1982) (clarifying that the distinction is abandonment, not mere territorial location of the LPR).

left itself room to reach a different constitutional conclusion, should Congress someday enact an unambiguous statute permitting indefinite detention, or (in the opposite direction) if a case squarely challenging *Mezei* were to be accepted for review.

A. INITIAL FACTORS BEARING ON THE LEVEL
OF CONSTITUTIONAL PROTECTION

The first possible explanation for allowing indefinite detention to turn on the exclusion-deportation line derives from physical location. This factor provides the majority's most clearly stated rationale for distinguishing *Mezei* in order to advance the liberty claim of Zadvydas and Ma. At various points Justice Breyer's opinion seems to say that the Due Process Clause does not apply at all until an alien officially enters the country.[92] The opinion later argues against Justice Scalia's dissent by emphasizing that the Supreme Court's approval of Mezei's indefinite detention "rested upon a basic *territorial* distinction."[93]

Territoriality counted for a great deal in the worldview of the nineteenth-century court, and echoes of that outlook contributed to the conclusions in *Knauff* and *Mezei*.[94] But in the twenty-first century one can hardly find geography a satisfying foundation for distinctions of this magnitude—particularly when the Court itself began to move away from a wooden territorial understanding of the Constitution's reach nearly fifty years ago in *Reid v Covert*.[95] The 1990 decision in *United States v Verdugo-Urquidez*, to be sure, breathed some renewed life into territoriality as a basis for certain constitutional dividing lines.[96] But the Court emphasized that the issue there concerned only the application of the Fourth Amendment to actions carried out entirely in Mexico—a search by Mexi-

---

[92] 121 S Ct at 2500.

[93] Id at 2501 (emphasis added).

[94] For the leading statement of the earlier territorial understanding, see *In re Ross*, 140 US 453, 464 (1891) ("The Constitution can have no operation in another country."). See also *Fong Yue Ting v United States*, 149 US 698, 754–57 (1893) (Field, J, dissenting) (the author of *The Chinese Exclusion Case*, which essentially forswore judicial review of exclusion provisions, passionately dissents from a case applying its severe doctrine to a deportable resident alien—explaining the distinction based on territoriality); id at 734–38 (Brewer, J, dissenting) (similarly explaining the distinction in the two cases).

[95] 354 US 1, 12 (1957).

[96] 494 US 259, 270–72 (1990).

can and American authorities of a home in Mexico belonging to a Mexican citizen with no voluntary ties to the United States.[97] In contrast, the inspection stations for U.S. ports of entry are clearly on U.S. territory, and the ongoing detention of Marielitos occurs at U.S. jails or prisons well within the interior. *Verdugo-Urquidez* does not purport to stretch the territorial notion to render such locations extraterritorial, even for Fourth Amendment purposes.[98]

In any event, Justice Breyer's dividing line is not truly territorial. Recall that after invoking the exclusion-deportation distinction from *Mezei*, he immediately discussed cases not of prototypical first-time arrivals but of long-time parolees, who had been living in the community for as much as seven years. Territoriality thus cannot tell the whole story. No less important in his framework of constitutional analysis is legal status, or at least some types of legal status. Conceivably one could be persuaded that a port of entry, though obviously located on U.S. soil, should still be considered extraterritorial for some purposes—where else could inspection stations be located? Maybe such a conception does not press geography too hard.[99] It becomes more difficult, though perhaps not impossible, to take that view when the person is held in a U.S. detention facility while the decision on admission is pending. But a parolee released with few restrictions into the interior of the country moves within the same territory and social space as a host of other aliens and citizens.

The traditional "entry fiction" is meant to reconcile the constitutional status of parolees with the embarrassing physical facts of their geographic location. But an honest devotee of that fiction must still acknowledge that legal status thereby becomes far more

---

[97] Verdugo was in the United States at the time of the search, following his arrest by Mexican authorities and his handover to U.S. officials at the border. But the Fourth Amendment challenge went to the search of his home in Mexico in the ensuing days, not to the treatment of his person in America. The Court emphasized that "[f]or purposes of this case, therefore, if there were a constitutional violation, it occurred solely in Mexico." Id at 264.

[98] The government at one time tried to use *Verdugo-Urquidez* to establish that undocumented aliens enjoyed insufficient ties to the country to have standing to invoke the Fourth Amendment against searches and seizures undeniably conducted on U.S. soil. One court initially accepted this position, but on reconsideration decisively rejected it. *United States v Guitterez*, 983 F Supp 905 (ND Cal 1998).

[99] See *United States v Ju Toy*, 198 US 253, 263 (1905) (per Holmes, J) ("The petitioner, although physically within our boundaries, is to be regarded as if he had been stopped at the limit of our jurisdiction, and kept there while his right to enter was under debate.").

important than territorial location, and territory no longer can carry the explanatory burden. Despite an alien's de facto entry into the territory on parole, usually with broad freedom to travel, work, develop friendships, and even marry and produce U.S. citizen offspring, legal status dictates that the alien be treated as if still confined at the port of entry, even years later. If legal status can thus be determinative, then Justice Breyer's conclusion as to Zadvydas and Ma is vulnerable. Constitutional entitlements then turn not on extralegal or prelegal characteristics of the individual, but on governmentally defined specifications. If this kind of positivism rules in the case of parolees—that is, if statute or regulation may simply decree that a person is in a constitutionally unprotected category, whatever the physical or social facts—why deny it the same power with regard to deportable aliens who have been duly issued a final order of removal? I shall further explore this key question in Part IIID below, after we put a few more considerations on the table.

Another factor that obviously played a role in the majority's liberty-affirming decision in *Zadvydas* derives from the Court's resolute insistence on viewing the situation from the perspective of the alien, not of the government. The human impact was this: Zadvydas and Ma were "condemned" to an "imprisonment" that has no discernible or predictable end, and they faced that fate even though they had served the full term meted out by the criminal law and were not to blame for any impasse with possible destination states. This empathetic factor seems clearly at work in energizing the majority's conclusions. But importantly, by itself it cannot explain the distinction from Mezei, the Marielitos, or excludable aliens generally whose nations will not accept their return. Looking through their eyes at the prospects for their physical treatment, one would be likely to judge that they face the same human reality, a doom of indefinite confinement.

It is just possible, however, that a more careful examination could bolster some part of the distinction. Perhaps the human impact the majority had in mind derives not only from current treatment in the detention facility, but also from awareness of alternatives that would be available to the individual if he were released while awaiting deportation. An alien who has entered and remained in the country for any significant period of time may have developed ties to the community through education, employment, friendships, or other engagement during his stay. This network of connections would distinguish the prototypical excludable alien, a first-time arrival on our shores who has not yet progressed past the inspection station or the associated detention facility. Both aliens may face the bleakness of indefinite detention if the home government refuses return, but the excludable alien's plight is not compounded by knowledge of a potentially supportive community just on the other side of the wall, a familiar alternative location to which he is already connected, where he could at least await the outcome of negotiations for his repatriation. For the prototypical excludable alien, the Court could be saying, the human impact is thus somewhat different. His center of emotional gravity is back in the country of nationality, and neither release nor confinement can restore him to that primary web of social connections, so long as the government of that country prevents his return. He might of course establish new ties here if released, even under the shadow of the looming removal order. Nonetheless there remains a qualitative social difference from the situation of Zadvydas and Ma, who had established social connections through many years of lawful residence. Perhaps it is the blockage, for the deportable alien, of these preexisting connections that sharpens the harshness of indefinite detention and dictates, for the *Zadvydas* majority, a different constitutional outcome as between deportables and excludables.

This approach opens a useful line of thinking, but again it hardly tracks the contours of most of the cases that Breyer's opinion divides by category. Long-time parolees, including most of the Marielitos, undoubtedly acquired social connections, whereas some persons traditionally classed as deportable aliens, if apprehended within a short time after unlawful entry or if admitted only for transient purposes like tourism, probably would not. If some assessment of social connections really made the difference, one would expect a due process rule that varies not by immigration category, but by individual. Some sort of balancing test, perhaps something like the *Mathews v Eldridge* calculus,[100] could be applied.

---

[100] 424 US 319, 334–35 (1976). That case deals with procedural due process, whereas detention issues are more properly viewed as implicating a mix of procedural and substantive due process. The *Eldridge* three-part test involves evaluating (1) the individual interest, (2) the risk of an erroneous deprivation under existing procedures and the probable value of the added procedural ingredient for which the individual contends, and (3) the government interest.

An unreturnable alien's right to release from detention then might turn on a fine-grained assessment of the individual's interest associated with release, balanced against the government's interest in continued incarceration. The strength of the individual interest would depend on a case-by-case showing of actual social connections in this country—which would not vary by legal status or immigration category, but rather by sociological reality. Some academic writings essentially urge such an approach—downplaying legal status and instead basing any difference of constitutional treatment solely on individualized assessments of stakes or circumstances.[101]

B. THE FOUNDATIONS FOR A CATEGORICAL APPROACH TO ALIENS' RIGHTS AND THE RELEVANCE OF RELATIONAL OBLIGATIONS

Is it then justified to apply categorical judgments when assessing at least certain constitutional rights for aliens, or should we regard such thinking as outdated, worthy of replacement by a more individualized balancing test? If a categorical approach is justified, how should we understand the differences among categories? Is there some broad reason why social connections (or other relevant facts) established by aliens on the favored side of the traditional exclusion-deportation line should count for more categorically, and be of enduring constitutional significance, even once the individual's legal status has been altered by a final removal order—while ostensibly similar connections would not override legal status for a parolee? The question is how and where the *social reality* counts and where the *legal status* is more authoritative. My thesis is that each plays a certain role, but the mix is intricate and nuanced, and decisions in this realm should be guided by underappreciated patterns of constitutional and political practice that have persisted throughout most of the history of systematic federal immigration controls, particularly the premier status given in law and social reality to lawful permanent resident status.

As a starting point, the Constitution unmistakably points us toward one fundamental categorical distinction in deciding certain questions of rights: that between citizens and aliens. Although we

---

[101] See, e.g., T. Alexander Aleinikoff, *Aliens, Due Process, and "Community Ties": A Response to Martin*, 44 U Pitt L Rev 237, 244–45.

are justly proud of the fact that our Constitution does not leave aliens bereft of rights,[102] the text unmistakably draws this categorical line for certain purposes. Most of these have to do with political rights. Only citizens—and at that, persons who have been citizens for certain specified durations—are eligible for elected federal office,[103] and the many constitutional amendments that touch on voting rights extend their protections only to citizens.[104] By important contrast, the Bill of Rights uses terms of broader scope (e.g., "persons," "the accused") that generally include aliens when rights to property or rights in the criminal justice system are at issue. The Fifth Amendment Due Process Clause applies to "persons," not some narrower category, as do the two workhorse provisions of the Fourteenth Amendment, the Due Process and Equal Protection Clauses.

For well over a century, the Court has tended to apply these latter, broadly worded protections vigorously to gain for aliens equal treatment with citizens in the economic realm and when subjected to criminal sanctions—important fields where categorical distinctions are generally not allowed. In the criminal justice arena, government must afford aliens the full range of constitutional protections, especially jury trial, when imposing criminal punishment, even with regard to federal penalties for immigration violations imposed on aliens duly adjudged to be present unlawfully. The Court established this principle in 1896 in *Wong Wing v United States*,[105] a decision justly regarded as a bulwark of constitutional

---

[102] Alexander Bickel, *The Morality of Consent* 33–54 (1975); Gerald L. Neuman, *Strangers to the Constitution* at 1–15 (cited in note 9).

[103] Art I, § 2, cl 2 (members of the House of Representatives must have been U.S. citizens for seven years); Art I, § 3, cl 3 (Senators must have been U.S. citizens for nine years); Art II, § 1, cl 5 (President must be a natural born citizen).

[104] US Const, Amends XIV, § 2 (reducing representation in the House of Representatives to the extent that male citizens are denied the right to vote), XV (the right of citizens to vote is not to be denied on account of race, color, or previous condition of servitude), XIX (extending the right to vote to female citizens), XXIV (citizens must not be denied the right to vote for failure to pay poll tax or other taxes), XXVI (extending the right to vote to citizens eighteen years of age or older). None of these provisions requires that the franchise be restricted to citizens; they simply set a floor insisting upon voting rights for citizens who meet certain criteria. In fact, until the 1920s many states allowed resident aliens to vote. See Jamin B. Raskin, *Legal Aliens, Local Citizens: The Historical, Constitutional and Theoretical Meanings of Alien Suffrage*, 141 U Pa L Rev 1391, 1401–16 (1993). For broader reflections on extending voting rights to noncitizens, see Gerald L. Neuman, *"We Are the People": Alien Suffrage in German and American Perspective*, 13 Mich J Intl L 259 (1992).

[105] 163 US 228 (1896).

liberty.[106] Constitutional protections in the economic realm trace to another landmark case of that era, *Yick Wo v Hopkins*, which struck down unequal administration of a San Francisco laundry ordinance that had systematically disadvantaged Chinese aliens.[107] *Yick Wo* emphatically applied to these plaintiffs the Fourteenth Amendment's guarantee of equal protection of the laws, despite their alienage. In 1915, in *Truax v Raich*, the Court denied the state of Arizona the power to restrict the employment of lawfully resident aliens in the private sector.[108] In 1971, in *Graham v Richardson*, a case involving state-administered welfare benefits, the Court seemed to go much further and to suggest that any state-law usage of alienage distinctions amounted to a suspect classification demanding a compelling justification.[109]

But the Court soon realized that *Graham's* conceptual approach could not hold up. For certain purposes, such as voting and the holding of certain public offices, the Court retreated and eventually allowed the states to draw categorical alienage distinctions without being subject to strict scrutiny. In *Sugarman v Dougall*, the Court struck down a blanket New York rule that barred aliens from all state civil service jobs, but it laid the groundwork for the coming retreat by suggesting that a narrower state rule barring aliens from eligibility for policy-making governmental positions might be justified. It explained the distinction by reference to the concept of community: a state's power to place such limits on high-level positions derived from its "obligation . . . 'to preserve the basic conception of a political community.'"[110] A few years

---

[106] See Henry Hart, *The Power of Congress to Limit the Jurisdiction of Federal Courts: An Exercise in Dialectic*, 66 Harv L Rev 1362, 1387 (1953).

[107] 118 US 356 (1886).

[108] 239 US 33 (1915). See also *Takahashi v Fish & Game Comm'n*, 334 US 410 (1948) (striking down a California regulation denying to resident aliens ocean fishing rights). Absent federal law to the contrary, the states have a wider field of action in regulating the employment of non-LPR aliens, and specifically those who have not been given federal permission to work in this country. *DeCanas v Bica*, 424 US 351 (1976) (upholding California law sanctioning employers hiring undocumented aliens; such state laws were later expressly preempted by federal statute).

[109] 403 US 365 (1971); see also *In re Griffiths*, 413 US 717 (1973) (striking down state rule requiring citizenship as a prerequisite to practicing law); *Plyler v Doe*, 457 US 202 (1982) (applying intermediate scrutiny to strike down, as violative of the Equal Protection Clause, a Texas statute that denied a free public education to children who were undocumented aliens).

[110] 413 US 634, 647 (1973), quoting *Dunn v Blumstein*, 405 US 330, 344 (1972).

later, in *Cabell v Chavez-Salido*, the Court expanded on its reasoning: "The exclusion of aliens from basic governmental processes is not a deficiency in the democratic system but a necessary consequence of the community's process of political self-definition."[111]

The Court also retreated from any suggestion, which might have been derivable from *Graham*, that the federal government would also have to provide compelling justification for differential treatment of aliens, even in realms, such as the design of welfare programs, where states were thus constrained. In *Mathews v Diaz*, the Court sustained a federal regulation disqualifying aliens from Medicare participation unless they had lived in the country for five years as lawful permanent residents. Significantly, it justified the wider federal power to distinguish among aliens or between aliens and citizens based on the federal government's authority, in contrast to the states, "to regulate the conditions of entry and residence of aliens."[112] In this respect, the restriction on access to federal welfare benefits fit rather tidily with a long-standing immigration-law requirement that aliens applying for admission must convince the relevant officials that they were not "likely to become a public charge," and a further provision permitting deportation, under some circumstances, if the alien did go on public assistance within five years of entry.[113] The Court explained the wider scope for federal distinctions: "In the exercise of its broad power over naturalization and immigration, Congress regularly makes rules that would be unacceptable if applied to citizens."[114] But the Court

---

[111] *Cabell v Chavez-Salido*, 454 US 432, 439 (1982). See also *Ambach v Norwick*, 441 US 68 (1979) (state may require teachers to be citizens); *Foley v Connelie*, 435 US 291 (1978) (same for police officers). Summary rulings on lower court judgments have clarified that states may bar aliens from voting and from jury duty. *Skafte v Rorex*, 191 Colo 399, 553 P2d 830 (1976), appeal dismissed for want of a substantial federal question, 430 US 961 (1977) (voting); *Perkins v Smith*, 370 F Supp 134 (D Md 1974), aff'd, 426 US 913 (1976) (jury duty).

[112] *Mathews v Diaz*, 426 US 67, 84 (1976).

[113] This provision is still reflected in the immigration laws at INA § 212(a)(4) (inadmissibility ground) and § 237(a)(5) (deportability ground, which itself is tied to persons who become a public charge within five years of entry, "from causes not affirmatively shown to have arisen since entry"), 8 USC §§ 1182(a)(4), 1227(a)(5) (2000). The deportation ground is rarely used, owing to a restrictive ruling by the Board of Immigration Appeals, which held that the ground could be applied only when the agency that provided the assistance made a demand for reimbursement and the alien failed to comply. *Matter of B–*, 3 I & N Dec 323 (1948). See Michael J. Sheridan, *The New Affidavit of Support and Other 1996 Amendments to Immigration and Welfare Provisions Designed to Prevent Aliens from Becoming Public Charges*, 31 Creighton L Rev 741, 742–43 (1998).

[114] 426 US at 79–80.

still manifested skepticism of the federal government's use of alien-age distinctions if they could not be sufficiently tied to the regulation of immigration or naturalization.[115] In a second decision issued the same day, *Hampton v Mow Sun Wong*,[116] the Court vacated a federal Civil Service Commission rule excluding aliens from federal employment. It conceded that categorical discrimination of this type by the federal government could possibly be justified (although *Sugarman* had ruled out such a broad regulation imposed by a state) if the proper authorities sought to use such a practice as an incentive for resident aliens to naturalize, or for certain foreign policy reasons. But it found that the Civil Service Commission was not institutionally competent to make rules of that type.[117]

The net effect of these distinctions could be described as a difference between immigration law on the one hand, where a discount in protections may give the federal political branches a freer rein in decisions about aliens, and immigrant or aliens law on the other hand, where all persons must be treated equally.[118] Even the restrictive reading of the Fourth Amendment in *Verdugo-Urquidez*, which relied on the amendment's language announcing "the right

---

[115] See also *Jean v Nelson*, 472 US 846, 881 (Marshall, J, dissenting) (offering a variant on this approach: "When central immigration concerns are not at stake, . . . the Executive must recognize the individuality of the alien, just as it must recognize the individuality of all other persons within our borders.").

[116] 426 US 88 (1976).

[117] The rule barring aliens from most civil service positions was eventually reinstated by means of an Executive Order issued by the President, who obviously does partake of wider powers in both the immigration and foreign policy fields. The renewed rule was sustained on judicial review. *Mow Sun Wong v Campbell*, 626 F2d 739 (9th Cir 1980), cert denied, 450 US 959 (1981). See Aleinikoff, Martin, and Motomura, *Immigration and Citizenship* at 535–38 (cited in note 17).

[118] For discussions of these distinctions, see Michael Scaperlanda, *Partial Membership: Aliens and The Constitutional Community*, 81 Iowa L Rev 707 (1996); Hiroshi Motomura, *Immigration and Alienage, Federalism and Proposition 187*, 35 Va J Intl L 201 (1994); Linda Bosniak, *Membership, Equality, and the Difference That Alienage Makes*, 69 NYU L Rev 1047, 1056–57 (1994); T. Alexander Aleinikoff, *Citizens, Aliens, Membership, and The Constitution*, 7 Const Comm 9 (1990). This distinction also corresponds to views about the respective spheres of action found in Michael Walzer, *Spheres of Justice: A Defense of Pluralism and Equality* 52–63 (1983). He argues that the distribution of national membership "is not pervasively subject to the constraints of justice." That is, in the realm of decisions about immigration, the nation has considerable discretion and freedom of action. But once persons are admitted as residents, Walzer argues, they must be able to live on terms of equality, subject only to a limited probationary period before full voting rights are obtained. For another fruitful and thought-provoking way to analyze these distinctions, see Hiroshi Motomura, *Alienage Classifications in a Nation of Immigrants: Three Models of "Permanent" Residence*, in Noah M. J. Pickus, ed, *Immigration and Citizenship in the 21st Century* 199 (1998).

of the People" to be free from unreasonable searches and seizures, did not leave all—or even most—aliens unprotected. The use of "the People," that decision explained, "refers to a class of persons who are part of a national community or who have otherwise developed sufficient connection with this country to be considered part of that community."[119] The Court there held, in essence, that aliens voluntarily present in this country are indeed part of "the People."

Aliens, in short, are part of the community for some purposes, but not for others. Or perhaps it would be phrased more accurately thus: Aliens, at least if present here, may be members of a relevant community they share with citizens, and are thus entitled to the respect of certain rights and subject to certain reciprocal duties. But there are different levels of membership, or different circles of community, and additional reciprocal duties and rights, or at least more stringent protections of rights, will come into being for persons as they move to higher circles of membership.

A certain range of constitutional entitlements, then, are already subject to categorical limitations. In these fields, we do not require the government to look to individual circumstance or social connections and weigh the relative claims of individual aliens, so that, for example, the better informed or those with longer periods of residence may claim a constitutional right to vote. Categorical distinctions, founded on but not wholly determined by legal status, are not permitted to overwhelm the proud tradition of *Yick Wo* and *Wong Wing* in the realms to which they apply, but they do continue to play an acknowledged role in deciding other constitutional questions.

Knauff and *Mezei*, then, were not methodologically aberrational in providing that some categorical judgments be made *before* applying the usual constitutional tests—or to allow for some discount in the operation of the usual tests based on the particularities of the person's status as an alien.[120] (Where they may have devi-

---

[119] 494 US 259, 265 (1990).

[120] This sequence of decision making is perhaps clearest in *Landon v Plasencia*, 459 US 21 (1982). The Court first had to decide which membership category applied. Once it determined that Mrs. Plasencia's two-day trip to Mexico did not take her out of the entitlement category occupied by LPRs, even though she was geographically at the border, it became clear that the *Eldridge* test applied, without discount, in the same fashion as to a citizen, in deciding her procedural due process claim.

ated, however, was in their refusal to recognize that these two individuals shared *any* membership in even one of the outer circles
of community that might give rise to even modest protections—
although one was married to an American and the other had long-
resident family members waiting for his return to their lawful
home of twenty-five years.) Moreover, to the extent that these
cases draw some sort of distinction between different categories of
aliens, they appeal to intuitions that are probably widely shared.
Most Americans, I suspect, would expect distinctions to be drawn
between longtime lawful permanent residents like Zadvydas or Ma
and excludable aliens who simply show up at our borders without
advance screening, as did the Marielitos, even if the latter group
eventually spends some time lawfully released inside the country.
The historical path followed by the two classes of claimants on
their way to their current, superficially similar, status as aliens who
are now subject to a final removal order simply cries out for some
kind of recognition. In encounters with the federal government,
it is not jarring to assume that the former would have a stronger
claim to protections than the latter. This is not necessarily to say
that the latter would have no constitutional claim. Even Justice
Scalia in *Zadvydas*, while disclaiming any court role in superin-
tending indefinite detention of unremovable aliens, hastens to add
that excludable aliens could not be tortured.

Or perhaps the intuition should be stated the other way around:
that our society somehow owes more in the way of protections,
both procedural and substantive, to the group that includes Zadvydas and Ma, in light of some kind of relevant difference in the
polity's connections, both legal and social, to the two classes. Due
process determinations amount to judgments about what is owing
to the claimant. "Due" derives from an Old French verb meaning
"to owe," and one meaning is "owing by right of circumstances
or condition."[121] The intuitively plausible notion of differences in
what is owed to aliens in these different circumstances amounts to
a statement about relational obligations. Relational obligations and
their corresponding rights are commonly recognized. Many arise
from voluntary acts or agreements, such as contract, but they can
also exist as a result of nonvoluntary circumstances, such as the

---

[121] The compact edition of the *Oxford English Dictionary* (1971).

relation of child to parent, or brother and sister. Though citizenship is largely an accident of birth, we commonly conceive of it as giving rise to special obligations to fellow citizens and to the polity that can serve as their representative. Citizens may owe military service. They may be required to pay taxes, even when they are not resident in the territory and therefore receive relatively little in the way of normal public services. The polity, in return, owes to citizens the recognition and fulfillment of a range of rights and certain kinds of support or services.

In talking about these kinds of relational rights and obligations, we often link them to the notion of community. To say that a certain town is a vibrant community is largely to suggest that this kind of interaction and sharing takes place there, that members recognize and fulfill reciprocal obligations of respect and assistance. The Court, as the quoted language from *Verdugo-Urquidez* and the *Sugarman-Cabell* line of state equal protection cases reveals, has often invoked the language of community to account for certain categorical differences in the constitutional treatment of aliens and citizens. But as indicated, our concept of national community does not coincide precisely with the boundaries of the class of citizens. Aliens who travel and work in our midst enjoy a form of membership in the community, and this form of membership gives rise to its own distinctive claims.[122]

Often unappreciated, however, is the fact that the character of that membership is marked, or at least affected, by certain fairly clear dividing lines that are an enduring feature of U.S. law and administration. They have developed and solidified in the practices of this country of immigration at least since the 1920s, when we first placed numerical limits on permanent immigration and therefore had to be more systematic in accounting for who was admitted temporarily and who more permanently.[123] But most of those dis-

---

[122] I have developed this line of thought at greater length, with a consideration of other possible objections, in David A. Martin, *Due Process and Membership in the National Community: Political Asylum and Beyond*, 44 U Pitt L Rev 165, 190–208 (1983).

[123] Immigration Act of May 26, 1924, 43 Stat 153; Quota Law of May 19, 1921, 42 Stat 5. It was apparently the 1924 law that first used the term "non-immigrant" (meaning a person coming for a temporary stay) in distinction to nonquota immigrants, such as the wife or minor child of a citizen, although the difference was not clearly marked; both categories were exempt from the national origins quotas established by those acts. The Act of July 1, 1932, 47 Stat 524, clarified the authority to place time limits and other conditions on nonimmigrant admissions by regulation, and to enforce them through bond requirements.

tinctions have antecedents in earlier immigration practices as well. The exclusion-deportation boundary marks one of these dividing lines. But it is neither the only such line nor, in all probability, the most important one. If we are going to use categorical distinctions among aliens in deciding on constitutional rights, as has been our constitutional practice for at least the fifty years since *Knauff*, we should derive a better and more justifiable set of constitutional delineations.

I do not assert that the dividing lines sketched in the next section were themselves constitutionally required, nor that they are necessarily immune to change. But the layered practice I will describe has been exceptionally stable and durable, even as Congress has seen fit to amend the details affecting both immigration benefits and enforcement tools and tactics. Because we do employ categorical distinctions among aliens for some constitutional purposes, borrowed from what initially began as optional statutory architecture, my claim is, at a minimum, that we should use a richer and more accurate understanding of that architecture in the future.

C. A HIERARCHY OF MEMBERSHIP LEVELS

The basic structure of community membership levels in this setting employs six distinct categories, clearly grounded in enduring features of U.S. immigration law and practice. In summary form, and roughly in order of decreasing community membership, these are:

—citizen
—lawful permanent resident (or immigrant)
—admitted nonimmigrant
—entrant without inspection
—parolee
—applicant at the border.

Citizens. Obviously, citizens occupy the highest rung of the community membership ladder. They are full members, with complete political rights such as voting and officeholding, and are entitled to the entire range of constitutional protections, without any categorical discount. The exact content of those protections as they apply to questions of ongoing membership of course has evolved. For example, through much of our early history, citizens could be subjected to banishment as a punishment for crime,[124] and could also have their citizenship taken away against their wishes.[125] But since the 1940s, the Supreme Court has steadily enhanced the protections that citizens enjoy against involuntary loss of membership, to the point that it now may be lost only when a citizen specifically intends to relinquish it.[126] And banishment of a citizen is no longer viewed as a permissible punishment.[127]

Lawful permanent residents. Since the 1920s, U.S. law has been characterized by administrative practices that clarify from the time of admission whether an alien is being admitted for permanent residence purposes or only for a temporary stay. Aliens are admitted either as immigrants, otherwise called lawful permanent residents (LPRs), or as nonimmigrants allowed to enter for a temporary purpose. Lawful permanent residents—green card holders—have wide access to the private employment market and are generally as protected as citizens in their rights to enter into contracts and acquire property, rights that have been bolstered by numerous Supreme Court rulings, as described in Part IIIB.[128] Lawful permanent residents are also subject to some obligations quite comparable to those imposed on citizens. In general, they are taxed on an equal footing with citizens, covering their worldwide income, not just that from U.S. sources.[129] They have historically been fully subject to conscription, in those times when this nation has had a military draft.[130] They can acquire citizenship through naturaliza-

---

[124] See *Cooper v Telfair*, 4 US (4 Dall) 14, 19 (1800) (dictum); Gerald L. Neuman, *Strangers to the Constitution: Immigrants, Borders, and Fundamental Law* 22–23 (1996).

[125] See *Perez v Brownell*, 356 US 44 (1958); *MacKenzie v Hare*, 239 US 299 (1915).

[126] *Vance v Terrazas*, 444 US 252 (1980); *Afroyim v Rusk*, 387 US 253 (1967); *Trop v Dulles*, 356 US 86 (1958); *Nishikawa v Dulles*, 356 US 129 (1958). Citizenship acquired through naturalization may be lost without such specific intent, but only upon a finding that it was originally acquired illegally or through fraud. *Schneider v Rusk*, 377 US 163 (1964). Moreover, the Supreme Court has made it clear that the government bears a heavy burden of proof in denaturalization cases. *Schneiderman v United States*, 320 US 118 (1943).

[127] *Trop v Dulles*, 356 US at 102 (dictum). The practice may perhaps survive in the form of pardons conditioned on departure from the country, see Neuman, *Strangers to the Constitution* at 23 (cited in note 9), although if so, its incidence is rare.

[128] Protecting resident aliens, especially Chinese, was also an objective of the civil rights laws passed after the Civil War. See *Runyon v McCrary*, 427 US 160, 200–06 (White, J, dissenting) (recounting the legislative history).

[129] See David M. Hudson, *Tax Problems for Departing Aliens*, 97-03 Immigration Briefings 1–3 (March 1997).

[130] See, e.g., Selective Service Act of 1948, c 625, Title I, § 3, 62 Stat 604, 605. Although no conscription currently takes place, resident aliens must register for the draft, while nonimmigrants are expressly exempt from registration. 50 USC App § 453 (2000). Unlike citi-

tion on fairly easy terms that have scarcely changed in 200 years: generally by showing five years' residence, a minimal ability in the English language, a record clean of serious criminal offenses, and a basic knowledge and acceptance of the principles of U.S. governance.[131] Unlike citizens, they of course cannot vote or hold certain public offices, and they can be subjected to restrictions on their access to welfare and certain other federal government programs.[132] They are not immune to deportation. Nonetheless, with very limited exceptions our laws have imposed expulsion on LPRs only for crimes and a narrow range of other individual bad behavior, such as engagement in terrorism or defined subversive activities. In practice, for the last forty years at least, LPRs have almost never been expelled on grounds other than conviction for a crime.[133] And even while the Court has been highly deferential to the political branches' plenary power over substantive deportation grounds, it has insisted that LPRs are entitled to an undiluted measure of procedural due process protection, under the *Eldridge* test, even if they are at the border seeking readmission.[134]

---

zens, LPRs have been permitted to opt out of subjection to conscription, but only at the cost of becoming ineligible for naturalization. See INA §§ 101(a)(19), 315, 8 USC §§ 1101(a)(19), 1426 (2000).

[131] INA §§ 313, 316, 8 USC §§ 1424, 1427 (2000).

[132] *Mathews v Diaz*, 426 US 67 (1976); *City of Chicago v Shalala*, 189 F3d 598 (7th Cir 1999), cert denied, 529 US 1036 (2000).

[133] Immediately before that time frame, national security cases gave rise to several well-publicized expulsions in the 1950s based on membership in the Communist party, without criminal convictions. Yet even in that era, the risk to LPRs generally of removal on grounds other than a criminal conviction was not great. In the 1950s, INS deported 230 aliens on grounds relating to subversion or anarchist beliefs, as compared to seventeen in the 1940s, fifteen in the 1960s, and eighteen during the 1970s. (INS stopped separate reporting for this category of deportation after 1980.) The published INS data do not record how many of these were LPRs. Department of Justice, *1998 Statistical Yearbook of the Immigration and Naturalization Service* 227 (table 68).

The Supreme Court justified upholding such expulsions by noting that membership in subversive organizations alone could then also be a ground for criminal conviction, under the doctrine of *Dennis v United States*, 341 US 494 (1951), and by comparing such expulsions to the loss of home and family that might be imposed on a citizen conscripted into the military in order to meet Communist aggression in foreign lands. *Harisiades v Shaughnessy*, 342 US 580, 591–92 (1952). Eventually the Court found ways to limit the imposition of deportation based only on membership in the Communist party, by construing the statute to cover only those who had a "meaningful association," one undertaken with awareness of the party's distinct and active political nature. *Rowoldt v Perfetto*, 355 US 115, 120 (1957); *Gastelum-Quinones v Kennedy*, 374 US 469, 473 (1963). See generally Harry Kalven, Jr., *A Worthy Tradition: Freedom of Speech in America* 403–22 (1988).

[134] *Landon v Plasencia*, 459 US 21, 34, insisting on application of the well-known three-part test from *Mathews v Eldridge*, 424 US 319, 334–35 (1976). See also *Rafeedie v INS*, 880 F2d 506 (DC Cir 1989), applying the full measure of due process protection to a

It was by no means inevitable that our immigration-control system would employ clear categorical distinctions between temporary and permanent admission, set forth from the time of admission—or typically earlier, from the time of visa issuance by a U.S. consulate. Some continental European systems have employed a different approach, regarding most migration as temporary at the outset but gradually recognizing greater rights, through the separate mechanism of internal work or residence permits, as the individual's period of stay lengthened or as she demonstrated other measures of social connection, such as learning the language.[135] Under such continental systems, only indistinct shadings may differentiate the rights of various aliens to continuing community membership, and it might be far more accurate to base assessments of reciprocal obligations on social connections or length of stay alone. Under the U.S. system, in contrast, for about seventy-five years it has been fundamental that the temporary or permanent character of admission is established from the beginning in explicit terms. This does not mean that nonimmigrants may never move into the ranks of lawful permanent residents in the American system. Consistently with this structural feature, however, such a change happens not by mere passage of time, but only as a result of a deliberate governmental decision in a process known as adjustment of status.[136] Even long-present nonimmigrants will not succeed in shifting categories unless they persuade the examining officer that they meet the more demanding criteria for LPR status.

Admitted nonimmigrants. Nonimmigrants—aliens admitted temporarily—have more restricted entitlements than LPRs. The exact shape of their privileges varies depending on the category of nonimmigrant admission, and in fact is closely linked to the purposes of the specific nonimmigrant category. But those privileges do decidedly add up to a significant recognition of a level of rights— to travel within our borders, to attend our educational institutions,

---

returning LPR placed in exclusion proceedings based on the government's charge that he had terrorist connections.

[135] See, e.g., Grete Brochmann, *The Mechanisms of Control*, in Grete Brochmann and Tomas Hammar, eds, *Mechanisms of Immigration Control: A Comparative Analysis of European Regulation Policies* 1, 9–14 (1999); Kees Groenendijk, Elspeth Guild, and Robin Barzilay, *The Legal Status of Third Country Nationals Who Are Long-Term Residents in a Member State of the European Union* (2000).

[136] INA § 245, 8 USC § 1255 (2000).

sometimes to undertake specified work on U.S. territory—well beyond those deliberately extended by this society to most of the world's population. The proliferation of nonimmigrant categories (there are now twenty-two, many with further intricate subdivisions[137]), each with its own eligibility requirements and limitations, may seem to defeat generalization. Perhaps the initially daunting technical differences have helped to forestall broader recognition of this group of individuals as belonging to a distinct level of community membership.

But in fact the exact details of those various categories are less important than the features they share, which have been reasonably durable since 1924, when the term "nonimmigrant" first entered the statute books.[138] Most significantly, in the course of obtaining their statuses, admitted nonimmigrants have respected the processing procedures established by this country and thereby afforded the government a clear opportunity to consider their qualifications before they begin their stay on U.S. soil. All receive documentation that either sets forth a specific date on which their right to remain terminates, or else, in a minority of cases, specifies that the status continues only so long as some other identifiable relationship (such as enrollment in a designated school) persists. Their presence is decidedly lawful, and they are certainly within their rights to establish social connections and familiarity with this society and its other members, of whatever level. But such connections are established under a formal understanding of temporariness, and deportation—that is, involuntary termination of these social connections on grounds well short of a criminal conviction—is regularly invoked by INS for persons in these categories, usually for overstaying the admission period or otherwise transgressing the conditions imposed at the time of admission.

Congress has on many occasions seen fit to lump nonimmigrants together with LPRs (and no other alien categories) for certain ameliorative purposes under the immigration laws. For example, when Congress chose in 1991, and again in 1996 for a limited transition period, to soften earlier provisions mandating preorder detention for aliens with criminal convictions, it did so by granting

---

[137] INA § 101(a)(15), 8 USC § 1101(a)(15) (2000).

[138] See note 123.

INS discretion to consider individual releases, provided that the alien had been lawfully admitted.[139] Thus this provision applied to LPRs and admitted nonimmigrants, but not to the remaining three categories of aliens. Such an enactment could be seen as paying some kind of reciprocal respect for the nonimmigrants' honoring of the border admission screening. These admitted aliens respected the polity's procedure for individualized consideration of qualifications on the way in. Congress's 1991 and 1996 enactments essentially afforded individualized consideration of release requests if the person was placed in removal proceedings after amassing a criminal record.

Unadmitted aliens (the final three categories). The respective rankings of the last three categories are less certain (though not their placement below the first three). Practice has traditionally treated an entrant without inspection (EWI) more favorably, for purposes of constitutional and statutory claims, than parolees or applicants for admission at the border. This was the precise purpose and impact of the exclusion-deportation line, a boundary marked by the concept of entry rather than admission following inspection. These individuals accomplish entry, but are not admitted. Perhaps a modestly higher placement for them on the membership spectrum may be defended on the assumption that most in fact are present longer than parolees (and certainly so in comparison to unsuccessful applicants for admission), and therefore typically establish stronger social connections and other stakes in the community. On the other hand, one could also argue that their constitutional placement should be below the other two groups, because they failed to respect elemental border procedures and simply established their presence here in defiance of the law. Several lower courts have noted the irony of giving EWIs a better constitutional status than those applicants for admission who did as they were supposed to do and presented their credentials to the border inspector.[140] The applicant for admission at the border has at least attempted to establish his community membership on the right footing, on a basis of respect for the laws and procedures of the national community

---

[139] See notes 36, 47.

[140] See, e.g., *Louis v Nelson*, 544 F Supp 973, 977 (SD Fla 1982); *Fernandez v Wilkinson*, 505 F Supp 787, 790 (D Kan 1980), aff'd on other grounds as *Rodriquez-Fernandez v Wilkinson*, 654 F2d 1382 (10th Cir 1981).

into which he seeks entrance. And from a less abstract and more functional perspective, the alien who comes through the inspection station at least gives the government one clear shot at applying the screening criteria meant to keep out those who do not qualify for entry or who may seek to do the nation harm.

Whatever the reason for such relative rankings, giving EWIs more favorable treatment *for statutory purposes* was indeed a proper reading of the pre-1996 statutes. Unlike the other two groups, they were subject to deportation, not exclusion, and Congress opened to them a somewhat wider array of opportunities to escape removal once placed in deportation proceedings. But whether the Supreme Court truly intended in *Mezei* to place EWIs on the favored side of the constitutional line could be questioned. The exact issue was not presented in the case; Mezei was an unsuccessful applicant for admission at a port of entry, not an EWI. In the course of distinguishing earlier precedents that applied more generous procedural protections for certain aliens, *Mezei* stated: "It is true that aliens who have once passed through our gates, even illegally, may be expelled only after proceedings conforming to traditional standards of fairness encompassed in due process of law."[141] But an EWI did not pass through the gates. Perhaps the 1953 Court's reference to an illegal gate-passer may have meant only someone whose factual ineligibility went unnoticed by the inspector at the time of admission. If that reading is correct, then the *Mezei* court did not intend to favor the EWI over the applicant for admission.

Congress, as recounted in Part I, deliberately marked EWIs down a statutory notch in 1996, throwing them, along with the traditional class of excludable aliens, into the new (and less favored) grouping of inadmissible aliens. It is possible that this change may have limited practical significance, particularly because, as mentioned, even at that moment Congress backed off from full equivalence. The statute still treats arriving aliens (the former excludable alien category, including non-EWI parolees) less favorably in several respects than it does EWIs. But that statutory change supports the view that the exclusion-deportation line is an inadequate dividing line to capture the full significance of the varying levels of alien membership in the national community. Both before and after

---

[141] 345 US at 212 (citations omitted).

1996, EWIs were not members on a par with admitted nonimmigrants, and certainly not with LPRs.

Still, this approach does not have to entail a complete surrender to positivism with regard to the EWI category. Although it accounts for the failure of initial respect for community rules at the time of the EWI's entry, it should not be overwhelmed by that fact. Particularly when EWIs remain present for a lengthy period, and even more so when (as is usually the case) they have worked hard and become a part of community life in the locality where they live, social connections amount to a significant element in the historical path they have pursued. Such connections then deserve some weight in deciding on the exact protections owed them in light of this complex relationship they hold to our polity and society—without of course moving them to the same position as LPRs. Perhaps over time such EWIs should not be seen as greatly different for these purposes from admitted nonimmigrants who have stayed far beyond their initial admission period. Though overstayers honored the initial admission requirements and presented themselves for border screening, their respect for the community's terms ceased when they failed to leave as initially promised. Perhaps the social connections established or deepened thereafter are as colored by this early default as are those of the EWI. If that perspective is taken, then EWIs rank lower than nonimmigrants during the latter's period of lawful presence, but not thereafter, or at least not when years have passed.

Probably it still makes sense to place aliens actually stopped at the border at the lowest rung, because if never allowed to move at large in U.S. society, they will not have the de facto community connections that an EWI can establish. (This could happen because they are detained throughout the controversy over their admission, or because they are asked to wait in a neighboring country, as the law sometimes contemplates,[142] until the question of their admissibility is resolved.) But the placement of parolees then remains problematic. Though not formally admitted, they are allowed a certain freedom to move at large in U.S. society, and unlike for EWIs, any social connections thereby established will have occurred with a form of deliberate permission from the U.S. gov-

---

[142] INA § 235(b)(2)(C), 8 USC § 1225(b)(2)(C) (2000).

ernment, following an opportunity for screening. That kind of permission would seem to argue for a higher membership placement as compared with EWIs. The more traditional view, according parolees a lower status, however, has been justified on highly pragmatic grounds. In a case rejecting the assertion that a parolee should be afforded certain statutory benefits otherwise reserved for deportable aliens, the Supreme Court described parole merely as a device to "avoid needless confinement while administrative proceedings are conducted." It feared that elevating the petitioner to a higher status based only on her parole "would be quite likely to prompt some curtailment of current parole policy."[143]

In sum, arriving aliens never released past the border may have the lowest claim to membership, but are not wholly beyond the pale of relational obligations. They share membership in a community of persons "having our common humanity,"[144] and so would be shielded against physical abuse[145] and, under *Wong Wing*, against criminal punishment without observance of the protections of the Fifth and Sixth Amendments. I will argue later that they are also constitutionally entitled to more than *Mezei* and *Knauff* gave them when faced with indefinite detention or secret evidence—not to release or full disclosure, but to modest yet important alternative safeguards. Entrants without inspection and parolees probably deserve recognition on higher rungs of the membership ladder, and we have identified plausible reasons to treat parolees, contrary to the trend of the case law, as having somewhat stronger relational claims. But we need not resolve all issues of

---

[143] *Leng May Ma v Barber*, 357 US 185, 190 (1958). See also *Kaplan v Tod*, 267 US 228, 230 (1925) ("When her prison bounds were enlarged by committing her to the custody of the Hebrew Society, the nature of her stay within the territory was not changed [from what it would have been had she been kept at Ellis Island]. She was still in theory of law at the boundary line and had gained no foothold in the United States."). In fact, parole has been used for a much wider array of purposes than simply release during exclusion proceedings. For a full discussion, see Aleinikoff, Martin, and Motomura, *Immigration and Citizenship* at 507–10 (cited in note 17). Furthermore, after the 1996 amendments that moved EWIs into the inadmissible category, INS now considers that EWIs too may be paroled following their apprehension, sometimes for lengthy periods of time. See 76 Interpreter Releases 1050, 1067 (1999) (INS General Counsel legal opinion discussing the availability of parole for EWIs).

[144] From a phrase used by Justice Field in his dissent in *Fong Yue Ting v United States*, 149 US 698, 754 (1893).

[145] *Lynch v Cannatella*, 810 F2d 1363 (5th Cir 1987). See Margaret H. Taylor, 22 Hastings Const L Q 1087, 1143–50 (cited in note 9).

relative placement among these three categories for present purposes.

D. MEMBERSHIP LEVELS AND A MORE THOROUGH EXPLANATION FOR THE MAJORITY'S RESULT IN ZADVYDAS

To be sure, this hierarchy of membership levels does not answer all questions having to do with the constitutional rights of aliens nor exhaust all pertinent considerations that might go into the final ruling on a specific constitutional claim by a person who is not a U.S. citizen. One still has to decide on just what questions membership level should make a difference, and if so, how much of a discount in protection is appropriate for the particular claim, as well as how much other factors, such as length of de facto residence or the nature of social connections, should count in deciding the ultimate outcome, no matter what the category.[146] Nonetheless, this analytical approach helps focus and structure the pertinent inquiry, and it can help us make sense of several portions of constitutional doctrine governing aliens' rights that might otherwise remain puzzling.

With this conceptual groundwork more fully developed, then, we are now equipped to take a closer look at justifications for the majority's ruling in *Zadvydas*. If *Mezei* had not constricted the gradational universe by reference only to the exclusion-deportation line, Justice Breyer might well have given far more attention to a central feature of the actual cases as they reached the Supreme Court—a feature he mentions only in passing. Both Ma and Zadvydas had been lawful permanent residents. They were not tourists or clandestine entrants, or even persons who had amassed several years in our society while here on an explicitly time-limited educational or business visa.

If we focus on LPRs, we can perhaps recast the majority as saying something important about the deep structure or the trans-statutory understanding of just what lawful permanent residence

---

[146] Additionally, I emphasize that the considerations described here should help guide decisions on *constitutional* protections, and are not meant to place limits on political choices to give more recognition to social or economic connections or other factors. For example, under certain circumstances, legislated amnesties for those who have been long present in violation of law (as EWIs or nonimmigrant overstayers) may make considerable policy sense. But such initiatives do not come with the momentum of some claim of constitutional right.

really means. Historically and psychologically, admission in this category amounts to an invitation to full membership in the society and eventually the polity. Immigrants—that is, aliens selected for lawful permanent resident status—pass through the most rigorous screening our immigration system imposes. But having done so, they are then invited to become part of our community, to sink roots—permanent roots—and to chart out life plans in reliance on enduring rights to remain. With minimal additional effort, an LPR can also graduate to the highest level of membership, by becoming a naturalized citizen after five years residence. And in general it is fair to say that our reigning national mythology, bolstered by certain practical inducements, reflects an expectation that immigrants should and will naturalize.[147] The exact holding in *Zadvydas*, which involved only LPRs, could be understood as saying that roots or connections established in that fashion, on the basis of such an invitation, simply count for more when calculating the constitutional limits on future treatment—even if the initially favorable legal status, for valid reasons, has been terminated. The historical paths these two aliens followed to a removal order leave them in a genuinely different constitutional position from a Marielito.

This understanding of the significance of LPR status is of course contestable. Justice Scalia, in fact, contests it with vigor, and the Fifth and Tenth Circuits spell out the argument in patient and tightly argued detail—an argument that Justice Breyer never really takes on.[148] They focus on the precise lawyerly content of LPR status, rather than the psychological impact or popular understanding or membership conception sketched above. The status of the LPR is clearly subject to express conditions set forth in the statute books, prescribing a limited and not overly demanding list of acts that will terminate even permanent residence and render the alien deportable. In this perspective, these provisions say to LPRs, in effect: If you commit a crime or otherwise violate the conditions of your continued residence, then your own act has given us warrant to insist once again that legal status (your new one—deportable alien) trumps social connections or community member-

---

[147] This orientation corresponds to the "transition model" for permanent residence, under the helpful framework described in Motomura, *Three Models* 206–09 (cited in note 118).

[148] *Zadvydas v Underdown*, 185 F3d at 294–97; *Ho v Greene*, 204 F3d at 1058–60.

ship—just as it would have done all along for parolees.[149] In this perspective, LPRs are on statutory notice that if they commit crimes, they not only are subject to deportation, but also run the risk of indefinite detention should no other country then agree to receive them.

Further, any alien who consults a knowledgeable lawyer would learn that courts have held, ever since the landmark 1893 case of *Fong Yue Ting*, that Congress is entitled to change the list of deportability grounds as it sees fit and without advance notice.[150] "Permanent" residence is thus exposed as a case of mislabeling, but the asterisk that explains its true impermanence, the Fifth and Tenth Circuits in effect say, is wholly clear to anyone who looks at statute and precedent. True security and permanence, in this view, would come only when the alien takes the initiative to cross the line into citizenship.[151] The Fifth Circuit emphasized: "The whole point of earmarking criminal aliens for deportation or exclusion is that while we must tolerate a certain risk of recidivism from our criminal citizens, we need not be similarly generous when it comes to those who have not achieved citizenship."[152]

---

[149] The Fifth and Tenth Circuit approach is also reminiscent of Justice Rehnquist's position in *Arnett v Kennedy*, 416 US 134, 154 (1974), arguing that the beneficiary of government largess must "take the bitter with the sweet," that the very definition of the government benefit comes qualified by the revocation procedures explicitly set forth in the same statute that confers the benefit. The majority in *Arnett* rejected this pure positivism, with the most extensive, but still unsatisfying, justification appearing in Justice Powell's concurrence. Id at 166–67. The exact rationale for ignoring the procedural specifications, if other sections of the act or regulation make ongoing entitlement depend on specific factual predicates, has remained something of a puzzle. See Thomas Grey, *Procedural Fairness and Substantive Rights*, in J. Chapman and J. Pennock eds, *XVIII Nomos: Due Process* 182 (1977).

[150] *Fong Yue Ting v United States*, 149 US 698, 705–07 (1893). This notion was strongly reinforced in *Carlson v Landon*, 342 US 524, 536–37 (1952) ("Mankind is not vouchsafed sufficient foresight to justify requiring a country to permit its continuous occupation in peace or war by legally admitted aliens, even though they never violate the laws in effect at their entry."). A few days before *Zadvydas* was decided, the Court protected certain permanent residents with criminal convictions from what it regarded as the retroactive imposition of changed rules that would have blocked their opportunity to seek a discretionary waiver of deportability under INA § 212(c). *INS v St. Cyr*, 121 S Ct 2271 (2001). But its ruling was wholly a matter of statutory interpretation; the opinion does not cast doubt on Congress's power to change the rules in such fashion, to the detriment of already settled LPRs, if it is clear enough about what it intends.

[151] Other decisions have justified this state of affairs by observing that failure to naturalize "leaves outstanding a foreign call on [one's] loyalties" and also brings unfair advantages, because a foreign citizen has certain immunities and avenues of protection, through diplomatic interposition, unavailable to citizens. *Harisiades v Shaughnessy*, 342 US 580, 585–86 (1952).

[152] 185 F3d at 296–97.

If the matter were to turn on a lawyer's understanding of the precise statutory contours of LPR status, these Circuits (and Justice Scalia) clearly have the better of the argument. Breyer never really seeks to contest Scalia's view that the national will is the same with regard to both excludables and deportables who are now subject to a final and (currently) uncontested order of removal. The appropriate organs of government have decided that these people do not belong here, and Breyer specifically reaffirms that there is no barrier to the government's proceeding with removal once travel can be arranged.

Nevertheless, Justice Breyer still insists that detention consequences are different. Thus the Supreme Court majority must be rejecting Scalia's positivist approach. It must be saying that in applying due process protections to aliens, at least in certain circumstances, technical legal boundaries count for less than some kind of trans-statutory understanding. People who come here as immigrants simply do not live as though their status were so tenuous as *Fong Yue Ting* formally decrees. In general, they come to stay, they shift their expectations about where home is, and they sink roots they rely on to be durable.

This understanding does not rest only on idiosyncratic expectations or exaggerated hopes adopted by the LPRs themselves. Instead it is anchored in a whole host of social and cultural expectations on the part of those around them about what it means to be an LPR, a green-card alien, as manifested in seventy-five years of consistent governmental practices. Enforcement agents of the INS take the notion of permanent residence seriously and do not regard it as an ironic jest. That the "permanent" label survives on official documents, including the very card[153] issued to each LPR by the government and which each is required, by law, to keep in his or her presence throughout his residence period,[154] reveals something about the way the polity understands the status. Most Americans also bring to this situation a similar understanding, including most other agencies of federal and state government. They seek ways to cement the identification of the individuals with this society and to promote their full integration, even to the point of promoting naturalization.

---

[153] The I-551 card, known popularly as the "green card," bears the legend at the top, in the largest type used: "Permanent Resident Card."

[154] INA § 264(e), 8 USC § 1304(e) (2000).

This set of governmental, social, and cultural practices, which decidedly do give emphasis to the "permanent" in lawful permanent residence, Breyer could be saying, carries constitutional significance, even if a knowledgeable immigration lawyer could find fault with its technical legal foundations. We are thus left with doctrine that incorporates a complex reliance on both legal and social determinations. The legal designation of permanence starts the process rolling. Shared social or structural understandings then take over, even if they outrun the technical legal boundaries. As Justice O'Connor observed for the Court in the last Supreme Court case to consider due process claims lodged by a lawful permanent resident in removal proceedings, "once an alien gains admission to our country and begins to develop *the ties that go with permanent residence*, his constitutional status changes accordingly"[155]—changes, in fact, in a way that may trump positive law.

In sum, to the *Mezei* court's assertion that unremovable aliens "are no more ours than theirs," this view would say, at least with regard to LPRs: not so fast. It is not that they are exclusively ours, but they remain also ours, because we invited them to build a home here. Even the breaking of certain terms of the entry compact represented by their criminal behavior does not wholly erase the significance of this level of membership. The social connections and the assumptions about "home" that they developed based on a legitimate and largely mutual expectation of permanency mean that they are also ours. When state-to-state relations break down and the normal responsibility for accepting the return of nationals fails to work, for whatever reason, then the "also ours" must be given constitutional weight.

One more inquiry regarding the interplay of the legal and the social needs attention, however. As noted, Justice Scalia and the Fifth and Tenth Circuits contest the *Zadvydas* majority's stance by placing full reliance on precise *legal* specifications of what comes with LPR status. The position sketched here about the unique significance of LPR status could also be contested from the opposite direction, by placing full reliance on *social* connections or subjective feelings about rootedness established by any alien who stays in this country for an extended period. After all, an estimated 7–

---

[155] *Landon v Plasencia*, 459 US 21, 32 (1982) (emphasis added).

8 million aliens are currently unlawfully resident in the United States, roughly 40 percent after overstaying a temporary admission and the rest after entering without inspection.[156] In view of these statistics, some contend that the message of the United States to unlawful migrants is at least equivocal, if not actually inviting.[157] In this view, statutory provisions limiting migration are window dressing, hypocritical enactments meant to placate a domestic constituency but rendered hollow by deliberate underresourcing of immigration enforcement and the demands and blandishments of U.S. business. Hence the social dimension serves not merely to qualify, but actually to overwhelm the legal dimension. If this conception were to be carried over into constitutional doctrine, there would be no room for use of categorical distinctions among classes of settled aliens; after all, the categories set forth here are artifacts of legal dividing lines. The weight of a due process claim would then vary depending only on assessments specific to the individual: the longer she was present or the more extensive her social, family, and community connections, the greater the weight that must be assigned to her individual interest in an otherwise uniform constitutional balancing process.

An initial response might be to say that migrants who consider themselves settled here but who lack LPR status have developed expectations that are not legitimate. After all, for some due process

---

[156] D'Vera Cohn, *Illegal Immigrant Total Is Raised*, Washington Post (Oct 25, 2001), at A24 (reporting on latest census estimates, raising previous estimates of the illegal population to 7 or 8 million); Department of Justice, *1998 Statistical Yearbook of the Immigration and Naturalization Service* at 239 (estimating that 41 percent of the undocumented population are nonimmigrant overstays).

[157] See Angela Cortez, *Bad Claim Is Just That*, Denver Post (Jan 26, 2000), at B9; Kitty Calavita, *U.S. Immigration and Policy Responses: The Limits of Legislation*, in Wayne A. Cornelius, Philip L. Martin, and James F. Hollifield, eds, *Controlling Immigration: A Global Perspective* 55, 73, 76–78 (1994); *Introduction: The Ambivalent Quest for Immigration Control*, id at 3–4.

I have argued elsewhere that this portrait of societal messages, while clearly carrying some force, often employs misleading baselines, particularly with regard to nonimmigrants who overstay their admission periods. It is true that the absolute number of such overstayers, perhaps 2–3 million de facto residents, is quite high. But the character of the enforcement signal this represents depends not only on absolute numbers but also, and perhaps more importantly, on a comparison to how many nonimmigrants actually refrain, as the law commands, from taking up permanent residence. Well over 99 percent of admitted nonimmigrants obey this legal command. The number of violators appears high only because the universe of admitted nonimmigrants is so huge, numbering well over 20 million in each of the last several years. David A. Martin, *On Counterintuitive Consequences and Choosing the Right Control Group: A Defense of Reno v AADC*, 14 Georgetown Immig L J 363, 378–79 (2000).

purposes the Supreme Court has emphasized that neither "unilateral expectations" nor an abstract need or desire for a government benefit are sufficient; the person must have "a legitimate claim of entitlement."[158] After *Zadvydas*, however, this response cannot carry the full burden. If we are to cut loose from positivism, as the *Zadvydas* majority has clearly done, we necessarily are relying, to some extent, on a separate source for weighing and grading constitutional claims of unlawful aliens. If that source encompasses broader societal messages and how they are perceived by migrants, we shall have to be prepared to argue about what those are and how they are to be counted. Nonetheless, I believe that the categorical approach still holds up and justifies a major distinction between LPRs and other aliens for constitutional purposes.[159]

From the standpoint of the long-staying migrant who lacks legal status, the issue is not solely the legitimacy of any expectations of permanence or rootedness, but also the credibility of those expectations. If a person is explicitly told upon admission into the country, as is the case with most nonimmigrants,[160] that his permission to remain ceases as of a specified date, then one may certainly doubt that he thereafter really develops a feeling that he is settled, a feeling that home is wholeheartedly in the country where he stays. Entrants without inspection of course receive no in-hand notice of an end date by which they must leave. But the very circumstances of their entry, sneaking across a border at night, often with the aid of a paid smuggler, surely impart a similar message

---

[158] *Board of Regents v Roth*, 408 US 564, 577 (1972) (the Court was specifically speaking about the definition of "property" for purposes of triggering due process scrutiny).

[159] I do not maintain that such a distinction should always be decisive for statutory purposes. Sound policy should indeed take account of the social and human ties developed through lengthy de facto residence, and immigration law should temper enforcement with carefully designed provisions to this end. One of the true deficiencies in the 1996 immigration amendments was their radical cutback on two forms of relief from removal (once known as suspension and 212(c) relief, now called cancellation of removal) that formerly allowed immigration judges to override formal deportability on an adequate showing of human connections here or hardship that would result from deportation. Compare INA § 240A, 8 USC § 1229b (2000) (current provisions for cancellation) with 8 USC §§ 1182(c), 1254 (1994) (earlier provisions for comparable relief). Under certain circumstances, broader amnesties or legalization programs may provide an appropriate way to recognize such connections. But I consider those questions of policy, to be decided by public and legislative debate, not matters that are resolved by constitutional law.

[160] Nonimmigrant students are often admitted with an INS document that allows them to stay for "duration of status," rather than setting a fixed end date. But other papers they typically receive from the sponsoring school provide details about what brings that status to an end—primarily ceasing studies or falling below the level of a full course load.

that their stay is tenuous at best. It is therefore implausible that either visa overstayers or EWIs develop a sense of rootedness that wholly ignores the vulnerability of their situation. This is not just a matter of statutory notice (as Justice Scalia relied on in his attempt to justify the imposition of indefinite detention on persons once admitted as LPRs), but of real-world signals through either the papers delivered to nonimmigrants or the circumstances of clandestine entry, coupled with the reality of ongoing worries that *la migra* will discover them.

Further support for this conclusion may be found if we turn to examine this claim closely from the standpoint of the expectations of the receiving society itself. Mixed messages no doubt do exist. Particularly in times of prosperity, the economy and even elements of the government may send to illegal migrants signals of welcome and invitation to stay. But even in those periods, enforcement does not cease. During the boom years of the late 1990s, in fact, the funding of the INS more than doubled, and the ranks of the border patrol along the southwest border more than tripled. Far from widely accepting the settling in of non-LPRs, the American public has been steadfast in regarding it as wrong. In his book *One Nation, After All*, Alan Wolfe points out that the distinction between legal and illegal immigrants "is one of the most tenaciously held distinctions in middle-class America; the people with whom we spoke overwhelmingly support legal immigration and express disgust with the illegal variety."[161] To be sure, this sentiment seems to translate into rigorous public policy only when stimulated by economic bad times or wider concerns and fears in the international arena. Nonetheless, its persistence undermines any claim that subjective feelings of rootedness on the part of EWIs or overstayers are truly founded in mutual understandings shared widely in the receiving society.

Therefore it is quite appropriate to conclude that the due process claims of persons once invited to make their homes here as lawful permanent residents rank higher than those of other noncitizens who may subjectively also think of the United States as home. But the critics' observations about conflicted messages to overstayers and EWIs should not be wholly ignored. That range

---

[161] Alan Wolfe, *One Nation After All* 147 (1998). See also Peter Skerry, *Why Amnesty Is the Wrong Way to Go*, Washington Post (Aug 12, 2001) at B1.

of trans-statutory societal practices helps give such persons some measure of cognizable membership in our constitutional community, which could be reflected in due process decisions. Their different status dictates a lower level of protection—but not necessarily an absence of protection.

E. FURTHER OBJECTIONS

Reconstructing the rationale for the majority's antipositivist outcome in *Zadvydas* in this fashion still leaves open two possible and weighty objections, coming from different directions. First, if invited rootedness counts for so much in giving persons who were initially admitted as LPRs such a strong constitutional claim, why does it wind up providing such a paltry benefit? In *Zadvydas*, it protects only against indefinite detention, a fate that befalls a tiny minority of those ordered deported, and seems to do nothing to call into question the more basic governmental assault on the person's roots, deportation itself. If this level of membership carries significant constitutional weight, shouldn't it work as well—or indeed more logically—to raise constitutional doubt about the very banishment of LPRs from their homes, at least after they have been present for a considerable period of time? After all, if deportation were deemed a constitutionally disproportionate sanction in these circumstances, the indefinite-detention question would never arise. Zadvydas and Ma would serve their criminal sentences and then simply resume life as LPRs. They would remain fully subject to the further discipline of the criminal law, and probably would enjoy a better chance at rehabilitation if released to a familiar community instead of being sent to a distant foreign land, where they might not even speak the language.

The second objection notes that the rationale sketched above does not account for what the majority in *Zadvydas* says it is doing. The majority opinion never suggests that the constitutional rationale it identifies applies only to LPRs. It seems to say that constitutional protection against indefinite detention goes well beyond the ranks of LPRs, covering at least other admitted aliens and possibly EWIs as well. I will take up these objections in turn.

1. *The banishment of rooted aliens—deportation itself.* Should the membership claims of LPRs also carry with them some stronger constitutional protection against banishment? This question seems

deeply impractical and academic, at a time when members of Congress often compete to demonstrate their toughness by thinking up new ways to provide for the deportation of criminal aliens. Taken for granted in these legislative debates has been Congress's constitutional power to deport LPRs for any reason it pleases, though some commentators have sought ways to reopen that issue.[162]

In contrast to the assumption underlying today's legislative battles, however, during at least two periods of our national history, a vigorous constitutional debate raged over the validity of imposing banishment on lawfully domiciled aliens (the term "lawful permanent resident" was not yet in currency). The Jeffersonian attack against the Alien and Sedition Acts of 1798 employed such an argument, and it appeared again a century later in the litigation over the deportation provisions of the Chinese Exclusion Laws.[163] A brief review of those debates may illuminate the question under discussion here.

The Alien Act of 1798, triggered by fears of subversion stemming from revolutionary France, provided for deportation of aliens whom the President judged "dangerous to the peace and safety of the United States."[164] Supporters of this measure argued that the removal of aliens was not punishment, but instead a precautionary measure, a mere revocation of a favor—admission to the country—which did not have to be granted, and whose termination was therefore wholly discretionary. Thus deportation decisions were

---

[162] See, e.g., Daniel Kanstroom, *Deportation, Social Control, and Punishment: Some Thoughts about Why Hard Laws Make Bad Cases*, 113 Harv L Rev 1889, 1931 (2000); Robert Pauw, *A New Look at Deportation as Punishment: Why at Least Some of the Constitution's Criminal Procedures Protections Must Apply*, 52 Admin L Rev 305, 337–45 (2000); Javier Bleichmar, *Deportation as Punishment: A Historical Analysis of the British Practice of Banishment and Its Impact on Modern Constitutional Law*, 14 Georgetown Immig L J 115, 160–63 (1999); Nancy Morawetz, *Rethinking Retroactive Deportation Laws and the Due Process Clause*, 73 NYU L Rev 97, 102 (1998).

[163] The characterization of deportation as akin to banishment or exile frequently appeared as well in opinions in the mid-twentieth century, often bolstering a highly protective interpretation of an ambiguous statute. See, e.g., *Bridges v Wixon*, 326 US 135, 160–61 (1945); *Harisiades v Shaughnessy*, 342 US 580, 600 (1952) (Douglas, J, dissenting); *Fong Haw Tan v Phelan*, 333 US 6, 10 (1948); *Woodby v INS*, 385 US 276, 285 (1966).

[164] Act of June 25, 1798, Ch 58, 1 Stat 570. This Act is often called the Alien Friends Act, to distinguish it from the Alien Enemies Act, Act of July 6, 1798, Ch 66, 1 Stat 577, which permitted internment and removal of aliens from nations at war with the United States. The latter provision was not objected to by the Jeffersonians, and remains on the books today with only minor modifications. 50 USC §§ 21–23 (2000).

appropriately placed within the prerogative of the chief executive rather than requiring a judicial decision.

The Jeffersonian criticism, most thoroughly worked out in Madison's 1800 report in defense of the Virginia and Kentucky Resolutions, refused to accept this characterization. Madison wrote:

> If the banishment of an alien from a country into which he has been invited as the asylum most auspicious to his happiness,—a country where he may have formed the most tender connections; where he may have invested his entire property, and acquired property of the real and permanent, as well as the movable and temporary kind; where he enjoys, under the laws, a greater share of the blessings of personal security, and personal liberty, than he can elsewhere hope for; and where he may have nearly completed his probationary title to citizenship; . . .—if a banishment of this sort be not a punishment, and among the severest of punishments, it will be difficult to imagine a doom to which the name can be applied.[165]

Importantly, this passage does not assert that all deportation is punishment. It limits its observations to those who have certain kinds of legal as well as social connections, in a manner consistent with the observations in Part IIIC. Only those *invited* to treat this country as an asylum—at the time, this covered all admitted to take up legal residence—fall within the assertion that deportation amounts to punishment. The Alien Act was allowed to expire in 1800, and the judgment of history has definitely sided with Madison.[166]

Federal law did not again provide for deportation until one of the later Chinese Exclusion Acts. The earliest acts in that series provided only for the exclusion of Chinese laborers at the border, and did not contain provisions for removal of any persons who had already immigrated. These earlier measures were upheld unanimously in *The Chinese Exclusion Case* of 1889, which ruled that the political branches have extensive powers, free of judicial supervision, to regulate the admission or exclusion of aliens at the border, even if the regulation violates a treaty obligation or an apparent preexisting understanding with a former resident.[167] But

---

[165] 4 *Elliott's Debates* 546, 555 (1836).

[166] See Neuman, *Strangers to the Constitution* at 52–63 (cited in note 9).

[167] *The Chinese Exclusion Case* (*Chae Chan Ping v United States*), 130 US 581 (1889).

Congress did not stop with the exclusion of newly arriving Chinese laborers. Motivated largely by a belief that some Chinese were defeating the earlier exclusion law by entering surreptitiously and then claiming to have migrated before the cutoff, Congress passed an 1892 law requiring those already in the country to register and obtain a certificate of residence from the collector of internal revenue for their district. Though the rationale was formally aimed only at aliens much further down the scale of membership—illegal entrants—the act in fact placed many lawfully resident Chinese at risk, because the statute and implementing regulations required that residence be proven, to the collector or a reviewing court, by the testimony of "at least one credible white witness."[168]

As litigation testing the 1892 act found its way to the Supreme Court, many observers, including the leading associations of Chinese residents, confidently expected the Court to assume a far broader supervisory role in applying constitutional constraints to deportation than it had to the earlier exclusion laws.[169] Furthermore, a district court judge hearing one of the key deportation actions that ultimately made it to the Supreme Court as *Fong Yue Ting v United States* bravely chose to frame his findings in such a way that the higher court would have to confront the issue in its starkest form. Based on all the testimony in the case, the judge entered a *factual* finding that the alien was in reality a lawful resident before the law took effect. But the court reluctantly reached the *legal* conclusion that he was still deportable, because he could not prove his residency through the statutorily required white witness.

The Supreme Court majority rather easily found for the government, in a leading plenary-power ruling. "The right of a nation to expel or deport foreigners who have not been naturalized, or taken any steps towards becoming citizens of the country, rests upon the same grounds, and is as absolute and unqualified, as the right to prohibit and prevent their entrance into the country."[170]

---

[168] *Fong Yue Ting v United States*, 149 US 698, 727 (1893). See Aleinikoff, Martin, and Motomura, *Immigration and Citizenship* at 180–82, 198–99 (cited in note 17).

[169] Lucy Salyer, *Laws Harsh as Tigers* 43–58 (1995) (reporting on expectations, before the *Fong Yue Ting* decision, of key Chinese-American organizations, which advised resident Chinese not to register under the law; only a small percentage did register before the deadline, which preceded argument in the Supreme Court).

[170] 149 US 698, 707 (1893).

Chief Justice Fuller and Justices Brewer and Field issued fierce dissents. But they did not focus on the blatant racial discrimination in the statute that immediately draws the attention of the modern reader. Their dissents focused instead on the very fact that the law permitted the removal of persons who had become lawfully domiciled. The Chief Justice attacked as antithetical to the Constitution the idea that "the residence of the alien, when invited and secured by treaties and laws, is held in subordination to the exertion against him, as an alien, of the absolute and unqualified power asserted . . . ." This amounted, he said, to a "legislative sentence of banishment."[171] Justice Brewer took up the banishment theme, and regarded such deportation as a punishment that could be imposed only in accordance with all the constitutional protections that apply to criminal punishments, including the Fifth, Sixth, and Eighth Amendments.[172] Justice Field expressly linked his dissent to Madison's remonstrances against the Alien Act of 1798, calling that act the only other instance when "any public man had the boldness to advocate the deportation of friendly aliens in times of peace."[173] A revealing difference in rhetoric also marks the approach of the majority versus the three dissents. The majority describes the removal of these aliens as merely "a method of enforcing the return to *his own country* of an alien who has not complied with the conditions" imposed by the government for his continuing stay.[174] It was the formal link of legal nationality, and not the social reality of lengthy residence, that determined for the majority which country is the alien's own—an obdurate positivist approach. But the dissents echo Madison and speak at several points about the United States as "home" to the Chinese appellants, noting prominently how deportation would sever the "relations of friendship, family and business there contracted."[175]

The approach of the dissents in *Fong Yue Ting* thus resonates with the kind of antipositivist approach finally given majority sanc-

---

[171] Id at 762–63 (Fuller, CJ, dissenting).

[172] Id at 738–42 (Brewer, J, dissenting).

[173] Id at 750 (Field, J, dissenting).

[174] Id at 730 (emphasis added); see also id at 717.

[175] Id at 734, 740, 743 (Brewer, J, dissenting); 759 (Field, J, dissenting). The majority never uses the word "home," except when quoting from the earlier U.S.-China treaty, which guaranteed a person's "inherent and inalienable right to change his home and allegiance."

tion in *Zadvydas*. But like *Zadvydas*, it is not one that wholly throws aside consideration of legal status. The dissents emphasize that the deportation here amounts to punishment because it is applied to "[a]liens from countries at peace with us, domiciled within our country *by its consent*."[176] Many who invoke the *Fong* dissenters in criticism of modern constitutional rules as applied to aliens overlook or choose to ignore that important distinction.[177] The dissenters do not call for full application of the Constitution to all who have subjectively made their homes here, but only to those who do so with consent of the polity.

The immediate question, however, is whether the rootedness of LPR status should protect a green-card holder altogether, as a matter of constitutional law, against deportation. Neither Madison nor the *Fong* dissenters go that far. They objected to the measures

---

[176] Id at 754 (Field, J, dissenting) (emphasis added). Justice Brewer also specifically distinguishes these appellants from persons who are mere travelers or persons "simply passing through, or temporarily in" the country. Id at 734 (Brewer, J, dissenting). This language indicates that the distinction between these two levels of membership was recognized long before federal statutes began expressly to distinguish immigrants from nonimmigrants.

[177] For example, in the keynote address at a December 1999 Harvard conference on immigration, Judge Stephen Reinhardt of the Ninth Circuit gave a passionate speech criticizing many of the changes made by the 1996 immigration reform laws, as well as the current Supreme Court's stance of deference toward such laws. He quoted at length Field's peroration, 149 US at 754, in support of his critique of new expedited removal procedures applied to applicants for admission at the border, but he selectively omitted (without indicating to the audience that he was doing so) all passages referring to Field's proviso requiring entry or domicile with national consent. Judge Reinhardt is of course entitled to criticize these new procedures and judicial deference, but he is simply incorrect in invoking Field or the other *Fong Yue Ting* dissenters with regard to border procedures or temporary sojourners.

Justice Murphy's justly famous concurrence in *Bridges v Wixon*, 326 US 136, 161–62 (1945), is often equivalently invoked out of context. See, e.g., *American-Arab Anti-Discrimination Committee v Reno*, 70 F3d 1045, 1063–66 (9th Cir 1995), later decision (119 F3d 1367 (9th Cir 1997)) vacated on related grounds, *Reno v American-Arab Anti-Discrimination Committee*, 525 US 471 (1999). Murphy there supported the majority's reversal of a deportation order with a passionate argument discussing "[s]uch rights [as] those protected by the First and the Fifth Amendments and by the Due Process Clause of the Fourteenth Amendment." He stated: "None of these provisions acknowledges any distinction between citizens and resident aliens. They extend their inalienable privileges to all 'persons' and guard against any encroachment on those rights by federal or state authority." But in the sentence immediately preceding this passage, he notes an important qualification that is often ignored: these protections begin to apply "once an alien *lawfully enters and resides* in this country" (emphasis added). That case involved neither EWIs nor nonimmigrants, but instead the well-known Harry Bridges, who had clearly entered legally for the equivalent of lawful permanent residence (though his entry in 1920 preceded the development of the modern category). Murphy's position is not premised on mere de facto residence (as the Ninth Circuit implies in *AADC*), but instead rests on residence acquired lawfully. Doubtless Justice Murphy would not view other aliens present in the country as rightless, but his opinion in *Bridges* does not rule out possible distinctions among such categories of aliens in fixing the contours of those rights.

before them because the banishment was imposed on grounds that did not amount to a crime and through procedures that did not provide the safeguards required in a criminal proceeding.

The actual practice of the federal government now conforms much more closely, by statute and administrative practice, to the kind of world that Field and his dissenting colleagues envisioned. Deportation is not visited upon LPRs for failure to complete certain administrative demands, particularly requirements that some otherwise innocent individuals, like the alien in *Fong Yue Ting* who knew no white witnesses, could not possibly have fulfilled. The only significant basis for the deportation of resident aliens today is their knowing commitment of a criminal act, and deportation ensues only upon conviction. It is true that such LPRs are not given the full array of Fifth and Sixth Amendment rights in the removal proceeding itself, but they did have such protections in the underlying criminal prosecution. It seems unlikely that Madison or Field would find fault with such a law, which simply accords decisive effect to the finding of criminal guilt, without relitigation.

A return to the views of Madison and Field about banishment of domiciled aliens therefore would not interfere with most deportations of LPRs, but it could still help harmonize other elements of Supreme Court doctrine and also provide modest additional protections in a few LPR deportation cases. The Court has frequently held, as a formal matter, that deportation is not punishment.[178] This doctrine has had the salutary and indispensable effect of permitting this country to develop an administrative rather than judicial system for removal of aliens, without having to satisfy all the procedural requirements, such as jury trial, that the Fifth and Sixth Amendments apply to criminal proceedings. It is hard to conceive of a functioning immigration enforcement system under modern conditions of global mobility if the doctrine were otherwise. But, on the other hand, the Supreme Court has often observed that "deportation is a drastic measure and at times the equivalent of banishment or exile."[179] These observations usually lead the court to read an ambiguous statute in a way that is favor-

---

[178] The proposition is conventionally traced to Justice Holmes's opinion for the Court in *Bugajewitz v Adams*, 228 US 585, 591 (1913).

[179] *Fong Haw Tan v Phelan*, 333 US 6, 10 (1948); see also *Woodby v INS*, 385 US 276, 285 (1966).

able to the alien. For some purposes, then, the Court treats deportation as punishment, but for other purposes—particularly when the realities of a modern administrative state require greater flexibility—it does not. A recognition of the heightened membership claims of LPRs might justly lead the court to expand modestly the range of circumstances in which it treats deportation as punishment for constitutional purposes as well, while still stopping short of importing all the protections of the criminal justice process. If such treatment were confined to LPR cases, it would not greatly threaten the capacities and the needed flexibility of our immigration enforcement system.

One prime candidate for a Madisonian approach of this sort might be applying nonretroactivity principles to the deportation of LPRs.[180] Such a step would avoid inflicting the pain of banishment on the basis of actions undertaken at a time when the alien had no reason to believe that the act might jeopardize residence rights. The 1996 immigration amendments gave rise to this kind of jeopardy in a host of poignant cases that were widely reported in the media, often involving individuals who had lived exemplary

---

[180] In *Harisiades v Shaughnessy*, 342 US 580, 593–95 (1952), and *Galvan v Press*, 347 US 522, 530–31 (1954), it must be recognized, the Court refused to apply the Ex Post Facto Clause to deportation. But it is worth noting that Justice Frankfurter's majority opinion in *Galvan* expressed agonized doubts about that refusal if the matter were to be considered anew, and Justice Jackson in *Harisiades* noted that this result is based on two propositions that might be debatable "as original proposals," but were clearly entrenched in case law: that the Ex Post Facto Clause applies only to penal legislation, and that deportation is not punishment. Jackson also devoted several paragraphs to a demonstration that the imposition was not truly retroactive in any event; earlier legislation had warned aliens against the kind of actions that there resulted in deportation. The Justices' doubts on this score were surely fed by the fact that both cases involved long-resident LPRs, not EWIs or persons admitted on a temporary basis. If the Court were to accept more openly the legitimacy of a graduated approach to constitutional protections for aliens, it might conceivably rethink such an application of the Ex Post Facto Clause, as limited to the specific setting of the deportation of LPRs.

Alternatively, and more comfortably, the Due Process Clause could be used as the source for such a holding based on a graduated understanding of constitutional claims. Due process already incorporates doctrine discouraging retroactive application of amendments to civil statutes. Although it is an anemic doctrine, ordinarily overcome merely by a clear congressional statement supported by a rational basis, see *INS v St. Cyr*, 121 S Ct 2271, 2287–88 (2001), and *Usery v Turner Elkhorn Mining Co.*, 428 US 1, 16 (1976), this body of law would require only modest adjustments in order to shelter LPRs against deportation based on acts that did not jeopardize residency when performed, while still maintaining workable practical limits. Using the Ex Post Facto Clause, in contrast, would doubtless call into question the two propositions, on which other vast bodies of constitutional law are now based, that Justice Jackson regarded as entrenched, thereby sparking abundant new litigation in immigration and other fields.

lives after a long-forgotten encounter with the criminal law.[181] Their fate resulted from Congress's vast expansion of the list of aggravated felonies and especially from a further section enacted in 1996 clearly stating that the expanded list is fully retroactive.[182] Ancient crimes that could not before have resulted in the LPR's deportation suddenly were rechristened as the most serious type of deportable offense. Before 1996, the system might still have avoided deportation in these circumstances, because of a waiver provision that allowed an immigration judge to override deportability for LPRs with seven years' residence. Aliens who had managed years of careful law observance following an earlier mistake, particularly those with family members who were themselves LPRs or citizens, were the most likely to secure this discretionary benefit. If granted, the waiver had the effect of erasing the earlier conviction for deportation purposes.[183] But in 1996 Congress also revised and restated that waiver and made it wholly unavailable to aliens who have been convicted of aggravated felonies.[184] It is hard to see how any rational purpose is served by deporting someone on the basis of an old offense years after they have abundantly demonstrated their rehabilitation and contributed to the community. To rule that type of deportation of an LPR unconstitutional would not intrude very far into Congress's authority over immigration, nor would it leave the nation exposed to unforeseeable dangers. Congress could still toughen its stance toward criminal activity by aliens; it simply could not do so with retroactive effect as applied to LPRs.[185]

---

[181] See Morawetz, 73 NYU L Rev at 103–05, 115–16 (cited in note 162); Nancy Morawetz, *Understanding the Impact of the 1996 Deportation Laws and the Limited Scope of Proposed Reforms*, 113 Harv L Rev 1936, 1940–43 (2000). I emphasize that any such extension of nonretroactivity principles should not apply to aliens other than LPRs. Such other aliens' legitimate expectations extended no further than for a temporary stay anyway. Further, even with admitted nonimmigrants, the government has reserved a power to decree an earlier termination of their stay, by regulation, if circumstances warrant. See, e.g., 8 CFR § 214.5 (2000) (blanket regulation adopted in 1983, terminating the stay of certain Libyans already in the United States).

[182] INA § 101(a)(43), 8 USC § 1101(a)(43) (2000) (final sentence); IIRIRA § 321(c) (cited in note 3).

[183] See Aleinikoff, Martin, and Motomura, *Immigration: Process and Policy* 689–714 (cited in note 7) (describing relief under former INA § 212(c)).

[184] INA § 240A(a)(3), 8 USC § 1229b(a)(3) (2000).

[185] The Madison-Field position still contemplated limited situations where individual responsibility could be overridden by other larger factors that result in deportability for reasons wholly divorced from the individual's actions. Justice Field in his dissent in *Fong Yue*

A more ambitious return to the Madisonian position would call for constitutional review of the proportionality of deportation when measured against the seriousness of the alien's underlying crime, by analogy to Eighth Amendment principles. Some commentators have urged such an approach,[186] but this seems more of a stretch. The Court has been retreating from proportionality review of criminal sentences, in a field to which the Eighth Amendment undeniably applies.[187] Deportation based on criminal behavior was clearly contemplated even by Madison and Field.[188] There seems less of a warrant to second-guess the legislative judgment

---

Ting accepted deportation of domiciled aliens based on crime or "as an act of war in view of existing or anticipated hostilities." 149 US at 746. That stance is entirely consistent with the Jeffersonian reaction to the Alien Acts of 1798, because the Jeffersonians accepted the Alien Enemies Act, which remains a part of our statutes today with only slight modifications. 50 USC §§ 21–23. See *Ludecke v Watkins*, 335 US 160 (1948) (sustaining application of the Act). It allowed the internment and removal of nationals of a state against which the United States has declared war, or in certain other circumstances involving threatened hostilities, upon the public proclamation of the President. Such a procedure is rife with potential for individual unfairness, but perhaps Madison accepted it because of the very extremity of the situation in which it applies, where a massive contest between nations may make indispensable or at least inevitable crude assessments of who is with us and who against us. See *Johnson v Eisentrager*, 339 US 763, 772–75 (1950) (discussing the Alien Enemies Act and the reasons for such treatment). Even so, Presidents have generally stopped short of using the Act to its fullest extent. See J. Gregory Sidak, *War, Liberty, and Enemy Aliens*, 67 NYU L Rev 1402, 1412–19 (1992). In the war against Hitler's Germany, for example, the President triggered this authority only selectively, not against all LPRs from Germany, but only those seen to have some personal culpability for support of the enemy effort. It is worth noting that the Alien Enemies Act was not, and could not have been, the legal foundation for the internment during World War II of Japanese-Americans who had been resident in the western United States; it covers only enemy nationals. See *Korematsu v United States*, 323 US 214 (1944). Even so, the United States did not intern all Japanese LPRs during World War II. Moreover, in a recent court settlement, the government agreed to pay reparations, albeit on a more modest scale than that given to the wronged Japanese-American internees, to certain Japanese nationals who were detained and deported in that era. This concession signals that we have come a long way from the Jeffersonian acceptance of such blanket measures, perhaps now insisting on individualized treatment even in the aggravated setting of declared war. See Natsu Taylor Saito, *Justice Held Hostage: U.S. Disregard for International Law in the World War II Internment of Japanese Peruvians—a Case Study*, 40 BC L Rev 275 (1998).

[186] See, e.g., Kanstroom, 113 Harv L Rev at 1931 (cited in note 162); Pauw, 52 Admin L Rev at 337–45 (cited in note 162).

[187] See *Harmelin v Michigan*, 501 US 957, 965 (1991) (plurality opinion by Scalia, J, asserting that proportionality review under the Eighth Amendment is improper); id at 997–98, 1001 (Kennedy, J, concurring in the judgment) (agreeing to great deference to the legislature in setting penalties, but maintaining judicial authority to override the legislative judgment if the punishment is grossly disproportionate).

[188] Cf. *Rummel v Estelle*, 445 US 263, 274 (1980) ("for crimes concededly classified and classifiable as felonies, that is, as punishable by significant terms of imprisonment in a state penitentiary, the length of the sentence actually imposed is purely a matter of legislative prerogative").

here; it is not that difficult to live one's life without committing serious crimes, and LPRs, at least when adequately warned before-hand that the particular offense will jeopardize the status, may validly be held to such a standard of individual responsibility.[189] Nonetheless, perhaps this more ambitious application of Madison's principles would be more appropriate in considering those currently rare instances wherein an LPR is placed in deportation proceedings for something other than a criminal conviction.[190]

2. *The actual indefinite detention limits from Zadvydas.* Earlier I noted a second possible objection to the analysis in Part IIID, namely, that the explanation offered here for the *Zadvydas* ruling, focusing as it does on lawful permanent residents, fails to track what the majority opinion appears to say about its own result. Indeed, it seems to extend the constitutional protections it discusses

---

[189] It is the greater American emphasis on individual responsibility that, in my view, will and should keep us from following the lead of the European Court of Human Rights in this realm. That court has applied treaty protections of privacy, home, and family life to develop a stringent form of proportionality review that often overrules the deportation of settled immigrants with serious and extensive criminal records. See, e.g., *Beldjoudi v France*, 234 Eur Ct HR (ser A) (1992); *Moustaquim v Belgium*, 193 Eur Ct HR (ser A) (1991); *Berrehab v Netherlands*, 138 Eur Ct HR (ser A) (1988). These cases in effect hold the state primarily responsible for maintaining home and family life, almost no matter what criminal acts the individual commits. (In more recent years, the Court has, however, sustained a few deportations when the alien's links to the country were more limited and the crimes especially serious. See, e.g., *Bouchelkia v France*, 1997-I Eur Ct HR 47; *El Boujadi v France*, 1997-VI Eur Ct HR 1980. For a helpful overview of the European court's rulings regarding deportation, see Kees Groenendijk et al, *Security of Residence of Long-Term Migrants* 8–16 (1998).) In arguing against American adoption of such proportionality review on the basis of human rights provisions of constitutional stature, I do not necessarily want to foreclose such review altogether. It should, however, be established and adjusted over time through political decisions embodied in legislation—and it should not in any case go as far as the more ambitious European rulings. With sufficient advance notice, it is just to ask of immigrants that they refrain from serious criminal behavior if they wish to retain their residence rights.

[190] For example, INA § 237(a)(2)(B)(ii), 8 USC § 1227(a)(2)(B)(ii) (2000), provides for the deportation of drug abusers and addicts. I am unaware of any examples in the last two decades where this deportability ground has been applied to an LPR. We are perhaps more likely to see in coming years efforts to deport LPRs on the ground of involvement in terrorist activity, under INA § 237(a)(4)(B), 8 USC § 1227(a)(4)(B) (2000). Such proceedings are less likely to raise questions about the proportionality of the remedy than issues about the adequacy of proof and the procedures employed to make the finding of terrorist involvement. Part IIIF discusses one part of this controversy, the use of secret evidence. It seems wholly unlikely that a modern court inspired by Madison and Field would require in this setting the full protections the Constitution applies to criminal proceedings, but it might demand administrative procedures that provide a high degree of comparable protection. See *Rafeedie v INS*, 880 F2d 506 (DC Cir 1989) (requiring full procedural protections in the administrative process for an LPR in exclusion proceedings who, the government alleged, had been involved in terrorist activities in Palestine).

beyond LPRs, at times even reaching all classically deportable aliens, including EWIs. Does such an approach undercut the argument for recognition of additional gradations of constitutional protections for different categories of aliens?

One possible response would be simply to note that application beyond the ranks of LPRs is dictum, because the two aliens in question had undeniably been admitted for lawful permanent residence. Indeed, it may well come about that future Court rulings confine the impact of *Zadvydas* on this basis. But even if that does not occur, *Zadvydas* can still be understood in a way that coheres readily with the view offered here.

To urge recognition of additional constitutional dividing lines within the broad category of aliens, or to assert that the boundary line between LPRs and other aliens is often more important for constitutional purposes than the exclusion-deportation line, is not to say that the LPR line should always be decisive. For some purposes, it might certainly still be appropriate to apply a stronger dose of constitutional protection farther down the membership scale. In *Zadvydas*, other factors may provide a solid basis for extending the protection against indefinite detention to all admitted aliens who cannot be removed—that is, to LPRs and admitted nonimmigrants.

The primary factor is the Court's insistent recognition of the actual human impact; the majority emphasizes that such post-order detainees are "condemned" to an "imprisonment" that has no discernible or predictable end. Because this is such a severe fate, the Court sees its constitutional oversight role as moving to the more demanding end of whatever scrutiny spectrum applies to the particular category of claim or claimant. Nonetheless, as noted earlier, a complete focus on human impact could easily result in a presumptive six-month limit on detention of any unremovable alien, even first-time applicants for admission at the border—an outcome the *Zadvydas* court disclaims. Another element of the Court's reasoning in *Zadvydas*, therefore, must be looked to in explaining why the six-month rule stops short of protecting all detained aliens.

There is such an element. I do not find it as persuasive a basis for the outcome as would a rationale based more firmly on the significance of the petitioners' LPR status, but perhaps it is what the Court had in mind. The majority repeatedly assures its audience that the decision leaves "no unprotected spot in the Nation's armor."[191] What then constitutes sufficient armor? With regard to ex-LPRs, the Court evidently deems adequate the ongoing deterrence and incapacitation afforded by the normal criminal justice system, to which a released alien is clearly subject, coupled with whatever additional assurances derive from the INS supervisory order. That order cannot guarantee against future crime. But if properly designed and implemented, it can minimize opportunities and temptations, add to deterrence, and improve the odds of apprehension, prosecution, and future criminal punishment if the alien commits crimes while on supervised release.

But *any* nonremovable alien could be placed under supervision, and of course all remain subject to the normal operation of the criminal law for as long as they remain on U.S. soil. Hence there must be another component of the Court's vision of sufficient protection that distinguishes Zadvydas from Mezei and the Marielitos. It would seem that this could only be the preentry screening to which admitted aliens were subject. Before admission, LPRs like Zadvydas underwent the most demanding forms of review our system routinely provides, including medical screening, background checks with police authorities in the countries where they have resided, and matching against lookout databases. Nonimmigrants are also screened before admission, albeit not as thoroughly, although all are subjected to a name check against a lookout system that contains information about aliens with a criminal history or other indications of risk. Although those databases are inevitably less than comprehensive, the very circumstances of the entry of nonimmigrants—presenting their credentials to a border inspector, often after a prior review by the consular officer who issued the visa—allow the immigration authorities to adjust and tighten that review process whenever they deem it necessary.[192]

From this perspective, what may distinguish excludable aliens from admitted aliens, in a way that is highly relevant to the release question, is the fact that the nation has had a clear shot at de-

---

[191] 121 S Ct at 2502, quoting from *Kwong Hai Chew*, 344 US at 602.

[192] As a response to the September 11 attacks, Congress and the executive branch are considering a host of proposals to tighten such nonimmigrant screening. See Mike Allen and Eric Pianin, *Bush Seeks Tighter Rules on Entry*, Washington Post (Oct 30, 2001) at A1; Doris Meissner, *After the Attacks: Protecting Borders and Liberties*, Carnegie Endowment Policy Brief, No 2001.

termining whether the alien's presence in the country presents undue risk *before* it is ever placed in the position of having to accept
the alien's indefinite presence. A proponent of this view could not
maintain that such screening is foolproof, of course. A criminal act
committed on U.S. soil may afford far more probative evidence
regarding future dangers (and certainly is more recent) than whatever could have been developed even by the most stringent screening before entry. Nonetheless, a distinction remains. It is a distinction between some preentry armor and none. Excludable aliens
may arrive at a border or port of entry without any prior screening.
If excludable aliens must be released whenever the home nation
refuses their return, then there is a genuinely unprotected spot,
one that could be exploited by a hostile foreign leader. The Mariel
boatlift, involving as it did the deliberate insertion of hundreds of
serious criminals into a migratory flow by a Cuban government
that then refused to take them back, remains an instructive and
disturbing memory, for judges and for administrators.[193] To apply
a firm six-month release rule to excludables would be to undermine
the court's assurance of adequate protection and open a real opportunity for foreign government manipulation—either to cleanse its
own jails and subject the United States to a large-scale public safety
problem, or else to aid in the successful entry of potential terrorists
simply by refusing to accept return. Perhaps even more than the
loss of an opportunity for advance screening, it is the greater
chance for deliberate manipulation by another government that
makes the normal criminal justice response inadequate in excludable alien cases.

If these public safety considerations provide the true ground for
distinction between admitted aliens and excludables, then they also

---

[193] Members of the Select Commission on Immigration and Refugee Policy (SCIRP),
which was chartered in 1978 and reported in 1981, commented on the profound impact
that the Mariel boatlift had on their deliberations, leading them to propose more restrictive
measures to deal with "mass asylum" situations than originally contemplated. SCIRP, *U.S.
Immigration Policy and the National Interest, Final Report and Recommendations* 165–68 (1981);
Aleinikoff, Martin, and Motomura, *Immigration and Citizenship* at 1155–56 (cited in note
17). The classic statement of judicial concern appeared in *Jean v Nelson*, 727 F2d 957, 975
(11th Cir 1984) (en banc), aff'd as modified, 472 US 846 (1985) (if longer detention of
excludable aliens were not allowed, a "foreign leader could eventually compel us to grant
physical admission via parole to any aliens he wished by the simple expedient of sending
them here and then refusing to take them back"), and has been echoed elsewhere. See,
e.g., *Gisbert v U.S. Attorney General*, 988 F2d 1437, 1447 (5th Cir 1993). Justice Kennedy
also appears to make reference to such a risk in *Zadvydas*. 121 S Ct at 2511.

furnish a clearer theoretical basis for deciding how the indefinite detention question should be answered in the case of an entrant without inspection.[194] By definition, such a person, unlike an admitted nonimmigrant, has been through none of the normal border screening. Moreover, a foreign leader could exploit this avenue of entry through refusals of return almost as readily as with excludable aliens. To be sure, much of the discussion in Justice Breyer's opinion speaks as though entry is the critical dividing line between aliens who can claim due process protection against detention and those who, like Mezei, may not. The EWIs would then be on the protected side of the line. But in the second paragraph of the Court opinion, Breyer seems to take pains to signal a more circumscribed approach. Before beginning his substantive analysis, he carefully states:

> We deal here with aliens who were admitted to the United States but subsequently ordered removed. Aliens who have not yet gained initial admission to this country would present a very different question.[195]

If the dividing line is admission, not entry,[196] then LPRs and admitted nonimmigrants, but not the other categories of aliens, benefit from the six-month rule.

Must we then conclude, as the *Mezei* Court did, that the excludable alien (along with the EWI) is consigned to indefinite detention without any kind of judicial monitoring under the Constitution? Again, a functional understanding of adequate "armor" points toward an answer. The detention should reach no further

---

[194] They would also justify putting other aliens who were once lawfully admitted as nonimmigrants under the umbrella of the presumptive six-month release rule, as the *Zadvydas* court's dictum clearly does. Although their admission was supposed to be only temporary, and although their screening typically is not as thorough as that applied to immigrants, they did give the government one clear chance at detecting dangers.

[195] 121 S Ct at 2495. In a comment on *Zadvydas*, Linda Bosniak offers a different theory for the Court's varying reliance on entry and admission, namely, that it simply reflects judicial confusion "conflat[ing] three distinct sorts of territorial distinctions in the opinion: the admission/nonadmission distinction, the entry/nonentry distinction, and the presence/nonpresence distinction." Linda Bosniak, *A Basic Territorial Distinction*, 16 Georgetown Immig L J (forthcoming 2002). If so, then I hope this article, along with hers, may serve as a guide warding off similar confusion in future decisions, when these kinds of rights questions are squarely presented by nonimmigrant, EWI, or parolee claimants.

[196] This is exactly the changed dividing line Congress implemented in 1996 when for statutory purposes it replaced the exclusion-deportation line with a new structure that for many purposes lumps EWIs with the group formerly known as excludable aliens.

than its underlying rationale. Indefinite detention is not desirable in itself, but only to guard against dangerousness or flight risk. For these lower-ranking categories, the kind of screening that was not possible in advance of the person's arrival is now essentially transferred to the back end of the process. The human impact of such detention, coupled with its inescapable effect as a deprivation of liberty, provides a justification for some sort of court review under the Constitution. Review need not be highly intrusive, but it should assure that the procedures afford a meaningful hearing to consider evidence bearing on whether release poses a threat. Perhaps the burden is appropriately be placed on the alien, as it would be if he were applying for a visa or for admission at the border, although views will doubtless differ on this point. Judicial review might look only to the structural adequacy of the procedures, or it could, as Justice Kennedy suggested (referring in his case to both inadmissible aliens and ex-LPRs), provide some measure of review of the substantive decision. In any case, this reading of the constitutional protection for EWIs and excludables does inevitably presuppose a certain measure of substantive constitutional protection, in that it confines the substantive grounds permitting continued detention to the two that have been commonly employed, flight risk and dangerousness. By insisting that release is required if a detainee can adequately allay those concerns, it basically provides that detention will not be "indefinite," in the sense of being beyond the reach of the individual's own actions. No person would be held based entirely on diplomatic negotiations with a distant government that are beyond his own control. Instead he could take action to compile a record of good behavior in detention and to demonstrate rehabilitation, such as by completing training programs and anger management classes.

To rule otherwise, to place these individuals entirely beyond the pale of any kind of constitutional review merely because of status (as *Mezei* did), would be to declare them, as some courts and many commentators have observed, "nonpersons" for purposes of the Due Process Clause.[197] Even Justice Scalia seems to take pains to

---

[197] See, e.g., *Zadvydas v Underdown*, 185 F3d at 296; *Lynch v Cannatella*, 810 F2d 1363, 1375 (5th Cir 1987). See generally Kevin R. Johnson, *"Aliens" and the U.S. Immigration Laws: The Social and Legal Construction of Nonpersons*, 28 U Miami Int-Am L Rev 263 (1996–97).

dissociate himself from that sort of attitude, by indicating that Mezei could neither have been imprisoned at hard labor nor tortured.[198] Some courts in the excludable alien cases have not only noted the ongoing provision of annual INS review of releasability, but have either hinted or stated that it was constitutionally required.[199] Justices Kennedy and Rehnquist clearly indicate that they take the same view, affording even excludables some kind of constitutional monitoring. Under that framework, the choice is not between due process protection switched off and such protection switched on. It is a choice between levels of protection, none of which is at zero. The proper conclusion when a Marielito case (or indeed an EWI case) reaches the Court, then, would be to hold that lengthy detention is not precluded, but that INS must accord some form of regular procedures for ongoing consideration of dangerousness and flight risk, subject to review if challenged on habeas corpus.

Finally, the "no unprotected spot" concern also may help to account for the *Zadvydas* majority's apparent exception countenancing extended detention, even of LPRs, in cases of "terrorism or other special circumstances" linked in some manner to national security.[200] As discussed, for most deportable aliens, the protection of the nation that the court envisions consists in preadmission screening, coupled with the normal operation of the criminal justice system. The majority in essence says to the government: if you are worried about criminal recidivism, address it the same way you would have if the detainee had naturalized before embarking on his crimes. Monitor, investigate, and arrest if evidence develops

---

[198] Discussing *Wong Wing v United States*, on which Justice Breyer placed reliance, Justice Scalia writes: "all it held is that they could not be subjected to the punishment of hard labor without a judicial trial. I am sure they cannot be tortured, as well—but neither prohibition has anything to do with their right to be released into the United States. Nor does *Wong Wing* show that the rights of detained aliens subject to final order of deportation are different from the rights of aliens arrested and detained at the border—unless the Court believes that the detained alien in *Mezei* could have been set to hard labor." 121 S Ct at 2506.

[199] See *Chi Thon Ngo v INS*, 192 F3d 390, 397–99 (3d Cir 1999) (so holding and collecting cases that "look[ed] to the existence of those procedures to turn back due process challenges").

[200] Strictly speaking, the Court merely says that it is not addressing such a case: "Neither do we consider terrorism or other special circumstances where special arguments might be made for forms of preventive detention and for heightened deference to the judgments of the political branches with respect to matters of national security." 121 S Ct at 2502.

showing new criminal activity. (And for the unremovable alien, the supervisory order may afford extra monitoring opportunities, beyond what would be allowed under the criminal law, for supervision of one who has completed a sentence of confinement.)

Terrorism, however, introduces a new element. As we have all been reminded in the aftermath of September 11, 2001, terrorism usually has an international dimension that cannot be adequately addressed through the operation of American criminal investigation and prosecution alone. If the terrorism is international, we are dependent to a greater or lesser degree on actions by foreign sovereigns—at least to cooperate in the provision of information, if not also in the actual apprehension, prosecution, or suppression of the people who are responsible. The United States cannot empanel grand juries and issue subpoenas on foreign soil, nor, on its own authority, send in police investigators or arresting officers. Without such steps, normal U.S. criminal justice initiatives may be insufficient to the task. This insufficiency probably poses a particular risk in the setting we are considering, because, with rare exceptions, post-order indefinite detention arises only when a foreign sovereign has already refused to cooperate in a fundamental respect required by international law—receiving back its own nationals. One can hardly then expect that sovereign to cooperate in the kind of mutual efforts needed to suppress terrorism through the application of the criminal law. In that setting, the majority may be saying, when international terrorism is involved, we cannot declare the normal operation of the criminal justice system ipso facto sufficient to provide the needed level of future public safety, even when there has been preadmission screening. If the Court does someday squarely permit a terrorism exception to the release obligation, however, it would be most in keeping with *Zadvydas* to hold that habeas courts must afford some measure of review of the government's finding that the person is actually involved in terrorism.

F. APPLYING THE GRADUATED PROTECTION FRAMEWORK: THE USE OF SECRET EVIDENCE

It may be useful, in conclusion, to demonstrate the advantages of the analytical framework sketched here by applying it to a set of current issues—the use of classified information not shared with the alien in the course of removal proceedings.[201] Indeed, this may be a particularly apt test, because this was the very issue that first clearly brought the Court, in the controversial *Knauff* case, into the business of graduated due process protections for different classes of aliens.

The use of secret evidence in immigration cases has been limited or ruled invalid in a host of recent reported cases,[202] and before the terrorist attacks on September 11, a Secret Evidence Repeal Act gained wide support in Congress.[203] The use of secret evidence implicates the highest possible stakes for the individual, because knowing the government's evidence may be critical to the ability to put on any sort of meaningful defense. Although the government typically provides an unclassified summary of the evidence in such cases, often such a summary is as brief and unhelpful as a one-

---

[201] Another important controversy where this approach could have ready application derives from the mandatory pre-order detention provision adopted in the 1996 immigration amendments. That section requires INS to detain throughout the proceedings, without individualized inquiry into flight risk or dangerousness, virtually any alien with a criminal record who is released after October 8, 1998 (and certain others). INA § 236(c), 8 USC § 1226(c) (2000). See *Matter of Adeniji*, Interim Dec 3417 (BIA 1999). The three circuits that have considered constitutional challenges have divided on the result: *Parra v Perryman*, 172 F3d 954 (7th Cir 1999) (upholding mandatory detention); *Patel v Zemski*, 275 F3d 299 (3d Cir 2001) (requiring individualized inquiry); *Kim v Ziglar*, 276 F3d 523 (9th Cir 2002) (requiring individualized inquiry but limiting its holding to release claims by lawful permanent residents).

[202] See, e.g., *American-Arab Anti-Discrimination Committee (AADC) v Reno*, 70 F3d 1045, 1070 (9th Cir 1995) (a later decision by the Ninth Circuit in the long-running AADC case was reversed by the Supreme Court in *Reno v AADC*, 525 US 471 (1999), but the Supreme Court did not consider the secret evidence issue); *Rafeedie v INS*, 880 F2d 506, 522–23 (DC Cir 1989); *Najjar v Reno*, 97 F Supp 2d 1329, 1349–60 (SD Fla 2000), vacated on mootness grounds, *Al Najjar v Ashcroft*, 273 F3d 1330 (11th Cir 2001); *Kiaraldeen v Reno*, 71 F Supp 2d 402, 407–14 (D NJ 1999). The use of secret evidence also aroused controversy when the Department of Justice sought to deny asylum, based on classified evidence, to six of 6,000 Iraqi Kurds evacuated to the United States in 1997 in the wake of an Iraqi offensive. Former CIA Director James Woolsey took up their cases and Congress called oversight hearings. Settlements with the government ultimately allowed full hearings for five of the six. See Niels Frenzen, *National Security and Procedural Fairness: Secret Evidence and the Immigration Laws*, 76 Interpreter Releases 1677 n 31 (1999); *Senate Holds Hearing on National Security Considerations in Asylum Applications*, 75 Interpreter Releases 1446 (1998); Alexander Cockburn, *The Radicalization of James Woolsey*, NY Times (magazine) (July 23, 2000). During this period the BIA also issued a nonprecedent ruling in Matter of Haddam (BIA Nov 30, 2000), granting asylum despite the secret evidence presented by the INS. A comprehensive account of the case appears in *BIA Nonprecedent Decision Grants Asylum in Secret Evidence Case*, 77 Interpreter Releases 1704 (2000). The Attorney General ordered a stay of the BIA decision. *Board's Decision in Secret Evidence Case "Not Final," Reno Holds*, 78 Interpreter Releases 334 (2001).

[203] See HR 1266, 107th Cong, 1st Sess (2001). This bill tracked a measure approved by the House Judiciary Committee in the previous session, HR Rep No 106-981, 106th Cong, 2d Sess (2000) (reporting on HR 2121 of that Congress).

sentence statement that the evidence concerns the respondent's "association . . . with the Palestinian Islamic Jihad."[204] It is logical to assume that the hidden evidence would contain dates and places of the individual's alleged contacts with persons believed to be associated with the terrorist organization. With such details, the individual could mount a focused defense, perhaps demonstrating presence elsewhere at the times indicated, or offering an innocent explanation for the contacts. Lacking such details, the defendant may be reduced to providing general character witnesses, completely failing to engage what might prove to be the crucial factual allegations underlying the government's case.

The second *Eldridge* factor[205] runs entirely in the direction of the individual here: the added procedural ingredient for which he contends (revealing the secret evidence) could have a potentially enormous impact on the accuracy of the adjudication. As a result, several lower courts have rejected the use of secret evidence or have imposed requirements apparently designed to force the government to provide added details.[206] At least initially that may seem like an unthreatening and reasonable request. There is also the wholly legitimate concern that secrecy permits government abuse and sloppiness—allowing the government to rely too much on unfounded conjecture or on information that might derive only from deliberate falsehood planted by someone with a personal grudge.[207]

On the other hand, the government may have compelling reasons not to reveal to the individual any details, innocuous as they may seem to an uninformed observer, concerning the basis for its conclusions regarding a national security threat. Much of such classified information comes from confidential informants, and such sources are likely to become more important in the future. A prominent theme of the reaction to the September 11 bombings, even from civil liberties groups, has been the need to rely more fully on human intelligence—that is, on operatives who can work their way into a terrorist organization and provide information on

---

[204] This was the summary provided in *Najjar v Reno*, 97 F Supp 2d at 1334.

[205] *Mathews v Eldridge*, 424 US 319 (1976). See note 100.

[206] See note 202.

[207] The decision in the Kiaraldeen case, 71 F Supp 2d at 413, 416–18, for example, suggests that the derogatory information was rumor sown by the deportation respondent's estranged ex-wife. Similar rumor seems to have been the source of Ellen Knauff's problems. See Weisselberg, 143 U Pa L Rev at 960–64 (cited in note 16).

its operations.[208] This is an extremely dangerous business, and those who undertake it need the strongest possible assurance that their identities will be shielded. If the deportation respondent is in fact associated with a terrorist organization, yielding up even the minor detail of the date of an alleged meeting could reveal that a government informant was present at that moment. Associates still at large could work back from that information to root out or kill the informant.

The dilemma could not be more acute. An innocent respondent is left virtually defenseless without the details buried in the classified evidence. But if the information is shared, a guilty respondent is given a key that leaves the government's informant frightfully exposed.

In proceedings where the fullest measure of due process protection unmistakably applies, criminal trials, secret evidence simply cannot be used as the basis for a prosecution.[209] The Fifth and Sixth Amendments generally require giving the defendant the details of the government's case and affording the right to cross-examine adverse witnesses. If the classified information is needed for the case in chief, the government is put to a choice whether to "burn the asset"—that is, pull in the informant and shield him in other ways after he testifies in open court, thereby losing future information—or else abandon the prosecution.[210] Should a similar

---

[208] See, e.g., *Making Our Immigration System More Secure*, National Immigration Forum Issue Paper at 1, December 2001 ("As the details of the terrorist plot have emerged, what has become clear is that any change in the way we manage our immigration system will have only a limited impact on our national security. Far more important is our capacity to collect and analyze intelligence. . . . Changes to the immigration system that will make us more secure involve, primarily, better access to and timely use of information collected by our intelligence agencies."). See also Edward Alden, *The CIA's Failure of Imagination*, Financial Times (Sept 15, 2001); Steve Goldstein, *High-Tech Spying Called Inadequate: U.S. Needs to Boost "Human Intelligence," Critics Now Saying*, Pittsburgh Post-Gazette (Sept 16, 2001), at A10; Editorial, *Boost Intelligence: Serious Thought Must be Given to Expanding the Human Component*, Orlando Sentinel (Sept 17, 2001).

[209] This limitation on the use of classified evidence in ordinary criminal cases appears to have provided a significant part of the reason why President Bush issued his Military Order authorizing the trial before military commissions of designated aliens implicated in "acts of international terrorism." 66 Fed Reg 57833 (2001). Whether any aliens resident, lawfully or unlawfully, in the United States (as opposed to persons seized and held overseas) will be prosecuted in that venue, and if so, whether such prosecutions will survive constitutional scrutiny, remains to be seen.

[210] The Classified Information Procedures Act, 18 USC app III, §§ 1–16 (2000), was developed primarily to assure that the defendant could not engage in "greymail," by threatening wide exposure of classified information in the course of making out a defense. It provides pretrial procedures to resolve questions of admissibility and discovery before such

rule apply to immigration proceedings? The black-letter law holds
that deportation is not punishment, thereby making criminal law
protections not directly applicable. But it also provides that deportable aliens are entitled to procedural due process protection,
superintended by the courts, in removal proceedings. If the potential for unfairness is so great, perhaps results similar to those in
criminal proceedings should obtain.

A better middle ground could be found by separating the cases
along the gradational spectrum laid out above and attending
closely to the exact issues that the secret evidence addresses. Consider first excludable aliens who can be returned promptly to the
country from which they came. They may be aggrieved by the
refusal of admission based on secret evidence, and may even be
the victims of injustice in such a determination, but their stakes
are generally low. Denial of admission at the border is not much
different, functionally, from the refusal of a visa, for which full
access to the adverse evidence has never been provided. *Knauff*
decided this precise issue, giving the government carte blanche to
use classified information, unshared with any other adjudicating
official or judge, in deciding on admission at the border.[211] Next
came *Kwong Hai Chew*, which held that a lawful permanent resident (whose status had not lapsed in the way Mezei's did) could
not be subjected to an adverse decision on the basis of classified
information.[212] That decision, strictly speaking, rested on construction of the governing regulations, but in the 1982 *Plasencia* decision, again involving a lawful permanent resident, Justice O'Connor emphasized that "the rationale was one of constitutional
law."[213] Her dictum thus strongly implied that the Constitution
would not permit subjection of LPRs to deportation based on confidential information they could not confront or effectively rebut.

What about the alien categories in between? Until 1996, the
government was not in a position to attempt to use classified information as part of the case in chief for removal, except in the setting
approved by *Knauff* and *Mezei*—that is, cases against excludable

---

information is used in open court. See *United States v Smith*, 780 F2d 1102 (4th Cir 1985);
United States v Lee, 90 F Supp 2d 1324 (D NM 2000). The Act does not permit the prosecution to use such information in its case in chief.

[211] 338 US 537 (1950).

[212] 344 US 590 (1953).

[213] 459 US at 33.

independently evaluated by, an immigration judge or a reviewing court.

If the government makes the classified information available to the immigration judge, he or she is in a position, first, to consider whether the information was properly classified, and second, to question the government's attorneys and, if necessary, its witnesses, in order to test for reliability and to be on the lookout for mere rumor, informant's vendetta, or possible agent abuse or sloppiness. It is true that this *in camera* procedure, away from the individual and his attorney, falls well short of the usual adversarial guarantees our common-law tradition holds in high esteem, and that sometimes judges will be ill-equipped to provide anything other than a rough test of the soundness of the evidence. But full adversarial testing is difficult to provide while still shielding the human asset (or other interests that led to the classification). The immigration judge's role, coupled with the now-standard procedure for the government to share the classified information with a reviewing court, should ordinarily be ruled sufficient under the Due Process Clause for arriving aliens and EWIs.

With regard to nonimmigrants, the case is closer. But if the government can prove its case in chief without such problematic evidence, so that the only issue for which the information is relevant is a discretionary waiver—as is overwhelmingly the case when nonimmigrants are placed in removal proceedings—the individual interest is considerably reduced, and the case for protecting the government's source appears proportionally stronger. Asylum claims, however, asserting protection because of a risk that the person will be persecuted if deported, may deserve special treatment. At least some forms of asylum-type protection are not discretionary,[221] and in any event courts have recognized that an asylum application represents "this most sensitive of human claims in the international community."[222] Perhaps such claims should be given

---

[221] Asylum under INA § 208, 8 USC § 1158 (2000), is discretionary, but the closely related relief known as withholding of removal, under INA § 241(b)(3), 8 USC § 1231(b)(3) (2000), is mandatory for those who meet its somewhat more demanding standards. Similarly, protection under Article 3 of the Convention Against Torture is mandatory. See Aleinikoff, Martin, and Motomura, *Immigration and Citizenship* at 1052–57, 1145–46 (cited in note 17); *INS v Cardoza-Fonseca*, 480 US 421, 429, 444 (1987).

[222] *Reyes-Arias v INS*, 866 F2d 500, 504 (DC Cir 1989) (per Starr, J).
Two of the more embarrassing misfires from the government's point of view, the *Knauff* and *Kiaraldeen* rejections, came in another class of invariably sensitive cases: those involving

a more extensive form of substitute safeguards. I shall return to that possibility after considering what the statute now provides with regard to secret evidence and LPRs.

What if the evidence is critical to the case in chief against a respondent who is still in status—which would ordinarily mean against an LPR charged under the terrorist grounds of deportability? (By the time such cases are developed against nonimmigrants, their status has usually expired or some other violation of the terms of their admission has been identified, all of which can be proved without reliance on the secret evidence.) If LPRs are to be considered nearly full members of the community, for whom the effect of deportation is akin to banishment (owing to their wholly legitimate rootedness in the community), then the case is extremely strong that deportation on the basis of secret evidence simply should not be permitted under the Due Process Clause. The situation of these aliens is markedly different from that of LPRs like Zadvydas and Ma who have been duly convicted, on a public record, of crimes that undeniably make them deportable. When secret evidence goes to the case in chief against an LPR, there is no equivalent nonsecret guarantee of deportability. The person could be wholly innocent, and therefore wholly at a loss as to how to contest the charge.

Until 1996, immigration law and regulations tacitly embodied this position. There was simply no authority to use secret evidence in the case in chief against a deportable alien. It could only be used against non-LPR excludable aliens and with regard to relief from deportation—far more defensible uses, as indicated above. In 1996, however, the Antiterrorism and Effective Death Penalty Act introduced an Alien Terrorist Removal Court (ATRC), essentially to permit secret evidence to be used against lawful permanent residents.[223] (The Court's jurisdiction also extends, if necessary, to nonimmigrants who remain in status when proceedings are initiated.) Although this institution has been denounced in some circles

---

spouses of U.S. citizens. When the genuineness of the marriage is uncontested (as was true in both those instances), the marriage itself generates a level of community membership that perhaps should be regarded as nudging the claimant up the gradational hierarchy. At the very least, there is no doubt that marriage makes the case a far more sympathetic one in the public and congressional arenas. Any statutory effort to provide selectively heightened safeguards against secret evidence should keep these sensitivities in mind.

[223] INA §§ 501–07, 8 USC §§ 1531–37 (2000).

as a Star Chamber,[224] in fact it represents a good-faith congressional effort to provide as many substitute safeguards as possible while still shielding the confidential information.[225] The court is staffed by five life-tenured federal judges named for five-year terms by the Chief Justice. The principal initial decision makers therefore, not simply those who will review a decision according to some more deferential appellate standard, are wholly independent of the executive branch. They are given a role in preliminary consideration of the charges and of custody determinations, in addition to the ultimate decision whether the evidence proves the charge. They superintend the creation of an unclassified summary of the secret information to be given to the respondent. The individual haled before the court is entitled to counsel paid by the government (appointed counsel is not available in any other immigration proceedings), and in most cases will be aided by a "special counsel" named from a list of attorneys with high-level security clearances.[226] The evident objective was to allow as much as possible the normal adversarial testing of the evidence, while still avoiding disclosure to the alien—because of the risk that she would share it with confederates still at large. The special counsel has full access to the secret evidence and participates in the *in camera* procedures considering it, including cross-examination of the government's witnesses.

The Justice Department has not yet brought any cases in the ATRC, but that quiescence may end with the new antiterrorism efforts sparked by the September 11 bombings. Hence we have as yet no body of practice that might help judge the institution's effectiveness and fairness. The critical factor may be the details of the role of special counsel: how closely can they replicate the kinds of adversarial testing we expect from normal procedures in open

---

[224] Secret Evidence Repeal Act of 1999, Part II: Hearing on HR 2121 Before the House Comm on the Judiciary, 106th Cong, 2d Sess 54 (May 23, 2000) (letter from sixty-three advocacy and service organizations, attached to prepared statement of Gregory Nojeim, Legislative Counsel, American Civil Liberties Union). See also Susan Akram, *Scheherezade Meets Kafka: Two Dozen Sordid Tales of Ideological Exclusion*, 14 Georgetown Immig L J 51 (1999).

[225] See Michael Scaperlanda, *Are We That Far Gone? Due Process and Secret Deportation Proceedings*, 7 Stan L & Policy Rev 23, 28–30 (1996).

[226] See Aleinikoff, Martin, and Motomura, *Immigration and Citizenship* at 872–74 (cited in note 17).

court? One can expect that they will be tough and demanding, but the requirement that they not divulge any of the classified information to their clients cannot help but impair their effectiveness. To return to an earlier example, if the government's case turns critically on the informant's testimony regarding meetings with known terrorists in which the LPR allegedly participated, dogged cross-examination can try to expose internal inconsistencies in the witness's testimony. But it seems nearly impossible for counsel to develop and present detailed countertestimony without tipping his client as to the crucial dates at issue—which could then compromise the secret information and thus violate the terms of counsel's role.[227]

For my part, I would conclude that the status of LPR commands the full measure of informed adversarial testing of the crucial evidence before the person can be uprooted from a domicile established with full permission of the U.S. government. The ATRC is an impressive effort at substitute safeguards, but as applied to LPRs, it is just not good enough.[228] Nonetheless, that special court and its distinctive procedures do show that there is a richer middle ground than some of the recent debate over secret evidence has conceded. It is not a choice between wholly disallowing the use of such evidence and complete discretion in the government, unmonitored by judicial officers. In some cases where *in camera* review of secret evidence by an immigration judge, followed by judicial review, is deemed insufficient to protect the particular alien's procedural rights, the ATRC could be used as a model for striking a better balance. For example, asylum and similar persecution-based claims, though rarely met by a government proffer of classified information, would be good candidates for assignment to a procedure like that provided in the ATRC when such information is introduced.[229]

---

[227] The counsel's role would be similar to that carried out by some defense counsel in the case of *United States v Bin Laden*, 2001 WL 66393 (SDNY 2001), under special discovery procedures ordered by the court under the Classified Information Procedures Act.

[228] Representative Rohrabacher introduced what he hoped would be a substitute for the proposed Secret Evidence Repeal Act, which he styled the "Secret Evidence Against Lawful Aliens Repeal Act of 2001." Consonantly with the conclusions reached here, its main function would have been to shield LPRs against such evidence, even while allowing such evidence, with specific safeguards, against aliens with lesser stakes in the community. HR 2113, 107th Cong, 1st Sess (2001).

[229] This would require a statutory change in the jurisdiction of the ATRC. But such an amendment might be hastened along if courts were to rule that at least some aliens in

IV. Conclusion

Zadvydas marks a milestone of moderate promise toward candid adoption of a sensible framework yielding graduated constitutional protections for different categories of aliens. It reached the right result for the two individuals then before the court, who had been lawful permanent residents before being ordered deported, for it gives them fairly demanding protection. It soundly indicates that not all aliens deserve the same recognition, and it refuses to take a wholly positivist stance toward the definition of the categories and their entitlements.

But far more needs to be done to build on this foundation. The Court needs to stop acting as if the exclusion-deportation line is of central importance. It should recognize that the line separating lawful permanent residents, domiciled with the clearest possible consent of the community, from other aliens temporarily or unlawfully present carries greater significance. And it should decide that those below that line, even those so far below it as Ellen Knauff and the Marielitos, are not wholly cast into outer constitutional darkness—a trail surprisingly blazed by Justices Kennedy and Rehnquist in their *Zadvydas* dissent. In identifying the various levels of protection, it needs to be far more careful in its use of categories and patterns that are now deeply entrenched in the architecture of our immigration control system—for which this article attempts to provide a clarifying blueprint. The Court needs to know the difference between admitted nonimmigrants and EWIs and parolees and to think carefully about how the incidents of their status, coupled with the social reality they have experienced and the community ties they enjoy, affect the constitutional calculus.

The task of building a clear and candid system of graduated protections for aliens has never been more urgent, for the Court doubtless will be asked over the next few years to rule on many constitutional questions posed by the nation's response to the grave challenge of foreign terrorism. The framework that I have sketched here in preliminary fashion should enable us to apply the Constitution in a way that is both appropriately protective of individuals and realistic in securing government's legitimate interests.

---

removal proceedings, depending on their membership level and the exact nature of their defense, deserve a higher level of protection than simply that provided by an immigration judge's *in camera* review of the classified evidence.

PAUL GEWIRTZ

PRIVACY AND SPEECH

We often disclose ourselves to the world at large, or at least we act as if indifferent to the world's eyes. But at other times, most of us try to control the disclosure of certain matters about ourselves. Sometimes we share thoughts, feelings, information, personality, or bodily appearance with no one at all. More commonly, we share these things with a limited number of other people. Privacy in this sense—the ability to control and to avoid the disclosure of certain matters about oneself—is a widely recognized value, an important precondition for human flourishing.

Freedom of speech and freedom of the press are also deeply cherished values. The right to generally say and publish what one wants is a bedrock element of human freedom and democratic self-governance, and this encompasses saying and publishing things about other people, including things they would prefer not be said or published about them. The tension between free speech and privacy is not so much a conflict among camps of adherents as it is a tension within ourselves. Both privacy and speech are values of great importance, and people typically embrace both of them. Louis Brandeis, the co-author of the most famous article on privacy ever written,[1] was also the author of some of the greatest prose ever written about free speech.[2]

Although the tension between speech and privacy is hardly a

Paul Gewirtz is Potter Stewart Professor of Constitutional Law, Yale Law School.

AUTHOR'S NOTE: I am grateful to Zoë Baird, Jack Balkin, Philip Chen, Jacob Katz Cogan, Owen Fiss, Linda Greenhouse, and Spiros Simitis for their very helpful comments on an earlier draft, and to Daniel Marx for his excellent research assistance.

[1] Samuel D. Warren and Louis D. Brandeis, *The Right to Privacy*, 4 Harv L Rev 193 (1890).
[2] *Whitney v California*, 274 US 357, 372 (1927) (Brandeis concurring).

new one, it has expanding significance. New technologies have opened up wonderful new possibilities for communication and expression, but also have created ominous new possibilities for diminution of privacy. Any breach in privacy, of course, can be greatly magnified if the media discloses it to the public—and the public's appetite for information about other people's private matters, and the media's willingness to satisfy that appetite, have never been greater. These and other developments have underscored the vulnerability of privacy and have created new concerns about the balance between free speech and privacy.

The Supreme Court has considered this tension in a number of cases over the past decades, and there is a clear pattern. Speech almost always wins. In rejecting privacy claims, the Court's broadly stated First Amendment rationales leave little room for privacy protection in cases of a speech-privacy conflict. In this article, I argue that the Supreme Court should give more weight to privacy protection than it has. My goal is to define a constitutional position that gives strong weight to speech, recognizing its central and indispensable role, but that also gives sufficient weight to privacy, recognizing its crucial role as well.

My starting point is last term's decision in *Bartnicki v Vopper*.[3] *Bartnicki* continues the Court's basic pattern of ruling for the media in cases of speech-privacy conflict. In *Bartnicki*, the Court held, by a vote of 6–3, that the media has a First Amendment right to broadcast certain information that had been illegally intercepted from a cell phone conversation. The "opinion of the Court" written by Justice Stevens makes some bows in the direction of protecting privacy, but ends up giving privacy little weight.

But the case may well represent a turn on the Court toward greater protection of privacy and greater restrictions on the media and speech. It is misleading to think of Justice Stevens's opinion as a true "opinion of the Court." Justice Breyer, joined by Justice O'Connor, wrote an important and unusually interesting concurring opinion analyzing the speech-privacy conflict in a way far more protective of privacy than Justice Stevens's opinion. Although Justices Breyer and O'Connor joined the Stevens opinion, their votes were needed to make up the six-member majority.

---

[3] 121 S Ct 1753 (2001).

When read alongside the opinion of the three dissenters, who thought the media should lose this case, the Breyer opinion makes clear that a majority of the Court is prepared to uphold significant restrictions on the media in order to protect privacy.

The time is now ripe to establish a new framework for considering speech-privacy cases that gives enhanced protection to privacy. Justice Breyer's opinion is a start in that direction, as well as a significant installment in his little observed but important ongoing effort to develop a new approach to the First Amendment generally. As Justice Breyer's opinion suggests, it will be difficult to enhance privacy protection without, to some extent, modifying First Amendment doctrine as it currently exists. The challenge is to find greater room for protecting privacy within our constitutional law without undermining the media's freedom to perform its crucial roles. In this article, I seek to advance that effort.

I

At issue in *Bartnicki* was the constitutionality of a provision in Title III of the Omnibus Crime Control and Safe Streets Act that sought to prevent invasions of privacy that occur through the interception and disclosure of wire, oral, or electronic communications. The statute provides sanctions against "any person who . . . intentionally discloses, or endeavors to disclose, to any other person the contents of any wire, oral, or electronic communication, knowing or having reason to know that the information was obtained through the interception of" such a communication.[4]

The case involved the unlawful interception of a cell phone conversation between two union officials during a period of collective bargaining negotiations involving the teachers' union and a local Pennsylvania school board. The conversation concerned various matters related to the status and handling of the negotiations and a possible strike. At one point, one union official said to the other, "If they're not gonna move for three percent, we're gonna have to go to their, their homes . . . To blow off their front porches, we'll have to do some work on some of those guys."[5] The telephone call was covertly and unlawfully intercepted and taped by

---

[4] 18 USC § 2511(1)(c).
[5] 121 S Ct at 1757.

an unidentified person who gave the tape to a prominent union opponent, who then gave it to a radio station broadcaster. The broadcaster played the tape on his talk show. The union officials whose conversation had been intercepted filed suit for damages under Title III. The case reached the Supreme Court after a divided U.S. Court of Appeals for the Third Circuit ordered entry of summary judgment for the broadcaster.[6]

Justice Stevens's opinion for the Court affirmed, declaring the Act unconstitutional as applied because it restricted media freedom to publish the illegally intercepted material. Two factors were critical for Justice Stevens. First, the media was not itself involved in the illegal interception of the conversation. Second, the information disclosed involved a matter of "public concern"; the intercepted conversation was between two union officials discussing negotiations over the proper level of compensation for teachers in the union.

Justice Stevens starts his opinion by stating that "these cases present a conflict between interests of the highest order—on the one hand, the interest in the full and free dissemination of information concerning public issues, and, on the other hand, the interest in individual privacy and, more specifically, in fostering private speech."[7] But there is very little in what follows that treats these interests as if they were of equivalent importance and both of the "highest order."

Justice Stevens's legal analysis begins with notable elusiveness in discussing the governing legal standard. Both the majority and dissent in the Court of Appeals had concluded that an "intermediate scrutiny" test should be used, not "strict scrutiny," because Title III is a "content neutral" law.[8] The Solicitor General, urging reversal, agreed that "intermediate scrutiny" was appropriate.[9] These conclusions were not surprising in light of prevailing First-

---

[6] 200 F3d 109 (3d Cir 2000).

[7] 121 S Ct at 1756.

[8] 200 F3d 109, 121, 131 (3d Cir 1999). The other two Courts of Appeals that had considered the issue before the case came to the Supreme Court also applied intermediate scrutiny. *Boehner v McDermott*, 191 F3d 463, 467 (DC Cir 1999), vacated and remanded, 121 S Ct 2190 (2001); *Peavy v WFAA-TV*, 221 F3d 158 (5th Cir 2000), cert denied, 121 S Ct 2191 (2001). Both courts found Title III constitutional as applied to the facts of those cases.

[9] Reply Brief for the United States at 11–13, 16–33, *Bartnicki v Vopper*, 121 S Ct 1753 (2001) (Nos 99-1687, 99-1728) (available at 1999 US LEXIS Briefs 1687).

Amendment doctrine. "Strict scrutiny," the Supreme Court has said, is applied "to regulations that suppress, disadvantage, or impose differential burdens upon speech because of its content," but content-neutral laws of general applicability are subject to "an intermediate level of scrutiny" because they "pose a less substantial risk of excising certain ideas or viewpoints from the public dialogue."[10]

Title III is a content-neutral law of general applicability. It protects all private communications from unlawful intrusions and prohibits the use and disclosure of all illegally intercepted communications, without regard to the content of what is intercepted. The prohibition on disclosure is triggered by the source of the communication—an illegal interception—not the substance of an interception. Indeed, exactly the same content can be published if its source is not an unlawful interception.[11] Moreover, Title III applies generally to all "uses" of the unlawfully intercepted communication—speech uses and non-speech uses (say, using the information in buying securities or developing a product), and expressive uses by all media. Title III's purpose is not to suppress disfavored ideas, but to protect the privacy of communications, without regard to the content of what is privately communicated. In doing so, Title III not only protects privacy but also promotes free speech itself by encouraging uninhibited expression and reducing the fear that uninhibited discussions might be intercepted, used, and disseminated. As such, Title III's use and disclosure restrictions meet all the criteria for "intermediate scrutiny."

But Justice Stevens does not apply intermediate scrutiny—indeed he does not mention it, except in his summary of the Court

---

[10] *Turner Broadcasting System v Federal Communications Commission*, 512 US 622, 641–43, 661 (1994). See also *Cohen v Cowles Media Co.*, 501 US 663, 669 (1991); *San Francisco Arts & Athletics, Inc. v United States Olympic Comm.*, 483 US 522, 536–37 (1987). A content-neutral law of general applicability will be sustained under "intermediate scrutiny," the Court has said, "if it furthers an important or substantial governmental interest; if the governmental interest is unrelated to the suppression of free expression; and if the incidental restriction on alleged First Amendment freedoms is no greater than is essential to the furtherance of that interest." *Turner Broadcasting System v Federal Communications Commission*, 512 US at 662 (quoting *United States v O'Brien*, 391 US 367, 377 (1968)).

[11] Cf. *Seattle Times Co. v Rhinehart*, 467 US 20, 34 (1984) (media defendant may be placed under protective order not to disclose information that had come from the defendant in the discovery process, although it could publish identical information that came from a different source).

of Appeals' opinion below.[12] Indeed, nowhere in the opinion does Justice Stevens say that he is applying either strict scrutiny or intermediate scrutiny. The closest he comes to articulating a governing legal standard is to say that the restriction here must be justified by "a need . . . of the highest order" (quoting *Smith v Daily Mail Publishing Co.*).[13] The dissent calls this "strict scrutiny,"[14] and perhaps it is—although Justice Breyer, who joins the Stevens opinion, says in his concurrence that "strict scrutiny" is "out of place" in this kind of case.[15]

Justice Stevens takes this "need . . . of the highest order" standard from a series of four cases that do not seem applicable: *Florida Star v B.J.F.*,[16] *Smith v Daily Mail Publishing Co.*,[17] *Landmark Communications, Inc. v Virginia*,[18] and *Cox Broadcasting Corp. v Cohn.*[19]

---

[12] Justice Stevens begins his legal analysis of the case (Part V of the opinion) by saying that "we agree with petitioners" that Title III is "a content-neutral law of general applicability," and explaining why:

> [T]he basic purpose of the statute at issue is to "protec[t] the privacy of wire[, electronic], and oral communications. . . ." The statute does not distinguish based on the content of the intercepted conversations, nor is it justified by reference to the content of those conversations. Rather, the communications at issue are singled out by virtue of the fact that they were illegally intercepted—by virtue of the source, rather than the subject matter.

121 S Ct at 1760. Characterizing Title III as a "content-neutral law of general applicability" was exactly what led the Court of Appeals below and the Solicitor General before the Supreme Court to argue that the intermediate scrutiny test was appropriate here. Yet instead of taking the seemingly next step of saying that therefore this case is governed by intermediate scrutiny, Justice Stevens simply moves on. "[O]n the other hand," he says, "the naked prohibition against disclosures is fairly characterized as a regulation of pure speech, . . . not a regulation of conduct. . . . [A]s such, it is the kind of 'speech' that the First Amendment protects." Id at 1761. Leaving to one side the revealing characterization of the regulation here as a "naked" prohibition (of "pure" speech no less), this "on the other hand" discussion seems beside the point. It is true that intermediate scrutiny, in addition to being used for "content-neutral laws of general applicability," is sometimes also used for laws that regulate "conduct" and have only an incidental effect on "speech." Justice Stevens sensibly appears to be rejecting this alternative basis for using intermediate scrutiny. But rejecting a second possible ground for using intermediate scrutiny is not an "on the other hand" counterargument to the first ground. Having made this "on the other hand" point, though, Justice Stevens simply moves on, drawing no conclusion here at all about the appropriate legal standard to be used. All of Part V of the opinion reads like a false start.

[13] Id at 1761 (citing the *Daily Mail* case at 443 US 97, 102 (1979)).

[14] Id at 1770 (Rehnquist dissenting).

[15] Id at 1766 (Breyer concurring).

[16] 491 US 524 (1989).

[17] 443 US 97 (1979).

[18] 435 US 829 (1978).

[19] 420 US 469 (1975).

In all of these cases, the Court sided with the media in concluding that the First Amendment prohibited the government from punishing the publication of information claimed to invade people's privacy. Although superficially similar to *Bartnicki*, these cases were very different in fundamental respects relevant to both the choice of legal standard and the outcomes.

Most significantly, these cases all involved the publication of information that was "lawfully obtained." This was the explicit and crucial predicate for the legal standard used. As the Court in *Florida Star* summarized the rule governing these cases (referred to commonly as "the *Daily Mail* principle"), when "a newspaper lawfully obtains truthful information about a matter of public significance then state officials may not constitutionally punish publication of the information, absent a need to further a state interest of the highest order."[20] In each of these cases, the information published by the media was not unlawfully obtained by the media or by anyone else. In *Cox Broadcasting*, a television station broadcast a rape victim's name that had been in "official court records open to public inspection."[21] In *Landmark Communications*, a newspaper printed information about proceedings pending before a judicial inquiry commission, information that the Supreme Court emphasized had not been "secure[d] . . . by illegal means."[22] In *Daily Mail*, a newspaper published the name and photograph of a fourteen-year-old boy arrested for murder after getting the information by "routine newspaper reporting techniques."[23] In *Florida Star*, a newspaper published the name of a victim of a sexual assault after learning the name from a police report placed in the police department's pressroom.[24] Some of these cases are critiqued below for giving insufficient weight to privacy interests, but at least the published information in these cases was not illegally secured, as it was in *Bartnicki*.

The fact that published information has been lawfully obtained properly structures First Amendment analysis. More directly relevant here, the fact that information is *unlawfully* obtained properly

---

[20] 491 US at 533 (quoting *Smith v Daily Mail Publishing Co.*).

[21] 420 US 469, 495 (1975).

[22] 435 US at 837.

[23] 443 US at 103.

[24] 491 US at 527.

structures First Amendment analysis, and justifies a very different legal standard. This is because, where information has been obtained unlawfully, very different values are predictably involved—most obviously, there are likely to be distinctively strong privacy (or confidentiality) interests as well as an understandable desire to arrange incentives (including the incentives of the media) to reduce the incidence of unlawfulness.[25] In *Florida Star*, the Court not only repeated the formulation of the *Daily Mail* standard that is limited to "lawfully obtained" information, but specifically stated that a case would fall "outside the *Daily Mail* principle" if the information were in private hands and obtained "nonconsensual[ly]."[26]

Because the information broadcast in *Bartnicki* was unlawfully intercepted,[27] the case involves a range of concerns outside the *Daily Mail* principle. Justice Stevens makes much of the fact that the initial unlawful obtaining of the information was done by a third party rather than the broadcaster. But it is hard to see why this should make any difference. Title III limits the media only where it knows or has reason to know that the information comes from an illegal interception.[28] Surely the knowing exploitation of an illegality is not an innocent state of mind. More fundamentally, the illegal interception is what makes the broadcast a distinctive invasion of privacy, which properly prompts a constitutional analysis different from that in the *Daily Mail* line of cases.

The particular laws challenged in the *Daily Mail* line of cases and the circumstances of their application involved other features that further demonstrate why *Bartnicki* should have triggered a different analysis under current First Amendment doctrine. First, in all four cases, the challenged law was content-specific—and, as

---

[25] Doctrinal rules are rules of thumb that take account of the predictably competing values at stake in applying legal provisions in particular types of circumstances. It would defeat the purpose of doctrinal rules not to use different tests when predictably very different values are involved.

[26] 491 US at 534. At another point in the *Florida Star* opinion, the Court adds that "the *Daily Mail* principle does not settle the issue whether, in cases where information has been acquired unlawfully by a newspaper or by a source, government may ever punish not only the unlawful acquisition, but the ensuing publication as well." 491 US at 535 n 8.

[27] In addition, the information came to the radio station through a series of "disclosures" that were themselves illegal.

[28] The statute also limits liability to those disclosures that are "intentional." 18 USC § 2511(1)(c). Negligent disclosure of the contents of an illegally intercepted conversation is not sanctioned.

noted above, content-specific laws generally trigger strict scrutiny. In *Cox Broadcasting*, *Florida Star*, and *Daily Mail*, the challenged statutes prohibited disclosures of certain specific types of information in criminal cases (the names of rape victims in the first two, and the names of juvenile offenders in the latter). In *Landmark Communications*, the statute prohibited disclosures of the content of judicial commission proceedings only. Indeed, in at least *Landmark Communications*, the state law had the earmarks of the government trying to censor unpleasant information about government officials and limiting criticism of the government (allegations that might harm a "judge's reputation" or public "confidence in the judicial system"). In *Bartnicki*, by contrast, the law is content-neutral and has none of the earmarks of government censorship of particular information or ideas.

Second, in all of the cases except *Landmark Communications*, the challenged law applied only to disclosures by the media or by some media. Thus, these were arguably not laws of general applicability.[29] The limited scope of the laws in these cases raised questions not only about evenhandedness but also about whether the state was effectively furthering its claimed interests. In *Bartnicki*, by contrast, Title III is a law of general applicability, prohibiting all use and disclosure of illegally intercepted communications.

Third, in all four cases, the government itself was the source of the information. As the Court noted in each case, this means that the government (at least in theory) could have taken steps to control the information rather than creating causes of action against media entities that learn of the information.[30] In *Bartnicki*, by contrast, the communication involved private parties rather than the government—and private parties who were victims of a deliberate illegal interception, not their own casualness with the information.

In spite of these differences, Justice Stevens applies the *Daily*

---

[29] In *Cox Broadcasting*, the statute prohibited only the disclosure of rape victims' names by print, broadcast, television, or radio media. In *Daily Mail*, the statute prohibited only newspapers from publishing the names of juvenile offenders. In *Florida Star*, the statute prohibited publishing rape victims' names only "in any instrument of mass communication." In *Landmark Communications*, the statute was not focused on particular media, but made it unlawful to "divulge" information about the proceedings.

[30] Arguably, the government should be allowed the additional tool of punishing further disclosures following a leak of its information that it failed to prevent. See text accompanying note 127. But the balance of interests in such a case is somewhat different from the balance in a case where information has been intercepted from private parties.

Mail standard in *Bartnicki*. He concludes that Title III does not advance a "need of the highest order" that would justify restrictions on the media's disclosures. The fact that the information broadcast was unlawfully obtained neither affects his choice of legal standard nor furnishes a justification to satisfy the standard.

The government identified two "interests" related to protecting privacy from illegal interceptions, but neither satisfies the Court. First, the government argued that punishing disclosures helps to "dry up the market" for illegally intercepted private conversations, and thus reduces the incentives to intercept in the first place. It is especially important to punish disclosures, including those by people who lawfully obtained the illegally intercepted material, because the original act of interception is often hard to detect and punish.[31] Justice Stevens states that "[t]he normal method of deterring unlawful conduct is to impose an appropriate punishment on the person who engages in it."[32] But in fact the law commonly tries to deter unlawful conduct by restricting those who try to piggyback on the illegality. Most obviously, the exclusionary rule in criminal cases rests precisely on the belief that police misconduct can be deterred by barring prosecutors and others from using the unlawfully seized evidence.[33] Moreover, the law regularly punishes the knowing receipt and sale of stolen property as a way of deterring thefts.[34]

Justice Stevens argues that it would be "quite remarkable" to "hold that speech by a law-abiding possessor of information can be suppressed in order to deter conduct by a non-law-abiding third party."[35] But there is nothing remarkable or novel about restricting speech that is the fruit of unlawful action as a means of deterring the unlawful action. For example, the First Amendment permits a ban on the distribution of erotic material portraying children, even though not legally obscene, as a means of controlling the illegal exploitation of children in the production of the material. As the

---

[31] 121 S Ct at 1773–75.

[32] Id at 1762.

[33] E.g., *Oregon v Elstad*, 470 US 298, 306 (1985); *Elkins v United States*, 364 US 206, 217 (1960). Indeed, Title III itself has an exclusionary rule barring the use of illegally seized communications as evidence, in order to deter illegal interceptions. 18 USC § 2515.

[34] 121 S Ct at 1773–74 (Rehnquist dissenting) (citing W. R. LaFave and A. W. Scott, Jr., 2 *Substantive Criminal Law* § 8.10(a) at 422 (1986)).

[35] Id at 1762.

Court said in *New York v Ferber*, "[t]he most expeditious if not the only practical method of law enforcement may be to dry up the market for this material by imposing severe criminal penalties on persons selling, advertising, or otherwise promoting the product."[36]

Illegal conduct that yields stolen information can be every bit as wrongful and offensive as illegal conduct that yields stolen goods, and there is no reason why deterrence of the former should be disfavored any more than deterrence of the latter. The fact that the fruit of an illegality is speech acts does not make it wrong to try to discourage the illegality, does not make distributing the fruits of the illegality praiseworthy, and does not make it improper to try to discourage the illegality by drying up the market for the illegally obtained material. To say otherwise is inescapably to say that we care less about deterring the illegal stealing of information than the illegal stealing of other things, and that is unjustified. Justice Stevens asserts that in most instances the identity of the person illegally intercepting the communication will be learned. Thus, he argues, there are few instances where prohibiting third party disclosures will help deter unlawful interceptions, and therefore no government interest of the "highest order" is involved. But Congress concluded that "[a]ll too often the invasion of privacy itself will go unknown. Only by striking at all aspects of the problem can privacy be adequately protected."[37] Especially since there is such plausibility to Congress's assumption that illegal acts will be deterred if wrongdoers are prevented from enjoying the fruits of their wrongdoing, the Court should not have substituted its own judgment.

---

[36] 458 US 747, 760 (1982). See also *Osborne v Ohio*, 495 US 103, 109–10 (1990) (it is "surely reasonable for the State to conclude that it will decrease the production of child pornography if it penalizes those who possess and view the product, thereby decreasing demand"). To be sure, the speech involved in *Ferber* and *Osborne*, although not legally obscene, is widely understood to have very limited value. It might be argued that suppressing speech that is related to public issues in order to deter the illegal conduct of others is a different matter (just as some object to an exclusionary rule that suppresses valuable probative evidence as a means to deter unlawful police searches). There is indeed a difference, which is one reason I would rest more on the government's second "interest" in limiting the media disclosures—protecting privacy by limiting the harm that the illegal conduct produces. See text accompanying notes 38–40. But *Ferber* and *Osborne* demonstrate that whether the fruit of illegal activity is property or speech, the Supreme Court has concluded that closing off outlets deters the illegal conduct.

[37] S Rep No 1097, 90th Cong, 2d Sess 69 (1968) (quoted in 121 S Ct at 1773 (Rehnquist, joined by Scalia and Thomas, dissenting)).

In any event, quite apart from deterring illegal interception, punishing the disclosure of illegally intercepted communications promotes a second and even clearer interest: protecting privacy by limiting the harm that the illegal conduct produces. Preventing media disclosure is more than a means to deter someone else's illegality (the government's first interest); it also directly protects privacy. As the Court has recognized in other contexts, disclosing illegally intercepted communications "compounds the statutorily proscribed invasion of . . . privacy."[38] Such disclosures also deepen the chill on private communication. It is as much an invasion of privacy to disclose an illegally intercepted communication as to make the illegal interception in the first place. Indeed, the intrusion on conversational privacy from the disclosure is often the more serious intrusion, for it allows a far wider audience to "overhear" the private communication. If a legislature has a weighty interest in protecting privacy from unwarranted interceptions of private communications, surely it has the same interest in protecting that privacy from disclosures that many times over "compound[ ] the statutorily proscribed invasion."[39]

Nor is it at all remarkable, as Justice Stevens suggests, to limit publication where publication is what produces the harm. If someone breaks into my home and steals my diary or personal letters, of course that person can be sanctioned for publishing the diary's or letter's contents. This is usually a rule of government-created intellectual property law, and nothing in the First Amendment prohibits it.[40] Similarly, nothing in the First Amendment should

---

[38] *Gelbard v United States*, 408 US 41, 52 (1972).

[39] There appears to be an inconsistency in how Justice Stevens characterizes the weight of the interest in protecting privacy. At the outset of his opinion, Justice Stevens states that "the interest in individual privacy" is an interest "of the highest order." 121 S Ct at 1756. But once he announces that the governing legal standard is the *Daily Mail* standard requiring the government to show a "need of the highest order" to justify regulating the media, he stops characterizing the government's interest in protecting privacy as having that rank. Instead, at the point where he assesses the government's argument that punishing media disclosures prevents compounding the harm from the illegal interception (the government's strongest argument), Justice Stevens starts calling the protection of privacy of communication only "an important interest," id at 1764, obviously something less than "an interest . . . of the highest order." He nowhere reconciles the inconsistency.

[40] Copyright law, as well as the common law, have long protected private letters from unauthorized publication. See *Salinger v Random House, Inc.*, 811 F2d 90, 94 (2d Cir 1987); *Birnbaum v United States*, 436 F Supp 967, 978–82 (EDNY 1977); David Nimmer, *Nimmer on Copyright* § 5.04 at 5–57 (1999). Far from being barred by First Amendment principles of free expression, copyright law is understood as itself "an engine of free expression." *Harper & Row, Publishers, Inc. v Nation Enterprises*, 471 US 539, 558 (1985). Moreover,

prohibit the government from creating an analogous rule of privacy law in Title III.

It is significant that Title III limits its sanctions for disclosures to those "knowing or having reason to know that the information was obtained through [an illegal] interception." First Amendment law properly reflects a concern about "timidity and self-censorship" by the press in the performance of its valued roles.[41] But legitimate press activities will not be chilled by a rule that prohibits disclosures of material that reporters know was illegally obtained. And to the extent that the press becomes "timid and self-censoring" about publishing illegally intercepted material that invades people's privacy, that is a good thing.

Title III's prohibition on disclosures by those "having reason to know" that the information was illegally obtained is potentially more troublesome. This standard might leave reporters uncertain whether, after the fact, a trier of fact will conclude that they "had reason to know" even though they did not in fact know. This could chill the reporting of legally secured information out of fear that its origins will be misjudged. On the other hand, a "reason to know" standard, unlike a "should have known" standard, "imposes no duty of inquiry; it merely requires that a person draw reasonable inferences from information already known to him."[42] Significantly, in his briefs in the Supreme Court, the Solicitor General took pains to dispel any chill by strictly construing the "reason to know" provision.[43] Nevertheless, had the Court pointed to distinc-

---

copyright protection may not be ignored simply because the work "contains material of possible public importance" or there is "social value in dissemination," id at 558, 559 (internal citations omitted). The fact that an author's words "may of themselves be 'newsworthy' is not an independent justification for unauthorized copying of the author's expression. . . ." Id at 557.

[41] *Florida Star*, 491 US at 535; see *Bartnicki*, 121 S Ct at 1765 n 22; *New York Times Co. v Sullivan*, 376 US 254, 271–72 (1964).

[42] *Novivki v Cook*, 946 F2d 938, 941 (DC Cir 1991).

[43] "Title III's prohibition applies only to those who either have actual knowledge of the nature of the interception or actual knowledge of facts that make those origins 'so highly probable that' one should assume such to be true. Restatement (Second) of Torts, § 12, cmt. a (1965). Indeed, the facts surrounding the interception must be apparent, because Title III imposes no duty of inquiry. Ibid.; U.S. Br. 45–46. Consequently, Title III does not deter (and for the past three decades has not deterred) the press from reporting the news. Far from requiring reporters to research sources for fear of illegality, it merely requires them to refrain from use if they know or all but know that the source was an unlawful interception." Reply Brief for the United States at 20, *Bartnicki v Vopper*, 121 S Ct 1753 (2001) (Nos 99-1687, 99-1728) (available at 1999 US Briefs LEXIS 1687).

tive First Amendment concerns with the "reason to know" standard, it would have highlighted a legitimate concern about chilling reporting that relies only on *legally secured* information; it would have rooted the decision in the right to report legally secured information, rather than extending the mantle of First Amendment protection over reporting information that the press knows to have been illegally secured. And of course it would not have invalidated the application of Title III in cases where the press actual knows that the information was illegally intercepted.

In the end, for Justice Stevens nothing turns on the fact that the information here was stolen. *New York Times Co. v Sullivan* put the mantle of First Amendment protection around the publication of factually false information, but not the publication of information the media knows to be false.[44] Neither should *Bartnicki* have protected the publication of information known to be illegally secured.

A case that hangs over *Bartnicki*, and may help to explain why Justice Stevens gives so little weight to the fact that the published information was illegally obtained, is *New York Times Co. v United States*,[45] the *Pentagon Papers* case. Justice Stevens invokes it at the very outset of his discussion of why it is irrelevant that the conversation was illegally intercepted.[46] Decided in 1971 when public debate about the ongoing Vietnam War was intense, the *Pentagon Papers* case was a suit by the U.S. government against *The New York Times* and *The Washington Post* to enjoin their publication of materials from a classified Defense Department study of the war. It was apparently undisputed that the newspapers were publishing classified material that they knew had been stolen and given to them by Daniel Ellsberg.[47] The *Pentagon Papers* case is a free press icon. How could the Court now rule that the press had no right to disclose illegally secured information?

But *Pentagon Papers* is easily distinguishable from *Bartnicki*. First, *Pentagon Papers* was a prior restraint case. The only issue before the Court was whether the publication of the papers could be en-

---

[44] 376 US 254, 279–80 (1964).

[45] 403 US 713 (1971).

[46] 121 S Ct at 1761.

[47] Although this fact was not discussed in the majority opinions, Justice Harlan emphasized it in his dissent. See 403 US at 754.

Amendment," it is uncertain whether media disclosures infringing on privacy can ever be limited consistent with the First Amendment. In other words, the Court's opinion does not mark out any area in which privacy trumps media prerogatives.[59]

II

At the outset, though, I said that *Bartnicki* takes steps forward in privacy protection, and that is because Justice Stevens's opinion is "for the Court" only in name. Justice Breyer, joined by Justice O'Connor, wrote a concurring opinion. Although Justices Breyer and O'Connor also joined Justice Stevens's opinion to make up a six-member majority, in fact their separate opinion is much less speech protective, and much more privacy protective, than the Stevens opinion. Because Chief Justice Rehnquist, Justice Scalia, and Justice Thomas dissented in an opinion that would have upheld the limitations on the media here and is broadly protective of privacy, the Breyer opinion is determinative. The controlling law is Breyer's law.

Justice Breyer's opinion sets forth an analysis that is different from Justice Stevens's on almost all of the key matters except for the result, that points to a quite narrow constitutional immunity for the media in privacy cases, and that further develops his evolving and innovative general approach to the First Amendment. As Breyer analyzes the press versus privacy issue in *Bartnicki*, there are constitutional interests "on both sides of the equation."[60] On

---

[59] These statements by Justice Stevens are inexplicable for other reasons. In a variety of other circumstances, the Court has upheld sanctions on the press for publishing truthful information. See, e.g., *Cohen v Cowles Broadcasting Co.*, 501 US 663 (1991) (First Amendment does not bar a promissory estoppel action against a newspaper for publishing truthful information about the source of a political news story in breach of its promise to keep the source's identity confidential); *Harper & Row, Publishers, Inc., v Nation Enterprises*, 471 US 539 (1985) (First Amendment does not bar an action against a magazine for publishing truthful copyrighted material); *Zacchini v Scripps-Howard Broadcasting Co.*, 433 US 562 (1977) (First Amendment does not "immunize the media [from damage liability] when they broadcast a performer's entire act without his consent"); *Seattle Times Co. v Rhinehart*, 467 US 20 (1984) (First Amendment does not bar an action against a newspaper for publishing truthful information learned during discovery in a civil suit that was covered by a protective order).

[60] 121 S Ct at 1766 (quoting his earlier separate opinions in *Turner Broadcasting System, Inc. v Federal Communications Commission*, 520 US 180, 227 (1997) (Breyer concurring in part), and *Nixon v Shrink Missouri Government PAC*, 528 US 377, 402 (2000) (Breyer concurring)).

one side is the media's constitutionally rooted interest in publish- •
ing what it wishes. On the other side is a privacy interest "that
includes not only 'the right to be let alone' . . . but also 'the interest
. . . in fostering private speech.' "[61] "The assurance of privacy,"
Breyer emphasizes, "helps to overcome our natural reluctance to
discuss private matters when we fear that our private conversations
may become public. And the statutory restrictions [in this case]
consequently encourage conversations that otherwise might not
take place."[62]

This interest in fostering private speech, Breyer says, is itself a
"constitutional interest" related to the system of free expression
guaranteed by the First Amendment. Breyer cites his own previous
separate opinions in which he characterizes the First Amendment's
purposes in affirmative terms, such as "encouraging . . . open discussion," rather than simply as a prohibition on state action restricting speech.[63] Thus, Breyer says, there are "competing constitutional interests"[64] in *Bartnicki*, and competing constitutional
interests related to free expression itself. Justice Stevens, by contrast, avoids saying that the interest on the privacy side is itself of
"constitutional" dimension. Rather, he says only that "there are
important interests to be considered on both sides of the constitutional calculus."[65] Justice Breyer himself hedges in one significant
respect: Although he recognizes that the privacy interest includes
both the "the right to be let alone" and "the interest . . . in fostering private speech," he labels only the speech-related aspect of privacy a constitutional interest and focuses his analysis on this
speech-related aspect—leaving unclear how he would evaluate a
case where only the nonspeech aspects of privacy were on the
"other side of the equation."[66]

---

[61] Id (citations omitted).

[62] Id.

[63] *Nixon v Shrink Missouri Government PAC*, 528 US at 402; *Turner Broadcasting System,
Inc. v Federal Communications Commission*, 520 US at 227. The relationship between Breyer's
general conception of the First Amendment and the traditional conception is discussed
further in Part IV.

[64] 121 S Ct at 1766.

[65] Id at 1764.

[66] There are suggestions in his opinion that Justice Breyer is in fact giving weight to
those nonspeech aspects of privacy. "As a general matter," Justice Breyer says, "the Federal
Constitution must tolerate laws of this kind because of the importance of these *privacy and
speech-related objectives.*" And the basic standard that Justice Breyer uses in deciding this case
is to ask whether the "restrictions on speech . . . are disproportionate when measured

Because Justice Breyer sees "competing constitutional interests" on both sides, he concludes that the Court should not apply "strict scrutiny." Rather, he would use a much more flexible and multifactored approach that gives greater leeway for protecting privacy:

> I would ask whether the statutes strike a reasonable balance between their speech-restricting and speech-enhancing consequences. Or do they instead impose restrictions on speech that are disproportionate when measured against their corresponding privacy and speech-related benefits, taking into account the kind, the importance, and the extent of these benefits, as well as the need for the restrictions in order to secure those benefits?[67]

Breyer then explains why the statute here "enhances private speech,"[68] prevents "serious harm" to privacy,[69] and "resemble[s] laws that would award damages caused through publication of information obtained by theft from a private bedroom."[70] In light of this, Breyer concludes, "As a general matter, despite the statutes' direct restrictions on speech, the Federal Constitution must tolerate laws of this kind because of the importance of these privacy and speech related objectives."[71] The phrasing of this conclusion is in direct, and presumably intended, contrast to Justice Stevens's statement that "As a general matter, 'state action to punish the publication of truthful information seldom can satisfy constitutional standards.'"[72]

In the end, however, Justices Breyer and O'Connor decide for the media, but only on the narrowest of grounds, and only with a clear endorsement of the power of legislators to take significant

---

against the corresponding *privacy and speech-related benefits.*" Id at 1766, 1767 (emphasis added). Thus, "privacy" benefits that are not "speech-related" appear to have some independent weight in the constitutional balance. Presumably, Justice Breyer is leaving open the possibility that he would uphold government action to protect privacy from media infringement where only the nonspeech aspects of privacy are involved, even though they are not themselves a "constitutional interest," just as in other cases he has concluded that nonspeech (and nonconstitutional) interests can sometimes justify a restriction on speech. See text accompanying notes 176–78.

[67] 121 S Ct at 1766.

[68] Id at 1766–67.

[69] "Media dissemination of an intimate conversation to an entire community will often cause the speakers serious harm over and above the harm caused by an initial disclosure to the person who intercepted the phone call." Id at 1766.

[70] Id at 1767.

[71] Id.

[72] Id at 1761 (citation omitted).

steps to protect privacy from media incursions. For Justice Breyer, there are two reasons why the media win this case. First, as Justice Stevens also had emphasized, the broadcaster was not involved in the illegal interception. Breyer suggests a further narrowing of the Stevens approach, however, by implying that Congress might have been able to reach the media in *Bartnicki* if it had made "receipt" of the illegally intercepted tape unlawful.[73]

Second, Justice Breyer says, "the information publicized involved a matter of *unusual* public concern, *namely a threat of potential physical harm to others.*"[74] This formulation is much narrower than the one used by Justice Stevens. Far from relying on a general "public concern" rationale to outweigh the privacy interests here, as Stevens does, Breyer emphasizes that the public concern in this case was an "unusual" and "special" one involving "threats to public safety," since one of the overheard speakers suggested "blow[ing] off . . . front porches" and "doing some work on some of these guys."[75] One might question whether these remarks should be interpreted as a true and continuing threat.[76] But the

---

[73] The meaning of the relevant passage on "receipt" is somewhat uncertain. In the context of explaining that the media "engaged in no unlawful activity other than the ultimate publication," id at 1767, Breyer says: "[A]s the Court points out, the statutes do not forbid the receipt of the tape itself. *Ante*, at 9. The Court adds that its holding 'does not apply to punishing parties for obtaining the relevant information *unlawfully*.' *Ante*, at 17 n.19 (emphasis added)." Id. The implication seems to be, although this is not certain, that punishing the receipt in these circumstances might be constitutional even if punishing "the ultimate publication" is not. Justice Breyer quite clearly seems to consider "obtaining" to include "receipt." However, the full text of Justice Stevens's footnote 19 suggests that he is probably using "obtaining" to mean no more than directly stealing or intercepting the information. Footnote 19 seems simply to make explicit that "of course" it would be "frivolous" to assert that the First Amendment protects such direct intrusions even by the press.

In any event, it is hard to see why this case should be decided differently if Congress had made the "receipt" of illegally intercepted information itself unlawful. Congress has made unlawful both the "interception" of certain electronic communications and the "disclosure" of that intercepted information. Why should the constitutionality of these provisions depend on whether an interim step between the unlawful interception and the unlawful disclosure is also explicitly made unlawful?

[74] Id at 1766 (emphasis added).

[75] Id at 1766, 1767, 1768.

[76] Perhaps anticipating such a question, particularly when that characterization is key to resolving a motion for summary judgment, Justice Breyer adds: "Nor should editors, who must make a publication decision quickly, have to determine present or continued danger before publishing this kind of threat." Id at 1768.

It is also reasonable to ask whether it would be more appropriate to report the threat, if there was believed to be one, to law enforcement authorities. It is not settled, however, that Title III would permit this "disclosure" any more than it permits media publication. Several lower court cases have construed Title III to prohibit certain disclosures of illegally intercepted material to law enforcement entities. *In re Grand Jury*, 111 F3d 1066, 1077–

allowing noncompliance with ambivalently supported laws; reducing unfair, out-of-context judgments of people; letting people bury their past; protecting human dignity; sustaining individualism; and developing a liberal and pluralistic society, to mention just some that have been discussed in the literature.[93] Privacy also promotes a system of free expression, for people are more likely to express themselves fully, openly, and robustly when they have confidence that what they say will be heard only by a known group of listeners. Fear of being overheard, fear of public exposure, fear of one's words becoming the subject of gossip, fear of intimacies being publicly scrutinized, fear of being sanctioned or disapproved of because of what one says—all of these have a profound inhibiting effect on expression, and make it crucially important for the law to protect a realm of privacy for communications. Far from threatening speech, protecting private communication is itself a central part of constructing a vibrant system of free expression.

Given the special status of free speech in the American constitutional firmament, it is easiest to argue for readjustments in the speech/privacy balance by emphasizing the ways in which protecting privacy itself promotes free expression. By doing so, one identifies speech interests "on both sides of the equation," and restricting speech to protect privacy can be justified as a speech-enhancing rather than a speech-restricting approach.[94] But not all concerns about privacy are related to expressive freedom. The other values that privacy serves may themselves at times be strong enough to justify some restriction on what the media may publish.

We need to see privacy in the same systemic way that we have come to see speech. Suppressing speech, we recognize, is not only a loss to the individual in question. It also deprives public debate and deliberation of the benefits of wide-open and robust discussion; it harms democratic self-government. Similarly, lost privacy is not only a diminishment to the individual directly concerned. It also reduces a sphere of life that is crucial for a particular kind

---

[93] See, e.g., Warren and Brandeis, 4 Harv L Rev 193 (cited in note 1); Ruth Gavison, *Privacy and the Limits of Law*, 89 Yale L J 421 (1980); Jeffrey Rosen, *The Unwanted Gaze: The Destruction of Privacy in America* (2000); Post, *The Social Foundations of Privacy* (cited in note 52); Charles Fried, *An Anatomy of Values* (1970); Amitai Etzioni, *The Limits of Privacy* (1999); Richard C. Turkington and Anita L. Allen, *Privacy Law: Cases and Materials* (1999); Spiros Simitis, *Reviewing Privacy in an Information Society*, 135 U Pa L Rev 707 (1987).

[94] 121 S Ct at 1766 (Breyer concurring).

of human functioning that sustains a pluralistic society. Moreover, when the media puts private matters into the public sphere, it has systemic consequences for the public sphere itself.

Those who do not participate in the public square at all can make the strongest claims to privacy protection. People only tangentially or episodically in the public eye—or those who have been forced into the public square because they are victims of crime or some other misfortune—also have strong claims. Cases involving public figures are the hardest privacy cases, since public figures seem to want it both ways, to embrace the public and yet evade it, and because the accountability of public officials and political candidates is a central element of democratic self-governance. But protecting some aspect of privacy for public figures is crucial for their own human functioning. Moreover, as discussed more fully below, protecting their privacy can further the values of democratic self-governance.[95]

But while privacy serves public values, at bottom privacy is antipublic. This is part of what makes it such a challenging concept for contemporary constitutional and political theory, and why many are reluctant to say that privacy should outweigh the public functions of a free press. Owen Fiss has written about a number of recent circumstances in which traditional supporters of free speech have supported restrictions on speech.[96] He discusses, for example, feminist support for restricting pornography in spite of liberalism's traditional support for freedom of sexual expression, support for hate speech laws among many in the civil rights movement in spite of their traditional opposition to censorship, and support of some civil liberties groups for campaign finance restrictions and regulations of the media to assure wider access and enhance the diversity of views available to the public. Some of these examples pit different conceptions of free speech against each other. Others, such as hate speech and pornography, can be seen as a conflict between free speech and equality, although Fiss sees them as a conflict within the First Amendment itself. But in each case, the argument in favor of restricting speech rests at bottom on a conception of the "public"—a revised sense of public debate, or

---

[95] See text accompanying notes 120, 135–36.

[96] Owen M. Fiss, *Liberalism Divided: Freedom of Speech and the Many Uses of State Power* (1996). See also Owen M. Fiss, *The Irony of Free Speech* (1996).

collective self-determination, or social roles, or social status. As Fiss puts it, these arguments in favor of restricting speech rest on an understanding of freedom "in more social terms."[97]

But the arguments in favor of restricting speech to protect privacy are largely anti-"social"—or at least they seek to preserve a realm of the social and personal that often refuses to contribute to a wider "public." "Private speech" might be related to public issues or might be preparation for an ultimately more "public" formulation, but its value does not depend only on that, and that is not the primary reason we protect it from disclosure. We protect its privateness. We protect the right to choose a narrow audience, or no audience except oneself—to be what William Carlos Williams called "lonely, lonely," and as such to be "the happy genius of my household."[98] So too for the elements of privacy having nothing to do with speech—we protect them from disclosure largely because we know that humans are constituted in part by refusing to be public. One can and should identify public purposes served by protecting the private, as I have done above, but privacy's effort to subvert the public's knowledge and control is at the core of what it is—and, I believe, the core of its unique value.

2) In assessing the importance of enhancing privacy protection, we also need to take account of technological developments that create greater society-wide threats to privacy. It is appropriate and common for legal rules to adapt to the development of new technologies.[99] This is because legal rules are typically premised on often unarticulated background assumptions about what the world is like. When reality changes, and the background assumptions no longer hold true, existing law may not achieve its original purposes. If we adhere to existing rules in the face of new technologies, the existing balance between liberty and order may be transformed. Concerning privacy, for example, the law may not protect certain private activities or zones because there are few perceived threats to those activities or zones. The law allows access, but since access in practice is rare, the law does not occasion significant inva-

---

[97] Fiss, *Liberalism Divided* at 5.

[98] William Carlos Williams, *Danse Russe*, in A. Walton Litz and Christopher MacGowan, eds, *The Collected Poems of William Carlos Williams 1909–1939* at 86–87 (1986).

[99] See Paul Gewirtz, *Constitutional Law and New Technology*, 64 Social Research 1191 (1997).

sions of privacy. Our technological crudity protects us from wider invasions of privacy. But if new technologies create new capabilities that facilitate access and therefore open up new threats to privacy, we may have to change the rules if we wish to preserve the old rules' purposes.

Another privacy case decided last term, *Kyllo v United States*,[100] nicely illustrates one way that legal rules adapt to new technologies—specifically, adapt to what the Court described as the "power of technology to shrink the realm of guaranteed privacy."[101] *Kyllo* involved the police use of a "thermal-imaging" device in the course of a drug investigation. When aimed at a building from outside, such a device can pick up relative amounts of heat emanating from the building. In *Kyllo*, a thermal-imaging device was aimed at a private home from the street and was able to pick up hot zones suggesting that halide lights were being used inside to grow marijuana. The constitutional question was whether use of the device was a "search" within the meaning of the Fourth Amendment.

The Court acknowledged that visual observation traditionally has not been deemed a "search," but also underscored that individuals traditionally have had a reasonable expectation of privacy in "the interior of their homes." With "old" technologies, the two concepts are not in conflict. But with the "technological enhancement of ordinary perception" permitted by the "advance of technology," a conflict can emerge. The Court in *Kyllo* concluded that the use of thermal imaging on a house constitutes a "search," even though observation from the same spot without "technological enhancement" would not have been a "search."

> To withdraw protection of this minimum expectation [of privacy] would be to permit police technology to erode the privacy guaranteed by the Fourth Amendment. We think that obtaining by sense-enhancing technology any information regarding the interior of the home that could not otherwise have been obtained without physical "intrusion into a constitutionally protected area" constitutes a search—at least where (as here) the technology in question is not in general public use. This assures preservation of that degree of privacy against gov-

---

[100] 121 S Ct 2038 (2001).
[101] Id at 2043.

ernment that existed when the Fourth Amendment was adopted.[102]

Technological changes creating new threats to privacy should also affect legal rules in a broader way, encouraging reexamination of the rules governing the speech/privacy balance. As new technologies make outsiders' access to private matters easier (allowing ready interceptions of phone calls or eavesdropping on bedroom conversations or hacking into electronically stored information, for example), and as new technologies facilitate the creation of permanent electronic records and footprints and simplify the ability to gather personal information from dispersed sources, laws protecting privacy become more important. At the same time, the media has a greater potential to produce more extensive harms by broadly disseminating private material, and new media technologies such as the internet and e-mailing make possible new threats to privacy.[103] A continuing reluctance to limit the media in the face of new technologies, in short, may result in a major diminishment of privacy.[104] It may well be that in the years ahead further techno-

---

[102] Id (citation omitted). The Court in *Kyllo* relies on an earlier case in which technological change fostered a change in Fourth Amendment doctrine, *Katz v United States*, 389 US 347 (1967). In *Katz*, the Court discarded a constitutional rule that the Fourth Amendment was triggered only by a physical trespass, in significant part because new electronic technologies were allowing widespread intrusions on areas where there was a reasonable expectation of privacy even without any physical intrusion.

[103] See A. Michael Froomkin, *The Death of Privacy?* 52 Stan L Rev 1461 (2000); Rosen, *The Unwanted Gaze* at 57–58, 159–95 (cited in note 93); Lawrence Lessig, *Code and Other Laws of Cyberspace* 142–64 (1999); Turkington and Allen, *Privacy Law* at 311–25 (cited in note 93).

[104] Cf. Geoffrey R. Stone, *The Scope of the Fourth Amendment: Privacy and the Police Use of Spies, Secret Agents, and Informers*, 1966 Am Bar Found Res J 1193, 1216 (suggesting a "principle of conservation of privacy," which seeks "to maintain a cumulative level of privacy comparable to that existing at the time the fourth amendment was drafted"). This point is a general one, and has often been lost in discussions about the tension between liberty and security after the events of September 11, 2001. Many of our civil liberties doctrines and rules rest on background assumptions about the risks to security that will follow from civil liberties of a certain scope. For example, when we say it is better that ten guilty people go free than that one innocent person be convicted, we are implicitly assuming that the risk to society of setting ten guilty people free is a tolerable risk. But if technologies and access to technologies develop so that the ten guilty people have access to footlocker-sized nuclear weapons and the will to detonate them, then we may want to adjust our epigram (and at least some of our rules in some circumstances). Not to do so is to end up with a real-world balance between liberty and security that is very different from the one we started with. The point is just as applicable in the other direction. If we do not adjust existing rules when new investigative technologies give law enforcement officials much greater capacity to reduce liberty, then we will end up with a much different liberty/security balance than we thought we had. Liberty-oriented rules of wider scope will be necessary just to keep pace.

logical developments will themselves create better ways of advancing communication while also protecting privacy—for example, by strengthening encryption methods—but for now privacy protections will be significantly shaped by where the law draws the line between permissible and impermissible invasions.

3) Giving more weight to privacy in constitutional disputes is also warranted because of the contemporary social and cultural context within which these issues arise. Just as legal rules are typically premised on background assumptions about technologies, so too are such rules usually premised on assumptions about social conditions, behaviors, and attitudes. As these change, legal rules may require reexamination. Often in partnership with new technologies, social and cultural factors have made privacy more vulnerable than before—and, I would argue, more vulnerable than the press today—suggesting that legal efforts to strengthen privacy deserve added weight when balanced against press prerogatives. The events of September 11, 2001, and ongoing fears of terrorism will continue to augment the government's already great powers to collect information and monitor behavior. Employers have become expansive data gatherers and monitors. Legally, as well as culturally, there is a wider sense of a "right to know." The greater role of litigation in our society over past decades has created a new and extremely powerful engine to compel the disclosure of hitherto private information. A wider "politics of scandal" and "criminalization of politics" has unleashed powerful investigative machinery and increased mainstream attention to the private misdeeds of public figures and to the lives of private figures caught up in the investigative onslaught. I have elsewhere referred to an "Oprahfication" of American culture.[105] By this I mean that Americans have become ready and unashamed voyeurs, stimulated and allowed to peer into and judge the private lives of others, even as we typically try to hold on to our own privacy and support laws to protect it. Cultural boundaries between the public and private have become blurred, with private intimacies more casually the subject of public discourse, and new expectations created about what we may know about others.

The press itself has been changed by the more mainstreamed

---

[105] Paul Gewirtz, *Victims and Voyeurs: Two Narrative Problems at the Criminal Trial*, in *Law's Stories* at 135, 152 (cited in note 54).

prurience of the American people, and in turn has become a greater cultural force in diminishing privacy.[106] It has often been noted that "entertainment values" drive news coverage these days,[107] and a large part of what this means is that news coverage has increasingly broken down distinctions between what is public and what is private. The mainstream media devote more attention to personalities, gossip, and reporting on private lives of both the famous and the ordinary. Although we may seek to hold on to our own privacy and support laws to protect it, these broader cultural forces, along with new technologies, present new and serious threats to privacy.

On the other hand, the press today is not seriously endangered by government restrictions, and individual speakers are not seriously threatened by government-imposed conformity of viewpoint. Debate about public issues and public figures is extremely vigorous. The boundaries of the permissible have been extended very far out. In earlier times, this was not the case: the press and other speakers were subject to government legal action that directly sought to restrict criticism of the government and sought to limit a broad range of ideas from being expressed and heard. Understandably, free speech law sought to push back on these restrictions. But the press today has great leeway and boldness. It is true that the terrorist attacks of September 11, 2001, and the resulting war in Afghanistan have led the current administration to criticize the media—for example (and disturbingly), the Attorney General has criticized the media and others for giving "aid" to terrorists by their "fearmongering" objections to administration policies on civil liberties grounds.[108] But the government has taken no legal steps to restrict media criticism, and the media remains bold (although this popular war is also generally popular in the media). The system of free expression still needs to be strengthened—es-

---

[106] The point here is one of degree. Concerns about the press invading privacy and pushing boundaries in that direction are hardly new, of course. In a different social context where there were different cultural boundaries, Warren and Brandeis's famous article on privacy expressed analogous sorts of concerns about press behavior.

[107] See, e.g., James Fallows, *Breaking the News* (1996); Neil Postman, *Amusing Ourselves to Death* (1985).

[108] *DOJ Oversight: Preserving Our Freedoms While Defending Against Terrorism*, hearing before Senate Judiciary Committee, 107th Cong 1 (2001) (testimony of Attorney General John Ashcroft, Dec 6, 2001), available at <http://www.usdoj.gov/ag/testimony/2001/1206transcriptsenatejudiciarycommittee.htm>.

pecially by counteracting the dominance of media giants and further diversifying the voices that can be heard (without thereby di-
luting the power of strong press entities to be a true check on
government[109])—but not by strengthening the press in its freedom to interfere with privacy. It is the latter value that is now
often seriously threatened, and at times threatened by the press.
In deciding how to strike the press/privacy balance, it is essential
to take account of where the greater vulnerabilities and dangers
are.

These various factors help to justify strengthening privacy protections. But freedom of the press from government abridgment
is explicitly protected by the Constitution, and freedom from nongovernmental interference with privacy is not.[110] There are only
two conceptual ways for privacy concerns to prevail in the face of
the press' claim of First Amendment protection: (1) to conclude
that the First Amendment right does not apply, or does not apply
at full strength, when the press infringes on certain private matters;
or (2) to conclude that privacy is a strong enough competing interest in particular circumstances to outweigh the First Amendment
interest. Each conception is plausible, and indeed they are related.

The freedom of the press protected by the First Amendment
must be seen as primarily about the press' contribution to democratic self-governance, to public debate, and to checking the power
of the state.[111] This core freedom is a broad one, and it includes

---

[109] Vincent Blasi, *The Checking Value in First Amendment Theory*, 1977 Am Bar Found Res
J 521 (1977).

[110] A right to privacy as the freedom to keep the government from having unwanted
access to personal information is protected through the Fourth Amendment and also as an
aspect of substantive due process under the Fifth and Fourteenth Amendments. *Whalen v
Roe*, 429 US 589 (1977). The Fourth Amendment is phrased as a "right of the people to
be secure . . . against unreasonable searches and seizure," and, as literally phrased, does
not have a state action requirement. But the Fourth Amendment has not been interpreted
as providing protections against nongovernmental interference, and I do not rest my argument on a claim that media interference with "privacy" violates a constitutional right of
privacy.

[111] The idea that the First Amendment as a whole has this core meaning has its contempo-
rary roots in the writings of Alexander Meiklejohn, e.g., *Free Speech and Its Relation to Self-
Government* (1948), and has been developed in recent years by Owen Fiss, e.g., *Liberalism
Divided* (cited in note 96); *The Irony of Free Speech* (cited in note 96), and Cass Sunstein,
Democracy and the Problem of Free Speech (1993). These writers do not distinguish between
freedom of speech and freedom of the press. However, this understanding of the First
Amendment seems to have distinctive force in understanding freedom of the press in partic-
ular, both because the institutional nature of media entities makes less relevant another
standard rationale for free speech—promoting self-fulfillment—and, more importantly (as

not only explicitly "political" speech but also a broad range of "cultural" expression, since cultural expression contributes to our public life[112] and since experience teaches us that cultural censorship so often has a political motivation.[113] This understanding of freedom of the press as primarily about the public sphere reflects both an affirmative concept about the press' role and also, I would argue, a recognition that a wider concept of press freedom would conflict with other values that a society properly cherishes, such as privacy. Thus concern about privacy is built into a proper conception of press freedom itself. Freedom of the press is not fundamentally about the freedom to disclose private matters or to invade the private sphere.[114] The freedom to publish the truth strikes many as the core of what freedom of the press is about; but truthful information about oneself is also at the core of what privacy protects. A plausible way to harmonize these ideas is to understand the press' freedom as focused primarily on the public sphere.

The alternative way to bring privacy protection into the constitutional analysis is to see privacy as a value that competes with the value of a free press. This is a plausible way of proceeding as long as we accept that interests not explicitly protected by the Constitution (here, the interest in protecting privacy from nongovernmental interference) can in certain circumstances outweigh interests that are.[115] In fact, almost all doctrinal "tests" in constitutional law

---

I note below), because a wider concept of freedom of the press would distinctively threaten privacy values.

[112] This was Alexander Meiklejohn's rationale, *The First Amendment Is an Absolute*, 1961 Supreme Court Review 245, 255–57. For a criticism of Meiklejohn's inclusion of culture, see Robert Bork, *Neutral Principles and Some First Amendment Problems*, 47 Ind L J 1, 26–28 (1971).

[113] See Sunstein, *Democracy and the Problem of Free Speech* at 135–36, 164–65 (cited in note 111). For a criticism of Sunstein's view—indeed, a broader criticism of approaches that see the First Amendment's primary purpose as promoting deliberation about public issues—see J. M. Balkin, *Populism and Progressivism as Constitutional Categories*, 104 Yale L J 1935 (1995).

[114] What differentiates freedom of the press from freedom of speech is that the former typically involves an institution of production and distribution. Since wide distribution of information is usually the main threat to privacy protection, arguably "freedom of the press" poses a greater danger to privacy than "freedom of speech" *simpliciter*—and therefore particular care should be taken in defining what comes within the constitutional concept of freedom of the press or particular receptivity shown when privacy values are balanced against it.

[115] There are countries in which both free press and privacy are explicitly protected by the Constitution—indeed, privacy is protected from both governmental and nongovernmental infringement. See text accompanying notes 140–55. In such countries it may not matter greatly which analytic route is followed and, in particular, whether a core conception of

reflect this, with, for example, "substantial" or "compelling" (but nonconstitutional) interests justifying restrictions on constitutional ones in certain circumstances. At bottom, under either approach, the task must be to reconcile protection for both a free press and for privacy, to reconcile protecting the need of the public to know with the competing need of individuals to keep things private. These are each things that we rightly cherish, and that the Constitution must be read as recognizing that we rightly cherish. Of course, "the right to be let alone [can] develop into an impediment to the transparency necessary for a democratic decisionmaking process."[116] But we must impose some limits on the transparency of the private, even where transparency might marginally enhance public deliberation, if we want to preserve a private sphere of meaningful scope.

In light of this, the concept of "public concern" is insufficient to mediate the press-privacy conflict. Superficially, this concept might appear to preserve the public/private distinction, but it does not. In fact, the notion that content of "public concern" justifies media attention protected by the First Amendment is an engine for destroying privacy. It is always possible to construct an argument that public knowledge about a "private" matter is relevant in some way to public understanding of public issues or public roles. It can always be said that some private fact is an exemplification of a wider public phenomenon and that informing the public about it will enhance public understanding.[117] If identifying "relevance" to

---

free press is defined. Even a very broad conception of free press will have to be reconciled with or "balanced" against the privacy values protected elsewhere in the constitution itself. But in our Constitution, the stakes in understanding the rationale for protecting a free press may be higher, for in our press-privacy cases freedom of the press is the only explicit constitutional right in the picture.

[116] Simitis, 135 U Pa L Rev at 731 (cited in note 93).

[117] There are endless varieties of these kinds of weak and privacy-destroying nexus arguments. To give just one example from a well-known case, Judge Richard Posner upheld on First Amendment grounds the reporting about private facts about an ordinary citizen (as summarized by Posner, "his heavy drinking, his unstable unemployment, his adultery, his irresponsible and neglectful behavior toward his wife and children") using the following argument in part: "Reporting the true facts about real people is necessary to 'obviate any impression that the [general social] problems raised in the [reporting] are remote or hypothetical.'" *Haynes v Alfred A. Knopf, Inc.*, 8 F3d 1222, 1233 (7th Cir 1993). Obviously, if personal and embarrassing private facts (here, from thirty years previously) can be published simply because they establish that some general social problem is not remote or hypothetical, no one with "problems" has any protection from media disclosure. See also text accompanying note 128, discussing the way that the Restatement (Second) of Torts limits the privacy protections for "involuntary public figures."

a "public concern" is sufficient to justify media publication, some relevance can always be found or created, and privacy will be only a matter of media grace and forbearance. To preserve some realm of the private from public disclosure, we need to develop more nuanced criteria, which inevitably will turn on matters of degree: how private, what degree of public significance, how much relevance between private fact and public concern, and so forth. Justice Breyer's concept of "legitimate public concern" in *Bartnicki* is a recognition that a limiting normative judgment is required. The need for limiting criteria is even clearer once we appreciate that in this context the usual nostrum that the remedy for problematic speech is more speech has no applicability. More speech following disclosure of a private matter would only deepen the loss of privacy, not protect it.[118] To permit the media to invoke "public concern" to justify publicizing private information means either that no one will fight back or that the fighting back will further undermine privacy.[119]

I would also argue that limiting invasion of the "private" actually enhances public debate. Information about the private lives of public officials easily distracts us from their official actions. The public has great curiosity about these private matters, and the media has financial incentives to satisfy that curiosity. The public and the press each push along these tendencies in the other, but the fundamental element here is an aspect of human nature, the weakness for voyeurism that we all have, a weakness that drives out (or at least diminishes) public attention to official actions and policies when offered more prurient alternatives. It is no accident—and only slightly hyperbolic to point out—that while the media were endlessly reporting and re-reporting details about Representative Gary Condit's sex life, they barely noted the Rudman-Hart Commission's Report on Terrorism and offered virtually no criticism of our ineffectual antiterrorism policies or our utter unpreparedness for terrorist attacks. Enhanced media prerogatives do not necessarily mean improvement in public discourse or enhance-

---

[118] See Geoffrey R. Stone, Louis M. Seidman, Cass R. Sunstein, and Mark V. Tushnet, *Constitutional Law* 1075 (4th ed 2001).

[119] Litigation of a privacy claim, of course, presents a similar problem. See Harry J. Kalven, Jr., *Privacy in Tort Law—Were Warren and Brandeis Wrong?* 31 L & Contemp Probs 326, 328 (1966). However, establishing a privacy right would presumably deter publication to some extent.

ment of the press' role in society. To the contrary, augmented leeway to publicize private matters almost surely means less coverage of more public matters and a diminishment of political discourse. What may be even worse, it can transform what we consider to be "public and political discourse"—with private matters coming to play a comparatively greater role both in what passes for "public and political discourse" and also in the ultimate public judgments of public figures. At times, enhanced media prerogatives not only can damage the competing value of privacy, but can distort public debate itself. Strengthening privacy protection will help reclaim both the "private" and the "public."[120]

For all these reasons, then, the Court should be more receptive to rules that protect privacy even when the media's desire to publish certain truthful information is restricted. The Supreme Court has allowed the speech/privacy balance to shift too far against privacy interests. And the problem is not only the rules the Court has adopted and the Court's repeated "refusal to answer whether truthful information may ever be punished consistent with the First Amendment."[121] The problem includes the fact that, in virtually every case that the Supreme Court decides involving a press/privacy conflict, the privacy claim loses. The Court sends signals by its patterns, not only by its rules.

What privacy protections will be, of course, is initially in the hands of state and federal lawmakers, and there have long been different views about the appropriate scope of privacy protection "simply" as a matter of statutory or common law.[122] It is clear, however, that for some time statutory and common law tort rules have developed in the shadow of perceived First Amendment re-

---

[120] Cf. Lee Bollinger, *Images of a Free Press* 133–45 (1991) (arguing that members of a democratic society, aware of their own "deficiencies," may use public regulation to improve "the quality of public discussion"); Geoffrey R. Stone, *Imagining a Free Press*, 90 Mich L Rev 1246, 1262–63 (1992) (arguing for "some limit" on what the press reports about political candidates, "designed not only to respect [their] legitimate privacy interests . . . , but also to reflect our right, as a society, to decide that some matters simply should not play a significant role in our political process" because "the information has a greater potential to distract and distort than to inform our better judgment"); Rosen, *The Unwanted Gaze* at 143 (cited in note 93) ("knowing everything about someone's private life inevitably distracts us from making reliable judgments about his or her character and public achievements").

[121] 121 S Ct at 1764, and text accompany notes 57–59.

[122] See, e.g., Marc A. Franklin and Robert L. Rabin, *Tort Law and Alternatives: Cases and Materials* 1098–1215 (2001); Turkington and Allen, *Privacy Law* (cited in note 93).

strictions resulting from Supreme Court decisions. The Restatement (Second) of Torts is explicit that its "model" privacy tort rules take the shape they do because of the drafters' efforts to fit those rules within the constraints of existing First Amendment doctrine.[123] If the Court placed fewer First Amendment restrictions on state and federal flexibility to strengthen privacy protections, not only would statutes like Title III have wider force in protecting privacy, but other federal and state protections of privacy could well expand.

In my judgment, where information has been obtained *unlawfully*, and the law prohibits further disclosures, the First Amendment should not be interpreted to stand in the way of damage actions for media disclosures, except where there is an extraordinary justification for the publication. Justice Breyer may be right that the situation in *Bartnicki* presented the kind of public security threat that counts as an extraordinary justification. If so, however, it is important to be clear that, generally speaking, the publication of unlawfully intercepted conversations, even conversations about matters being publicly debated, is not protected by the First Amendment. Even when they have a public content, they come from a private zone that the state may protect from media intrusion. Although Justice Breyer emphasizes that *Bartnicki* involves an "unusual" public concern, and that he would "not create a 'public interest' exception that swallows up the statutes' privacy protecting general rule," his examples of information that the government may protect from disclosure are all from a polar extreme—"situations where the media publicizes *truly private matters*,"[124] by which he appears to mean "truly private" content (his examples concern sexual relations and divorce). Where information has been secured unlawfully, however, and a private zone has been unlawfully invaded, privacy law should be permitted to limit the media more substantially, restricting it from disclosing conversations from that zone which concern public issues as well as personal matters.

Where information is obtained *lawfully*, but the law seeks to prevent publicity and protect privacy, the First Amendment analysis is rightly more complex. The goal is to strike a balance that pro-

---

[123] Restatement (Second) of Torts, § 652D (1977) ("Special Note on Relation of § 652D to the First Amendment of the Constitution").

[124] 121 S Ct at 1768 (Breyer concurring) (emphasis added).

tects privacy but does not unduly restrict the press. A variety of factors should be relevant, similar to those identified in Justice Breyer's *Bartnicki* opinion.[125] One element of the analysis is the substantiality of the public concerns—put another way, the substantiality of free press concerns in light of the purposes of the First Amendment. This turns in part on the identity of the figure receiving public attention. A fuller range of a public figure's life is properly a subject of public scrutiny, and the media must have a wider "breathing space" in its coverage of such figures in order effectively to contribute to political deliberation and democratic self-governance. The nature of the information involved is also relevant. Information about "truly private matters," even concerning public figures, should generally be protectable. A second element of the analysis is the interrelated question of the extent and degree of the privacy invasion. This turns in part on content, whether intimate private characteristics or behavior is concerned. It also turns on the circumstances involved, whether the information comes from a zone of reasonably expected privacy.[126] Final elements in the constitutional analysis concern what might be called the "need" for the particular restriction involved. Are there reasonable and practical alternatives to restricting publication that would protect privacy? Does the law operate with undue selectivity, suggesting either a censorial motive concerning certain ideas or singling out of particular media unrelated to the privacy-protection rationale?

This approach would recalibrate the press/privacy balance and lead to different outcomes in some familiar cases. One example is

---

[125] See text accompanying note 67.

[126] As an element of the tort of "Publicity Given to Private Life," § 652D of the Restatement (Second) of Torts requires that the disclosure of a private fact be "highly offensive." See note 86. This is an incomplete measure. Even where a disclosure about intimate details of someone's life is not "highly offensive," protection may be justified. Consider a touching and tasteful story and photograph about a terminally ill teenager, published without his family's consent, or simply the publishing of ordinary personal details about a child. These may not be "highly offensive," but that should not end the inquiry. See also Rosen, *The Unwanted Gaze* at 50 (cited in note 93) ("In an age that is beyond embarrassment, it's rarely clear what a 'reasonable person' would find highly offensive.").

The Restatement also states that the tort cannot be established if the matter publicized is of "legitimate concern to the public." The word "legitimate" is in effect a placeholder, for it operates here essentially as a conclusion that the public concern is appropriate—a judgment that, as I indicate in the text, reflects a range of factors and normative trade-offs, including not only the substantiality of the public concern but also the degree to which privacy is invaded.

Florida Star v B.J.F.[127] A Florida statute made it unlawful to "print, publish, or broadcast . . . in any instrument of mass communication" the name of a victim of a sexual offense. The *Florida Star* violated the statute and its own internal policy of not publishing such names, and was sued by a rape victim for damages. The Court held that the First Amendment barred recovery, emphasizing that the information was "truthful" and "lawfully obtained." But why should that count for almost everything? Publicizing a rape victim's name is a cruel invasion of privacy concerning a matter of great sensitivity to the victim. Furthermore, in most cases, why is the name of a rape victim a matter of legitimate public concern? The fact of the rape or even the name of the alleged perpetrator is one thing, but the victim's name is ordinarily not something the public profits from knowing. If the rape victim is a public figure or limited public figure, it is only because she has been dragged into the public square against her will as a victim of crime. It is hard to see that publicizing her name contributes to the crucial role the press plays in promoting democratic self-governance. The balance in these circumstances seems very much on the side of privacy. In addition, the Florida law in question was clear and specific. It is hard to see how enforcing this law would "chill" any valuable reporting.

The Court, invoking the *Daily Mail* test requiring the state to show a "need of the highest order" to justify limiting publication of lawfully acquired and truthful information, points to two main factors to explain its holding. First, the *Florida Star* obtained the rape victim's name from a police incident report that had inadvertently included her name. Although the Sheriff Department could in theory have prevented the name from becoming public, the department's error cannot be seen as evidence that the state lacked a commitment to protecting rape victims' privacy. The privacy interests belonged to the victim. An error by the Sheriff's Department should not put her at the mercy of the newspaper, which knew full well that it had a legal obligation not to disclose the victim's name and itself had an internal policy against doing so. Protecting privacy should not be a game of gotcha. Second, the Court said that the Florida statute was underinclusive in that it

---

[127] 491 US 524 (1989).

prohibited publication only by "an instrument of mass communication," not by other means. But since Florida's primary concern was to prevent the widespread dissemination of rape victims' names, the statute's focus is understandable. This is not a case where the state has singled out one segment of the news media for adverse treatment in a manner suggesting that there are favored and disfavored media entities. It is hard to see how the interest in press freedom and free expression is harmed by this "underinclusiveness."

The flavor of the Court's opinion in *Florida Star* is that the Court will find any conceivable escape hatch for media liability. The Court gives only token recognition to the value of implementing legal protections of privacy. This extreme solicitude for the one and sharply limited solicitude for the other is what should be reversed.

Florida Star involved a private figure victimized by crime. Unfortunately, other types of "involuntary public figures" also receive too little privacy protection under current law. The official comments to Section 652D of the Restatement (Second) of Torts ("Publicity Given to Private Life"),[128] clearly influenced by existing First Amendment law, state:

> There are other individuals who have not sought publicity or consented to it, but through their own conduct or otherwise have become a legitimate subject of public interest. They have, in other words, become "news." . . . These persons are regarded as properly subject to the public interest, and publishers are permitted to satisfy the curiosity of the public . . . . As in the case of the voluntary public figure, the authorized publicity is not limited to the event that itself arouses the public interest, and to some reasonable extent includes publicity given to facts about the individual that would otherwise be purely private. (Comment f.)

I would not interpret the First Amendment to prohibit protections against disclosures of "purely private" and tangential matters. Consider the case of Oliver Sipple, who, while standing in a crowd of onlookers, blocked Sara Jane Moore's arm as she was about to shoot at President Gerald Ford. The *San Francisco Chronicle* thereafter disclosed that Sipple was gay. When Sipple sued the newspa-

---

[128] See note 86.

per for invasion of privacy, his case was dismissed on First Amendment grounds. The California appellate court noted that Sipple had not completely concealed his sexual identity (although the court did not dispute that Sipple had kept the information from his family and that, as a result of the publicity, Sipple's family abandoned him). But the court's main argument was that "the publications were not motivated by a morbid and sensational prying into appellant's private life but rather were prompted by legitimate political considerations, i.e., to dispel the false public opinion that gays were timid, weak and unheroic figures. . . ."[129] Given the intensely personal nature of Sipple's sexual identity and the care many homosexuals take to limit general knowledge about that identity, and given that Sipple did not seek notoriety, this asserted connection between the private fact and "political considerations" was simply too weak to warrant the *Chronicle*'s disclosure.[130]

The privacy protections permitted to a true public figure—a political official, an entertainment personality—must be more limited. Most obviously, the media must have a very broad right to cover the actions of political figures because of the presumptive connection between such coverage and the process of democratic self-governance and because the media must be given "breathing space . . . to ensure the robust debate of public issues."[131] Voters assess public officials on a wide variety of grounds, and the scope of press coverage properly reflects this. But this rationale should not make every aspect of a public figure's life fair game for media attention.

Public officials have some legitimate expectations of privacy because they are human beings as well as "public officials." They magnify and reconfigure, but do not abandon, our own complex and ambivalent relations to the public as we assume multiple roles in day-to-day life. Indeed, since public figures are typically our

---

[129] *Sipple v Chronicle Publishing Co.*, 201 Cal Rptr 665, 670 (Cal App 1st 1984).

[130] For a different view, see Rosen, *The Unwanted Gaze* at 48 (cited in note 93). Rosen describes "the brutal outing of Oliver Sipple" and recognizes the "psychological distress" it caused (Sipple eventually committed suicide), but concludes: "[D]espite the tragic personal consequences that often result from the disclosure of true but embarrassing private facts, it's appropriate, in a country that takes the First Amendment seriously, that invasion of privacy suits against the press rarely succeed."

[131] *Dun and Bradstreet, Inc. v Greenmoss Builders*, 472 US 749, 776 (1985); *New York Times Co. v Sullivan*, 376 US at 271–72.

proxies and representatives in the public space and perform so many public functions for us—letting us preserve more of the private than we otherwise could—we arguably owe them space for at least some reciprocal measure of our own ambivalence and our own needs for privacy. When Justice Stevens says in *Bartnicki* that "[o]ne of the costs of participation in public affairs is an attendant loss of privacy,"[132] he is making a descriptively true statement. But he seems to be using this inevitable descriptive truth as a justification for allowing the law itself to undermine privacies that can be preserved. Some people, of course, will enter public life even if they know that their lives will be lived on the front pages of newspapers; and there always will be some public figures complicitous in destroying their own potential privacy. Nevertheless, our legal regime should not compel those interested in public affairs to pay such a price against their will.

Reporting on sexual habits or on intimate family matters of public figures should generally be outside First Amendment protection, particularly when the information comes from circumstances of reasonably expected privacy. To be sure, media disclosures concerning these private matters can always be said to promote the greater accountability of public officials because there will always be some citizens who view those private matters as relevant to the official's suitability for office.[133] But that, by itself, cannot justify First Amendment protection for such disclosures. Accountability in this expansive sense should not trump all other values. It is a very important value, but not our democratic society's only value. If public figures should have some zone of protected privacy, then some limits on the media's leeway to invade privacy will have to be accepted, even if this also means some limit on accountability. I am prepared to accept this, although many will disagree and al-

---

[132] 121 S Ct at 1765.

[133] See Post, *The Social Foundations of Privacy* at 74–85 (cited in note 52); Geoffrey R. Stone, 90 Mich L Rev at 1262–63 (cited in note 120); Owen M. Fiss, *Do Public Officials Have a Right to Privacy?* in Dieter Simon and Manfred Weiss, eds, *Zur Autonmie des Individuums: Liber Amicorum Spiros Simitis* 91–98 (2001). For example, Professor Post writes: "The claims of public officials to a 'private' information preserve are simply overridden by the more general demands of the public for political accountability. . . . Because American law views the public, in its role as the electorate, as ultimately responsible for political decisions, the public is presumptively entitled to all information that is necessary for informed governance." Id at 76, 78.

though I recognize, and would seek to minimize, the risks of chilling more legitimate press coverage. The law already recognizes some of these limits on the media. As Justice Stevens himself notes in *Bartnicki*, we forbid reporters from stealing documents and from wiretapping, even if these activities would provide newsworthy information.[134] A prohibition on publishing certain lawfully obtained information involves different concerns, of course. But where a democratically elected legislature seeks to give limited additional protection to the privacy of public officials, neither First Amendment principles nor a commitment to democratic self-government should necessarily bar this.

Indeed, as I argued above, information about the private lives of public officials so readily distracts us from their official actions that limiting press coverage of these private matters would likely enhance public discourse and public debate that is at the heart of the First Amendment's purposes. Such limitations could also strengthen the process of democratic self-government in other respects. In the name of improving the quality of official actions by enhancing public scrutiny, media coverage that intrudes on private matters can distort the personalities of public officials and damage their performance. In addition, it is widely believed that many talented people are being deterred from running for office or assuming senior political appointments because of a concern about the extreme loss of privacy that now must be expected for oneself and one's family. If there were greater protections for privacy, the political system as a whole could be strengthened by drawing greater numbers of talented people into public service.[135] As Justice Breyer has argued in a recent speech,[136] we should see the Constitution as a whole and read the First Amendment as a part of that whole—a document seeking to advance a system of effective democratic self-governance. Certain media restrictions to protect privacy, even though limiting the press' leeway, may in overall effect contribute positively to advancing public debate and democratic self-governance.

---

[134] 121 S Ct at 1764 n 19. See also *Wilson v Layne*, 526 US 603 (1999) (Fourth Amendment violated by media "ride-along" to accompany police during attempted execution of arrest warrant in a person's home).

[135] See, e.g., Fiss, *Do Public Officials Have a Right to Privacy?* at 94 (cited in note 133).

[136] Breyer, *Our Democratic Constitution* (cited in note 89).

There are too many special circumstances related to President Clinton's relationship with Monica Lewinsky to make that a prime example here (the presidency is arguably a special case; the information about President Clinton's relationship with Monica Lewinsky developed out of the Paula Jones legal proceeding and then became relevant to a possible perjury prosecution and impeachment, raising distinctive questions regarding the proper scope of discovery, sexual harassment law, and "high crimes and misdemeanors"; and adulterous sexual relationships had already become an issue in President Clinton's political campaigns and in political judgments about him). But whatever one thinks about that episode (I consider it to have been a distraction from the public's business), I would not interpret the First Amendment as categorically barring efforts to prevent media disclosures about the private sexual behavior of public officials. Nor should it bar restrictions on the publication of other intimate personal matters, such as information about their children or private photographs. Once again, relevance to matters of public concern could undoubtedly be drawn in most cases—sexual behavior may suggest something about a person's character or general willingness to take risks, family details may reveal something relevant to the public policies the official has articulated, etc. At times the relevance to public matters may indeed be substantial, and therefore publication addresses a legitimate public concern. But if we allow any articulated relevance to a public concern to justify publication, however weak that relevance is, we have eliminated privacy protection for public figures, and that is too extreme.[137]

The constitutional law of other countries reinforces the reasonableness of the approach suggested here, or at least makes clear that our own Supreme Court's approach has judicial competitors. Other countries often take a significantly more privacy-protective and media-restrictive approach than we do. These countries, of

---

[137] "Public figures" from the entertainment world present somewhat different issues because such figures are typically less connected than public officials to the process of public deliberation and democratic self-government. Matters of public significance that might justify media publicity may therefore be less clearly involved. On the other hand, entertainment figures often utilize publicity about their private lives (including their sexual partners) to enhance their public image, so the interest in the privacy of personal facts may sometimes be less apparent. Nevertheless, in my judgment, there should still be protectable zones of privacy that the media may not invade—for example, publishing intrusively (if lawfully) secured photographs of entertainment figures with their children.

course, have somewhat different constitutional provisions, and I do not suggest that comparisons can be made in any simple fashion. But a few examples will illustrate that our Court has struck the speech/privacy balance quite differently from many other democratic countries with highly developed constitutional systems and a vibrant free press.

In Great Britain, for example, a well-known case quite analogous to *Bartnicki* was decided against the media, with more weight given to the fact that the published material had been unlawfully obtained. In *Francome v Mirror Group Newspapers Ltd.*,[138] an unknown person illegally bugged telephone conversations made to and from the home of a champion jockey—a criminal offense under British law. The *Daily Mirror*, a newspaper that had nothing to do with the bugging, obtained tapes of the telephone conversations and wanted to publish material based on them. Publication, the *Daily Mirror* said, was justified because the tapes revealed actions contrary to the public interest and possible criminal conduct by the jockey. The jockey sought to enjoin the *Daily Mirror*'s publication of the material. The Court of Appeal upheld the trial judge's granting of an injunction pending full trial. Sir John Donaldson wrote, "I regard [the *Daily Mirror*'s] assertion as arrogant and wholly unacceptable. . . . If . . . the *Daily Mirror* can assert this right to act on the basis that the public interest, as [it] sees it, justifies breaches of the criminal law, so can any other citizen."[139]

The Supreme Court of Germany and the German Constitutional Court, the most influential constitutional court in Europe, have developed a rich speech/privacy jurisprudence that is very different from ours conceptually, and that yields quite different results in particular cases, including one quite similar to *Bartnicki*. What we in the United States call the right to privacy is protected in Germany by the constitutional right to "the free development

---

[138] 2 All ER 408 (CA 1984).

[139] Sir John Donaldson added: "The media . . . are an essential foundation of any democracy. In exposing crime, anti-social behavior and hypocrisy and in campaigning for reform and propagating the views of minorities, they perform an invaluable function. However, they are peculiarly vulnerable to the error of confusing the public interest with their own interest. . . . In the present case, pending a trial, it is impossible to see what public interest would be served by publishing the contents of the tapes which would not equally be served by giving them to the police or to the Jockey Club. Any wider publication could only serve the interests of the *Daily Mirror*." Id at 413.

of one's personality"[140] in conjunction with the right to "human dignity."[141] The personality right "comprises the authority of the individual to decide for himself—based on the idea of self-determination—when and within what limits facts about one's personal life should be disclosed."[142] The right is conceptualized as a right to "informational self-determination."[143] The individual, however, "has to accept limitations on his right to informational self-determination for reasons of a predominant public interest." "In formulating enactments," the Constitutional Court has said, the legislature "has to observe the principle of proportionality"[144]— "proportionality" being the widely invoked concept of balancing in many constitutional courts and supreme courts around the world.[145]

The German courts have decided several cases addressing the balance between the right to "informational self-determination" and "freedom of the press." The courts' analysis, of course, depends upon a constitutional context quite different from ours: the privacy right is expressly protected by the German Constitution and applies to relationships among citizens, not simply between the citizen and the state. But the comparison is instructive. The *Bartnicki*-type case involved a suit against the magazine *Stern* for publishing the transcript of an illegally taped telephone call between two senior political party officials about political matters in Germany.[146] *Stern* knew that the information had been obtained unlawfully but had not participated in the intrusion. The German Supreme Court concluded that the plaintiffs' "personality" right was violated and that the defendant's "free press" right was not.

---

[140] Grundgesetz (Basic Law), Art 2. The English translations of the German materials discussed here are taken from Paul Gewirtz and Jacob Katz Cogan, *Global Constitutionalism: Privacy, Proportionality, The Political Case* (2001) (hereafter cited as *Global Constitutionalism*). Grundgesetz (Basic Law), Art 2, appears in *Global Constitutionalism* at II-27.

[141] Grundgesetz (Basic Law), Art 1, in *Global Constitutionalism* at II-27.

[142] *Census Act Case*, BVerfGE, 1 (1983), in *Global Constitutionalism* at I-3.

[143] Id at I-4. The right is understood as not only contributing to an individual's personal development but as also contributing to "the common good" because informational self-determination fosters important elements of a "free democratic community" such as "communication" and "participation." Id.

[144] Id.

[145] See Part IV (discussing proportionality).

[146] *On the Limits Placed on the Press by the Personality Right*, BGHZ 73, 120 (1978), in *Global Constitutionalism* at II-25.

"[B]alancing the conflicting interests,"[147] the Court concluded that "[o]nly a very grave public need to be informed could possibly justify" publishing the transcript of the phone call, which exposed the "personal sphere . . . in an unusually intrusive form."[148] That "grave public need" did not exist in this case, even though public officials were involved and the conversation concerned their public functions.

In another important decision, the German Constitutional Court ruled that Princess Caroline of Monaco's "personality" rights were violated by magazines that published photographs of her and her boyfriend in a garden cafe which had "the characteristics of . . . a sphere of seclusion" even though members of the public were present, as well as photographs of Princess Caroline with her children on a street and in a canoe.[149] The publication of other photographs showing Princess Caroline in "the public sphere" was held not to violate her personality rights.

In a well-known Indian speech/privacy case, the Supreme Court of India stated that "[t]he sweep of the First Amendment to the United States Constitution and the freedom of speech and expression under our Constitution is not identical though similar in their major premises."[150] Among these differences, the Indian Court concluded that a "proper balancing of the freedom of press" and the "right to privacy" means that "the victim of a sexual assault, kidnap, abduction or alike offense should not further be subjected to the indignity of her name and the incident being publicised in press/media."[151]

Lastly, the Supreme Court of Canada, which is generally strongly press-protective, has upheld a damages action for the un-

---

[147] Id at II-30. As a general matter, the Court observed, "[t]he more the information is private in character and the more it involves personal interests in keeping it secret and the more it involves personal harm, the greater the 'public value' will have to be if the press wants to disregard the person's wish in keeping it [private]." Id at II-31. Note the similarity to Justice Breyer's balancing approach in *Bartnicki* and his conclusion there that "the speakers' legitimate privacy expectations are unusually low, and the public interest in defeating those expectations unusually high." 121 S Ct at 1768.

[148] *Global Constitutionalism* at II-27. The Court, in a crucial conceptualization, observed that the taped conversation "addressed very *personal* concerns, even though these were still related to their *public* occupations." Id at II-26 (emphasis added).

[149] *Princess Caroline of Monaco Case*, BVerfGE 101, 361 (1999), in *Global Constitutionalism* at II-33.

[150] See *Rajagopal v State of Tamil Nadu*, 6 S C C 632, 648 (1994).

[151] Id at 648, 650.

authorized publication of a photograph that a magazine photographer had taken of the plaintiff in a public place and published without that person's consent.[152] In doing so, the Canadian Court specifically disagreed with American constitutional law. The Court held that "the right to one's image is included in the right to respect for one's private life" protected by the Quebec Charter, that the "freedom of expression" was also involved here, and that it was necessary "to balance these two rights."[153] The Supreme Court of Canada rejected the approach of the Court of Appeal that "the public's right to information will prevail where the expression at issue concerns information that is 'socially useful.'"[154] The Court stated:

> This notion seems to have been borrowed from American law
> . . . . A photograph of a single person can be "socially useful"
> because it serves to illustrate a theme. That does not make its
> publication acceptable, however, if it infringes the right to privacy. We do not consider it appropriate to adopt the notion
> of "socially useful" for the purposes of legal analysis. . . . Only
> one question arises, namely the balancing of the rights at issue.
> It must, therefore, be decided whether the public's right to
> information can justify dissemination of a photograph taken
> without authorization. . . . In our view, the artistic expression of
> the photograph, which was alleged to have served to illustrate
> contemporary urban life, cannot justify the infringement of the
> right to privacy it entails. It has not been shown that the public's interest in seeing this work is predominant. . . . [F]reedom
> of expression must be defined in light of the other values
> concerned.[155]

No other democratic country forbids restrictions on expressive conduct as completely as the United States. Supreme courts and constitutional courts in most other democracies give greater weight to values of privacy and human dignity when they conflict with free speech claims, and they therefore are more inclined to permit legal actions against privacy invasions, libel, and hate speech. They also permit the state to play a much greater role in assuring wider public access to the media even though some restriction on the speech of others is involved. Although the consti-

---

[152] *Aubry v Editions Vice-Versa Inc.*, 1 S C R 591 (1998).

[153] Id at 615, 616.

[154] Id at 617.

[155] Id at 617–18.

tutional rules in these countries are somewhat different, the press is vibrant and robust. The glories of the American free speech tradition have had great and greatly beneficial influence worldwide. But to other countries, our current free speech doctrines seem to have become quite extreme, and our current law indeed is at the far end of the spectrum. Thus, far from being aberrational, giving more weight to privacy in speech/privacy cases would move American free speech law closer to the global democratic mainstream.

IV

Justice Breyer's concurring opinion in *Bartnicki*, while directly relevant for its treatment of the speech/privacy tension, deserves further comment because of its wider implications for First Amendment analysis generally. Many of Justice Breyer's key moves in *Bartnicki*—his conceptualization of speech on both sides of the constitutional analysis, his receptivity to some restrictions on speech where doing so would produce important "privacy and speech-related benefits," his utilization of flexible proportionality analysis—are part and parcel of an important new approach to First Amendment analysis that Justice Breyer has been developing in various separate opinions over the last several years.[156] He has recently developed these views further in his ambitious Madison Lecture,[157] placing his First Amendment views in the context of a wider constitutional theory that emphasizes "participatory self-governance" as a central theme in constitutional law generally.

Breyer's First Amendment approach has several key elements:

1) The First Amendment's protection of "the freedom of speech" seeks not only to prevent government restrictions on speech, but also to "enhanc[e]" speech,"[158] "to facilitate . . . public discussion and informed deliberation,"[159] and to help advance "the

---

[156] See *Turner Broadcasting System, Inc. v Federal Communications Commission*, 520 US 180, 225–29 (1997) (Breyer concurring in part); *Nixon v Shrink Missouri Government PAC*, 528 US 377, 399–405 (2000) (Breyer concurring); *United States v Playboy Entertainment Group, Inc.*, 529 US 803, 835–47 (2000) (Breyer dissenting); *Bartnicki v Vopper*, 121 S Ct 1753, 1766 (2001) (Breyer concurring); *United States v United Foods, Inc.*, 533 US 405, 450–59 (2001) (Breyer dissenting).

[157] Breyer, *Our Democratic Constitution* (cited in note 89).

[158] *Bartnicki v Vopper*, 121 S Ct at 1766.

[159] *Turner Broadcasting System, Inc. v Federal Communications Commission*, 520 US at 227.

Constitution's general participatory self-government objective."[160] In others words, the freedom of speech is not only a negative liberty but also an "active liberty,"[161] concerned with "encouraging the exchange of ideas,"[162] "encouraging . . . public participation and open discussion,"[163] " 'assuring that the public has access to a multiplicity of information sources,' "[164] "facilitat[ing] . . . informed deliberation,"[165] and "prevent[ing]" the speech of "a few from drowning out the many."[166]

2) Current First Amendment cases tend to see the restriction of speech as the only free speech interest in the picture. However, many challenged laws enhance the speech of some people while restricting the speech of others. The "speech-enhancing"[167] dimensions of such laws promote First Amendment interests even though other aspects of these laws restrict First Amendment interests. Thus, in one of Breyer's central ideas, reiterated in *Bartnicki,* "[C]onstitutionally protected interests lie on both sides of the legal equation."[168]

3) Once one accepts that "constitutionally protected interests lie on both sides of the legal equation," conventional First Amendment doctrine becomes less useful and less appropriate. Under the conventional doctrines, laws that directly restrict speech typically trigger "strict scrutiny"—a strong presumption against a law's constitutionality, which almost always condemns the law to invalidation. But where laws have speech-enhancing elements as well as speech-restricting ones, Justice Breyer says, the proper constitutional analysis must involve balancing of these interests. The key question should be one of "proportionality"—whether the "laws impose restrictions on speech that are disproportionate

---

[160] Breyer, *Our Democratic Constitution* at 6 (cited in note 89).

[161] Id.

[162] Id.

[163] *Nixon v Shrink Missouri Government PAC,* 528 US at 401.

[164] *Turner Broadcasting System, Inc. v Federal Communications Commission,* 520 US at 227 (citation omitted).

[165] Id.

[166] *Nixon v Shrink Missouri Government PAC,* 528 US at 402.

[167] *Bartnicki v Vopper,* 121 S Ct at 1766.

[168] Id at 400.

Justice Breyer's approach is also significant in its method. His opinions reveal a growing skepticism about the complex array of doctrinal formulas that now make up First Amendment law, a concern that they invite "mechanical"[181] applications and do not keep in view the purposes of the First Amendment or take open account of the full complexities and likely consequences of decisions or readily accommodate new social realities. Justice Breyer favors a more explicit and multifactored balancing of interests. In *Bartnicki*, for example, he rejects strict scrutiny, but does not embrace any other existing "test." Rather, he says:

> I would ask whether the statutes strike a reasonable balance between their speech-restricting and speech-enhancing consequences. Or do they instead impose restrictions on speech that are disproportionate when measured against their corresponding privacy and speech-related benefits, taking into account the kind, the importance, and the extent of these benefits, as well as the need for the restrictions in order to secure those benefits?[182]

As the word "disproportionate" in this passage indicates, one of the most striking things about Breyer's approach is that he has begun to embrace a formulation of balancing widely used by supreme courts and constitutional courts in other leading democracies: "proportionality." "Proportionality" is a general element of constitutional analysis used by these courts in diverse areas of constitutional law,[183] but it has not in so many words entered American

---

[181] *Nixon v Shrink Missouri Government PAC*, 528 US at 400; *United States v Playboy Entertainment Group, Inc.*, 529 US at 841.

[182] 121 S Ct at 1766.

[183] An analysis of the concept of "proportionality" as used by other countries' supreme courts and constitutional courts is beyond the scope of this article. For a fuller discussion, see Paul Gewirtz and Jacob Katz Cogan, *Global Constitutionalism* at IV-1-98 (cited in note 140). Examples of cases from other jurisdictions discussing and applying the proportionality concept include: *Lebach Case*, BVerfGE 35, 202 (1975) (Constitutional Court of Germany); *Cannabis Case*, BVerfGE 90, 145 (1994) (Constitutional Court of Germany); *Reiten im Walde Case*, BVerfGE 80, 137 (1989) (Constitutional Court of Germany); *R. v Oakes*, 1 S C R 103 (1986) (Supreme Court of Canada); *Dagenais v CBC*, 3 S C R 835 (1994) (Supreme Court of Canada); *Thomson Newspaper v Canada* (A.G.), 1 S C R 877 (1998) (Supreme Court of Canada); *Decision Dated April 26, 1995 (K.11/94)* (Constitutional Court of Poland), in *Constitutional Tribunal, a Selection of the Polish Constitutional Tribunal's Jurisprudence from 1986 to 1999*, at 153–58 (1999); *United Mizrahi Bank Ltd. v Migdal Village*, 49 (4) P D 221 (1995) (Supreme Court of Israel). See also P. van Duk and G. J. H. van Hoof, *Theory and Practice of the European Convention on Human Rights* 80–82 (3d ed 1998); Walter van Gerven, *The Effect of Proportionality on the Actions of Member States of the European Community: National Viewpoints from Continental Europe*, in Evelyn Ellis, ed, *The Principle of Proportionality in the Laws of Europe: A Comparative Study* (1999).

constitutional law. Justice Breyer has been the boldest of the current U.S. Supreme Court Justices in drawing upon concepts and examples from the constitutional jurisprudence of other countries, including "proportionality."[184] His concurrence in *Nixon v Shrink Missouri Government PAC*, for example, explicitly cited "proportionality" cases from the European Court of Human Rights and the Supreme Court of Canada, with Breyer writing:

> [W]here a law significantly implicates competing constitutionally protected interests in complex ways[,] the Court has closely scrutinized the statute's impact on those interests, but refrained from employing a simple test that effectively presumes unconstitutionality. Rather, it has balanced interests. And in practice that has meant asking whether the statute burdens any one such interest in a manner out of proportion to the statute's salutary effects upon the others (perhaps, but not necessarily, because of the existence of a clearly superior, less restrictive alternative).
> . . . [This approach] is consistent with that of other constitutional courts facing similar complex constitutional problems.[185]

In his dissent in *United States v Playboy Entertainment Group, Inc.*, he counsels the Court "not to apply First Amendment rules mechanically, but to decide whether, in light of the benefits and potential alternatives, the statute works speech-related harm (here to adult speech) out of proportion to the benefits that the statute seeks to provide (here, child protection)."[186] His recent Madison

---

[184] In addition to the "proportionality" concept, Justice Breyer has referred to other countries' constitutional law in other respects. See, e.g., *Printz v United States*, 521 US 898, 976–77 (1997) (Breyer dissenting) (discussing other countries' approach to federalism); *Nixon v Shrink Missouri Government PAC*, 528 US 377, 403 (2000) (Breyer concurring) (discussing other countries' approach to campaign finance); Breyer, *Our Democratic Constitution* at 7 (cited in note 89) (referring to same); *Knight v Florida*, 528 US 990 (1999) (Breyer dissenting from denial of certiorari) (discussing other countries' treatment of delays in capital punishment executions). In speeches he has also spoken approvingly of the fact that "[j]udges who enforce the law as well as those who write it increasingly turn to the experience of other nations when deciding difficult open questions of substantive law, particularly human rights law. . . ." He notes that U.S. courts "less frequently refer to judicial opinions from abroad" than other courts do, and has called upon American lawyers and academics to "themselves become familiar with foreign material relevant to particular legal disciplines and facilitate the judicial use of that material." Stephen Breyer, Dinner Keynote Speech, International Symposium on Democracy and the Rule of Law in a Changing World Order, New York University Law School, March 9, 2000 (copy on file with author).

[185] 528 US at 402, 403 (citations omitted).

[186] 529 US at 841. Citing his own separate opinion in *Bartnicki*, Justice Breyer also invoked the idea of proportionality in last term's dissent in *United States v United Foods, Inc.*, a commercial speech case:

> Several features of the program indicate that its speech-related aspects, i.e., its compelled monetary contributions, are necessary and proportionate to the legiti-

Lecture is the most direct: "The basic question the Court should ask is one of proportionality."[187]

It is fair to ask whether this balancing or "proportionality" review invites too much subjectivity and arbitrariness from judges. The question, of course, is not whether we trust judges like Justice Breyer to engage in this kind of balancing, but whether we trust our adjudicative system as a whole. I remain of two minds about this. Concerns about subjectivity and arbitrariness in balancing are altogether legitimate. But the system of doctrinal rules that we have now itself invites subjectivity and arbitrariness, both in deciding what rule to apply in a particular circumstance and in applying the selected rules. The variety of different doctrinal rules in contemporary First Amendment law—"strict scrutiny," "intermediate scrutiny," the *Daily Mail* principle, "clear and present danger," the *New York Times Co. v Sullivan* test, content neutrality, prior restraint, "public forum" rules, rules for commercial speech and other "low-value" speech, etc.—reflects the complexities of the balances that need to made and continuing disagreements about the appropriate approach. As the invocation of both "intermediate scrutiny" and "the *Daily Mail* principle" in the *Bartnicki* litigation itself demonstrates, the current doctrinal cacophony creates remarkable leeway for choosing which doctrinal rule to apply as well as what result to reach. Interest balancing often occurs, but not in a fully open way.

In this rather chaotic doctrinal situation, and in circumstances of social and technological change that create new background conditions, an open recognition of the factors at stake and a more direct consideration and debate about the values in the balance have distinctive value. With more open balancing, a fuller range of factors can be made visible. Justice Breyer's use of balancing and proportionality analysis has a refreshing candor and lucidity, and his very openness about the factors at work for him is a constraint on subjectivity.[188] What he says in his Madison Lecture

---

mate promotional goals that it seeks. . . . [At] the same time, those features of the program that led [dissenters in an earlier case] to find its program disproportionately restrictive are absent here. . . . In consequence, whatever harm the program may cause First Amendment interests is proportionate.

533 US at 457.

[187] Breyer, *Our Democratic Constitution* at 7 (cited in note 89).

[188] See Rosen, *Modest Proposal* at 25 (cited in note 173).

about his pragmatic attention to "consequences" is as applicable to his balancing approach generally: An approach that exclusively emphasizes "language, history, tradition, or prior rules," at least in the "borderline" cases, will "produce a decision which is no less subjective but which is far less transparent than a decision that directly addresses consequences in constitutional terms."[189] In addition, many of the existing rules would still have value as guidelines because they reflect and crystalize past experience about where the balance should lie. The balancing inquiry may eventually lead to new guidelines. The debate about rules versus balancing is a perennial one in law, of course, and such persistence is usually a sign that there are real advantages and disadvantages to the contending approaches.[190] But in this context, the case for more open balancing appears strong, at least when compared to the current doctrinal rules.

Justice Breyer is developing the most important new ideas about the First Amendment on the Supreme Court since Justices Brennan and Black. To say the least, it will be interesting to watch how his ideas evolve, and to see whether they will come to shape First Amendment doctrine on the Court as a whole.

CONCLUSION

In the particular area of privacy and speech, *Bartnicki* demonstrates that there is currently no single view that a majority of the Justices shares. But a majority does seem prepared to allow some new restrictions on speech to protect privacy. This is a development to be praised. But even in this area, working out the details of a new approach will be difficult, requiring elaboration of the complexities of privacy in its speech and nonspeech dimensions,

---

[189] Breyer, *Our Democratic Constitution* at 22 (cited in note 89).

[190] See, e.g., Richard H. Fallon, Jr., *The Supreme Court, 1996 Term—Foreword: Implementing the Constitution*, 111 Harv L Rev 54 (1997); Kathleen M. Sullivan, *The Supreme Court, 1991 Term—Foreword: The Justices of Rules and Standards*, 106 Harv L Rev 22 (1992); T. Alexander Aleinikoff, *Constitutional Law in the Age of Balancing*, 96 Yale L J 943 (1987); Stephen E. Gottlieb, *Compelling Governmental Interests: An Essential but Unanalyzed Term in Constitutional Adjudication*, 68 BU L Rev 917 (1988); Paul Kahn, *The Court, the Community and the Judicial Balance: The Jurisprudence of Justice Powell*, 97 Yale L J 1 (1987); Charles Fried, *Two Concepts of Interests: Some Reflections on the Supreme Court's Balancing Test*, 76 Harv L Rev 755 (1963).

the complexities of different understandings of the role of speech and press in society, and a finely tuned accommodation of the competing interests. Above all, it will require the most sensitive attention to the risks that always attend limitations of speech. The only justification for taking these risks is the judgment—which I have now reached—that the risks of not doing so are greater.

exercises of this authority based on the identity of the final agency decision maker and then to reward, through more deferential judicial review, interpretations offered by more responsible officials. This approach would make the institutional choice reflected in the *Chevron* doctrine—the choice, that is, between agencies and courts in ultimately resolving statutory ambiguities—dependent on a matter of prior institutional design that courts today fail to consider: the decision of the agency as to whether, within the agency's four walls, the congressional delegatee or, alternatively, a lower-level official is to exercise interpretive authority.

Our reflections on this score arise from *United States v Mead Corp.*,[2] the latest and most important in a line of cases in which the Supreme Court has attempted to demarcate the scope of the *Chevron* doctrine, or what one recent article has termed "*Chevron*'s domain."[3] The question in *Mead* was whether the *Chevron* deference rule applied to a tariff classification ruling of the U.S. Customs Service. The Court held that the tariff ruling fell outside the scope of *Chevron* and so could not claim its strong brand of deference. The eight-member majority first framed the issue as an inquiry into whether Congress, in enacting the statute at issue, had intended for the courts to defer to this kind of interpretive decision. The majority then reasoned that the lack of formal procedures preceding the decision, as well as its highly particularistic nature, indicated to the contrary. Surveying the landscape after *Mead*, Justice Scalia in lone dissent charged that an "avulsive change in judicial review of federal administrative action" had taken place.[4] No longer was an agency's interpretation of its own organic statute—regardless of the interpretive decision's pedigree, form, or character—presumptively entitled to *Chevron* deference.

The issue addressed in *Mead* assumes its consequence from the heavy reliance of agencies today on relatively informal, "non-rulelike," or decentralized forms of administrative action. *Chevron* arose from a major rule, which the administrator of the EPA issued in accordance with the notice-and-comment procedures of the Administrative Procedure Act (APA).[5] But many—indeed, the vast

---

[2] 121 S Ct 2164 (2001).

[3] Thomas W. Merrill and Kristin E. Hickman, *Chevron's Domain*, 89 Georgetown L J 833 (2001).

[4] 121 S Ct at 2177 (Scalia dissenting).

[5] 5 USC §§ 551–59, 701–06 (1994 & Supp IV 1998).

majority of—agency decisions have nothing like this aspect. They may emerge, like the tariff ruling of *Mead*, from processes considerably more streamlined than those detailed in the APA. They may apply, like the tariff ruling, in this case and this case only, rather than as a general prescription. And they may proceed, as in *Mead*, not from the central hierarchy of the agency but from branch offices or limited subject matter divisions. Assuming *Chevron* to have even a fraction of the significance that the countless judicial decisions and law review articles on the case would indicate, the question whether or which of these various administrative actions merit *Chevron* deference thus becomes of critical importance to the operation of the administrative state.

We first argue in this article that an inquiry into actual congressional intent, of the kind the *Mead* Court advocated, cannot realistically solve this question. Although Congress has broad power to decide what kind of judicial review should apply to what kind of administrative decision, Congress so rarely discloses (or, perhaps, even has) a view on this subject as to make a search for legislative intent chimerical and a conclusion regarding that intent fraudulent in the mine run of cases. (The statute at issue in *Mead* complicates but also underlines our basic point; although the statute contains unusual indicia of legislative intent, these point in the exact opposite direction from the one the Court took, thus demonstrating the hazards of the Court's approach.) Given the difficulty of determining actual congressional intent, some version of constructive—or perhaps more frankly said, fictional—intent must operate in judicial efforts to delineate the scope of *Chevron*. After considering other alternatives, we aver that this construction should arise from and reflect candid policy judgments, of the kind evident in *Chevron* itself, about the allocation of interpretive authority between administrators and judges with respect to various kinds of agency action.

Underneath the rhetoric of legislative intent, an approach of this kind in fact animates the *Mead* decision, but the Court's reliance on the two stock dichotomies of administrative process failed to generate the most appropriate distribution of interpretive power. The Court emphasized most heavily the divide between formal and informal procedures, suggesting that, except in unusual circumstances, only decisions taken in formal procedural contexts merit *Chevron* deference. But this preference for formality in administration, even in cases when not statutorily required, fails to acknowledge the costs associated with the procedures specified in the APA, which only have increased in significance since that statute's enactment. The Court similarly noted at times the divide between generality and particularity in administrative decision making, suggesting that actions exhibiting the former trait should receive greater judicial deference. But administrative law doctrine long has resisted, for good reason, the temptation to pressure the choice between general and particular decision making, in light of the many and fluctuating considerations, usually best known to an agency itself, relevant to this choice. None of this is to say that interpretive authority in areas of statutory ambiguity or silence always should rest with agency officials; it is only to say that in allocating this power in a way consistent with important administrative values, courts can do better than to rely on the two usual (indeed, hoary) "either-ors" of agency process.

We contend that the deference question should turn on a different feature of agency process, traditionally ignored in administrative law doctrine and scholarship—that is, the position in the agency hierarchy of the person assuming responsibility for the administrative decision. More briefly said, the Court should refocus its inquiry from the "how" to the "who" of administrative decision making. If the congressional delegatee of the relevant statutory grant of authority takes personal responsibility for the decision, then the agency should command obeisance, within the broad bounds of reasonableness, in resolving statutory ambiguity; if she does not, then the judiciary should render the ultimate interpretive decision. This agency nondelegation principle serves values familiar from the congressional brand of the doctrine, as well as from *Chevron* itself: by offering an incentive to certain actors to take responsibility for interpretive choice, the principle advances both accountability and discipline in decision making. At the same time, the nondelegation principle, as applied in the administrative context to determine the appropriate deference regime, escapes the well-known difficulties of the congressional nondelegation doctrine: the administrative principle will neither lead to excessive centralization nor prove incapable of judicial enforcement. Critical to this analysis is a more general phenomenon often disregarded in discussions of administrative law, yet highly significant for the creation of doctrine: the interplay of political with judicial constraints in shaping agency behavior.

The aspect of institutional design we emphasize here—call it the high level/low level distinction—justifies the result the Court reached in *Mead*, but only by fortuity. In other cases our approach would diverge significantly from the Court's—in granting deference even in the absence of formality or generality and, conversely, in refusing deference even in the face of these attributes. This approach also would diverge from Justice Scalia's, given the nearly unlimited deference he favors. But oddly enough, we see our approach as in some sense, even if in a sense unrecognized by the Justices themselves, present in all of their different views on the issue: because this is so, we see some potential for the Court to move toward, and even converge on, the *Chevron* nondelegation doctrine we advocate.

The article proceeds in five parts. Part I sets the stage by describing the emergence after *Chevron* of issues relating to that decision's reach and summarizing the contrasting approaches to these issues taken in the *Mead* opinions. Parts II and III are critique. Part II argues that the Court's reliance on congressional intent should give way to a frankly policy-laden assessment of the appropriate allocation of power in the administrative state. Part III contends that the underlying policy evaluation of the Court misidentifies the criteria that should govern this allocation by focusing on the presence of formal procedures and generality. Parts IV and V offer our alternative approach. Part IV describes and defends the *Chevron* nondelegation principle as facilitating responsible agency decision making. Part V applies our analysis to *Mead* and discusses its potential application in other contexts.

I. Background

In the beginning (at least for the purposes of this article), there was *Chevron*. The question in that case concerned whether the Environmental Protection Agency (EPA) had acted lawfully when it issued a rule, in accordance with applicable notice-and-comment procedures, defining the term "stationary source" in the Clean Air Act to refer to whole plants, rather than each pollution-emitting device within them. In sustaining the rule, the Court prescribed a by now well-known, two-step inquiry to govern judicial review of an agency's interpretation of a statute that the agency administers. The first question is "whether Congress has directly spoken to the precise question at issue";[6] if so, the agency must comply with that judgment. The second question, reached only if Congress failed to speak clearly, is whether the agency has adopted a "reasonable" interpretation of the statute;[7] if so, the courts must accept that interpretation.

Nearly as soon as *Chevron* issued, questions began to arise about its reach—in particular, its application to agency interpretations rendered in contexts other than notice-and-comment rulemaking. The Court in several subsequent cases granted *Chevron* deference to interpretive decisions issued in formal adjudications,[8] but the Court's failure specifically to address the question left some lower courts and commentators uncertain as to whether all or only some of these decisions now stood beneath the *Chevron* umbrella.[9] The Court gave even less guidance as to whether more informal agency interpretations, of both the general and the particular variety, should receive *Chevron* deference. The range of possible questions stretched as wide as the range of decisional formats used by agencies. Should *Chevron* deference extend to interpretations contained in rules exempted from notice-and-comment procedures by virtue of their subject matter or exigency, but identical in force to the rule in *Chevron?*[10] Should deference extend to legal conclusions in what Peter Strauss has termed "publication rules,"[11] including general statements of interpretation and policy as well as staff man-

---

[6] *Chevron,* 467 US at 842.

[7] Id at 845.

[8] See, e.g., *INS v Aguirre-Aguirre,* 526 US 415 (1999); *ABF Freight System, Inc. v NLRB,* 517 US 392 (1996); *Fort Stewart Schools v FLRA,* 495 US 641 (1990).

[9] See, e.g., *Bob Evans Farms, Inc. v NLRB,* 163 F3d 1012, 1018–19 (7th Cir 1998) (holding that the NLRB's adjudicative decisions merit *Chevron* deference only when they have an inherently rulemaking quality); *Trans Union Corp. v FTC,* 81 F3d 228, 230–31 (DC Cir 1996) (addressing but not deciding the question whether *Chevron* deference applies to the adjudications of an agency lacking rulemaking authority); Robert A. Anthony, *Which Agency Interpretations Should Bind Citizens and the Courts?* 7 Yale J Reg 1, 47–52 (1990) (proposing a multifaceted scheme for determining which agency adjudications are entitled to *Chevron* deference).

[10] See 5 USC § 553(a), (b)(B) (stating subject matter and "good cause" exemptions from notice-and-comment requirements); Merrill and Hickman, 89 Georgetown L J at 905–07 (cited in note 3) (discussing these issues).

[11] Peter L. Strauss, *The Rulemaking Continuum,* 41 Duke L J 1463, 1467 (1992).

uals and instructions, which issue without notice and comment, but which may form the basis for enforcement proceedings against regulated parties?[12] Should deference extend to interpretations arising in informal adjudicative settings, or through the initial issuance of case-specific opinion and no-action letters?[13] The inquiries could (and did) go on and on.

Although these questions might appear to be arcana, they are anything but. Notice-and-comment regulations doubtless have, on average, both a higher profile and a greater import than other administrative forms of decision. The mass of agency action today, however, occurs in these other modes. One study showed that well over 40 percent of even the regulations published in the Federal Register in the first half of 1987 went into effect without notice and comment, usually in either overt or implicit reliance on the APA's "good cause" exemption;[14] and there is little reason to think that this percentage has declined since that time. Peter Strauss has calculated that publication rules appearing in a variety of informal media take up tens or even hundreds of times the library shelf space of regulations printed in the Federal Register.[15] And adjudicative or other particularistic action swamps general regulation in many agencies, with as many as 95 percent of administrative adjudications occurring without the formal procedures specified in the APA.[16] Amid this mass of non-notice-and-comment decision mak-

---

[12] Compare, e.g., *Wagner Seed Co. v Bush*, 946 F2d 918, 922–23 (DC Cir 1991) (granting *Chevron* deference to interpretive rules), with, e.g., *S. Ute Indian Tribe v Amoco Production Co.*, 119 F3d 816, 832–34 (10th Cir 1997) (denying *Chevron* deference to interpretive rules), revd on other grounds, 526 US 865 (1999).

[13] Compare, e.g., *Owsley v San Antonio Independent Sch. D.*, 187 F3d 521 (5th Cir 1999) (denying *Chevron* deference to an opinion letter), with, e.g., *Herman v Nationsbank Trust Co.*, 126 F3d 1354 (11th Cir 1997) (granting *Chevron* deference to an opinion letter).

[14] Juan J. Lavilla, *The Good Cause Exemption to Notice and Comment Rulemaking Requirements Under the Administrative Procedure Act*, 3 Admin L J 317, 339–40 nn 86–87 (1989). Of the 2,061 rules (excluding technical corrections) published in this time period, 900 issued without notice and comment—547 explicitly relying on the good-cause exemption, 164 implicitly doing so, and 189 resting on another APA exemption. See id. In about one-fourth of the good-cause cases, however, the agency requested post hoc comments for consideration prior to the agency's issuing the rule in final form. See id at 412.

[15] See Strauss, 41 Duke L J at 1469 (cited in note 11). As Strauss notes, "formally adopted regulations of the Internal Revenue Service occupy about a foot of library shelf space, but Revenue Rulings and other similar publications, closer to twenty feet; [and] the rules of the Federal Aviation Administration (FAA), two inches, but the corresponding technical guidance materials, well in excess of forty feet." Id.

[16] See Peter L. Strauss, *An Introduction to Administrative Justice in the United States* 142 (Carolina Academic Press, 1989).

ing reside some agency actions of great significance, not only to individual parties but to whole classes of regulatory beneficiaries and targets. Whether courts will accept agency resolutions of statutory ambiguity made in these various forms or, alternatively, will apply independent judgment in such cases thus becomes a principal question of administrative law.

The Supreme Court first addressed this question directly in *Christensen v Harris County.*[17] The case concerned the legality under the Fair Labor Standards Act of Harris County's policy of compelling employees to take, rather than continually accrue, compensatory time (time off earned in exchange for overtime worked).[18] Prior to commencement of the litigation, the Department of Labor's Wage and Hour Division had issued an opinion letter to the county stating that the implementation of such a policy would violate the Act. The employees challenging the policy, as well as the United States, urged the Court to give *Chevron* deference to this interpretation. The Court refused, contrasting an "interpretation contained in an opinion letter" with one "arrived at after, for example, a formal adjudication or notice-and-comment rulemaking."[19] The former, the Court declared—"like interpretations contained in policy statements, agency manuals, and enforcement guidelines, all of which lack the force of law"—do not warrant *Chevron* deference.[20] These modes of agency decision making were entitled only to the "respect" that the half-century-old decision in *Skidmore v Swift & Co.* had instructed courts to give to agency positions that have (but only those that have) the "power to persuade."[21] Finding the view expressed in the opinion letter "unpersuasive," the Court sustained the county's policy.[22]

Mead followed hard on *Christensen*'s heels. *Mead* involved a tariff classification ruling, issued under the authority of the Tariff Act and pursuant regulations. The Tariff Act provides that the Cus-

---

[17] 529 US 576 (2000).

[18] The county adopted the policy to avoid paying monetary compensation to employees who left their jobs with substantial reserves of compensatory time or who exceeded a statutory cap on accrual.

[19] 529 US at 587.

[20] Id.

[21] 323 US 134, 140 (1944).

[22] 529 US at 587.

toms Service "shall, under rules and regulations prescribed by the Secretary [of the Treasury] . . . fix the final classification and rate of duty applicable to [imported] merchandise"[23] under the Harmonized Tariff Schedule of the United States (HTSUS),[24] which sets forth taxation rates for specified categories of imports. The Act further provides that the Secretary "shall establish and promulgate such rules and regulations . . . (including regulations establishing procedures for the issuance of binding rulings prior to the entry of the merchandise concerned) . . . as may be necessary to secure a just, impartial, and uniform appraisement of imported merchandise and the classification and assessment of duties thereon at the various ports of entry."[25] According to the Secretary's regulations, the Customs Service, through an official of either one of the forty-six port-of-entry offices or the headquarters office, will endeavor, on request, to "issue a ruling letter setting forth a determination with respect to a specifically described Customs transaction."[26] This letter, from the time of issuance, "represents the official position of the Customs Service with respect to the particular transaction . . . and is binding on all Customs Service personnel . . . until modified or revoked."[27] Further, the "principle" contained in the ruling letter "may be cited as authority in the disposition of transactions involving the same circumstances."[28] But because a ruling letter, under the regulations in effect at the relevant time, was subject to change without notice to any person except the initial addressee,[29] the regulations provided that "no other person should rely on the ruling letter or assume that the principles of that ruling will be applied in connection with any transaction other than the one described."[30]

---

[23] 19 USC § 1500(b).

[24] 19 USC § 1202.

[25] 19 USC § 1502(a).

[26] 19 CFR § 177.8(a); see 19 CFR § 177.2(b)(2)(ii)(B).

[27] 19 CFR § 177.9(a).

[28] Id.

[29] See 19 CFR § 177.9(c). Subsequent to the Customs decision in *Mead*, Congress amended the Tariff Act to provide for public notice and an opportunity to comment prior to any modification of a ruling in effect for at least sixty days. See 19 USC § 1625(c). Even prior to the statutory change, which had no effect on *Mead*, the Treasury Department's regulations provided that the Customs Service would give notice to the initial addressee before modifying a ruling letter and would refrain from retroactively applying the modification to that person except in unusual circumstances. See 19 CFR § 177.9(d)(2).

[30] 19 CFR § 177.9(c).

The Mead Corporation imported "day planners," three-ring binders with pages on which users could note their daily schedules, phone numbers and addresses, and the like. If classified as "bound" "diaries" under the HTSUS, these products were subject to an import duty; if, conversely, viewed as either not "bound" or not "diaries," the products could enter the country without any duty applying.[31] An initial ruling letter regarding Mead's day planners, issued at Mead's request by a port-of-entry official, found that Mead's day planners were not bound diaries and thus not subject to tariff.[32] But two subsequent rulings, issued by the director of the Commercial Rulings Division at Customs Headquarters, found to the contrary.[33] Mead accordingly filed suit. Although the Court of International Trade, the specialized court with jurisdiction over such challenges, sustained the Customs Service,[34] the Federal Circuit reversed on appeal, holding that Customs classification rulings should not receive *Chevron* deference.[35]

Justice Souter's opinion for the Supreme Court reached the same conclusion as to *Chevron*, relying on a theory of the *Chevron* doctrine as a reflection of congressional intent and at least partially equating that intent with a preference for proceduralism and generality in agency decision making. Whether *Chevron* should govern, the opinion averred, depends on whether "the agency's generally conferred authority and other statutory circumstances" make apparent that "Congress would expect the agency to be able to speak with the force of law when it addresses ambiguity in the statute or fills a space in the enacted law."[36] Implicitly recognizing that Congress seldom makes this expectation plain, the Court approved the use of a "variety of indicators" to determine if Congress would want, given statutory ambiguity, an agency's conclusions to control.[37] Though the opinion refrained from cataloguing

---

[31] Subheadings 4820.10.20, 4820.10.40, of the HTSUS, 19 USC § 1202.

[32] See NY 864206 (June 19, 1991) (Jean F. McGuire, Area Director, New York Seaport), 1991 US Custom NY LEXIS 344.

[33] See HQ 955937 (Oct 21, 1994), 1994 WL 712863; HQ 953126 (Jan 11, 1993), 1993 WL 68471. The first headquarters ruling followed from a request by the port-of-entry official for central review of her decision, the second from Mead's own administrative protest.

[34] 17 F Supp 2d 1004 (1998).

[35] 185 F3d 1304 (1999).

[36] 121 S Ct at 2172.

[37] Id at 2176.

these indicators, it suggested that chief among them is the degree of procedural formality involved in the action. Said the Court, pointing to both notice-and-comment rulemaking and formal adjudication: "It is fair to assume generally that Congress contemplates administrative action with the effect of law when it provides for a relatively formal administrative procedure tending to foster . . . deliberation."[38] More submerged but also present within the opinion was reference to the level of generality of the agency action: did the decision "bespeak the legislative type of activity that would naturally bind more than the parties to the ruling[?]"[39] Because the ruling in *Mead* proceeded from no formal procedures and purported to bind no party other than Mead, only weak, *Skidmore*-style deference should apply.

And so the contours of *Chevron* seem set, running alongside the two great fault lines of administrative law (formality vs. informality and generality vs. particularity), though subject always to change in the event that a reviewing court sees indicia of a contrary congressional desire. Procedural formality creates a usually safe haven, enabling an agency to ensure that a court will defer to, and not just respectfully consider, its judgments about how to proceed in the face of congressional silence. Outside that haven, *Chevron* remains potentially applicable—"we have," cautioned the Court, "sometimes found reasons for *Chevron* deference even when no such administrative formality was required and none was afforded"[40]—but less likely to provide the standard of review. The presumption against deference for informal action appears especially strong when an agency acts in an individual case only, in effect adopting the decision-making paradigm associated with judges rather than legislators. Exactly what it takes to reverse this presumption the Court did not say, but even in this reticence lies the suggestion of a heavy burden.

For Justice Scalia, in dissent, the question of deference to agency action, even given its manifold forms, ought to have been simpler. In line with his usual preference for rules, Scalia objected to the

---

[38] Id at 2172.

[39] Id at 2174.

[40] Id at 2173 (citing *NationsBank of NC, NA v Variable Annuity Life Insurance Co.*, 513 US 251, 256–57, 263 (1995) (deferring, on grounds of long-standing precedent, to the Controller of the Currency's determination to grant a national bank's application to broker annuities)).

variability and unpredictability of the Court's analysis; in line with his frequent taste for executive power, Scalia protested the diminution of agencies' discretion to interpret ambiguous statutory language. For him, a single question was determinative of the deference inquiry (assuming Congress had not said anything explicit about the matter): was the interpretation in question "authoritative" in the sense that it "represents the official position of the agency"?[41] Because the interpretation contained in the Customs ruling letter met this test—evidenced by the signatures of the Solicitor General of the United States and the General Counsel of the Department of the Treasury on a brief stating so much—the *Chevron* deference rule should govern.

II. Congressional Intent

Mead represents the apotheosis of a developing trend in *Chevron* cases: the treatment of *Chevron* as a congressional choice, rather than either a constitutional mandate or a judicial doctrine. In one sense, this new focus is fitting: Congress indeed has the power to turn on or off *Chevron* deference. In another and more important sense, however, this focus is misdirected. Although Congress can control applications of *Chevron*, it almost never does so, expressly or otherwise; most notably, in enacting a standard delegation to an agency to make substantive law, Congress says nothing about the standard of judicial review. Because Congress so rarely makes its intentions about deference clear, *Chevron* doctrine at most can rely on a fictionalized statement of legislative desire, which in the end must rest on the Court's view of how best to allocate interpretive authority. Behind all its rhetoric about actual congressional intent, even the *Mead* Court may have understood these points: *Chevron* is a congressional doctrine only in the sense that Congress can overturn it; in all other respects, *Chevron* is a judicial construction, reflecting implicit policy judgments about what interpretive practices make for good government.

The *Chevron* doctrine began its life shrouded in uncertainty about its origin. *Chevron* barely bothered to justify its rule of deference, and the few brief passages on this matter pointed in disparate

---

[41] Id at 2187.

directions. Most prominent in the Court's explanation were functional considerations, relating to the accountability and deliberativeness of interpretive decisions. The Court stressed that agencies
had a link, through the President, to a public "constituency," and
averred as well that they would consider complex regulatory issues
in a "detailed and reasoned fashion."[42] These references implied
that the rule of deference sprang from legal process principles: in
effect, the Court was creating a common law of judicial review
responsive to institutional competencies. But interspersed with
these ideas ran a strand of thought relating the deference regime
to Congress: here, the Court emphasized that "Congress ha[d] delegated policy-making responsibilities" to the agency and that in
this context gaps and ambiguity in legislation themselves might
count as delegations to the agency to "elucidate . . . the statute
by regulation."[43] On this theory, the Court's decision to defer was
an act of obeisance to congressional dictate. In the years following
Chevron, courts and commentators discussed the deference rule in
both these ways,[44] while occasionally also arguing that *Chevron*
arose from separation-of-powers principles, which favor agencies
over courts in making the policy decisions inherent in the resolution of statutory ambiguity.[45]

In recent Supreme Court decisions, the statutory theory of
Chevron has become dominant, largely (if, after *Mead*, ironically)
at the hands of Justice Scalia. In an early law review article on
the subject, Justice Scalia dismissed the institutional competence
argument, arguing that it provided "a good practical reason for
accepting the agency's views, but hardly a valid theoretical justification for doing so."[46] That theory, Justice Scalia wrote, could

---

[42] 467 US at 865–66.

[43] Id at 865, 845.

[44] For discussion of these competing rationales and their treatment in the courts, see
Merrill and Hickman, 89 Georgetown L J at 867–72 (cited in note 3); John F. Duffy,
Administrative Common Law in Judicial Review, 77 Tex L Rev 113, 203–07 (1998).

[45] For variants of this argument, which has received more attention from scholars than
courts, see Douglas W. Kmiec, *Judicial Deference to Executive Agencies and the Decline of the
Nondelegation Doctrine*, 2 Admin L J 269, 278, 287–90 (1988); Kenneth W. Starr, *Judicial
Review in the Post-Chevron Era*, 3 Yale J Reg 283, 308 (1986); Richard J. Pierce, Jr., *The
Role of Constitutional and Political Theory in Administrative Law*, 64 Tex L Rev 469, 520–24
(1985).

[46] Antonin Scalia, *Judicial Deference to Administrative Interpretations of Law*, 1989 Duke L
J 511, 514.

come only from congressional command: "The extent to which courts should defer to agency interpretations of law is ultimately a function of Congress's intent on the subject."[47] The *Chevron* deference regime proceeded from this insight along with a preference for broad rules over case-by-case determinations: *Chevron* represented a presumption that when Congress gave an agency the power to implement a statute, Congress also gave the agency broad interpretive authority. In his article, Justice Scalia spoke in realist terms about this justification, stating that the relevant congressional intent was in fact "fictional."[48] In his opinions, however, this concession dropped out of the description. "We accord deference to agencies under *Chevron*," Justice Scalia wrote, "because of a presumption that Congress when it left ambiguity in a statute meant for implementation by an agency, understood that the ambiguity would be resolved, first and foremost, by the agency, and desired the agency (rather than the courts) to possess whatever degree of discretion the ambiguity allows."[49] Other Justices acceded to this claim as the primary basis for *Chevron* deference.[50]

Mead goes a step further, hoisting Justice Scalia on the petard of his own "valid theoretical justification."[51] Take a theory emphasizing *Chevron*'s legislative origins, place that theory in the hands of Justices not overly concerned with the "rulelike" nature of law, and the result is a search for actual legislative intent in each instance. Indeed, the *Mead* Court criticized Justice Scalia's dissent primarily on the ground that his "efforts to simplify" by using a presumption would produce results at odds with Congress's wishes.[52] For the Court, the scope of *Chevron* deference should emerge from a particularistic consideration of Congress's views on this issue.

---

[47] Id at 516 (quoting *Process Gas Consumers Group v Department of Agriculture*, 694 F2d 778, 791 (DC Cir 1982) (en banc)). Justice Scalia also rejected the constitutional rationale, arguing that separation-of-powers principles permitted courts to engage in the kind of policymaking incident to statutory interpretation. See id at 515–16.

[48] Id at 517.

[49] *Smiley v Citibank (SD), NA*, 517 US 735, 740–41 (1996).

[50] See Merrill and Hickman, 89 Georgetown L J at 863 (cited in note 3) ("The Court, in recent descriptions of the *Chevron* doctrine, has rather consistently opted for the congressional intent theory.").

[51] Scalia, 1989 Duke L J at 514 (cited in note 46).

[52] 121 S Ct at 2177.

The *Mead* Court's emphasis on actual legislative intent serves one useful, if limited function: it underlines that Congress has ultimate authority over whether and when *Chevron* deference should operate. Scholars occasionally have raised doubts about this proposition, relying on constitutional claims of directly opposing character. If *Chevron* arises from the Constitution because courts must refrain from "policymaking,"[53] or if, conversely, *Chevron* violates the Constitution because courts must possess dispositive power over "legal interpretation" (the authority "to say what the law is"[54]), then Congress could have nothing to say about *Chevron* deference one way or the other. But both these arguments are fallacious. The functions of policymaking and legal interpretation in the context of statutory ambiguity (the only context in which *Chevron* operates) are so intertwined as to prevent any strict constitutional assignment of the one to agencies and the other to courts. And even to the extent that the Constitution dictates some separation of these functions, once Congress has designated either the courts or an agency to resolve statutory ambiguity, other constitutional interpreters should assume, if only by virtue of the doctrine of constitutional avoidance,[55] that the resulting scheme involves the exercise of appropriate authority.[56] In focusing on legislative intent, *Mead* thus clears away some constitutional underbrush associated with the *Chevron* doctrine and places Congress in its rightful position of control.

But to say that Congress has this authority is not to say that Congress uses it, and by suggesting the latter as well as the former,

---

[53] For arguments along this line, see sources cited in note 45.

[54] *Marbury v Madison*, 5 US (1 Cranch) 137, 177 (1803). For an argument to this general effect, see Cynthia R. Farina, *Statutory Interpretation and the Balance of Power in the Administrative State*, 89 Colum L Rev 452, 476 (1989) ("It is surely a far more remarkable step than *Chevron* acknowledged to number among Congress's constitutional prerogatives the power to compel courts to accept and enforce another entity's view of legal meaning whenever the law is ambiguous.").

[55] See *Edward J. DeBartolo Corp v Florida Gulf Coast Building & Construction Trades Council*, 485 US 568, 575 (1988) ("[W]here an otherwise acceptable construction of a statute would raise serious constitutional problems, the Court will construe the statute to avoid such problems unless such construction is plainly contrary to the intent of Congress."); *Ashwander v TVA*, 297 US 288, 348 (1936) (Brandeis concurring).

[56] Consider *Bowsher v Synar*, 478 US 714, 749 (Stevens concurring) ("[A]s our cases demonstrate, a particular function, like a chameleon, will often take on the aspect of the office to which it is assigned. For this reason, '[w]hen any Branch acts, it is presumptively exercising the power the Constitution has delegated to it.'") (quoting *INS v Chadha*, 462 US 919, 951 (1983)).

the *Mead* Court obscured the nature of the judicial task involved in defining *Chevron*'s domain. Judges can put into effect congressional decisions about the scope of the *Chevron* doctrine only if Congress, as an initial matter, makes these decisions. If Congress does not, then the courts, whatever their rhetoric, must resort to other sources and rely on other methods to shape the law in this area. And in fact, Congress usually does not make decisions about *Chevron* review, thus forcing courts to consider how best to fill the vacuum.

Federal statutes almost never speak directly to the standard of review of an agency's interpretations. Congress surely believes that the allocation of interpretive authority as between agencies and courts rests within its constitutional prerogatives. And since *Chevron*, both judges and commentators essentially have invited Congress to exercise this prerogative.[57] Yet only a few times has Congress made clear a desire to flip the *Chevron* rule of deference so as to give to courts, rather than agencies, primary interpretive authority.[58] To be sure, Congress's usual silence on this matter may express agreement with a broad rule of deference to agency interpretations. But this explanation seems improbable given (1) Congress's similar passivity on this issue prior to *Chevron*, and (2) Congress's certain appreciation of variety in both administrative statutes and administrative decision-making processes. It is far more likely that Congress, unless confronting a serious problem in the exercise of some interpretive authority, simply fails to think about this allocation of power between judges and agencies.

Some Justices and scholars may protest that this conclusion comes too soon. A burgeoning theory in *Chevron* scholarship holds that Congress does speak to the issue of interpretive authority, although in a kind of code. This argument posits that when Congress grants an agency the power to implement a statute in a way that has binding legal effect on parties, whether by issuing rules

---

[57] See, e.g., Scalia, 1989 Duke L J at 517 (cited in note 46) (describing *Chevron* as "a background rule of law against which Congress can legislate"); Thomas W. Merrill, *Judicial Deference to Executive Precedent*, 101 Yale L J 969, 978 (1992) (referring to *Chevron* as a "default rule," which Congress can change).

[58] See, e.g., Gramm-Leach-Bliley Act, Pub L No 106–102, 113 Stat 1409 (1999), codified at 15 USC § 6714(e) (2000) (providing that in a dispute between federal and state insurance regulators over the preemptive effect of a federal statute, the court shall decide the issue "without unequal deference").

or by conducting adjudications, Congress necessarily grants the agency the power to resolve ambiguities in the statute.[59] Stated otherwise, a delegation to an agency to take action having the "force of law" as to parties logically entails a command that any interpretations made in the course of that action (but only those interpretations) should have the "force of law" as to judges.[60] This argument has appeared in several recent Supreme Court decisions. In *Christensen*, for example, the Court distinguished agency actions having the "force of law" from those lacking this quality and stated that *Chevron* deference should extend only to the former.[61] And the argument played a significant, if confusing, role in *Mead*. Although an unadorned version of the theory cannot explain the result in *Mead*, given that the Customs ruling had binding legal effect on the party to whom issued, the Court's initial statement of its holding declared that an agency interpretation "qualifies for *Chevron* deference when it appears that Congress delegated authority to the agency generally to make rules [through rulemaking or adjudicative proceedings] carrying the force of law, and . . . the agency interpretation claiming deference was promulgated in the exercise of that authority."[62]

---

[59] See Merrill and Hickman, 89 Georgetown L J at 873–89 (cited in note 3); Duffy, 77 Tex L Rev at 199–203 (cited in note 44); Anthony, 7 Yale J Reg at 36–40 (cited in note 9).

[60] Merrill and Hickman, 89 Georgetown L J at 837 (cited in note 3); Anthony, 7 Yale J Reg at 3 (cited in note 9).

[61] See text accompanying note 20; see also *EEOC v Arabian American Oil Co.*, 499 US 244, 257 (1991) (declining to give deference to the EEOC's interpretation of Title VII because that statute does not give the EEOC rulemaking authority); *Martin v Occupational Safety and Health Review Commission*, 499 US 144, 157 (stating in dicta that the interpretive rules of an agency lacking rulemaking power are not entitled to "the same deference as norms that derive from the exercise of . . . delegated lawmaking powers").

[62] 121 S Ct at 2171; see id at 2172 (also making reference to the "force of law"). The oddity of this statement, given that the ruling letter had the force of law as to the importer in question, is explicable in either of two ways. First, the Court may have used the phrase "force of law" here to refer only to an agency action that would have controlling effect on a reviewing court, as distinct from an action that would have binding legal effect on a party. But if that is the case, the "force of law" concept is doing no work at all: the Court might just as well have said that an agency interpretation "qualifies for *Chevron* deference when it appears that Congress delegated authority to the agency generally to make rules qualifying for *Chevron* deference," with the question still left open how to determine whether such a delegation has taken place. Second, the Court may have believed it necessary for the agency action in question to have binding legal effect not only on the single importer but on all others in the same position. See id at 2174 (noting that "a letter's binding character as a ruling stops short of third parties"); text accompanying note 39. The Court's position then would comport with Merrill and Hickman's view that to have the "force of law," for purposes of *Chevron*, an agency action must legally bind not only the parties involved,

But this equation—of delegations to make binding substantive law through rulemakings or adjudications with delegations to make controlling interpretations of statutory terms—has little to support it. Contrary to the theory, Congress might wish for an agency, in implementing a statute, to issue binding rules and orders subject to an understanding that the courts, in the event of a legal challenge, will review fully any interpretations of ambiguous terms made in the course of these actions. The power to make binding substantive law, after all, involves much more than the power to make controlling interpretations of ambiguous statutory terms; to deny the agency the latter is in no way to make meaningless the grant of the former. Indeed, the point here is even stronger. Prior to *Chevron* (when the most important regulatory statutes were enacted), Congress must have contemplated (to the extent it thought about the issue) some division of substantive lawmaking authority from interpretive authority; the APA's provision on judicial review permits this division,[63] and courts at the time put it into practice in countless administrative law decisions.[64]

---

but also "other agency personnel," in the sense that they will treat the action as controlling in future cases, involving other parties, that raise the same issue. See Merrill and Hickman, 89 Georgetown L J at 908 (cited in note 3). But this reasoning ill comports with ordinary notions of when a decision has force of law—in Merrill and Hickman's own words, "when, of its own force and effect, it commands certain behavior and subjects parties to penalties or sanctions if they violate this command." Id at 881. The reasoning in fact substitutes another criterion—generality—for the supposed criterion of force of law in the effort to determine congressional intent as to deference. We consider later in this part, see text accompanying notes 68–70, the relationship of generality, as well as of procedural formality, to understandings of this congressional intent.

[63] Section 706 of the APA provides that "[t]o the extent necessary to decision and when presented, the reviewing court shall decide all relevant questions of law [and] interpret constitutional and statutory provisions." 5 USC § 706. Some scholars have suggested that this provision in fact *requires* independent judicial review of interpretive judgments, thus precluding *Chevron* deference. See, e.g., Cass R. Sunstein, *Law and Administration After Chevron*, 90 Colum L Rev 2071, 2080–81, 2086 (1990); Farina, 89 Colum L Rev at 472–73 (cited in note 54). The issue never has troubled the Court unduly, nor do we think it should. As Sunstein himself concedes, the interpretive decisions that the court shall render under Section 706 may incorporate some measure of judicial deference; the courts, in other words, can decide the relevant legal question by holding that the agency is entitled to deference in some sphere and then policing its limits. See 90 Colum L Rev at 2081 n 46. The APA thus may well leave the level of deference to the courts, presumably to be decided according to common law methods, in the event that an organic statute says nothing about the matter. See John F. Manning, *Constitutional Structure and Judicial Deference to Agency Interpretations of Agency Rules*, 96 Colum L Rev 612, 635 (1996) (noting that the APA's provisions on judicial review contain "faint expressions of legislative purpose" and "came from a tradition that used flexible common law methods to review administrative action").

[64] Pre-*Chevron* law on judicial review was highly complex and variegated, but rarely did courts provide the equivalent of *Chevron* deference to agency interpretations, even when these interpretations arose in the course of rulemakings or adjudications having binding

And just as Congress might desire this division, Congress might desire the converse: to give interpretive authority to an agency separate and apart from the power to issue rules or orders with independent legal effect on parties. Again, the point follows from an understanding that the connection between the power to resolve statutory ambiguity and the power to issue binding rulings under that statute is situational rather than logical, contingent rather than necessary. Consider, for example, the National Labor Relations Board (NLRB), whose adjudicative orders become legally binding only when brought to and ratified by a court. Perhaps this statutory structure signifies, as some scholars have suggested, that Congress so distrusted the NLRB's adjudications as to preclude legal interpretations made there from receiving judicial deference;[65] but perhaps this structure signifies only that Congress wanted some other aspect of the agency's decision making—its fact-finding, for example—subject to prompt judicial review, thus leaving the NLRB, consistent with both pre- and post-*Chevron* decisions,[66] with primary interpretive authority when acting in its adjudicative, no less than in its legally binding rulemaking, capacity.[67]

Nor does it aid in the effort to determine congressional intent respecting *Chevron* deference to ask, as the *Mead* Court did, whether the agency action possesses the attributes of proceduralism and generality. These two aspects of agency action, of course, overlap but do not coincide with "force of law" effect (as well as with each other); as the Court discovered, these factors may point in opposing directions.[68] But more significant, neither

---

effect. For a cogent account of this doctrine, see Merrill, 101 Yale L J at 972–75 (cited in note 57).

[65] See Merrill and Hickman, 89 Georgetown L J at 892 (cited in note 3).

[66] See, e.g., *NLRB v Curtin Matheson Scientific, Inc.*, 494 US 775, 786–87 (1990); *Beth Israel Hospital v NLRB*, 437 US 483, 499 (1978); *NLRB v Hearst Publications*, 322 US 111, 131 (1944).

[67] We do not mean to claim here that the nature of a substantive delegation never implies a congressional intent as to *Chevron* deference. To take an extreme example that helps to make the point, a delegation to the Department of Labor to implement a workplace safety statute naturally will prevent the Department of Health and Human Services from gaining deference for its interpretations of that statute. For similar reasons, a very limited delegation of substantive authority to an agency may suggest a legislative decision as to the impropriety of granting *Chevron* deference. This is to say no more than what every Justice since *Chevron* has accepted: that an agency must "administer" a statute to obtain *Chevron*'s benefits. See, e.g., *Smiley*, 517 US at 739; *Chevron*, 467 US at 865.

[68] See text accompanying note 62 (noting that the Customs decision in *Mead* had binding legal effect, although lacking generality and procedural formality).

procedural formality nor generality has any apparent relevance to the question of actual (as opposed to fictive) legislative intent. It may be thought good regulatory policy to promote these traits by rewarding them with *Chevron* deference—though in the next part of this article, we contest this notion. But with all due respect to Congress, the ascription of the "best" regulatory policy to that institution's handiwork is not a reliable, and therefore not a usual, method for reflecting legislative desires. And nothing in the structure of administrative statutes suggests such a policy. As we will discuss,[69] Congress sometimes has authorized agencies to act without procedural formality and often has enabled them to choose between general and particular decision-making modes. In the areas in which such legal choice exists, Congress never has suggested a differential scheme of judicial review (or indeed any other set of differential incentives). To the contrary, the provision on review in the APA, to take the most notable example, cuts across all these distinctions, notwithstanding that they form the very core of the statute.[70]

Our general point regarding the unreliability of attempting to define *Chevron* doctrine through a search for congressional intent takes a strange twist in *Mead* itself, though in the end emerging all the stronger. The statute at issue in the case contains unusual indicia of legislative intent regarding judicial review of agency decisions, thus suggesting that we have condemned the Court's analysis too quickly. The problem for the Court is that the statute appears to command the precise reverse of the Court's holding. According to the statute, a tariff classification decision "is presumed to be correct" in a legal action.[71] The most natural understanding of this provision, as applied to a case like *Mead*, is that it directs a court to defer to a Customs Service determination that a particular statutory term encompasses a particular imported good, unless in the words of *Chevron* that determination is "unreasonable."[72] The Court conceivably could have shown that this interpretation would overread the provision—that, taken in context, the provision does no more than place the burden of proof on the

---

[69] See text accompanying notes 102–04.

[70] See 5 USC § 706.

[71] 28 USC § 2639.

[72] 467 US at 845.

importer. The Court, however, essayed no such argument, relegating the statute's "presumption of correctness" language to a footnote and briefly noting two provisions—one enabling the reviewing court to consider new grounds for decision and the other requiring the court to develop a record—which not two years earlier the Court had held in no way to preclude *Chevron* deference.[73] The failure of the Court to engage all this language in any sustained or coherent way bodes ill for a method of defining *Chevron*'s domain that focuses on statutory interpretation.[74]

But if the Court usually cannot give content to the *Chevron* doctrine in this way—most importantly, if perhaps not in *Mead*, because Congress usually does not give the Court the material to do so—then how is the Court to proceed? The Court inevitably must create a set of background rules against which Congress can (but should not be expected to) operate—otherwise put, must establish a constructive substitute for an actual statement of legislative desire. These default rules potentially could reflect any of three considerations. First, the Court could appeal to constitutional principles.[75] Second, the Court could resort to notions of legislative self-interest. Here the Court would select the set of rules most likely to give Congress the greatest influence, on the theory that Congress, were it to consider the matter, usually would prefer these rules to any other.[76] And third, the Court could refer to its own sense of sound administrative policy. We believe that the third option is alone capable of sustaining a forthright and productive discussion of the appropriate allocation of interpretive authority.

---

[73] See *United States v Haggar Apparel Co.*, 526 US 380, 391 (1999) (discussing the relevance of 28 USC §§ 2638 and 2640(a) to the *Chevron* inquiry).

[74] The Court's cavalier attitude toward the relevant statutory language also suggests a certain disingenuousness in describing the *Chevron* doctrine as a product of legislative decision. See text accompanying notes 85–87.

[75] See, e.g., Michael Herz, *Deference Running Riot: Separating Interpretation and Lawmaking Under Chevron*, 6 Admin L J 187, 189–90, 202–03 (1992) (invoking constitutionally based understandings of institutional roles as a reason for the Court to distinguish in deference analysis between legislative rules and interpretive rules); Randolph J. May, *Tug of Democracy: Justices Pull for America's Separation of Powers*, Legal Times 51 (July 9, 2001) (applauding *Mead* on the ground that its limitation of *Chevron* comports with constitutional principles relating to government structure).

[76] Professor Einer Elhauge offers a complex version of this position in *Preference-Estimating Statutory Default Rules* (forthcoming). He argues that *Chevron* doctrine (including *Mead*) both should and does allocate authority between courts and agencies in the way best designed to ensure that the resolution of statutory ambiguity will match "current governmental preferences," by which he means policies that Congress would enact into law.

An appeal to constitutional principles cannot give content to the *Chevron* doctrine because the only clear principle does nothing more than restate the dilemma. We have argued earlier, in accord with the Court's apparent view, that separation-of-powers law usually neither prohibits nor requires *Chevron* deference.[77] Indeed, this law fails to suggest even a tiebreaking principle in the event of congressional silence, given the equally plausible (or implausible) constitutional claims made on both sides of the deference question. All the constitutional structure suggests is that Congress has control over the allocation of authority to resolve statutory ambiguity. But if that is so, the appeal to constitutional norms is a strategy of infinite regress, as the failure of Congress to exercise its power forces the Court to look to constitutional principles, which then merely point back to Congress.

The resort to an implicit legislative intent reflecting legislative self-interest similarly cannot solve the problem. As an initial matter, the assumption that Congress always (or even usually) wants the administrative structure that increases its own institutional power finds little support in either practice or theory.[78] Consider the many legislative decisions inconsistent with this assumption: to delegate broadly to agencies in the first instance, to lodge most of this power with executive rather than with independent agencies, and to accede to ever greater assertions of presidential control over the entire sphere of administrative activity. As these decisions reflect, Congress protects its own institutional interests sporadically at best when it allocates governmental authority. And this frequent "failure" makes perfect sense given that Congress is far less a unitary institution than a congeries of members with crosscutting partisan, ideological, geographical, and constituency interests. In highly fact-dependent ways, a majority coalition of these interests often will conflict with and subordinate considerations of institutional prerogative.

And even if this were not the case, the Court would confront an impossible task in translating a goal of legislative aggrandizement into a scheme for judicial review of interpretative decisions.

---

[77] See text accompanying notes 53–56.

[78] See Elena Kagan, *Presidential Administration*, 114 Harv L Rev 2245, 2314–15, 2330 (2001); Terry M. Moe and William G. Howell, *The Presidential Power of Unilateral Action*, 15 J L Econ & Org 132, 143–48 (1999).

Congressional self-interest may comport with a deference rule because Congress more easily can control agencies than courts through oversight proceedings and budgetary and other legislation.[79] But congressional self-interest just as easily may dictate the opposite result because agencies, especially but not exclusively those in the executive branch, are subject to the authority of the President, Congress's principal competitor for governmental power.[80] Once again, then, Congress's view on deference (were Congress to consider the matter) likely would hinge on numerous case-specific and agency-specific variables, not readily susceptible to judicial understanding or analysis.

The only workable approach is the approach that *Chevron* took in the beginning: to fill in legislative silence about judicial review by making policy judgments based on institutional attributes, with Congress then free to overrule these conclusions.[81] Recall that in *Chevron* the Court nodded to the idea of a congressional delegation, but stressed more heavily the virtues of placing interpretive decisions in the hands of accountable and knowledgeable administrators. This method is endemic in administrative law when Congress has left its intentions unclear. Consider, for example, *Vermont*

---

[79] See Mark Seidenfeld, *Syncopated Chevron: Emphasizing Reasoned Decisionmaking in Reviewing Agency Interpretations of Statutes*, 73 Tex L Rev 83, 136 (1994) (arguing that, as compared with stringent judicial review, *Chevron* "gives Congress greater control over the interpretive process").

[80] See Herz, 6 Admin L J at 187 (cited in note 75) (stating that the "rivalry between the legislative and executive branches" should make Congress "prefer relatively stringent judicial review of agency interpretations"). That an agency is formally "independent," in the sense that the President cannot remove its head at will, may but need not affect the analysis; Presidents often have a good deal of actual control over independent agencies—sometimes more than they have over executive branch agencies—by virtue of their appointments and other powers.

Judge Posner and Professor Landes make a different argument to the same ultimate effect in claiming that an enacting Congress may desire strict judicial review "in order to assure that the agency, in its eagerness to serve the current legislature, will not stray too far from the terms of the legislative 'deal'" that the agency is charged with implementing. See William M. Landes and Richard A. Posner, *The Independent Judiciary in an Interest-Group Perspective*, 18 J L & Econ 875, 888 (1975).

[81] Cass Sunstein has described the Court's task in much this way. In Sunstein's words:

[I]f Congress has not made a clear decision one way or the other [on the question of deference], the choice among the alternatives will call for an assessment of which strategy is the most sensible one to attribute to Congress under the circumstances. This assessment is not a mechanical exercise of uncovering an actual legislative decision. It calls for a frankly value-laden judgment about comparative competence.

Sunstein, 90 Colum L Rev at 2086 (cited in note 63).

Yankee Nuclear Power Corp v NRDC[82] (which held that agencies, but not courts, may add to the APA's procedural requirements) and *SEC v Chenery Corp*[83] (which held that agencies may choose to proceed by adjudication rather than rulemaking free from judicial constraint). These decisions at least implicitly concede the indeterminacy of statutory language and focus on the policy consequences of placing certain kinds of decisions in the hands of administrative or judicial actors. Regardless whether the Court attempts to frame these efforts to promote better lawmaking as "interpretive," they are in fact judicial constructions. But that is not to say they should arouse suspicion. When Congress has not spoken to the allocation of authority between courts and agencies, the choice inevitably falls to courts, and courts can do no better than assess how and when different institutions promote accountable and considered administrative governance.[84]

Indeed, this approach lies beneath *Mead*'s surface rhetoric about congressional intent, even though the Court cannot bring itself to put the matter plainly.[85] When the Court says that "[i]t is fair to assume generally" that Congress intends for the courts to give *Chevron* deference to agency actions emerging from formal procedures because these procedures "foster . . . deliberation,"[86] the

---

[82] 435 US 519 (1978).

[83] 332 US 194 (1947) (*Chenery II*).

[84] The APA's provision on judicial review, discussed in note 63, fairly invites, though does not require, such policy-based analysis. The very open-endedness of this provision suggests that, in the absence of an organic statute to the contrary, courts should set the level of deference in accordance with common law methods, which (as the examples in the text suggest) may include consideration of comparative institutional attributes and their relation to interpretation. Consider Manning, 96 Colum L Rev at 635 (cited in note 63) (noting that courts since the APA have "draw[n] upon their own sensibilities" about good government in giving content to that statute's judicial review provision).

[85] Justice Breyer, in extrajudicial commentary, years ago made the identical point about judicial decisions defining the scope of review of agency interpretations:

> For the most part courts have used "legislative intent to delegate the law-interpreting function" as a kind of legal fiction. They have looked to practical features of the particular circumstance to decide whether it "makes sense," in terms of the need for fair and efficient administration of that statute in light of its substantive purpose, to imply a congressional intent that courts defer to the agency's interpretation.

Stephen Breyer, *Judicial Review of Questions of Law and Policy*, 38 Admin L Rev 363, 370 (1986); see text accompanying note 48 (noting Justice Scalia's recognition that the delegation rationale for *Chevron* is fictional).

[86] 121 S Ct at 2172.

Court is making its own determination of when agencies should be "assume[d] generally" to make better interpretive decisions than can courts. And when the Court, again ostensibly as a matter of statutory interpretation, asks whether the agency interpretation "bespeak[s] . . . legislative type of activity,"[87] binding more than the parties in a single proceeding, the Court is following the same course. Perhaps the Court attributes its policy judgments to Congress to emphasize that Congress can reverse the decision. Perhaps the Court does so to emphasize the "judicial" nature of what it is doing. Perhaps, and least generously understood, the Court does so to cloak judicial aggrandizement; it may be no coincidence that when ceding power in *Chevron*, the Court spoke the language of policy, whereas when reclaiming power in *Mead*, the Court abandoned this language. The explanation, in the end, is of no great importance. What matters is that the Court's rhetoric not becloud the essential nature of its judgment, and that this judgment not escape evaluation on its actual, policy-based terms. We accordingly turn to that analysis.

III. PROCEDURALISM AND GENERALITY

Because the *Mead* Court's discussion of policy issues is veiled, it is susceptible of two readings. On one interpretation, which Justice Scalia adopts, *Mead* suggests an unstructured, case-by-case inquiry into whether deference to an agency interpretation "makes best sense." If courts take this approach, it will prove harmful, given the need for clarity and predictability in *Chevron* doctrine. But this understanding of *Mead* misses what is most significant about the decision. A truer interpretation would recognize in *Mead* two dominant (though not congruent) dichotomies, widely used in administrative law—the first, and most notable, between procedural formality and informality, and the second between general and particular action. *Mead* rewards more formal and general forms of decision making—particularly, notice-and-comment rulemaking—in the implicit hope that these forms will correspond with accountability and discipline in administrative decision making. In encouraging agencies to adopt these forms, *Mead* threatens

---

[87] Id at 2174.

to impose substantial costs—to diminish needed flexibility in, and enhance existing pathologies of, the administrative system. And as we will discuss in the remainder of this article, in linking deference to these forms, *Mead* fails to serve as well as it could the very values that underlie it.

Mead naturally lends itself to interpretation as a classic ad hoc balancing decision, and so a partial reversion to the doctrine of judicial review that prevailed before *Chevron*. The Court adverted to the "multifarious" nature of administrative action and declared as its aim "to tailor deference to variety."[88] The Court refused to articulate any simple test, on the ground that none could capture the range of considerations relevant to the question of deference.[89] The opinion thus provides more than enough material for (and, indeed, seems to revel in) Justice Scalia's critique: "The Court has largely replaced *Chevron* . . . with that test most beloved by a court unwilling to be held to rules (and most feared by litigants who want to know what to expect): th' ol' 'totality of the circumstances' test."[90] This approach would bear more than a passing resemblance to the law that *Chevron* replaced. Although *Mead* does not revive the distinction between pure questions of law and mixed questions of law and fact that in part determined the level of deference prior to *Chevron*,[91] the "it all depends" attitude that Justice Scalia saw as pervading *Mead* featured notably in pre-*Chevron* doctrine, which also took into account the scope and nature of the delegation,[92] the importance and complexity of the interpretive question,[93] the degree of the agency's expertise,[94] and the thoroughness and history of the agency's interpretation.[95]

---

[88] Id at 2176. Although Justice Souter wrote *Mead*, the part of the opinion most fully expounding this approach echoes Justice Breyer's scholarly writing. See Breyer, 38 Admin L Rev at 377 (cited in note 85) (arguing that *Chevron* "cannot reasonably apply to all questions of statutory interpretation . . . [because] the way in which [these] questions . . . arise are too many and too complex to rely upon a single simple rule to provide an answer").

[89] See, e.g., 121 S Ct at 2173 ("That said, and as significant as notice-and-comment is in pointing to *Chevron* authority, the want of that procedure here does not decide the case, for we have sometimes found reasons for *Chevron* deference even when no such administrative formality was required and none was afforded.").

[90] Id at 2178 (Scalia dissenting).

[91] See, e.g., *Hearst Publications*, 322 US at 130.

[92] See, e.g., *Skidmore*, 323 US at 137; *Pittston Stevedoring Corp. v Dellaventura*, 544 F2d 35, 49–50 (2d Cir 1976) (Friendly, J).

[93] See, e.g, *Packard Motor Car Co. v NLRB*, 330 US 485, 491–93 (1947).

[94] See, e.g., *Pittston*, 544 F2d at 50.

[95] See, e.g., *Packard*, 330 US at 492; *Skidmore*, 323 US at 140.

Were this understanding of *Mead* accurate, we would join Justice Scalia in lamenting the absence of clarity and predictability in the new doctrine. The problem with an absence of structure in this sphere is not what Justice Scalia has stressed in the past—that Congress must have a stable background rule against which to legislate.[96] Given the scarce interest Congress has demonstrated in the judicial review of agency interpretations,[97] such solicitude is wasted. The real problem concerns "litigants," as Justice Scalia noted in *Mead*—and, more particularly, the administrative agencies. Unclear law regarding judicial review no doubt would lead potential challengers of administrative action to make more errors in their selection of cases, but many of these parties would prefer unpredictability to near-automatic deference. For agencies, the shift in doctrine would count as no such mixed blessing. Agencies factor the scope of judicial review into their decisions, and uncertainty on this score would result in both excess caution and wasted effort.[98] And this problem is not one for agencies alone, but for the public as well. As the uncertainties associated with "hard look" review of an agency's decision-making processes have shown,[99] these consequences can exact a considerable toll on an agency's ability to perform coherently and effectively its regulatory mission.

But properly read, *Mead* imposes far more structure on the deference inquiry than this critique implies: *Mead* in fact counsels an administrative law variant of "categorical balancing." As noted earlier, the Court establishes safe harbors, defined by the kind of procedure an agency uses, within which interpretations will receive *Chevron* deference; whenever an agency engages in either notice-and-comment rulemaking or formal adjudication, the agency will

---

[96] See Scalia, 1989 Duke L J at 517 (cited in note 46) (praising *Chevron* on the ground that "Congress now knows that the ambiguities it creates . . . will be resolved, within the bounds of permissible interpretation, not by the courts but by a particular agency, whose policy biases will ordinarily be known").

[97] See text accompanying notes 57–58.

[98] Nor does the availability of *Skidmore* deference assist on this score. Even if *Skidmore* deference amounts to something more than a court saying "we will defer to the agency if we believe the agency is right," the application of *Skidmore* deference depends so much on context and circumstance—the kind of agency, the kind of issue, the kind of decision—as to preclude an agency from relying on it.

[99] See Jerry L. Mashaw and David L. Harfst, *Regulation and Legal Culture: The Case of Motor Vehicle Safety*, 4 Yale J Reg 257, 315–16 (1987) (discussing the adverse consequences to traffic safety regulation arising from the uncertainties involved in hard look review).

know that its reasonable resolution of statutory ambiguity will govern.[100] Although leaving some uncertainty outside these categories, the Court also indicates that in this sphere an absence of generality will deprive an agency of any real possibility of interpretive control.[101] Questions of course remain—the resulting structure lacks the rigorously rulelike nature of *Chevron*—but no agency counsel will find herself at a loss when asked to render advice on the consequences, for purposes of judicial review, of taking administrative action in a particular form. To a greater extent than Justice Scalia acknowledged in *Mead*, his repeated admonitions about the importance of predictability in *Chevron* doctrine have entered the consciousness of the Court.

The critical question in evaluating *Mead* thus has to do with the consequences of selecting the categories noted above as a way to give structure to *Chevron* doctrine. Administrative statutes, of course, often allow agencies to take action without formal procedures. The APA, which controls agency processes in the absence of more specific statutory provisions, exempts rulemaking from notice and comment when the rule concerns certain subject matters or takes certain forms or, more generally, when the agency has good cause to dispense with this procedural requirement;[102] similarly, the APA permits deviation from formality in adjudication except when the applicable organic statute requires a hearing and perhaps also an "on the record" determination.[103] And administrative law, ever since *Chenery*, has left to agencies, again in the absence of a statute addressing the matter, the decision whether to proceed by general rulemaking or by more particular adjudicative processes.[104] *Mead* exerts pressure on an agency selecting among

---

[100] See text accompanying note 38.

[101] See text accompanying notes 39–40. This is not to say that generality will ensure *Chevron* deference in the absence of formal procedures; the Court's slighting reference to interpretive rules—that they "enjoy no *Chevron* status as a class," 121 S Ct at 2174—makes clear that generality alone often will not suffice. The point here is only that *Mead*, in addition to favoring formality over informality in procedures, expresses a preference for general over particular decision-making forms.

[102] See 5 USC § 553(a), (b)(A), (b)(B).

[103] See id at § 554(a); compare *Seacoast Anti-Pollution League v Costle*, 572 F2d 872 (1st Cir 1978) (requiring formality when another statute requires a hearing) with *Chemical Waste Management, Inc. v EPA*, 873 F2d 1477 (DC Cir 1989) (requiring formality only when another statute requires an "on-the-record" hearing).

[104] 332 US at 201.

these legal options by means of denying the agency a valued benefit if it proceeds in one way rather than the other; the decision thus effectively narrows the scope of administrative discretion over (otherwise and previously) legitimate decision-making modes. We think this judicial channeling unfortunate.

Consider the matter of formal (including nominally informal, notice-and-comment) procedures. Two different arguments can support giving peculiarly deferential treatment to agency action that emerges from formal process. The first is essentially prophylactic in nature. Under this rationale, withholding *Chevron* deference from agency action that lacks a formal procedural pedigree ensures that agencies will provide such procedures when the law so requires. The second argument is straightforwardly preferential. On this reasoning, an agency should reap a benefit (deferential review) for acting through formal procedures because this kind of decision making better serves accountability and deliberative values. Whereas the first rationale intends merely to keep agencies within legal bounds, the second aims to influence the manner in which agencies exercise legal choice.

The prophylactic argument is insufficient to justify the decision. The problem to which the prophylaxis responds is of uncertain dimension; although courts sometimes invalidate administrative action for failing to comply with the APA's (or other statutes') required procedures,[105] no evidence points to systematic evasion of the law in this area.[106] More important, a prophylactic remedy does little except guarantee *over*enforcement. In any case in which a party can claim that an agency's interpretation of a statute should not receive *Chevron* deference, the party also can claim that the interpretation arose from an illegal (because not sufficiently formal) set of procedures. Nothing about this claim makes it peculiarly difficult for either a party to prove or a court to vindicate: the claim, for example, involves no exploration of motive or ma-

---

[105] See, e.g., *United States Telephone Association v FCC*, 28 F3d 1232 (DC Cir 1994); *Community Nutrition Institute v Young*, 818 F2d 943 (DC Cir 1987).

[106] We do not mean to deny here that agencies happily avail themselves of exceptions to formal procedural requirements, and indeed that they actively look for opportunities to do so. See Thomas O. McGarity, *Some Thoughts on "Deossifying" the Rulemaking Process*, 41 Duke L J 1385, 1393–96 (1992). But if the Court's aim in *Mead* is to deter these perfectly legal avoidance practices, then the rationale of the decision is, in the terminology we used above, more preferential than prophylactic. We address this reasoning in the next few paragraphs.

nipulation of hazy standards. Direct policing thus should safeguard adequately against violations of procedural law; the *Mead* rule works, in addition, only to promote thick proceduralism when it is *not* required.

This simple promotion of proceduralism disregards the considerations underlying the APA's exemptions from formal requirements. The "good cause" exception to notice-and-comment rulemaking, for example, arose from a recognition that the "public interest," in the language of the statute—more specifically, the interest in fulfilling the agency's statutory mission—might call for more expedition than rulemaking procedures permit and thus less participation than they require.[107] The same section's exception for interpretive rules similarly acknowledged the common need of agencies to interpret a statute without the delays involved in notice and comment, along with the strong interest of regulated parties in learning of these interpretations in advance of an enforcement action.[108] By depriving the rules issued under these exceptions of *Chevron* deference, *Mead* increases the likelihood that agencies will use notice and comment where it is inappropriate or that they will forgo any announcement of their interpretive views prior to embarking on enforcement. Much the same holds true in the sphere of adjudication, as *Mead* pushes toward greater proceduralism even when the matter at issue and the surrounding context suggest that informality better advances statutory objects. *Mead*, in short, upsets a balance reflected in the APA (as well as in other administrative procedure provisions) between procedural formality and procedural informality. The decision recognizes the values that counsel the former, but not the countervailing values that counsel the latter.

The dangers of this one-sidedness emerge starkly when account is taken of the current rulemaking context, which we and many

---

[107] 5 USC § 553(b)(B).

[108] See 5 USC § 553(b)(A) (using the term "interpretative" rules). As Judge Posner explained in *Hoctor v United States Department of Agriculture*, 82 F3d 165 (7th Cir 1996), "the agency would be stymied in its enforcement duties if every time it brought a case on a new theory it had to pause for a bout, possibly lasting several years, of notice and comment rulemaking"; given that this is so, and the true alternative to an interpretive rule is therefore often not a notice-and-comment rule but a simple enforcement action preceded by no rule at all, the agency does regulated interests "a favor if it announces the interpretation in advance of enforcement." Id at 167, 170.

others view as, even without *Mead*, too formal.[109] The story behind the so-called ossification of notice-and-comment rulemaking is by now familiar. To increase the influence of underrepresented interests, as well as to facilitate "hard look" judicial review, courts interpreted the APA, contrary to the design of its drafters, to compel agencies to conduct full-scale "paper hearings," involving extensive and often repeated notice of a proposed rule to affected groups, provision to them of the factual and analytical material supporting the rule, and detailed responses to any group's adverse comment or alternative proposal.[110] These procedures consume significant agency time and resources and thereby inhibit needed regulatory (or, for that matter, deregulatory) initiatives. *Mead* inevitably will channel additional agency action into this already overburdened administrative mechanism, as agencies sometimes adopt notice-and-comment procedures for no other reason than to gain *Chevron* deference.[111] By placing this new strain on notice and comment, *Mead* exacerbates a systemic problem impeding the development of optimal regulatory programs.

Even the ostensible virtues of notice-and-comment procedures are today open to serious question. As practiced in the shadow of the courts, notice and comment often functions as charade—or what one administrative expert has called "Kabuki theater."[112] The more courts have required agencies to give detailed notice of proposed regulatory action to interest groups, the more pressure agen-

---

[109] See, e.g., Jerry L. Mashaw and David L. Harfst, *The Struggle for Auto Safety* (Harvard, 1990); McGarity (cited in note 106); Richard J. Pierce, Jr., *Seven Ways to Deossify Agency Rulemaking*, 47 Admin L Rev 59 (1995); Paul R. Verkuil, *Rulemaking Ossification—a Modest Proposal*, 47 Admin L Rev 453 (1995).

[110] See, e.g., *Horsehead Resource Development Co., Inc. v Browner*, 16 F3d 1246, 1267–69 (DC Cir 1994); *Solite Corp. v EPA*, 952 F2d 473, 484 (DC Cir 1991); *Portland Cement Association v Ruckelshaus*, 486 F2d 375, 394 (DC Cir 1973).

[111] We do not mean to say that agencies always will adopt this course when they have a choice between formal and informal procedures; given the cost of formal procedures, they may do so only on the margin. Cf. text following note 165 (discussing the impact of our alternative deference regime on agency decision making). We mean only to say that some shift will occur and that it runs in the wrong direction.

[112] Professor E. Donald Elliott, a former General Counsel of the EPA, has written:

No administrator in Washington turns to full-scale notice-and-comment rulemaking when she is genuinely interested in obtaining input from interested parties. Notice-and-comment rulemaking is to public participation as Japanese Kabuki theater is to human passions—a highly stylized process for displaying in a formal way the essence of something which in real life takes place in other venues.

Re-Inventing Rulemaking, 41 Duke L J 1490, 1492 (1992).

cies have felt to complete the bulk of their work prior to the onset of the rulemaking process. And the more work agencies put into their proposals, the less flexibility they show during rulemaking to respond to the concerns of affected parties. At the same time, notice-and-comment rulemaking today tends to promote a conception of the regulatory process as a forum for competition among interest groups, rather than a means to further the public interest.[113] This is not a necessary result of participatory opportunities, which may provide agencies with valuable information and prevent the factional domination of policymaking that sometimes occurs in nonpublic settings. But as ritualized by the courts and as appropriated by interest groups more than ever divorced from their nominal constituents,[114] notice and comment has taken on the aspect of an end in itself, both symbolizing and amplifying all that the public finds most distasteful in government. These facets of the process make *Mead*'s preference for procedural formality all the more doubtful.

The case against *Mead*'s secondary distinction, between general and particular agency action, is shorter and simpler, in part because it mirrors the half-century-old reasoning of *Chenery II*. In suggesting that informal agency action should get *Chevron* deference only (though not necessarily) when that action has a "legislative" quality[115]—or, otherwise put, when the action formally binds parties outside the proceeding—*Mead* appears to assume that generally applicable agency action betokens more considered judgment than action limited in its operation. This notion, in turn, may derive from two lines of reasoning: that the process of reflecting on a general rule forces an agency to engage in more comprehensive analysis,[116] or that the decision to issue a general rule shows a

---

[113] For discussion of these disparate understandings of the administrative process, see Cass R. Sunstein, *Interest Groups in American Public Law*, 38 Stan L Rev 29, 31–35 (1985).

[114] See Theda Skocpol, *Advocates Without Members: The Recent Transformation of American Civic Life*, in Theda Skocpol and Morris P. Fiorina, eds, *Civic Engagement in American Democracy* 461, 498–504 (Brookings, 1999).

[115] 121 S Ct at 2174.

[116] See Richard J. Pierce, Jr., *Two Problems in Administrative Law: Political Polarity on the District of Columbia Circuit and Judicial Deterrence of Agency Rulemaking*, 1988 Duke L J 300, 308 ("Rulemaking yields higher-quality policy decisions than adjudication . . . because it encourages the agency to focus on the broad effects of its policy rather than the often idiosyncratic adjudicative facts of a specific dispute.").

firmer commitment by the agency to the decision.[117] But as the APA implied in providing for both adjudications and rulemaking, and as *Chenery II* stated, an agency decision to proceed case by case may reflect a deeply reasoned judgment that this method will promote the sensible development of law in an area, either because the issues are inherently "specialized and varying" or because they are too new to suggest an appropriate general resolution.[118] In using this method, the agency shows no more uncertainty about the choice it has made in the given case—which is the only choice to which a court would defer under *Chevron*—than a court does in deciding to cabin a holding. The denial of deference on this ground, rather than promoting more "serious" agency decisions, thus encourages a form of decision making that in some contexts will produce overbroad, premature, or otherwise ill-advised judgments.

The perverse incentives that *Mead* creates emerge from a consideration of that very case. To obtain *Chevron* deference under *Mead*, the Customs Service would have to forgo issuing a ruling letter as to a specific import in favor of announcing a general view, "bespeak[ing] . . . legislative . . . activity,"[119] on the meaning of the relevant tariff classification.[120] More, this general interpretive view would have to arise from full-scale notice-and-comment procedures. At the least, this mode of proceeding would entail substantial time and expense, no less adverse to the importer's than to the agency's interests. In addition, this method might produce worse results, insensitive to the varying ways and contexts in which the interpretive question might arise in the future. It is, indeed, hard to see who would support a move from the current fast, inex-

---

[117] Thomas Merrill and Kristin Hickman appear to take this view in support of their claim, essentially adopted in *Mead* as to informal (though not formal) adjudication, that an agency action must control more than the immediate case to qualify for *Chevron* deference. See note 62. On their reasoning, "[i]t would be extremely odd to give [adjudicative] decisions greater legal force in court than they have within the agency itself." See Merrill and Hickman, 89 Georgetown L J at 908 (cited in note 3).

[118] 332 US at 203.

[119] Id at 2174.

[120] Perhaps alternatively (if the Tariff Act permitted), the Customs Service could amend its procedural rules to provide for formal adjudications in tariff cases and thereby obtain *Chevron* deference. But because the agency probably would have to adopt this procedure across the board, this "option" seems a non-starter.

thority (subject only to *Skidmore*-style deference) if, alternatively, this named person passed her decision-making authority to lower-level officials. In short, decisions that statutory delegatees make their own would receive *Chevron* deference, and decisions they delegate would not.[125] We call this the *Chevron* nondelegation doctrine.[126]

In this part, we first flesh out the proposal and then turn to its normative basis. The initial task involves specifying in detail the institutional design characteristics that should trigger *Chevron* deference: the identity of the decision maker and the mode and timing of her decision. As we lay out the proposed prerequisites for *Chevron* deference, we will discuss rationales for the choices we make, but more to demonstrate the cogency and realism of our standard than to present affirmative reasons for its adoption. We then will offer the normative case, explaining how our standard would promote appropriately accountable and considered decision making—much as the congressional nondelegation doctrine is intended to do—by pushing responsibility toward (and away from) certain officials. This argument inevitably raises the question whether an administrative nondelegation doctrine would suffer from the same flaws that have made its legislative counterpart so weak. We accordingly close this part by showing that the different context and way in which our standard operates ensure that it will neither over-

---

[125] A more dramatic version of this approach would save *Chevron* deference for cases in which the President has assumed some responsibility for an administrative decision. One of us has suggested just such a revision of *Chevron* doctrine, implemented primarily through a distinction between executive branch and independent agencies. See Kagan, 114 Harv L Rev at 2372–80 (cited in note 78). The normative case for this change has distinct similarities to the one we lay out here, but this greater revision depends on contested understandings of the role of the President within administration that do not enter into the analysis offered in this article.

[126] Our approach has affinities to several constitutional decisions that suggest a link between the courts' posture toward a governmental decision and the identity of the institution responsible for that decision. See Laurence H. Tribe, *American Constitutional Law* 1677–87 (Foundation, 2d ed 1988) (discussing these decisions). In *Hampton v Mow Sun Wong*, 426 US 88 (1976), for example, the Court invalidated on equal protection grounds the Civil Service Commission's ban on the federal employment of aliens, but suggested that Congress or the President might impose such a ban consistently with the Constitution. See also *Regents of the University of California v Bakke*, 438 US 265 (1978) (Powell concurring) (rejecting an affirmative action policy in part because the state's Board of Regents, rather than the legislature, had adopted it). These decisions effectively prevent a legislature from delegating certain kinds of decisions to certain kinds of institutions. Our proposed nondelegation doctrine differs in looking within an institution and making doctrinal distinctions on the basis of the decisional structure that the institution has adopted prior to taking an action.

centralize the decision-making process nor depend for enforcement on a standardless judicial inquiry.

The key player in our approach is the statutory delegatee—the officer to whom the agency's organic statute has granted authority over a given administrative action. Almost all delegations of power to agencies designate such a person—perhaps the secretary of the department, perhaps the head of a departmental bureau—to take action within the scope of the delegation.[127] The critical question for *Chevron* deference should be whether this statutory delegatee took the action at issue, rather than subdelegating that action to other officials or employees within the agency.[128]

The question whether to defer to action taken under a subdelegation arises because most administrative statutes permit these subdelegations.[129] The result is that lower- (and sometimes simply low-) level officials carry out a wide range of agency action pursuant to internal delegations. In particular, the vast majority of agency action taken outside of notice-and-comment or good-cause rulemaking or formal adjudicative processes issue under the name of these officials.[130] So agencies exercise delegated power not in

---

[127] In the rare cases when a statute names only an office, our standard uses, as noted in the final part of this article, the head of that office as the relevant delegatee. See text accompanying notes 203–04.

[128] If a statute authorizes the named delegatee to delegate the decision making to another specifically named actor within the agency—as opposed to any other officer or employee—the second named actor likewise should count as a statutory delegatee.

[129] See, e.g., *Touby v United States*, 500 US 160, 169 (1991) (upholding the Attorney General's delegation of power to establish classifications of controlled substances pursuant to a statute authorizing her to delegate this power "to any officer or employee of the Department of Justice"); Cass, 66 BU L Rev at 3–7 (cited in note 122) (discussing statutory provisions that allow agency heads to deny review of adjudicative decisions). An occasional statute will make certain functions nondelegable by the designated official. For example, the statutory provision authorizing the Attorney General to approve wiretaps specifically limits her delegation power. See *United States v Giordano*, 416 US 505 (1974). Similarly, statutes that provide for formal adjudication may grant adversely affected parties the right to appeal all the way to the Secretary before a decision may take effect against them. See Cass, 66 BU L Rev at 3–7 (cited in note 122). Assuming that a party invokes this right, a statutory provision of this kind effectively prohibits delegation of the decision. When such a nondelegation provision is in effect, final action almost always will merit *Chevron* deference because (by statutory command) the delegatee herself will have issued the decision. For a qualification to this statement, deriving from the need not only to issue formally but to assess the decision in a meaningful way, see text accompanying notes 132–33.

[130] See Strauss, 41 Duke L J at 1467 (cited in note 11) (contrasting legislative rules, which are "invariably an act of the particular individual or body to whom that authority has been delegated," with other interpretive rulings, which are "typically effected by agency staff without participation at the agency's head").

one but in two senses—the first (and often discussed) relating to Congress's statutory grant, the second (and rarely mentioned) relating to the agency's own establishment of a decision-making structure.

In proposing to limit *Chevron* deference to action of the statutory delegatee, we claim not that Congress intended this result, but that policy considerations counsel it. In Part II of this article we showed the fallacy of grounding deference doctrine in congressional intent, and particularly of contending that deference to an administrative interpretation follows from a congressional delegation to the agency.[131] Similarly here. That Congress has delegated power to a named person within an agency does not mean that Congress has instructed courts to defer to that person's actions; and, conversely, that Congress has made this delegation does not mean that Congress has instructed courts to review independently any other agency official's actions, especially given that Congress has authorized, either explicitly or implicitly, the internal delegation. Our designation of the statutory delegatee as the key figure in the *Chevron* deference inquiry follows from two facts. First, the statutory delegatee is likely to be the secretary of a department, commission of an independent agency, or other high policy official whose participation in administrative action will promote, in ways that we discuss below, accountable and disciplined policymaking. Second, even assuming that the designation of the named delegatee functions as an imperfect (both overinclusive and underinclusive) mechanism for advancing these policy goals, that designation results in an easily identifiable actor to stand at the center of the *Chevron* inquiry.

But what must this statutory delegatee do to qualify an agency interpretation for *Chevron* deference? What does it mean for this person to make the interpretation hers in the way we would require? As an initial matter, the delegatee must issue the interpretation under her name. Authorship is a familiar concept in agency practice; indeed, agencies today are admirably (if surprisingly) punctilious about this feature of their interpretive rulings and other actions. Though agencies may seem faceless bureaucracies, they demonstrate daily that their decisions have human sources.

---

[131] See text accompanying notes 57–70.

Neither the Federal Register nor the agency web pages that now serve much of the Register's traditional function set forth disembodied pronouncements. Like judicial opinions, agency interpretations have authors, sometimes the statutory delegatee, but often not—perhaps the secretary of a department, perhaps the head of a division, perhaps a lower-level officeholder. This practice reflects a desire on the part of agencies to make clear that not all of their interpretations issue from the top and, in so doing, provides a hook for applying the contingent deference rule we propose. Only when an interpretation bears the name of the statutory delegatee has she adopted it as her own.

Adoption in the delegatee's name, however, should not be sufficient; this adoption must follow a meaningful review of the interpretation by the delegatee or her close advisors. This aspect of the standard perhaps is superfluous: we know of no agency that routinely affixes its top official's name to agency interpretations in the absence of such review; and, as we explain below, we doubt that any agency will adopt a practice of "rubberstamping" just to gain *Chevron* deference.[132] An explicit statement of the requirement nonetheless makes clear the purpose of hinging deference on the identity of the agency decision maker; it is, after all, the substantive impact, and not the mere form, of high-level involvement that promotes sound administration. This substantive review (unlike the ultimate formal adoption) of agency action could involve, or even fall wholly to, members of the delegatee's immediate staff (say, a chief of staff or special assistant) or members of other offices with general supervisory responsibility (say, a deputy secretary or general counsel).[133] Given the extensive responsibilities and time commitments of most statutory delegatees, they necessarily—and indeed, wisely—will rely on their senior advisors in important respects.[134] We will return below to the question whether the

---

[132] See text accompanying notes 173–82.

[133] We contrast these "central" advisors to advisors located within a given substantive unit of the agency. So, for example, if a statute assigned the Secretary of Health and Human Services the power to issue rulings concerning welfare benefits, she would not receive deference for a ruling reviewed only by the assistant secretary of the office responsible for formulating welfare policy.

[134] The Court has recognized, in the context of enforcing the principle that "the one who decides must hear," that agency heads necessarily will rely on staff-level assistance. See *Morgan v United States*, 298 US 468, 481 (1936) (*Morgan I*). In *Morgan*, the Court noted that the requirement that a departmental head "hear" the evidence in a case before rendering a decision did not preclude him from relying on reviews and summaries that his

involvement of these other central actors in a secretary's (or other delegatee's) decision undermines the benefits that accrue from lodging responsibility at this level.[135] For now, we note only that a sizable distinction remains between an agency head using her top aides to make a decision that she will issue and an agency head delegating wholesale to a subordinate the authority to make and publish the decision.

Finally, given that our standard is designed to preclude *Chevron* deference for agency decisions made pursuant to internal delegations, the statutory delegatee must adopt the agency's decision as her own prior to its final issuance.[136] Postdecisional ratification of a judgment made and published in final form lower down the chain of command does not withdraw the delegation of decisional power. That action merely stamps the exercise of the delegation with approval post hoc. The standard we propose thus would go unmet by, say, a statutory delegatee's assertion in a brief that she agreed with a ruling previously issued by a hearing examiner.[137]

---

staff had compiled. See id at 481–82. As Judge Friendly explained in a later, similar case, a prohibition on such staff-level input would beggar reality:

> With the enormous increase in delegation of lawmaking power which Congress has been obliged to make to agencies, both independent and in the executive branch, and in the complexity of life, government would become impossible if courts were to insist on anything of the sort. It would suffice under the circumstances [which involved a record comprised of tens of thousands of documents] that [the Commissioner] considered the summaries of the objections and of the answers contained in the elaborate preambles and conferred with his staff about them.

National Nutritional Foods Association v FDA, 491 F2d 1141, 1146 (2d Cir 1974).

[135] See text accompanying note 151.

[136] Whether to gain *Chevron* deference or to achieve some other objective, agencies can (and even now do) structure their internal processes in a variety of ways to select matters appropriate for the statutory delegatee to decide herself prior to the issuance of a ruling. The agency can leave it to lower-level officials to make case-by-case determinations as to which matters should go to the top. This method places control over the decisional flow in the hands of employees with intimate knowledge of an issue, but also with a potential incentive to avoid scrutiny and reversal. Alternatively (or in some combination), the agency can establish categorical rules or presumptions respecting which decisions to handle at the delegatee's level. This method enables the delegatee to set her own priorities, independent of the potentially conflicting judgments of lower-level employees, but risks substantial imprecision (both overinclusion and underinclusion) in the selection of cases for high-level resolution. Finally, the delegatee herself may become aware of and reach out for matters otherwise ensconced in the bowels of the bureaucracy. The appropriate choice among (or mix of) these approaches depends on context and circumstance, which the delegatee can best evaluate.

[137] We discuss further the normative basis for this position at text accompanying notes 197–202.

The normative case for applying *Chevron* in this way rests on the capacity of an agency nondelegation doctrine to promote the values of accountable and disciplined decision making, in much the way the congressional nondelegation doctrine is meant to do in another context. We have noted that these values explicitly underlay *Chevron* and implicitly underlay *Mead*, and we have argued that they provide the best touchstones to guide the deference inquiry, given Congress's usual silence.[138] With this much accepted, a nondelegation principle offers itself as a potential key to the *Chevron* question. The congressional nondelegation doctrine, after all, long has rested on the twin propositions that it places decision making in the hands of politically accountable actors[139] and that it serves to discipline administrative behavior.[140] The two doctrines, to be sure, are not identical. The congressional nondelegation doctrine is a tenet of constitutional law, the administrative variant a policy-based default rule of statutory interpretation. The former determines the very lawfulness of delegations, the latter only the rigor of judicial review due in their wake. But the established, congressional nondelegation doctrine remains suggestive in that it responds to concerns about the accountability and discipline of administrative action by focusing on the identity of the decision maker. This focus, when applied within the administrative context,

---

[138] See text accompanying notes 42, 75–87.

[139] See *Industrial Union Department, AFL-CIO v American Petroleum Institute*, 448 US 607, 685 (1980) (*Benzene Case*) (Rehnquist concurring) (stating that the congressional nondelegation doctrine "ensures to the extent consistent with orderly governmental administration that important choices of social policy are made by Congress, the branch of our government most responsive to the popular will"); John Hart Ely, *Democracy and Distrust: A Theory of Judicial Review* 133 (Harvard, 1980) ("That legislators often find it convenient to escape accountability is precisely the reason for a nondelegation doctrine.").

[140] See Cass R. Sunstein, *Is the Clean Air Act Unconstitutional?* 98 Mich L Rev 303, 337 (1999) (noting that the congressional nondelegation doctrine fosters "rule of law" values, in part by "cabining the discretionary authority of enforcement officials, who might otherwise act abusively or capriciously"). Kenneth Davis originated this strand of justification for the congressional nondelegation doctrine. See Kenneth Culp Davis, *A New Approach to Delegation*, 36 U Chi L Rev 713 (1969). A nondelegation doctrine premised on rule-of-law values need not require Congress to establish limits on agency action; indeed, Davis suggested that agencies themselves could establish such limits. See id at 729. The D.C. Circuit recently advocated a similar approach, but the Supreme Court reversed, pointedly noting that an agency's own adoption of disciplining mechanisms could not "cure an unlawful delegation." *Whitman v American Trucking Associations, Inc.*, 531 US 457, 472 (2001). The Court thus refused to sever the accountability and rule-of-law rationales for the nondelegation doctrine.

mitigates many of the usual concerns about deferring to an agency's exercise of broad delegated authority.[141]

Consider first accountability. *Chevron* posited that this value supports a rule of deference because agency officials have connections to political institutions and through them to the general public that the judiciary does not.[142] But is this true of all agency officials? We think not. Career agency staff, as a rule, are (proudly) resistant to broad political influence;[143] not for them the kind of "responsive[ness] to the popular will" that then-Justice Rehnquist heralded in a famous opinion concerning the congressional nondelegation doctrine.[144] To the extent that politics colors these employees' judgments, it is likely to be of the special interest variety, which may enter into their decision making as a result of enduring ties with and significant dependence on repeat players in the administrative process (often regulated parties).[145] The appropriate inquiry, to be sure, is comparative in nature, contrasting the public accountability of agency decision makers with that of courts. But still the conclusion remains much the same: the notion that low-level agency employees have a significant advantage on this dimension stretches the imagination.

It is only the presence of high-level agency officials that makes plausible *Chevron*'s claimed connection between agencies and the public; and it is only the involvement of these officials in decision making that makes possible the kind of political accountability that

---

[141] Some scholars might claim that our approach undermines, rather than runs parallel to, the congressional nondelegation doctrine by demanding that courts grant *Chevron* deference in some circumstances. See Farina, 89 Colum L Rev at 487–88 (cited in note 54) (arguing that *Chevron* and the congressional nondelegation doctrine work at cross-purposes). But there is no tension, much less conflict, between *Chevron* and the congressional nondelegation doctrine. Under the nondelegation doctrine, Congress may set the terms of a delegation so long as those terms provide an "intelligible principle." And under *Chevron*, agencies must conform their interpretations to the terms that Congress has established. *Chevron* thus does not enhance Congress's constitutional power to delegate authority, but only provides the background principles for construing delegations that conform to constitutional requirements.

[142] See 467 US at 865–66 (focusing on an agency's link to the President).

[143] See James Q. Wilson, *Bureaucracy: What Government Agencies Do and Why They Do It* 59–62 (Basic, 1989) (discussing the substantial influence that independent professional norms have on low-level agency actors).

[144] *Benzene Case*, 448 US at 685.

[145] See Richard B. Stewart, *The Reformation of American Administrative Law*, 88 Harv L Rev 1669, 1684–87 (1975) (discussing the causes, scope, and limits of interest group capture of agency personnel).

Chevron viewed as compelling deference. The delegatee named in an administrative statute, as contrasted with lower-level officials, usually has more frequent and direct links with a wide range of political institutions and public constituencies. A statutory delegatee typically assumes her position as the result of action by both the President and the Senate.[146] Once appointed, she remains subject to the direct oversight of the White House and Congress in a way not true of employees lower down the bureaucratic chain. She is the person most likely to appear before Congress on a regular basis; indeed, agencies may prohibit many of their nonpolitical appointees from giving congressional testimony. And the statutory delegatee has greater visibility than her subordinates to the public. The press (both general and specialized) covers her more extensively; the full panoply of interested parties attends to her more closely. As a result, a decision made by this official usually is both more responsive and more transparent to the public than a decision made in the depths of the bureaucracy.

Even when the statutory delegatee is not a cabinet secretary or similarly prominent official, a distinction between the delegatee and her subordinates, for purposes of according deference, will serve these accountability values. By pushing key decision making (the kind of decision making for which agencies desire deference) to a small set of identifiable actors, the deference regime we propose will counter the tendency of agencies to diffuse and cloak responsibility. As one of us has argued elsewhere, "to the extent possible, consistent with congressional command and other policy objectives, there is good reason to impose clear lines of command and to simplify and personalize the process of bureaucratic governance."[147] This method of structuring an agency's internal processes, by enhancing intelligibility and transparency, encourages a certain attitude on the part of decision makers; understanding that they possess—and that others will see that they possess—the last

---

[146] The Court has posited that the Appointments Clause establishes this mode of selection as the default rule for the appointment of all "officers of the United States" precisely to promote values of political accountability. See *Freytag v Commissioner*, 501 US 868, 883–84 (1991).

[147] Kagan, 114 Harv L Rev at 2332 (cited in note 78); see Charles Fried, *Order and Law: Arguing the Reagan Revolution—a Firsthand Account* 153 (Simon & Schuster, 1991) (arguing that "[t]he lines of responsibility [within the administrative state] should be stark and clear, so that the exercise of power can be comprehensible, transparent to the gaze of the citizens subject to it").

word on a matter, these officials will approach decision making with an increased attentiveness to political and public reaction.

At the same time, the confinement of judicial deference to the statutory delegatee—and the consequent centralization of agency decision making—promotes the disciplined consideration of policy throughout the agency, even (or especially) at the lower levels. Decisions that the statutory delegatee reviews and issues still will involve extensive work at the civil servant rank, but now the quality and rigor of this work will assume greater significance. The prospect of high-level review occasions scrupulous consideration of proposed agency action within the bureaucracy. Participants in decisions headed for review want to make a good showing before the Secretary (or other statutory delegatee)—to have persuasive reasons for a recommendation and ready answers to her potential questions. The spotlight of the secretary's own attention, focused on the shadowy world of administrative action, enhances preparation; as a decision advances from line actors to unit heads to the secretary's political advisors to the secretary herself, so too does deliberation step up and, accordingly, improve agency decisions.

High-level review similarly furthers the coherence of administrative action, both by preventing deviations from agency policy and establishing a mechanism to implement that policy in a coordinated manner. A General Accounting Office survey published some two decades ago reached the unsurprising conclusion that agency heads exercise discretionary authority over the decisions of administrative law judges as a way of ensuring that these decisions are "in accordance with agency policy."[148] That high-level review often is needed to accomplish this object surely remains true today—and not only with respect to administrative law judges' decisions. A deference rule contingent on secretarial review and action would protect against agency outliers, acting through ignorance or guile inconsistently with general policy.[149] More affirmatively, such

---

[148] Peter L. Strauss et al, *Gellhorn & Byse's Administrative Law: Cases and Comments* 891 (Foundation, 8th ed 1987) (quoting 1978 GAO survey).

[149] See McGarity, *Reinventing Rationality* at 183 (cited in note 121) ("[T]o the extent that upper-level decision makers carefully monitor the decision making process, it helps ensure that lower-level staff continue to adhere to the policy preferences of politically-appointed decision makers, rather than following their own hidden agenda."); Ronald A. Cass, *Agency Review of Administrative Law Judges' Decisions*, in Administrative Law Conference of the United States, *Reports and Recommendations* 115, 133 (1983) ("[A]bsent some form of review, it is difficult to reward conforming behavior or punish behavior that departs from [the agency head's] wishes, the stuff incentives are made of.").

a rule would promote the integration of diverse agency actions into a coordinated stream of policy aimed at achieving set objectives. Standing at the apex of many agency components, the statutory delegatee can see the interrelationships among different interpretive positions (and the bodies of expertise giving rise to them), determine the combination that most effectively will advance the agency's substantive goals, and choose the order, timing, and form of action that best will support this combination. In short, the delegatee's involvement militates against administrative ad hocery.[150]

That our scheme would provide deference even when a statutory delegatee relies on central advisors to review administrative action undermines none of these arguments. The delegatee, as noted earlier,[151] necessarily operates less as a person than an office. She does not—and cannot—handle all matters herself; like every Washington "principal," she uses assistants to perform a range of functions: to select the matters that require her personal attention, to speak for her to persons within and outside the agency, and even to speak in her own name by writing "her" speeches, preparing "her" memos, and so forth. But this concession to reality in no way renders the delegatee either a cipher or a puppet. Given the typically small size of a delegatee's central staff, the loyalty and understanding that this intimacy breeds, and the usual coincidence of interests of this staff and the delegatee, slippage between the principal and these agents usually remains at tolerable levels. Consider the analogous argument in the context of the congressional nondelegation doctrine. No one would say that the existence of legislative staffs undermines the doctrine; no one would say that congressmen's decisions do not remain congressmen's decisions in a way that mat-

---

[150] This point holds even though a high-level official's intervention may cause shifts in agency policy. None of what we have said is meant to suggest that a statutory delegatee's involvement in decision making necessarily will support the status quo. To the contrary, such an official may have less compunction than a lower-level employee about breaking with past practice or setting out in an uncharted direction. See Wilson, *Bureaucracy* at 230 (cited in note 143) (discussing the unique role that high-level actors can play in altering an agency's course). A deference rule that encourages high-level agency decision making thus may lead to aggressive rather than to cautious interpretations. But a rule permitting altered policy is not equivalent to a rule permitting aberrant or ad hoc policy. If confined to high-level decision making, *Chevron* would function as the first kind of rule, but not as the second. That result, allowing the transformation but not the subversion of agency policy, is correct. The goal here, reflecting the value of disciplined consideration evident in *Chevron*, *Mead*, and the congressional nondelegation doctrine, is to prevent arbitrariness and unruliness, not to arrest all capacity for change.

[151] See text accompanying note 134.

ters. So too here, when the relevant principal is an agency secretary or other top official.

In suggesting an approach to *Chevron* doctrine that focuses on the assignment of decision-making responsibilities within an agency, we have drawn a broad analogy to the congressional nondelegation doctrine. We have done so to highlight the ways in which our constitutional tradition in general, and administrative law in particular, have expressed concern with delegated decision-making authority. Our analysis suggests similar reasons to worry about internal agency delegations and similar reasons to believe that agency decision making will improve if pushed upward.

We cannot disregard, however, the apparent archaicism of our approach. The congressional nondelegation doctrine had its last good year in 1935 (and perhaps its first good year then as well).[152] Just last term, a few months before announcing *Mead*, the Court dealt another and seemingly lethal blow to calls to revive the doctrine as a working part of the Constitution.[153] And the Court did so for good reason. We find sound the principal criticisms of the congressional nondelegation doctrine—that it insists on too much centralization of decision-making authority in the hands of Congress and that it resists any principled method of judicial enforcement.[154] We accordingly must address why our proposal to reformulate *Chevron* as a kind of internal nondelegation doctrine would not fall prey to the same concerns.

Consider first the argument respecting centralization. Critics of the congressional nondelegation doctrine aver that given the complexity of modern government, Congress cannot address all issues demanding resolution and that, even if Congress could do so, its decisions often would reflect deficient knowledge and experience.[155] For this reason, the objection proceeds, a meaningfully enforced nondelegation doctrine would have severe adverse consequences for effective governance.[156] Similarly, some administrative

---

[152] See Sunstein, 98 Mich L Rev at 330–35 (cited in note 140) (chronicling the rise and fall of the doctrine).

[153] See *American Trucking*, 531 US 457.

[154] See Sunstein, 98 Mich L Rev at 337–39 (cited in note 140) (summarizing the arguments against the doctrine).

[155] See id at 338–39.

[156] See id. Even proponents of a revived nondelegation doctrine appear to concede that members of Congress could respond to its demands only by increasing their reliance on legislative committees. See Ely, *Democracy and Distrust* at 133 (cited in note 139); cf. David

experts might claim, an internal agency nondelegation doctrine would result in excessive centralization.[157] Agency heads (even with their central staff), like members of Congress (with their staffs), cannot as a practical matter review and render a final determination on every matter of policy. And even were this supervision possible, it would succeed only in diminishing the quality of agency decision making by subordinating the knowledge, experience, and professionalism of lower-level employees. For these reasons, the argument might go, an agency nondelegation doctrine has a (familiarly) deficient warrant.

For two reasons, however, the charge of impracticality loses its punch when applied to the doctrine we propose. The most important relates to the divergent effects of applying a robust congressional nondelegation doctrine and reformulating *Chevron* as an administrative analogue. Under the congressional nondelegation doctrine, the consequence of a too-broad delegation is prohibition—or, conversely put, a command that Congress decide the matter, even against all evidence that it can do so. The proposal at issue here, by contrast, does not invalidate internal delegations;[158] all that it would do is affect *Chevron* deference. Agency decision making could proceed identically except that the courts would review it more independently. There is nothing "unthinkable" about this consequence; it merely reverts to the world before *Chevron*.

Moreover, a nondelegation doctrine can work more easily in the administrative than in the legislative sphere because of the greater capacity of high-level agency officials than of members of Congress to comply with the doctrine while leaving most of the effort associated with policymaking in the bureaucracy. In the legislative context, the nondelegation doctrine effectively forces Congress to take very burdensome action or to do nothing. Although Congress conceivably could erect a system to review and vote on agency

---

Epstein and Sharyn O'Halloran, *Delegating Powers: A Transaction Cost Politics Approach to Policy Making Under Separate Powers* 237–38 (Cambridge, 1999) (discussing the effects of a revived nondelegation doctrine on Congress's decision-making processes). Opponents of the doctrine might find yet a further reason for objection in this "cure," given the special interest orientation of many congressional committees. Consider Kenneth A. Shepsle, *The Giant Jigsaw Puzzle: Democratic Committee Assignments in the Modern House* 231–34 (Chicago, 1978) (discussing the factional leanings of many congressional committees).

[157] See McGarity, *Reinventing Rationality* at 119 (cited in note 121) (discussing the disadvantages associated with upper-level officials' monitoring the rulemaking process).

[158] We discuss this issue further at text accompanying notes 173–74.

recommendations,[159] the enormous mass of agency action, combined with the existence of other congressional responsibilities,
combined with the constitutionally mandated form and cumbersome nature of legislative decision making (which requires coordinated action of 535 individuals with different party and geographic
affiliations who are divided into numerous committees within two
separate chambers) would make the effective operation of this system contingent on an unprecedented feat of governmental engineering.[160] A statutory delegatee within an agency, by contrast, has
resort to more feasible means of monitoring and controlling, while
taking advantage of, the efforts of the bureaucracy. As compared
with Congress, she has a more limited body of decisions to review
and a more limited set of nonreview functions. She is usually a
unitary actor, or at most a board or commission made up of several
members, and so can act with greater expedition. And because she
both sits within the agency itself and faces no constitutional constraints on the form of her action, she can select from a variety
of processes—relying on close staff or not, operating at an early
or late stage, and so on—to perform the meaningful review necessary to satisfy the nondelegation requirement.[161]

Such a combination of "central" and "local" influence on
agency decision making promises the highest quality administration, contrary to the claim that high-level supervision inappropri-
ately suppresses professionalism and expertise. We in no way deni-
grate the importance of these bureaucratic attributes. Neither do
we deny that high-level review of agency decision making will inject more "political" concerns into that process. (This result is but
the corollary of the greater accountability of top officials to political institutions and the public.) The point here is that the inclusion
of the central, more political perspective, even aside from serving

---

[159] Congress of course could not satisfy a strong nondelegation doctrine through the use
of a legislative veto mechanism; indeed, Congress cannot any longer adopt this mechanism
for any purpose. See *INS v Chadha*, 462 US 919 (1983).

[160] Justice (then Judge) Breyer proposed in the wake of *Chadha* that Congress experiment
with a scheme of this kind, incorporating the use of fast-track procedures to facilitate the
"confirmation" of agency policy. See Stephen Breyer, *The Legislative Veto After Chadha*, 72
Georgetown L J 785, 788–89 (1984). That Congress never considered seriously the idea
suggests much about its feasibility.

[161] See McGarity, *Reinventing Rationality* at 31, 76–77, 120 (cited in note 121) (describing
the variety of processes by which high-level officials and their staffs communicate policy
preferences as to particular matters to lower-level employees).

accountability values, counters the excesses—most notably, the excesses of tradition and inertia—of local, more bureaucratic decision makers.[162] The very professional norms and institutional memory that these actors possess often blind them to new and beneficial policy approaches. Precisely because central decision makers are less rooted in existing agency culture, they add value to the administrative process. The ideal, then, is neither pure centralization, in which high-level actors execute directives for ministerial application, nor pure decentralization, in which lower-level actors decide matters autonomously. It is, instead, a system that encourages a relationship between the organization's parts and captures the benefits each can offer.[163]

The deference regime we have proposed likely will promote this kind of interactive, iterative exchange between high- and low-level perspectives. Almost everything about agencies—their size and scope, their strong institutional cultures, their attachment to past practice, the complexity of the issues they decide, the distribution of information within them, the interests of their permanent employees in avoiding political influence, and the existence of long-term relationships between employees and outside parties—all conspire to ensure that a statutory delegatee is greatly bounded in her ability to impose her judgments on the agency. Even when a statutory delegatee makes a final decision, she rarely will have considered the matter from scratch. Lower-level employees compile and scrutinize documents, offer legal opinions, provide regulatory analyses, and effectively shape and limit decisional options. This preparatory work powerfully influences the delegatee's judgments.[164]

---

[162] See Wilson, *Bureaucracy* at 62 (cited in note 143) (noting the way professional norms can cause "blind spots" within agencies); Bruce Ackerman, *The New Separation of Powers*, 113 Harv L Rev 633, 701 (2000) ("Bureaucracies are intellectually conservative creatures—full of old-timers who have invested heavily in obsolete conventional wisdom.").

[163] See McGarity, *Reinventing Rationality* at 118–21 (cited in note 121) (urging agencies to establish decision-making structures that have this consequence); consider Michael C. Dorf and Charles F. Sabel, *A Constitution of Democratic Experimentalism*, 98 Colum L Rev 267, 314–23 (1998) (advocating a complex relationship between central and local decision makers, though in a way that focuses less than we do on the actual participation of central officials in decisions).

[164] See McGarity, *Reinventing Rationality* at 179 (cited in note 121) ("Because institutions lack a centralized nervous system steered by a single brain, institutional decision making tends to be very different from individual decision making. Most regulatory decisions are the products of numerous encounters between the various institutional entities that have roles to play in the decision making process, and they therefore represent a synthesis of many views."). For a description of how low-level actors may constrain the choice-set of a high-level agency actor, see id at 61 (discussing decision making in the EPA in the 1980s).

The real danger is that high-level review will insufficiently, rather than excessively, crowd out the orientations of lower-level officials.[165]

And even if high-level review suppresses expertise in a way more hazardous than we acknowledge, the deference regime we propose inevitably would have a self-limiting quality. No rule of deference will prompt high-level review of anything approaching all agency interpretations, given the agency's (including the delegatee's) interest in providing timely interpretations to regulated parties and the burdens to the agency (including to the delegatee) that necessarily accompany high-level review. The centralizing effects of an internal nondelegation principle on the agency's decision-making processes will occur at the margins—in those cases (or categories of cases) for which judicial deference seems most important, which likely are also those cases (or categories of cases) in which more than professional expertise is involved.

Still, this does not end the matter. There is another argument against the congressional nondelegation doctrine—relating to the feasibility of judicial enforcement—which also might cut against our approach to *Chevron*. This claim is that judges cannot distinguish in a principled way between permissible and impermissible delegations and that they therefore should refrain from applying the doctrine.[166] So too, the skeptic might say, courts cannot draw a principled line between internal agency delegations that meet our test for *Chevron* deference and those that do not. Indeed, the "meaningful review" requirement incorporated in this test (alongside the necessity of the delegatee's formal adoption of the agency action) may appear even more resistant to judicial application than the notoriously squishy "intelligible principle" requirement of the congressional nondelegation doctrine.[167]

---

[165] Indeed, by encouraging the involvement of high-level officials in decision making, our standard may enhance their responsiveness to policy proposals initiated within the ranks of the bureaucracy. See Peter L. Strauss, *Rules, Adjudications, and Other Sources of Law in an Executive Department: Reflections on the Interior Department's Administration of the Mining Law*, 74 Colum L Rev 1231, 1247 (1974) (noting the tendency of high-level agency officials to fail to respond to policy suggestions from below).

[166] See *Mistretta v United States*, 488 US 361, 415–22 (1989) (Scalia dissenting) (arguing that courts cannot distinguish between permissible and impermissible delegations); Stewart, 88 Harv L Rev at 1696–97 (cited in note 145) (claiming that "[s]uch judgments are necessarily quite subjective, . . . almost inevitably appear partisan, and might often be so").

[167] *National Broadcasting Company v United States*, 319 US 190 (1943) (upholding the Communications Act on the ground that its "public convenience, interest or necessity" standard

But the prospects for effective implementation of an internal nondelegation rule far exceed those for administration of the congressional nondelegation doctrine because of the way political constraints reinforce judicial constraints in the administrative context. Courts mainly can enforce the agency nondelegation rule through the simple expedient of insisting on the statutory delegatee's formal adoption of the administrative action; they then can rely primarily on a preexisting set of political incentives (and disincentives) to ensure satisfaction of the additional "meaningful review" requirement. In effect, political and institutional realities obviate the need for judges to police the agency's decision-making process to prevent "rubberstamping." Recognition—or perhaps better said, exploitation—of these realities will enable courts to limit their own inquiry and yet rest confident that the inquiry will achieve effective enforcement of the agency nondelegation principle within the application of *Chevron* doctrine.

Judges easily can enforce the requirement that a statutory delegatee formally adopt an agency interpretation. The adoption requirement means only that the delegatee must affirm and publish the interpretation, in all its specificity, as her own. It is not sufficient for the delegatee to indicate general agreement with a decision that lower-level employees have reached; she must make that decision hers by putting forward both the decision and the rationale for it. There is nothing complicated about this matter; courts need only check that the delegatee has placed her name on the decision and all its supporting materials. Courts today enforce a similar adoption requirement in policing the APA's provision that an adequate statement of "findings and conclusions, and the reasons or basis therefor,"[168] accompany an agency's adjudicative decisions. In that context, courts have made clear that the final decision maker must take responsibility for this full statement. So, for example, the Third Circuit in *Armstrong v Commodity Futures Trading Commission*[169] invalidated an adjudicative decision because the commission, on appeal, said only that the administrative law judge's

---

provides an "intelligible principle" for the FCC to enforce); see Gerald E. Frug, *The Ideology of Bureaucracy in American Law*, 97 Harv L Rev 1276, 1303 (1984) (arguing that all delegations both do and do not satisfy the "intelligible principle" test).

[168] 5 USC § 557(c).

[169] 12 F3d 401 (3d Cir 1993).

initial determination was "substantially correct."[170] This statement, the court reasoned, left unclear which aspects of the judge's decision the commission meant to endorse and so "d[id] not rise to the level of adoption."[171]

The dilemma for courts arises from the second aspect of our principle—that the statutory delegatee or her central aides engage in meaningful review of an agency interpretation prior to the delegatee's adoption of it. Assuming the delegatee does not attempt to "adopt" low-level action before it is taken (in which case courts can say that no review, meaningful or not, has occurred), the review requirement appears to confront courts with two unpalatable alternatives. First, a court could attempt to assess the quality of the delegatee's review of the low-level action. But this inquiry places the courts in a more hazardous position than does even the analogue in the congressional context: the former calls on judges to evaluate officials' conduct, whereas the latter calls on them to evaluate only statutory language. Are the courts to compel a statutory delegatee and her staff to submit timesheets detailing the quantum of high-level input? How will courts decide whether this input has reached a sufficient level? Such a judicial endeavor would be unenviable at best.[172] Second, a court could disdain enforcement of the requirement of meaningful review. But if a court adopts this route, the agency nondelegation principle would appear to become purely formal. For at that point, the statutory delegatee would need only to rubberstamp low-level interpretations to obtain *Chevron* deference.

But this dilemma disappears if, as we believe to be the case, the review requirement would be self-enforcing. Administrative norms may play some role in restraining delegatees from formally adopting all agency action; the delegatee's sense of her professional responsibility—and, sometimes more important in Washington, the delegatee's sense of her importance—may make her reluctant to attach her name indiscriminately to every action taken within her department.[173] More critical, though, are high-level officials' political and

---

[170] Id at 404.

[171] Id at 406.

[172] Courts traditionally have expressed reluctance, for the reasons suggested in the text, to conduct a factual inquiry into the way agency officials reach their decisions. See, e.g., *Morgan v United States*, 304 US 1, 18 (1938) (*Morgan II*).

[173] In addition, the delegatee or her legal staff may resist evasion of the requirement of meaningful review out of a felt obligation to give effect to the courts' pronouncements. Congress, to be sure, has failed to demonstrate any analogous scruples when it comes to

institutional interests, which support the nondelegation standard within agencies in a way wholly foreign to the congressional context. How could such an interest-based calculation protect the requirement of meaningful review? Very simply—if the delegatee would find it more advantageous to decline to adopt a decision than to adopt it without meaningful review (i.e., to rubberstamp the decision). What is striking here is that, given the political and institutional pressures the delegatee faces, this will almost always be true. The delegatee will want to adopt a decision only if she or someone she trusts has subjected that decision to close review.

Key to the analysis here is that the delegatee suffers no dire consequences from simply declining to adopt the typical agency interpretation. Under the administrative (as opposed to the congressional) nondelegation doctrine, delegation of the decision will not result in automatic invalidation; all that will happen is that the decision will not receive *Chevron* protection. That protection, to be sure, is a valued good in agency culture. But its existence often will not be decisive. Perhaps no one will challenge the interpretation; perhaps a court will uphold the interpretation under a stricter standard; perhaps a court will strike down the interpretation even under *Chevron*. From an ex ante perspective the delegatee has something less than an overwhelming reason to flout the internal nondelegation principle by formally adopting agency interpretations without meaningful review.

Now add to the delegatee's calculation the substantial political risks of attempting to end-run the agency nondelegation principle. Consider here an incident from the end of the Clinton Administration involving an opinion letter of the kind issued in *Mead*. In response to a company's request for a legal interpretation, the Occupational, Safety, and Health Administration (OSHA), located within the Department of Labor, ruled that federal workplace safety standards applied to home offices.[174] The letter, once posted on the department's website, drew the attention of the press and

---

delegations of authority. But in the congressional context, the Court more often has denied the existence of a robust nondelegation doctrine than recognized that doctrine but left its enforcement to Congress. Perhaps more important, both the greater ease of compliance and the lesser effect of noncompliance with a nondelegation principle in the agency context may enhance the effect of a simple judicial pronouncement.

[174] See *OSHA Advisory Opinion, Re: Application of OSHA Rules to People Who Work at Home* (Nov 15, 1999), available online at <http://www.techlawjournal.com>.

triggered a firestorm of protest from individuals, companies, members of Congress, and even the White House.[175] Caught in the middle of the controversy, both the Secretary of Labor and the administrator of OSHA were quick to point out that a lower-level OSHA employee had signed and issued the letter.[176] Replying to press and congressional inquiries, the secretary noted that her office had never received the letter for review[177] and the administrator insisted that the letter resulted from a "breakdown in internal clearance mechanisms" and did not represent OSHA's official policy.[178] At a congressional hearing, one member of Congress responded to the administrator's explanation with the comment, "If you can't come back here and tell us that you've held someone accountable for this, maybe you ought to consider resigning."[179] No resignation took place; presumably the administrator found someone else to hold accountable.[180]

This dispute highlights both the political hazards instinct in interpretive materials and the distancing mechanisms available to high-level officials. A statutory delegatee may face criticism from the President, Congress, constituency groups, and the press when any person within her agency issues an ill-considered, aberrant, or unpopular decision. But when the delegatee cannot disclaim responsibility—when she cannot point the finger of blame at some hapless, faceless bureaucratic official—her political peril increases. And deniability becomes less plausible when the delegatee personally has signed a decision. This fact of political life partly explains why statutory delegatees place the prestige of their offices behind only a small subset of agency decisions; and it explains why any

---

[175] For accounts of the controversy, see Kent Hoover, *OSHA Criticized After Home-Office Debacle*, Denver Bus J 1 (Feb 4, 2000); Frank Swoboda, *Labor Chief Retreats on Home Offices; OSHA Position Drew Criticism*, Wash Post A1 (Jan 6, 2000).

[176] Richard E. Fairfax, Director of the Directorate of Compliance Programs for OSHA, had signed the letter. See *OSHA Advisory Opinion* (cited in note 174).

[177] See Swoboda (cited in note 175).

[178] See Hoover (cited in note 175) (quoting Administrator Jeffress).

[179] Id (quoting Representative Schaffer).

[180] A similar flap, complete with the same downward finger-pointing, occurred in the first months of the Bush Administration when the website of the Department of Agriculture highlighted a new policy to abandon a contract provision requiring salmonella testing of ground beef served in federal school lunch programs. The Secretary withdrew the policy, explaining that a "low-level employee" had issued it without seeking review from her office. See Marc Kaufman and Amy Goldstein, *USDA Shifts Stance on Testing of School Beef; Agency to Continue Salmonella Screen*, Wash Post A1 (April 6, 2001).

increase in this practice responding to a *Chevron* nondelegation principle will go hand in hand with an increase in high-level review of bureaucratic decisions (which we expect to be incremental rather than dramatic[181]). Unless she knows and has confidence in what she is personally affirming, no amount of judicial deference will persuade a delegatee to make her own an interpretive decision.

In addition, the statutory delegatee likely will confront pressures from within her agency to resist practices that would evade the requirement of meaningful review. This point may be counterintuitive: Why would the bureaucracy spurn a system in which the delegatee rubberstamped—thus giving weight to without impinging upon—bureaucratic decisions? But an agency bureaucracy is not a monolith. It is a congeries of components that have separate or even antagonistic missions and interests.[182] Some components, most notably the litigating sections, may want the delegatee to gain *Chevron* deference for as many decisions as possible; some components may so desire deference for their decisions that they will accede to processes that also provide deference for the decisions of others. But other components—perhaps the majority—will think this trade-off not worthwhile. Consider, for example, whether the Civil Rights Division of the Department of Justice would support a proposal that automatically would place the Attorney General's name on interpretations of the Immigration and Naturalization Service (INS). The division surely would prefer that it have an advance opportunity to confer with the Attorney General on these decisions, or that the decisions issue only under the authority of the INS, so the Attorney General later has latitude to disclaim them. So, too, for many components in many agencies, which desire broad influence on, rather than broad deference for, other components' interpretative decisions.

Perhaps within some agencies, these political and institutional pressures will have less force than we believe. If so, courts can reinforce them by precluding *Chevron* deference on a finding that a delegatee consistently has approved low-level decisions without providing for their review. In making these determinations, courts rightly can take note of the sophisticated, as well as the simple-

---

[181] See text following note 165.

[182] For discussion of this point see McGarity, *Reinventing Regulation* at 160–61, 185–86 (cited in note 121); Wilson, *Bureaucracy* at 105–07 (cited in note 143).

minded, ways in which cheating can occur. At the same time, however, courts should draw the line at investigating and dissecting
an agency's decision-making processes with respect to particular
decisions.[183] The best analogue here is the kind of "systemic" review contemplated in *Heckler v Chaney*[184] for claims that an agency
has failed to enforce a statutory scheme. The Court there explained that it usually would confine its review to allegations that
an agency had " 'consciously and expressly adopted a general policy' that is so extreme as to amount to an abdication of its statutory
responsibilities."[185] So too in this context, courts can show vigilance as to claims of wholesale evasion, while declining to explore
the review that a delegatee has accorded to any particular interpretive decision.[186]

In this way, courts can put in place a standard that conditions
Chevron deference on the decision-making structure that an agency
adopts to resolve an issue—and, more particularly, on the involvement of a high-level official within the agency. This standard will
encourage high-level officials to assume full and visible responsibility for interpretive rulings, while ensuring that meaningful review
lies behind these public acclamations. The standard demands no
intensive, case-by-case investigation of internal agency decision-
making processes. Courts can rely for effective implementation on
the extralegal (political and bureaucratic) incentives and disincentives that follow from the simple requirement that a high-level official adopt a ruling to entitle it to *Chevron* deference. In essence,
courts gain the ability to shape an agency's decision-making pro-

---

[183] See text accompanying note 172.

[184] 470 US 821 (1985).

[185] Id at 833 n 4.

[186] In handling these claims of systematic evasion, courts should adopt a high threshold
for permitting discovery, consistent with their traditional (and appropriate) reluctance to
require agencies to reveal their internal deliberative processes. See *Morgan v United States*,
313 US 409 (1941) (*Morgan IV*). But for our standard to have bite, courts must permit
inquiries into these processes when the challenger of agency action has made a strong
preliminary showing. Consider *National Nutritional Food Association v FDA*, 491 F2d 1141,
1145 (2d Cir 1974) (noting that courts after *Morgan IV* have required "strong preliminary
showings of bad faith . . . before the taking of testimony has been permitted with regard
to internal agency deliberations."). For example, evidence that a statutory delegatee had
signed hundreds of opinion letters on many matters within a short period of time might
justify a court in permitting discovery into the issue of high-level review. More direct evidence of rubberstamping, such as that obtainable form news reports or Freedom of Information Act requests, also might suffice.

cesses by recognizing a set of nonlegal factors that also affect these processes. Judicial sensitivity to an agency's organizational incentives thereby grounds judicial influence over an agency's organizational characteristics.[187]

V. Mead and Delegation

It is now time to return to *Mead*. So far, it might appear that our approach to *Chevron* deference is foreign to the Justices' analysis. In fact, this is not the case. Both the majority and the dissent in *Mead* refer to the agency's internal decision-making structure—and, specifically, to the level of the decision maker; these references count as the single point of commonality between the two warring opinions. In the end, however, each opinion, in different ways, reverts to the conventional understanding of the administrative agency as a unitary actor. After describing these forays and retreats, we apply in this part our *Chevron* nondelegation principle to the agency ruling in *Mead*. We then expand this analysis to suggest how the principle would apply more generally.

Justice Souter's majority opinion takes note of the extreme decentralization of agency decision making in the case, but then submerges this point in articulating the appropriate legal standard. Three times the majority opinion points out that "46 different Customs offices" issue classification rulings.[188] "[T]here would have to be something wrong with a standard" that accorded deference to the decisions of all these offices,[189] the Court proclaimed; any suggestion that deference should apply in such cir-

---

[187] The above analysis suggests why ours is only a plea to the courts to reshape the *Chevron* inquiry to respond to internal delegations and not a plea to Congress to limit the power of agency heads (and other delegatees) to subdelegate. Congress no doubt can promote responsible decision making by prohibiting subdelegation in a few select areas. But for Congress to do much more risks defeating its objects. If the delegatee takes a broad nondelegation command seriously, overcentralization indeed will result, as the delegatee does too much—and because too much, also too little (of import). If, alternatively, as seems likely, the delegatee recognizes this danger, she will develop means of perfunctory compliance, confident that the political risks of doing so are less than those of ignoring her other responsibilities. It is when the delegatee retains the core power to subdelegate that nondelegation will reflect a conscious, considered judgment about the decision-making process and will entail her meaningful participation in that process. It is that judgment and that participation which is integral to any sound scheme of promoting responsibility in agency decision making.

[188] 121 S Ct at 2174; see id at 2175, 2177 n 19.

[189] Id at 2177 n 19.

cumstances would "ignore . . . reality,"[190] and indeed be "simply self-refuting."[191] All these references point toward a test that would make *Chevron* deference contingent on a decision by a central, high-level official. But rather than articulating this test, the Court resorted to the vacuities of congressional intent and the irrelevancies of proceduralism and generality. Indeed, the opinion strongly indicates that formal decisions issued by diverse, low-level officials are more worthy of deference than informal decisions of a single high-level official.[192]

Justice Scalia's dissenting opinion attacks just this result of *Mead*, suggesting the significance of the level at which agency decision making occurs. Justice Scalia observes that some statutes require Cabinet Secretaries personally to resolve disputes without any prescribed procedures; under such a statute, for example, the Secretary of Transportation must determine (often in a politically salient setting) that no feasible alternatives exist to the use of public parkland for a highway.[193] "Is it conceivable," Justice Scalia asks, "that decisions specifically committed to these high-level officers" are ineligible for *Chevron* deference when "decisions by an administrative law judge" receive it?[194] And in response to his own question: "This seems to me quite absurd."[195]

Yet Justice Scalia also backs away from a doctrine that would respond to this analysis, instead adopting a test that more often requires deference. Justice Scalia's test, as noted earlier, accords *Chevron* deference to any "authoritative" agency interpretation.[196] The "authoritative" character of an interpretation in turn resides in a subsequent decision—by, say, the agency general counsel or the Solicitor General—to defend the interpretation in litigation. The *Chevron* inquiry thus depends not on the participation of high-level officials in making a decision, but only on the involvement of these officials (though not necessarily the statutory delegatee) in defending the decision against legal challenge. Because

---

[190] Id at 2174.

[191] Id at 2175.

[192] See 121 S Ct at 2172–73.

[193] See id at 2189 (Scalia dissenting).

[194] Id.

[195] Id.

[196] Id at 2187; see text accompanying note 41.

this postdecision ratification will exist in almost any case that comes before a court, *Chevron* will follow as a matter of course—regardless (despite Justice Scalia's posing of the question) whether an ALJ or the Secretary of Transportation initially made the decision.

But postdecision ratification cannot substitute for predecision participation in advancing the values of accountability and consideration in agency decision making. Ratification often will occur within agencies in near automatic fashion; at this stage, a high-level official is unlikely to influence an agency's interpretations in any of the ways she would have prior to adoption (including by doing something other than accepting or rejecting in toto the proposed interpretation).[197] It is difficult to reverse a course once set, and perhaps especially so within large organizations.[198] A high-level official will confront greater resistance from the bureaucracy in changing a decision already taken than one in the process of formulation. She may believe that the agency will suffer embarrassment from an admission of error. Or she may think that a reversal will lead to a decline in the morale and loyalty of employees. For all these reasons, she often will refuse to reverse a decision she believes in error, decline to consider the merits of the decision at all, or even succeed in persuading herself that a decision she earlier would have rejected in fact constitutes sound policy.

The procedural costs and litigation risks involved in reversing a recent, final agency action reinforce this bias toward the status quo. The reversal of a prior agency interpretation requires at least the extent of procedural formality initially used in adopting the interpretation.[199] To change direction at this late stage (unlike be-

---

[197] Of course, if a statutory delegatee reverses a decision after it issues, the new decision would receive deference under our standard. The reasons for withholding deference when a statutory delegatee ratifies a decision post hoc do not apply when she reverses it.

[198] See Donald C. Langevoort, *Organized Illusions: A Behavioral Theory of Why Corporations Mislead Stock Market Investors (and Cause Other Social Harms)*, 146 U Pa L Rev 101, 135 (1997) (noting strong biases against revisions in corporate behavior); Susan T. Fiske and Shelley E. Taylor, *Social Cognition* 149–51 (McGraw-Hill, 2d ed 1991) (arguing that "[w]ell-developed schemas generally resist change"); Richard E. Nisbett and Lee Ross, *Human Inference: Strategies and Shortcomings of Social Judgment* 167 (Prentice-Hall, 1980) (stating similar findings).

[199] See *National Family Planning and Reproductive Health Association, Inc. v Sullivan*, 979 F2d 227 (DC Cir 1992) (prohibiting an agency from revising a notice-and-comment regulation through an interpretive rule issued without notice and comment). This requirement almost surely obtains even if the agency provided more procedural formality than necessary in the first instance.

fore the action becomes final) essentially doubles the cost of issuing an interpretation. At the same time, such a change may decrease the probability that the new agency interpretation will prevail against a legal challenge. Although the issue is far from settled, the Court sometimes has indicated that administrative interpretations in conflict with previously stated views should receive diminished deference on review.[200] No agency head can view with equanimity the prospect that her reversal of a final interpretation will force the agency to embark three times on its interpretive mission.

All these points increase in force when the decision whether to reverse an action occurs in the course of litigation. Agencies are loathe to admit error when confronted with a legal challenge. It is natural for agencies, no less than any other entities, to bunker down when attacked. In addition, an agency can justify a decision to defend a final action less as a firm commitment to the merits than as a reasonable means of giving the courts the final say on a disputed question. Litigation, to be sure, can force an agency to face the weaknesses of the arguments it originally proffered for an interpretation. But even when this result occurs, the agency more likely will attempt to reverse engineer its decision than to incur the cost of starting over.[201] Given the probability of ratification, Justice Scalia's approach reflects anything but a nondelegation principle. Despite the apparent attention he gives to agency hierarchy, his focus would serve not to distinguish (and influence the choice) between different structures of decision making, but instead to deny legal effect to, and indeed to disguise, these differences.[202]

---

[200] See *Good Samaritan Hospital v Shalala*, 508 US 402, 417 (1993) (stating that "the consistency of an agency's position is a factor in assessing the weight that position is due," but ultimately deferring to an agency's changed interpretation); *Pauley v Bethenergy Mines, Inc.*, 501 US 680, 698 (1991) (stating that the "case for judicial deference is less compelling with respect to agency decisions that are inconsistent with previously held views," but finding that the interpretation at issue was not so inconsistent); *Bowen v Georgetown U. Hospital*, 488 US 204, 212–13 (1988) (declining to give deference on the alternative ground that the interpretation at issue was "contrary to the narrow view of that provision advocated in past cases"). But see *Rust v Sullivan*, 500 US 173, 186–87 (1991) (reading *Chevron* to hold that a revised interpretation deserves deference and sustaining agency action on this ground).

[201] Courts usually refuse to sustain agency action on grounds that the agency offers for the first time in litigation. See *NLRB v Yeshiva U.*, 444 US 672, 685 n 22 (1980) ("We do not, of course, substitute counsel's post hoc rationale for the reasoning supplied by the Board itself."). Agency counsel, however, routinely massage agency decisions to strengthen their prospects in litigation.

[202] Justice Scalia's standard, by conferring deference on essentially any agency interpretation that arrives in court, does avoid one potential disadvantage of our approach. Under current law, when a court interprets statutory language without deference to an agency,

What the Justices in *Mead* should have said goes something as follows. The tariff classification ruling was not entitled to deference (contra Justice Scalia). The reasons bear no relation to the ruling's lack of procedural formality or generality of application, still less to notions of congressional intent (contra the majority). Deference should not attach because the relevant decision maker did not adopt the decision after meaningful review. Here, we must concede, there is some uncertainty about who this decision maker is. The organic statute at issue, rather than designating (as most statutes do) a particular agency official to exercise delegated power, assigned the power to issue tariff classifications only to the "Customs Service."[203] This peculiarity, however, cannot save the ruling. In a case involving such a statutory delegation, the values of accountable and disciplined decision making indicate that the head of the named agency—the Customs Commissioner—should count as the critical decision maker for *Chevron* purposes. This official did not issue the classification ruling in question. Neither the commissioner's nor any other official's post hoc decision to defend the ruling in litigation provides the necessary high-level input to qualify the ruling for *Chevron* deference (contra Justice Scalia again). Conversely, the ex ante issuance of a regulation providing that all classification rulings represent the official position of the Customs Service fails to meet the standard;[204] as earlier noted, prospective "adoptions," because they preclude meaningful review, do not suffice.[205] The ruling still may qualify for *Skidmore* deference. But the ruling has no claim on courts independent of the qualities of expertise and persuasiveness it reflects.

This approach doubtless would preclude most rulings of this kind from gaining *Chevron* deference. Because these decisions are so numerous, and because most are so mundane, no statutory delegatee will—or should—usually concern herself with them.[206] Rela-

---

the judicial decision forever locks in the agency, depriving it of the ability to claim deference for a different interpretation in the future. See *Neal v United States*, 516 US 284 (1996); *Lechmere, Inc. v NLRB*, 502 US 527 (1992). This doctrine, which we think may be misguided, means that the agency may have only one shot on a given issue to satisfy the conditions for judicial deference. The agency, however, retains the ability to factor in this danger when deciding whether the statutory delegatee herself should issue an interpretation.

[203] See 19 USC § 1500; text accompanying note 23.

[204] See 19 CFR § 177.9.

[205] See text following note 171.

[206] See text following note 165.

tively low-level officials will dispatch these opinions secure in the knowledge that the statutory delegatee (or her central staff) has neither the time nor the inclination to provide supervision. And in the absence of this supervision, for all the political and institutional reasons we noted earlier,[207] the delegatee almost always will decline to issue these decisions in her name; or if these constraints somehow fail to operate, a judicial backstop meant to detect policies of rubberstamping, also described earlier, should work to prevent the attachment of deference.

In select cases, however, our standard would accord deference to such rulings. A component within an agency may refer an issue like that in *Mead* to the statutory delegatee, or she may reach down herself to decide the issue. The reason for her participation might bear no relation to *Chevron*. She might become involved because the issue is especially nettlesome or sensitive; because the issue matters to more than one component of the agency; because the issue calls for a creative decision-making process, which she can best initiate; or because the issue has broad ramifications, which may make general, rather than case-by-case, resolution appropriate. Or the reason for her participation might flow from the *Chevron* nondelegation principle itself—because the agency has special reasons, not apparent in *Mead*, for wanting the courts to defer to a given interpretation. However the matter reaches the statutory delegatee's in-box and with whatever cause, if the delegatee adopts a decision, *Chevron* deference should follow.

This approach should govern all kinds of administrative action. It should apply regardless whether the action is accompanied by formal or informal procedures and regardless whether it is general or particular in nature. The proposed standard would decline to give *Chevron* deference to the result of a formal proceeding (either a rulemaking or an adjudication) conducted pursuant to an internal delegation. So, for example, if the Board of Immigration Appeals in the Department of Justice, which operates under authority delegated from the Attorney General, desires deference for a decision, the Attorney General would have to adopt that decision, as she occasionally does.[208] On the other hand, the proposed standard

---

[207] See text accompanying notes 173–87.

[208] This result would conflict with current doctrine. See *INS v Aguirre-Aguirre*, 526 US 415 (1999) (conferring *Chevron* deference on a decision of the Board of Immigration Appeals). Similarly, the proposed approach would decline to give deference to a formal rule

would accord *Chevron* deference to even informal decisions (either general or particular) that a statutory delegatee herself renders. Consider, for example, the Comptroller of the Currency's interpretive letters regarding the National Banking Act; whereas the *Mead* Court could not explain how its analysis comported with prior caselaw according deference to these interpretations,[209] our approach would provide a rationale for this precedent (assuming the comptroller signed the letter). Or consider, more importantly, the mass of rules that almost all agencies issue under the good-cause and other exceptions to the APA's notice-and-comment requirements;[210] whereas *Mead* would deny deference to these rules, our standard usually would confer deference on them.

Nothing in this approach, of course, would legitimize agency action that violates legal requirements relating to formal procedures or generality; *Chevron* deference would attach only to lawful action. The APA or other statutory law imposes a variety of constraints on the means by which and form in which agencies can issue interpretations. When an agency fails to comply with these requirements, the action is invalid and the question of *Chevron* deference does not arise.[211] But as demonstrated earlier, the range of legal agency action lacking formality or generality is broad.[212] The scope of *Chevron* deference should be correspondingly broad. An agency should not have to conform its decision making to some idealized notion of either general lawmaking or courtlike formality to receive judicial deference. Within the sphere of legality, all the agency need do is set up its decision-making processes and structures to ensure that a high-level official takes appropriate responsibility for the interpretation.

---

that a subordinate of the statutory delegatee adopts. The Court appears never to have addressed this issue. Consider *United States v Touby*, 500 US 160 (1991) (upholding a controlled substance classification that the Administrator of the Drug Enforcement Agency issued pursuant to a delegation from the Attorney General, but not addressing the *Chevron* question).

[209] See 121 S Ct at 2173 (affirming, but without explanation, *NationsBank of NC, NA v Variable Annuity Life Insurance Co.*, 513 US 251 (1995)).

[210] See text accompanying notes 14–16.

[211] An agency, for example, violates section 553 of the APA by giving final binding effect to a general policy statement adopted without notice and comment. Regardless whether a statutory delegatee has adopted the policy statement, this prohibition applies. So if an agency applies a policy statement to a party without conducting a separate enforcement proceeding, in which the party has an opportunity to contest the position taken in the statement, the court should invalidate the action without considering *Chevron*.

[212] See text accompanying notes 14–16, 102–04.

VI. Conclusion

Administrative law, as practiced and discussed, too much rests on two stock, though not parallel, dichotomies: that between formal and informal procedures and that between general and particular rulings. Once the *Mead* Court reached beyond its unhelpful rhetoric of congressional intent, the Court relied on just these categories to structure the deference inquiry. The Court's analysis rewards and thereby promotes procedural formality (principally) and generality (secondarily) on the view that these characteristics enhance the accountability and deliberativeness of agency action. But in ways that now should be familiar to observers of administrative law, the Court's emphasis on these dual features threatens to increase the ossification and inflexibility of agency process. And the Court's focus both denies and accords judicial deference in the wrong places—denying it to interpretations that, when measured against the Court's own values, properly should reside in agency hands and conferring it on interpretations that, when measured against those same values, should be subject to independent scrutiny.

The alternative approach offered in this article, which is within reach of the Court, makes the institutional choice question of *Chevron* dependent on a key aspect of agency organization—the level in the administrative hierarchy at which final decision making takes place. The congressional nondelegation doctrine, which aims to promote (as most of administrative law aims to promote) similar values as *Chevron* and *Mead*, suggests and informs this approach. An internal agency nondelegation doctrine, like the congressional analogue, would recognize the comparative responsiveness and visibility of certain officials (here, high-level administrators) to the public. And an agency nondelegation doctrine, once again like the congressional analogue, would acknowledge the ability of certain officials to discipline decision making throughout a large and unwieldy bureaucracy. This doctrine, implemented through *Chevron*, would avoid the well-known pitfalls of its congressional cousin. Given the likely interaction between legal incentives and political and institutional pressures in the administrative sphere, often overlooked in discussions of judicial review, the doctrine neither would lead to overcentralization of decision making nor prove incapable of principled enforcement.

In advocating this approach, we have in mind an objective beyond, as well as within, its boundaries. Both administrative law doctrine and administrative law scholarship, in focusing on the two stock dichotomies noted above, have disregarded other matters pertaining to administrative decision-making structures. We have emphasized a single variable: the vertical distribution of decision-making authority within an agency. But others might well have equivalent importance in one context or another: the horizontal distribution of this authority (for example, as between and among different agency components), the nature of the relationship between the agency and the White House, even the budgetary resources available to the particular agency decision maker. Any full understanding of agency process must take into account these institutional elements; administrative law scholarship thus should focus more than it does now on them. And administrative law doctrine—and, in particular, various doctrines of judicial review—profitably might reflect in ways beyond what we have discussed here these features of agency decision-making structure. Courts have disregarded most of the ways in which agencies organize their decision making; the state of administration and administrative law today suggests that it is time for courts to expand their field of vision.

FREDERICK SCHAUER

THE DILEMMA OF IGNORANCE: PGA TOUR, INC. v CASEY MARTIN

Hans Kelsen observed, famously, that no legal act was completely determined by the law.[1] And although the truth of Kelsen's statement is obviously contingent upon adopting a particular and contested understanding of just what the law is,[2] his observation is a useful reminder that even those who subscribe to the possibility of strong constraint by legal rules and legal precedents must acknowledge that those rules and precedents can only take us so far. Like a frame without a picture, to employ another Kelsenian observation,[3] legal rules and legal precedents may determine the

Frederick Schauer is Academic Dean and Frank Stanton Professor of the First Amendment, John F. Kennedy School of Government, Harvard University.

AUTHOR'S NOTE: The research and writing of this article were supported by the Joan Shorenstein Center on the Press, Politics and Public Policy, John F. Kennedy School of Government, Harvard University. I am grateful to the participants at the Kennedy School Faculty Research Seminar for their comments and their challenges, to Jack Donahue and Christine Jolls for useful comments, and to Larry Alexander for valuable conversation about golf as well as about law.

[1] Hans Kelsen, *Pure Theory of Law* 349 (M. Knight trans, California, 2d ed 1967) ("[E]very law-applying act is only partly determined by law . . . "). See also Richard H. Fallon, Jr., *Ruminations on the Work of Frederick Schauer*, 72 Notre Dame L Rev 1391, 1402 (1997) (judicial decision making can be "bound, but not necessarily determined, by law.").

[2] Under a range of antipositivist views, law is not a separate and pedigreed domain, but is better understood in terms of what judges do, and in terms of the ability of judges and other legal decision makers to draw on the full universe of socially recognized political acts. See Ronald Dworkin, *Law's Empire* (Harvard, 1986); Ronald Dworkin, *Taking Rights Seriously* (Harvard, 1978); Ronald Dworkin, *A Reply by Ronald Dworkin*, in Marshall Cohen, ed, *Ronald Dworkin and Contemporary Jurisprudence* 261–63 (Duckworth, 1984) (describing as "law" all of the standards that judges have a duty to apply). Under this view, of course, every legal act is tautologically entirely determined by law.

[3] Kelsen, *Pure Theory of Law* 245 (cited in note 1). See also Hans Kelsen, *Introduction to the Problems of Legal Theory* 80 (Bonnie L. Paulson and Stanley L. Paulson trans, Clarendon/Oxford, 1992).

boundaries of plausible legal decision without determining precisely what is to be done within those boundaries.

If legal decision making often, to take the weaker view, or inevitably, to take the stronger, leads us into the realm of "non-law," then the looming question is what judges are to do when they enter this realm. H. L. A. Hart suggested that judges find themselves exercising "discretion" when law runs out,[4] but offered little help in thinking about what a judge actually *does* when she exercises discretion, and what sources of information and enlightenment are relevant to its exercise.[5] Indeed, in likening the exercise of discretion to the practice of legislation, and in describing the exercise of discretion as "a fresh choice between open alternatives,"[6] Hart might have been suggesting either that the nature of judicial discretion was not the concern of the legal theorist, or perhaps that judges were as legally unconstrained in looking for guidance in exercising discretion as legislators were in enacting legislation.

That judicial discretion is legally unconstrained is, given these understandings of "law," tautologically true. Yet the tautology is singularly helpful in thinking more broadly about what judges actually *do* in exercising their discretion, and in thinking more normatively about what judges *should* do when they are compelled to exercise discretion. This question of judicial behavior within the domain of discretion is especially important in considering the role of judges in courts of general jurisdiction, for such judges will necessarily be cast into the role of making decisions about matters as to which their antecedent knowledge is most likely to be negligible, and also cast into the role of using methodologies far afield from anything they would have been required to study in law school.[7] And although the information-providing functions of tri-

---

[4] H. L. A. Hart, *The Concept of Law* 125–30 (Clarendon/Oxford, 1961).

[5] Hart did observe that the judge's decision would not simply be arbitrary, H. L. A. Hart, *Problems in the Philosophy of Law*, in *Essays in Jurisprudence and Philosophy* 106–07 (Clarendon/Oxford, 1983), an observation that is consistent with Hart's (correct) view that nonlegal judgments can be more or less sound as a matter of morality, politics, or policy. For useful elaboration of Hart on indeterminacy and the discretion that follows from it, see Brian Bix, *Law, Language, and Legal Determinacy* 18–35 (Clarendon/Oxford, 1993); John Gardner, *Concerning Permissive Sources and Gaps*, 8 Oxford J Legal Stud 457 (1988). See also Marisa Iglesias Vila, *Facing Judicial Discretion: Legal Knowledge and Right Answers Revisited* (Kluwer, 2001), especially at 4–76.

[6] Hart, *The Concept of Law* at 125 (cited in note 4).

[7] If law consists of everything that judges do or everything that judges should do, see note 2, and if legal education, legal training, legal reasoning, and thinking like a lawyer

als, appeals, and judge-initiated research can often take judges some way down the road leading from ignorance to expertise, there are limits to just how much we can expect judges to know about the full range of domains into which their docket takes them. As a consequence, judicial discretion will often be a process in which judges would ideally be required to have a degree of expertise that they simply do not possess. Yet although judges may often lack the degree of expertise to decide the issues before them, they may also find themselves compelled by their docket or the legal indeterminacy of the relevant law to make just those decisions. How judges, individually and collectively as the judicial system, react to what we might uncharitably call the "dilemma of ignorance" is one of the central issues in judicial decision and in the design of judicial institutions.

The dilemma of ignorance has rarely been presented with such clarity—and such publicity—as it was in *PGA Tour, Inc. v Casey Martin*,[8] a case that but for *Bush v Gore*[9] would have attracted more public attention than any other during the 2000 Term. For *PGA v Martin* not only had all of the elements of a morality play—a likable and talented but physically disabled underdog takes on the uncaring, tradition-bound, and country-club-based establishment of the sport of the rich—but also presented the issues in the widely followed context of professional sports. More specifically, by being centered on the publicly understandable issue of what accommodations to Martin's physical handicap were inconsistent with the essence of golf, *PGA v Martin* presented the issue of judicial expertise, or lack thereof, with a clarity that matched its publicity. *PGA v Martin* is important, therefore, in part because its very publicness is likely to increase its impact, but even more because it is such an important example of judges grappling explicitly with the di-

---

are defined as anything that would help a judge or lawyer perform that task, then considering what judges do when the law and their legal skills run out is tautologically uninteresting. But if we think of law as at least a partially limited or differentiated domain, in which law school is different from a school of public policy, and a bar examination tests for skills narrower than all of the skills necessary to good decision making, then my distinction between legal and nonlegal decision, a distinction that guides this article and the consciousness of most judges and most lawyers, makes sense. See Frederick Schauer and Virginia J. Wise, *Legal Positivism as Legal Information*, 82 Cornell L Rev 1080 (1997).

[8] 121 S Ct 1879 (2001).

[9] 121 S Ct 525 (2000).

lemma of what to do when they are forced to make decisions requiring knowledge that they simply do not possess.

I. Casey Martin's Case

Casey Martin is a young and talented professional golfer.
A college teammate of Tiger Woods on the Stanford University
golf team, Martin had won a large number of amateur tournaments
before turning professional, and it is fair to say that he is one of
the two or three hundred best golfers in the world, no mean ac-
complishment in a sport played by tens of millions. Martin also,
however, suffers from Klippel-Trenaunay-Weber Syndrome, a
congenital and degenerative circulatory disorder that, in Martin's
case, obstructs the flow of blood from his right leg back to his
heart. The consequences of this for Martin are that his right leg
has atrophied, that he suffers from severe pain in that leg, and that
he consequently has great difficulty walking significant distances.
Moreover, walking for an extended time subjects Martin to a
heightened risk of hemorrhaging, blood clots, bone fractures, and,
conceivably, having his right leg amputated.
     The game of golf that ordinary recreational golfers play is not
a game in which walking between shots is a requirement. Neither
the formal nor informal rules of golf prohibit the employment of
motorized carts, and their use has become widespread. Indeed,
many upscale golf courses, especially in resort areas, require their
use, partly to speed up play, and partly because the rental fees
provide a substantial revenue source for golf courses. For vast
numbers of casual golfers and a great many quite serious ones, golf
is a game in which the player is transported between shots in an
electric cart holding golf clubs, lunch, beverages, and spare cloth-
ing in addition to the two golfers who ride in it.
     At the highest competitive levels, however, the situation is dif-
ferent. The National Collegiate Athletic Association requires golfers playing in NCAA tournaments to walk the entire course and
to carry their own golf clubs. And although professional golfers
are not required to carry their own clubs, the Professional Golf
Association requires players to walk the entire course when playing
in tournaments on the PGA Tour, on the Buy.com Tour (formerly
the Nike Tour, and the highest level of American professional golf
except for the PGA Tour), and when competing in the final stage

of the qualifying tournament (Q-School) to determine which golf-ers will earn regular playing privileges on either the PGA or Buy.com tours.[10]

Because of his affliction, Martin had secured from the NCAA and the PAC-10 athletic conference an exemption from their "walk and carry" requirements when he was a college golfer at Stanford. When playing in golf tournaments in college, therefore, Martin was permitted to ride in a golf cart rather than walk, and to use the golf cart rather than his shoulder to carry his clubs. Upon attempting to qualify to play in PGA tournaments, however, no such exemptions were forthcoming. Martin's application for an exemption from the "no-carts" rule was denied by the PGA, which insisted that all competitors play under the same conditions, and insisted as well that the element of fatigue that comes from walking the entire golf course (a typical professional level golf course is about four miles long taking the shortest distance from tee to hole, although no golfer would be able to traverse it in such a direct line) is an essential part of the conditions of competition for competitive professional golf at the highest levels.

Martin sued the PGA under the Americans with Disabilities Act (ADA) of 1990,[11] claiming that the PGA's failure to allow an ac-commodation to Martin's disability violated 42 USC § 12182 (b)(2)(A)(ii), which includes within the statutory definition of "dis-crimination" the "failure to make reasonable modifications" for disabled individuals.[12] According to Martin, permitting him to ride in a golf cart while playing in PGA tournaments was just such a "reasonable modification," so that the PGA's failure to allow him to ride constituted a failure to make a reasonable modification and was thus a violation of the Act.

In response, the PGA relied on a different clause of the same

---

[10] These rules are discussed in the Court's opinion, 121 S Ct at 1884–85.

[11] 42 USC § 12101 et seq (1998).

[12] It is important to recognize at the outset that the Americans with Disabilities Act is not simply an antidiscrimination law. It requires that accommodations be made to persons with disabilities, although there is a disagreement within the literature over the extent to which accommodation differs from antidiscrimination. See generally Samuel Issacharoff and Justin Nelson, *Discrimination with a Difference: Can Employment Discrimination Law Accommo-date the Americans with Disabilities Act?* 79 NC L Rev 307 (2001); Christine Jolls, *Antidiscrim-ination and Accommodation*, 115 Harv L Rev 642 (2001); Christine Jolls, *Accommodation Man-dates*, 53 Stan L Rev 223 (2000); Pamela S. Karlan and George Rutherglen, *Disabilities, Discrimination, and Reasonable Accommodation*, 46 Duke L J 1 (1996).

tise for the question of judicial power. Although the issue of judicial expertise about golf is not one likely to arise with great frequency, the question of judicial expertise about areas in which judges and Justices have limited familiarity is omnipresent. Rarely has a case presented this question with such clarity and with such public understandability, and golf as a case study in the consequences of judicial ignorance is what makes *PGA v Martin* of potentially enduring importance.

II. The Supreme Court on the Nature of Golf

On the merits of controversy, Casey Martin's case turned on the question whether allowing Martin to use a motorized golf cart in PGA tournaments would "fundamentally alter the nature" of competitive professional golf at the highest level, as the PGA claimed, or would instead be no more consequential to the "nature" of the activity than, say, the attire of the competitors. Even if the "fundamentally alter the nature" language had not appeared in the statute, it is conceivable that the same issue would have arisen in the context of trying to determine which accommodations to a disability were "reasonable" and which were not, but the explicit inclusion of the "fundamentally alter the nature" language focuses the inquiry, and focused the debate in the Supreme Court.

In concluding that allowing Martin to use a cart would not fundamentally alter the nature of the activity, Justice Stevens said that "[a]s an initial matter, we observe that the use of carts is not itself inconsistent with the fundamental character of the game of golf."[21] This is a curious statement, since what Justice Stevens describes as an "initial matter" subject to preliminary "observ[ation]" is what might reasonably be thought to be the very matter at issue. If using carts is inconsistent with the fundamental character of the game of golf, then the PGA would plainly have the right to prevail under the "fundamentally alter" language in the statute. But if the use of carts is consistent with the fundamental character of the game, then Martin's use of a cart could hardly be said to fundamentally alter the nature of the activity. It is true, of course, that riding in a golf cart could be consistent with the fundamental character of

---

[21] Id at 1893.

golf but not consistent with the fundamental character of high-level professional competitive golf, and presumably this possibility explains why Justice Stevens treats the question of the fundamental character of (all of) golf as an "initial matter." But the conclusion that inquiry into the fundamental nature of high-level professional golf is largely dependent on the fundamental nature of ordinary golf played by ordinary people is just what the PGA denied, so this conclusion can hardly be thought of as preliminary. Treating as an initial matter something so close to the major point of contention is thus a curious way of proceeding, although it does turn out to explain much of the majority's reasoning.

To support the conclusion that high-level professional competitive golf is not fundamentally altered by allowing one or even several competitors to ride in carts, Justice Stevens relies heavily on the unstated assumption that high-level professional competitive golf is a member of the category "golf," rather than on the plausible alternative assumption that high-level professional competitive golf is a member of the category "high-level professional competitive sports." The latter is hardly ridiculous, and it is possible that this latter categorization explains part of the PGA's motivation in insisting on the no-carts rule. Professional golfers, like professional bowlers and professional pool players, tend to obsess about whether they are "really" athletes, worried that to far too many people professional golf seems more akin to competitive bass fishing than it does to "real" sports like football, basketball, and the decathlon. Accordingly, it would not be surprising to find the PGA exaggerating the importance of physical endurance in the course of trying to explain to outsiders to that domain the nature of professional golf.[22]

But once the Court sees professional golf as a member of the category "golf," perhaps in part because it may also suspect that the PGA and its witnesses are exaggerating the importance of fitness and stamina for success as a professional golfer, the Court must then inquire about the nature of that category. It is clear that the word "golf" is correctly, as a matter of ordinary linguistic us-

---

[22] One of the witnesses at trial was Jack Nicklaus, 121 S Ct at 1887 n 14, who testified that "physical fitness" as well as "fatigue" were "part of the game of golf." Nicklaus himself, however, although now plainly fit at age sixty-two, could charitably have been described as portly during the early years of his greatest professional success. Indeed, he was then routinely chided as "Fat Jack" in the press and by jealous competitors.

age, applied to variations on the rules of golf ranging quite far from the formal rules of golf.[23] Justice Stevens implicitly relies on this common understanding about the fundamental nature of golf, but rests his conclusion even more heavily on the history of the game. He insists that "[f]rom early on, the essence of the game has been shot making—using clubs to cause a ball to progress from the teeing ground to a hole some distance away with as few strokes as possible."[24] Drawing on both early (1744) and current golf rules,[25] and on secondary sources describing the history of golf, the Court concludes that walking, although obviously a necessary feature of golf in its early days when motorized transportation had not been invented, was not even then part of the concept of golf, and consequently that recent developments in golfer transportation and golf club carriage are peripheral to the "essential" character of the game. Whatever the answer might be to the question "Is it chess without the queen?" the answer to the question "Is it golf without walking?" is to the majority plainly yes.

All this turned out to be too much for Justice Scalia. Arguing that competitive sports were necessarily defined by arbitrary rules (Why eighteen holes and not nineteen? Why three strikes rather than four?), he accused the majority of treating golf as if it were a matter of Platonic essences[26] when in fact it was simply a matter of arbitrary rules.[27] And as long as the rules were arbitrary, Justice

---

[23] In recent times the most prominent example of this phenomenon is former President Clinton, whose liberties with the rules of golf go well beyond winter rules, mulligans ("do-overs") on the first tee, and other modifications of the rules common among casual golfers of Clinton's skill level. For a sample of published accounts, see Glenn F. Bunting, *Game Fits President to a Tee*, Los Angeles Times (Nov 13, 1997), p E1; Melinda Henneberger, *Tom DeLay Holds No Gavel, but a Firm Grip on the Reins*, New York Times (June 21, 1999), p A1; Tim Tucker, *Shooting a 60 with President Mulligan*, Atlanta Constitution (Aug 16, 1999), p 1D.

[24] 121 S Ct at 1894.

[25] Id. The official rules of golf provide at best ambiguous support for the majority's position, since those rules explicitly permit tournament organizers to require that "[p]layers shall walk at all times during a stipulated round." Id at 1885 n 3.

[26] Id at 1902, 1903, 1905.

[27] This prompted the rejoinder from Justice Stevens that Justice Scalia was taking an [uncharacteristically] "postmodern" position. Id at 1897 n 57. The charge of postmodernism seems a bit confused, however, since one can in decidedly nonpostmodern fashion believe that certain facts are institutionally contingent without believing that all facts are contingent or socially constructed. John R. Searle, *The Construction of Social Reality* (Free Press, 1995). Believing that law, golf, the game of bridge, and the Brooklyn Bridge are socially constructed does not entail believing that gravity, giraffes, and the Grand Canyon are social constructions.

Scalia argued, there was no way around treating the rules as set by the sport's governing body as final, and, more importantly, no way around treating the answers given by the sport's governing body as the definitive answers to what properties could be eliminated or modified without "fundamentally alter[ing]" the nature of the activity. For Justice Scalia, professional golf is what the PGA says it is.

That the subject of the litigation was golf added fuel to Justice Scalia's ire. It is difficult to determine whether Justice Scalia objected to the majority's venture into determining the essence of golf because it was beyond the Justices' expertise or simply beneath their dignity.[28] But to the dissenters the determination of which of the features of the rules of professional golf were essential and which were not—which rules would, if changed, fundamentally alter the nature of the activity and which would not—would take the Court well beyond its area of competence, and well beyond the proper deployment of the judicial function.

"Blame Congress and not us," Justice Stevens and the majority can be understood as responding. Pointing out that the "fundamentally alter the nature" and "reasonable modification" language is in the statute itself,[29] Justice Stevens argued that the task of determining whether golf without walking is really golf was a task that Congress had through the explicit words of the Americans with Disabilities Act compelled the courts to take on. For the majority the question and the task that Justice Scalia found silly were nevertheless a question and a task that was compelled by the ADA's language. By including the words "fundamentally alter," Congress had explicitly and knowingly, or so the majority insists, put the courts in the business of determining the "fundamental nature" of a host of enterprises required by the ADA to make accommodations. That the Supreme Court found itself engaged in the enterprise of determining the fundamental nature of golf was not at all about golf, insists the majority, but was instead a function of the fact that golf is one of myriad enterprises whose fundamen-

---

[28] "Is someone riding around a golf course from shot to shot *really* a golfer? . . . Either out of humility or out of self-respect (one or the other) the Court should decline to answer this incredibly difficult and incredibly silly question." 121 S Ct at 1902–03 (Scalia, J, dissenting).

[29] Id at 1897 n 51.

tal nature it has become the statutory duty of the courts to determine.

III. On the Nature of Judicial Expertise

The debate between the majority and the dissent in *PGA v Martin* is not primarily about golf, and not even primarily about the "fundamentally alter the nature" language in the Americans with Disabilities Act. Rather, it is about the nature of judicial expertise. For Justice Scalia the courts have ventured into an area outside of their competence, and even if Congress has with its language statutorily authorized the excursion the courts would be better off interpreting that authorization as narrowly as possible. For the majority, by contrast, the statutory authorization should be taken at face value,[30] with the courts being no more authorized to fail to go where Congress sends them than they are to go where Congress has not sent them.

The debate about judicial expertise, however, is unlikely to be illuminated by rehearsing generations-old disputes about the proper sources for statutory interpretation. Rather, we can perhaps shed some light on the issue by examining just what the Supreme Court does when it finds itself—whether willingly or not—venturing into an area in which its expertise is not immediately apparent. And golf is just such an area. By all accounts the Supreme Court contains just one serious golfer—Justice O'Connor—although it is highly likely that most of the others have played occasionally and that all of the others have a basic understanding of the idea of the game. But it is highly unlikely that any of the Justices have anything approaching serious expertise about the game, its history, or its traditions. If we frame the question in terms of whether any of the Justices could have been qualified at trial as an expert witness

---

[30] Indeed, the majority's jibes at Justice Scalia might have avoided the misdirected charge of postmodernism, see note 27, and have been better directed against the inconsistency between his reluctance to take the congressional mandate to look at the "fundamental . . . nature" at face value and his oft-stated commitment to the text when engaged in statutory interpretation. See *Green v Bock Laundry Machine Co.*, 490 US 504, 527–30 (1989) (Scalia concurring in the judgment); *Chisom v Roemer*, 501 US 380, 404–05 (1991) (Scalia dissenting); Antonin Scalia, *Common-Law Courts in a Civil-Law System: The Role of United States Federal Courts in Interpreting the Constitution and Laws*, in Amy Guttman, ed, *A Matter of Interpretation: Federal Courts and the Law* 3, 16–17, 23–37 (Princeton, 1997). See also Bradley C. Karkkainen, *"Plain Meaning": Justice Scalia's Jurisprudence of Strict Statutory Construction*, 17 Harv J L & Pub Pol 401 (1994).

on golf according to the standards of the Federal Rules of Evidence, there is no indication that the answer would have been yes.

It is, of course, central to the judicial function that judges determine controversies involving topics about which the judges themselves are not expert. Instead, judges, at trial, listen to competing stories, hear the testimony of experts, and determine, when there is no jury, which side has the better of the argument. Whether the controversy be about the existence of conspiracies in restraint of trade, the causes of automobile or airline accidents, or for that matter the nature of the game of golf, it is (possibly) too late in the day to suggest that courts should be limited in their jurisdiction to topics about which the judges (and, a fortiori, juries) have antecedent and genuine expertise. Although having decisions made on the basis of just such expertise is at the heart of the idea of decisions made by specialized administrative agencies—the Securities and Exchange Commission, the Occupational Safety and Health Administration, and the National Endowment for the Arts, for example—this quite plausible approach to institutional design has rarely been thought to supplant the role of courts of general jurisdiction. And although there are courts whose jurisdiction is defined by the expertise of the judges—the Court of Military Appeals, the Court of Customs and Patent Appeals, the Court of International Trade, and the bankruptcy courts, for example—these are again best thought of as the exceptions and not the rule.

The traditional picture of the catholic capacities of courts of general jurisdiction, however, relies heavily on the nature of the trial. At trial witnesses can testify, documents can be introduced, and properly qualified experts can offer their opinions. The process of making a trial record, so the traditional picture has it, is precisely the process by which the judiciary informs itself about matters that would otherwise have been beyond its ken. If to determine the matters before it a trial courts needs to know about the structure of the airline industry, the harmfulness of cigarettes, or the norms of the stock markets, the law of evidence and the rules of procedure stand ready to facilitate obtaining that information.

On appeal, however, things are different, for the capacity of appellate courts to obtain new information, especially new information whose accuracy is likely to be contested by one or the other of the parties—and therefore not subject to judicial notice—is drastically limited. Indeed, the most famous exceptions to this principle turn out to be hardly exceptions at all. The psychological tests cited by the Supreme Court in *Brown v Board of Education*[31] to support the proposition that separate but equal education was not equal at all were, even apart from questions about their soundness,[32] tests that had been presented at trial and were there subject to cross-examination. And even the early uses of the so-called "Brandeis Brief"[33] were not uses to establish the contested question of which social policies were wise, sound, or optimal, but rather were uses to establish the far less contested questions of which social policies had such a minimal degree of empirical and public support that they could satisfy the standards of what later was to become rational basis scrutiny.[34] But when the question is whether the appellate court is the appropriate forum for the presentation of new and centrally contested nonlegal information, the traditional answer is that it is not.

Under this traditional picture, the Supreme Court's approach to the "what is the essence of golf?" question that was at the heart of *PGA v Martin* might have been expected to be an approach relying heavily on the findings below. Yet there is very little in the majority opinion to suggest that the Court's conclusion that walking is not part of the essence of golf was simply an affirmation of a finding below. There is nary a word about a deferential posture to findings of fact below, nor about a standard of review— abuse of discretion, substantial evidence, arbitrary and capricious, or whatever—that gives primacy to findings of fact at the trial level. All of the language in Justice Stevens's opinion is the language of his having decided the issue, along with six of his colleagues, and not the language of having affirmed someone else's decision of the issue. Twice the majority refers to the District Court's findings about fatigue,[35] but the overwhelming tone of the majority opinion is that, to quote directly, "we have demon-

---

[31] 347 US 483 (1954).

[32] See note 55 and accompanying text.

[33] As in, most prominently, *Muller v Oregon*, 208 US 412 (1908).

[34] See the discussions in Dean Alfange, *The Relevance of Legislative Facts in Constitutional Law*, 114 U Pa L Rev 637 (1966); David Bryden, *Brandeis's Facts*, 1 Const Comm 281 (1984); Kenneth Karst, *Legislative Facts in Constitutional Litigation*, 1960 Supreme Court Review 75; Jeffrey Shaman, *Constitutional Fact: The Perception of Reality by the Supreme Court*, 35 U Fla L Rev 236 (1983).

[35] 121 S Ct at 1895–96, 1897.

strated"[36] that the walking rule is not essential to the game of golf, even at the highest professional competitive levels, and that allowing a waiver of the rule would not "fundamentally alter the nature" of that enterprise. What emerges clearly from the majority opinion is the conclusion that it is the majority and not the trial judge who has determined that riding in a golf cart is not inconsistent with the fundamental nature of high-level competitive professional golf.

That the language of *PGA v Martin* is the language of independent Supreme Court decision and not the language of deference to findings below is not surprising. In the first place, the Court took the case, at least in part, because of a circuit split between the Ninth and Seventh Circuits. And when the circuits are split on the crucial issue, there would be no point in using the language of deference, because deciding to defer to one decision below rather than to another that reached the opposite conclusion on the very matter in issue is ordinarily to independently decide the issue and not to ratify a lower court decision. Deciding for *A* rather than *B* on the very issue on which *A* and *B* differ is typically not to defer to *A* or to *B*.[37] It is to decide. In addition, the notoriety of the case likely made it less possible for the Court to base its decision on simple deference to a decision below. It is hard enough for the Court to succeed in conveying to the public and to the press that its denials of certiorari do not represent decisions on the merits. It would be even harder to suggest, for one of the cases the Court did decide on the merits during the term, that it was only ratifying a decision below, an outcome that could be different in the Supreme Court were there to have been a different conclusion at trial. Finally, and relatedly, relying too heavily on the fortuity of a particular trial judge having decided in a particular way on the basis of a particular case presented by particular parties is inconsistent with a Supreme Court that routinely decides fewer than a hundred cases a year out of the close to eight thousand with

---

[36] Id at 1896.

[37] On occasion the decision for *A* rather then *B*, or vice versa, may be a product of one of the options presenting reasons for deference not presented by the other—a more careful opinion, a more experienced judge, or a more extensive record, for example. But more commonly such characteristics will not be determinative, and a reviewing court deciding which of two conflicting opinions below to prefer will find itself delving into the merits of the controversy.

the essence of torts, relied on *Torts in a Nutshell* and the "Torts" headings in *Corpus Juris Secundum* or *American Jurisprudence?*[45]

There is no need to belabor the point further, because it should be fairly obvious that the knowledge the Court uses to make its central decision is nonexpert knowledge on an issue as to which expertise is in theory available.[46] If it is central to the very idea of courts of general jurisdiction that they will function more as disinterested generalists than as sources of knowledgeable analysis of the nonlegal areas with which the law frequently intersects and relies, then few cases demonstrate this more clearly than *PGA v Martin*.

Although the infrequent appearance of golf on the dockets of the nation's appellate courts makes the point about nonexpertise especially clear in the context of *PGA v Martin*, it would be a mistake to assume that the issue is in any way a limited one. Consider, for example, the Sherman Antitrust Act,[47] whose mandate to the courts to determine which "contract[s], combination[s] . . . or con-spirac[ies]" are in restraint of trade, is not dissimilar to the ADA's mandate to the courts to determine which enterprises would be fundamentally altered by making accommodations to the disabled. And just as the determination of the fundamental nature of golf might better be assessed by golf insiders than by Supreme Court Justices, so too might the determination of which forms of corpo-

---

[45] I am not so naive as to ignore the possibility, indeed the probability, that the Justices, having made their decision, simply sent the clerks and librarians out to find nonlegal support for a decision already made. But of course much the same could be said about legal sources as well. If we accept (perhaps counterfactually, to the legal realist) that legal sources are decision-guiding rather than just decision-justifying, then it is certainly plausible that much the same can be said about nonlegal sources. To be skeptical about the use of nonlegal sources while not skeptical about legal sources assumes the very matter in issue, which is the question of the sources of judicial guidance in hard cases. Moreover, even if the exact nonlegal sources the Court uses are little more than the product of law clerks and librarians filling in the blanks for decisions already made, the sources found and then used may still provide a useful surrogate for contemplating the question of just how the Court obtains its knowledge of golf, or economics, or anything else. On all of this, see Frederick Schauer and Virginia J. Wise, *Nonlegal Information and the Delegalization of Law*, 29 J Legal Stud 495 (2000).

[46] That expertise is available is not the same as disinterested expertise being available, and a special problem in *Martin* was the extent to which the available expertise on golf was closely aligned with the PGA Tour, and the available expertise on Klippel-Trenaunay-Weber syndrome was closely aligned with Martin. Specialists in particular diseases rarely take the position that the diseases are not so bad, and specialists in particular sports rarely take the position that the sports are not so demanding.

[47] 15 USC § 1 (1998).

rate behavior would interfere with trade be better assessed by those with training in microeconomics, particularly those with a specialization in the economics of industrial organization. Similarly, when the Racketeer Influenced and Corrupt Organizations (RICO) Act limits its coverage to "patterns" of criminal activity,[48] again it is plausible to suppose that the knowledge required to determine what should or should not be a "pattern" under the act would be knowledge much more likely to be possessed by law enforcement experts or congressional investigating committees than by Supreme Court Justices.[49] And increasingly in recent years, Justice Breyer has been lamenting the fact that the Supreme Court finds itself having to decide issues involving and requiring scientific knowledge that none of the members of the court possess, and that are often at best dimly illuminated by the briefs and other formal materials before the Court.[50]

Given the pervasive presence of what Justice Jackson referred to as the "majestic generalities" of the Constitution,[51] the phenomenon of appellate courts in general and the Supreme Court in particular engaging in fact-based policy determinations on the basis of information contained neither in the record nor in the Justices' own expertise is even more pervasive in constitutional adjudication. When the Supreme Court in *New York Times Co. v Sullivan*[52] drastically limited the scope of libel law because of a commitment to the policy of unchilled criticism of public officials (and later public figures[53]), it based its judgment on the empirical and economic judgment, not supported either in the record or in any empirical

---

[48] 18 USC § 1965(5) (1998).

[49] For the Supreme Court debate on this very issue, compare the opinions of Justice Brennan for the majority and Justice Scalia, concurring in the judgment, in *H.J., Inc. v Northwestern Bell Telephone Co.*, 492 US 229 (1989). For a sample of resistance to taking on such a statutorily mandated policy-making task, see *Georgia Ass'n of Retarded Citizens v McDaniel*, 716 F2d 1565, 1581–82 (11th Cir 1983) (Hill, dissenting). See generally Bernard W. Bell, *R-E-S-P-E-C-T: Respecting Legislative Judgments in Interpretive Theory*, 78 NC L Rev 1253, 1307–17 (2000); Harry T. Edwards, *The Role of a Judge in Modern Society: Some Reflections on Current Practice in Federal Appellate Adjudication*, 32 Cleve St L Rev 285, 424–27 (1984).

[50] See Stephen Breyer, "Closing Address" at Conference on DNA and the Criminal Justice System, John F. Kennedy School of Government, Harvard University, Nov 21, 2000.

[51] *West Virginia Bd of Educ. v Barnette*, 319 US 624, 639–40 (1943).

[52] 376 US 254 (1964).

[53] *Curtis Publishing Co. v Butts*, 388 US 130 (1967); *Associated Press v Walker*, 388 US 130 (1967).

information then available, that the media would refrain from criticizing public officials and public policy if the common law of libel were allowed to continue. This may well be true, but there are plausible reasons to believe it may be false, and equally plausible policy alternatives not explored by the Court.[54] This is not to say that the Court's judgment casting aside the common law was wrong; but it is to say that its judgment, right or wrong, was based on what was at best armchair economics and at worst casual speculation, not about the law itself, but about the newspaper industry, its organization, and the incentives of its inhabitants. Much the same can be (and has been) said about the empirical and policy basis for the exclusionary rule,[55] and it has been a recurrent criticism of the Court's reliance on psychological studies in *Brown*.[56] And the Court's statistical misstatements in *Craig v Boren*[57] provide little basis for confidence that the Court can handle the empirical and statistical analyses that are an important, even if not complete, part of a full-blown policy analysis.

None of this, however, may be merely about statutes or the Constitution, or merely about American courts. Rather, the phenomenon of lawmaking on the basis of dimly informed policy speculation can arguably be said to be an accurate, even if possibly mean-spirited, characterization of the entire common law process. When common law courts modify a common law rule, they do so not only on the basis of principles, as Ronald Dworkin has long maintained,[58] but also on the basis of policy, as Dworkin denies but Melvin Eisenberg has persuasively demonstrated.[59] In ways

---

[54] See Frederick Schauer, *Uncoupling Free Speech*, 92 Colum L Rev 1321 (1992).

[55] See Yale Kamisar, *Does (Did) (Should) the Exclusionary Rule Rest on a "Principled Basis" Rather Than an "Empirical Proposition"?* 16 Creighton L Rev 565 (1983).

[56] See especially Edmund Cahn, *Jurisprudence*, 30 NYU L Rev 150 (1955). See also Charles Black, *The Lawfulness of the Segregation Decisions*, 69 Yale L J 421 (1960); Frank Goodman, *De Facto School Segregation: A Constitutional and Empirical Analysis*, 70 Calif L Rev 275 (1972).

[57] 429 US 190 (1976), in which Justice Brennan's opinion for the Court inferred from a .18 percent arrest rate for females and a 2.00 percent arrest rate for males that the correlation between gender and driving while intoxicated in the relevant age group was only 2 percent.

[58] Ronald Dworkin, *A Matter of Principle* (Harvard, 1987); Ronald Dworkin, *Law's Empire* (Harvard, 1986); Ronald Dworkin, *Taking Rights Seriously* (Harvard, 1978).

[59] Melvin A. Eisenberg, *The Nature of the Common Law* (Harvard, 1988).

that Holmes identified more than a century ago, the path of the common law is a path consisting of empirical assessment, behavioral speculation, and normative analysis far more than it is a path of logical deduction or any other form of distinctively legal reasoning.[60] Once we recognize that the common law at its heart is a process in which what had previously been thought to be the rules are modified in the process of application, we recognize as well that this is not and cannot be a process that is entirely rule-based.[61] Rather, like any rule-making or rule-remaking process, it is a process in which determining what the rule should be on the basis of knowledge about the state of the world and knowledge about the nature of human behavior in response to rules is of the essence.

In struggling to identify the essence of golf, therefore, the Supreme Court in *PGA v Martin* does not appear to have departed nearly as much from traditional judicial practice as the dissent appears to suggest. It is true that the Court's knowledge of golf at the highest level may have been amateurish, but there is no reason to believe it was any more amateurish than the Court's knowledge of newspaper practices in *New York Times v Sullivan*, its knowledge of educational psychology in *Brown*, or for that matter its knowledge of the empirical dimensions of voting behavior in *Bush v Gore*.[62] If there is indeed a dilemma of ignorance plaguing the common law process, and plaguing in similar fashion adjudication centered on linguistically indeterminate statutes or constitutional provisions, then this is not a dilemma anywhere near unique to *PGA v Martin*. Instead, *PGA v Martin* may have only presented in a

---

[60] This appears to be the best understanding of Holmes's view that the life of the law is not logic but experience. Oliver Wendell Holmes, *The Common Law* 1 (Little Brown, 1881). See also Oliver Wendell Holmes, *The Path of the Law*, 10 Harv L Rev 457 (1897).

[61] See Frederick Schauer, *Is the Common Law Law?* 77 Calif L Rev 455 (1989).

[62] The Court in *Bush* places some weight on the fact that 2 percent of the ballots in any presidential election fail to select a candidate for President, 531 US at 103, and relies in significant part for that proposition on an article in the *Omaha World-Herald* on Nov 15, 2000, entitled "Balloting Problems Not Rare But Only in a Very Close Election Do Mistakes and Mismarking Make a Difference." It turns out that the author of the article was one Matt Kelley, a twenty-nine-year-old reporter for the *World-Herald* who was so junior upon his arrival at the paper a few years earlier that the only office that could be found for him was a quickly converted closet, resulting in his colleagues referring to him as "Closet Boy." See Michael Kelly, *'Closet Boy' Makes History*, Omaha World-Herald (Dec 14, 2000), p 19. Closet Boy's information may well have been accurate, but it does give pause about the Court's sophistication in locating nonlegal information, even the nonlegal information that seems important to the Court's decisions.

particularly accessible way a problem historically ignored by the blind faith in the ability of the common law to "work itself pure."[63]

IV. The Management of Ignorance

We can identify (at least) four strategies for dealing with the dilemma of ignorance. The first is the one represented by the majority opinion in *PGA v Martin*, and might best be seen as a form of muddling through. Yes, appellate decision making requires more factual knowledge not contained in the record than the traditional Blackstonian view of adjudication recognized,[64] this strategy acknowledges, but that does not conclusively condemn the process. By having multimember appellate courts, and nine members in the Supreme Court, the process ameliorates some of the dilemma of ignorance by increasing the range of skills and experiences represented on the court. And with diligent assistance in the form of law clerks and library staffs, the judges have the ability to remedy some of their ignorance by doing their own research as and when the nature of the case demands it. Moreover, it is commonly the case, especially in the Supreme Court, that an adversary process coupled with liberal allowance of amicus briefs[65] will bring to the Court a vast amount of information otherwise unavailable to the Justices. If *PGA v Martin* had not been about golf but had been about a more obscure sport—curling, for example—it still would have been the case that the materials available to the Justices from the record below, from the parties, and from the amici would have given nine people of considerable experience, a diversity of opinions, and presumably good judgment most of the raw material they would have needed to make an intelligent, even if not demonstrably correct, decision.

From a somewhat different perspective, the muddling through represented by the majority opinion in *PGA v Martin* and the overwhelming bulk of most appellate constitutional and common law adjudication, as well as much appellate statutory adjudication,

---

[63] *Omychund v Barker*, 26 Eng Rep 15, 33 (1744) (Lord Mansfield). See also Lon L. Fuller, *The Forms and Limits of Adjudication*, 92 Harv L Rev 353, 377–81 (1978).

[64] I take Blackstone to be the exemplar of the belief that legal decision is not very much a matter of experience and largely a matter of logic and discovery.

[65] See Stephanie Tai, *Friendly Science: Medical, Scientific, and Technical Amici Before the Supreme Court*, 78 Wash U L Q 789 (2000).

might be little cause for alarm. Although it may seem scary to have major issues of policy determined by nine relatively uninformed people assisted by thirty-odd twenty-somethings surfing the Web, similarly dismal characterizations can be applied to the alternatives. Legislation is as often based on anecdote as analysis, interest group influence in legislative determinations is rampant,[66] staff influence is considerable,[67] and legislative hearings are typically performances rather than attempts by the legislature or one of its committees to obtain information. Although romantic glorification of the judicial process may be the characteristic pathology of many lawyers and most American law professors, correcting for this by unwarranted glorification of the legislative process is no more justified. And even if so-called expert decision making, whether by administrative agencies or blue-ribbon commissions, may solve some of the dilemma of ignorance, the process is not immune from regulatory capture, the agendas of the experts, and numerous other pathologies.[68] So even if muddling through is the best we can say about the process in cases like *PGA v Martin*, perhaps muddling through by a group of moderately intelligent, moderately electorally unaccountable, and moderately disinterested decision makers does not look nearly so bad when we compare it to the likely alternatives.

At the opposite pole from muddling through and being comfortable with it is the second approach, represented by Justice Scalia's dissent. For Justice Scalia the courts should be protective of their own comparative advantage, and should not venture into domains in which they have little expertise and little hope of obtaining it. And although the majority in *PGA v Martin* properly points out that the task that Justice Scalia finds distasteful for the judiciary appears to be compelled by the open-ended and policy-laden statu-

---

[66] See John Ferejohn and Barry Weingast, *Limitation of Statutes: Strategic Statutory Interpretation*, 80 Georgetown L J 565 (1992); Jonathan R. Macey, *Promoting Public-Regarding Legislation Through Statutory Interpretation: An Interest Group Model*, 86 Colum L Rev 223 (1986).

[67] See *Hirschey v Federal Energy Regulatory Commission*, 771 F2d 1, 7–8 (DC Cir 1985) (Scalia concurring); *Wallace v Christensen*, 802 F2d 1539, 1559–60 (9th Cir 1986) (Kozinski, concurring in the judgment); Roger H. Davidson, *What Judges Ought to Know About Lawmaking in Congress*, in Robert A. Katzmann, ed, *Judges and Legislators: Toward Institutional Comity* 90 (Brookings, 1988).

[68] See Jerry L. Mashaw, *Greed, Chaos, and Governance: Using Public Choice to Improve Public Law* (Yale, 1997).

merely as the traces of something deeper, as Dworkin maintains,[76] then Dworkin could well have come to a conclusion in *Martin* more aligned with the majority than the dissent. For present purposes, however, that is a side issue, less important than identifying a view that, like Justice Scalia's, takes policy as outside of the judicial ken, and that would also, albeit perhaps in different ways, seek to ensure that the courts in their decisions stayed away from making the kinds of policy determinations that characterized the majority in *Martin*.[77]

Most interesting, however, is the fourth strategy for dealing with the dilemma of ignorance, a strategy best exemplified on the Supreme Court by Justice Breyer and most actively promoted off the Supreme Court by Judge Posner.[78] Both Breyer and Posner recognize the necessity of nonlegal expertise in the making of judicial decisions, and recognize as well that judges are unlikely to have or to be able to obtain by traditional methods the necessary expertise. But unlike Justice Stevens, whose opinion Justice Breyer did join, neither Posner nor Breyer in their extrajudicial writings endorses the status quo of just muddling through. Rather, both, and especially Justice Breyer, advocate structural and procedural changes in the judiciary that would make it easier for judges to obtain the kinds of information they need in order to make the decisions that modern society requires of them. Whether it be more intensive training of judges in the techniques of empirical analysis, as Judge Posner has long advocated, or an increased ability for courts themselves to call on expertise without having to rely

---

[76] Ronald Dworkin, *Law's Empire* (cited in note 58), at 20–23. More recently, Dworkin has, consistent with the view articulated by Justice Stevens in *Martin*, taken broad legal language as representing a mandate or even a command to take on the tasks encompassed by the broad language. Ronald Dworkin, *Freedom's Law: The Moral Reading of the American Constitution* 2–9 (Harvard, 1996).

[77] There is a substantial risk, however, that these avoidance strategies will at times turn out to be less successful than their proponents suppose. Will Justice Scalia and those following him mask contested empirical issues as questions of law? Will Dworkin and those following him announce as principle and not policy issues that in fact contain contested empirical and policy judgments? To the extent that these pathologies are possible—if you have a hammer, every problem looks like a nail—the Scalia/Dworkin approach of defining judicial jurisdiction by reference to judicial comparative advantage may turn out to be illusory, and alternative approaches, including muddling through, may turn out at least to bring the benefits of transparency about what it is that the judges are actually doing.

[78] Richard A. Posner, *Overcoming Law* 208–10 (Harvard, 1995); Richard A. Posner, *The Problems of Jurisprudence* 132–36 (Harvard, 1990). More generally, see Richard Posner, *The Problematics of Moral and Legal Theory* (Harvard, 1998).

on the expertise hired by the parties, as Justice Breyer has famously urged,[79] both of them depart dramatically from the approach of Justice Scalia.[80] For Scalia the competence of the courts is a given, and the docket and the issues the courts take on need to be adjusted accordingly. But for Justice Breyer and Judge Posner, the docket and the issues are the given, and it is the competence of the courts that needs adjustment.

When applied to *PGA v Martin*, the Breyer-Posner approach opens up numerous possibilities at both trial and appellate levels. Most modestly, judges could simply recognize their own shortcomings, and self-consciously try to remedy them, not by on-the-fly web surfing but by semi-intensive immersion in the issues as and when they arise. Or, as suggested by Justice Breyer,[81] judges could wait to decide issues until extrajudicial policy debates have ripened, and could themselves even be part of these larger discussions. More radically, judges at trial could call their own experts,[82] and more radically yet, appellate courts could retain more ability than they now have to obtain information not offered by the parties, or to suspend proceedings and require the parties to provide additional information.

More broadly yet, judges could continue to press against the

---

[79] *General Electric Co. v Joiner*, 522 US 136, 147 (1997) (Breyer concurring); Stephen Breyer, *The Interdependence of Science and Law*, 82 Judicature 24 (1998).

[80] It is possible, however, that Justice Breyer, Judge Posner, and many others will misapprehend the nature of the relevant expertise. Is the relevant expertise about science policy, for example, the expertise of the scientist, as the scientists would have us believe, or the policy analyst, as the policy analysts would have us believe, or the science policy specialists, as the science policy specialists (some but not all of whom are scientists) would have us believe? Is the relevant expertise in *Martin* the expertise of the golfer, the sports physiologist, the physician, or someone else? Given that the identity of the expert is likely to be contested, and that claims of expertise will be clothed with the self-interest of experts in asserting that their expertise is most important, the role of the judge as ignorant but disinterested arbiter may become more appealing.

[81] Breyer, "Closing Address" (cited in note 50).

[82] Fueled by Justice Breyer, this has been an area of active debate and prescription. See *MediaCom Corp. v Rates Technology, Inc.*, 4 F Supp 2d 17, 29–30 (D Mass 1998); Joe S. Cecil and Thomas E. Willging, *Accepting Daubert's Invitation: Defining a Role for Court-Appointed Experts in Assessing Scientific Validity*, 43 Emory L J 995 (1994); Thomas M. Crowley, *Help Me Mr. Wizard! Can We Really Have "Neutral" Rule 706 Experts?* 1998 Detroit Coll L Rev 927; Ellen E. Deason, *Court-Appointed Expert Witness: Scientific Positivism Meets Bias and Deference*, 77 Or L Rev 59 (1998); Samuel Gross, *Expert Evidence*, 1991 Wis L Rev 1113, 1220 (1991); Laurel Hooker, Joe S. Cecil, and Thomas E. Willgang, *Assessing Causation in Breast Implant Litigation: The Role of Science Panels*, 64 L & Contemp Probs 139 (2001). For a more general look at the question, see Scott Brewer, *Expert Testimony and Intellectual Due Process*, 107 Yale L J 1535 (1998).

hold that two of the most important of litigation traditions have on judicial decision making. The first of these is that the ideal number of parties to a lawsuit is two. Although class actions, derivative suits, interpleader, impleader, cross-claims, institutional litigation, and numerous other devices of twentieth-century civil procedure have made inroads against the traditional model of one plaintiff and one defendant,[83] that model still shapes the legal and judicial consciousness[84] and still stands as a barrier to the kind of policy approach that would recognize that outside of traditional litigation the number of interests is likely to be more than two, and that the all-or-nothing, winner-take-all approach of traditional litigation is likely to be unsatisfactory.

Second, the traditional litigation model is based on litigation as a contest under strict rules. Among the most constraining of these rules is that the parties and not the judge control the informational terrain on which the contest will be contested. This is most apparent in traditional English practice, according to which judges are prohibited from conducting their own research, even legal research. If an authority is not cited by the parties, then it cannot be part of the decision, however important it might be. And although this approach, which still holds sway in Great Britain and many other common law countries, is substantially more constraining than the American approach, the nature of litigation, at both trials and appeals, is still within the penumbra of the English tradition, and is still a procedure in which the parties and not the judge are the primary controllers of the information that determines the outcome. The capacity of a court to depart from party-provided information—whether factual, legal, or expert—and obtain the information it needs is a valuable advance from thinking

---

[83] See Abram Chayes, *Foreword: Public Law Litigation and the Burger Court*, 96 Harv L Rev 4 (1982); Abram Chayes, *The Role of the Judge in Public Law Litigation*, 89 Harv L Rev 1281 (1976); Owen M. Fiss, *Foreword: The Forms of Justice*, 93 Harv L Rev 1 (1979). See also Malcolm M. Feeley and Edward L. Rubin, *Judicial Policy Making and the Modern State: How the Courts Reformed America's Prisons* (Cambridge, 1998); Theodore Eisenberg and Stephen C. Yeazell, *The Ordinary and the Extraordinary in Institutional Litigation*, 93 Harv L Rev 465 (1980); William A. Fletcher, *The Discretionary Constitution: Institutional Remedies and Judicial Legitimacy*, 91 Yale L J 635 (1982).

[84] See Lon L. Fuller, *The Forms and Limits of Adjudication*, 92 Harv L Rev 353 (1978); Donald L. Horowitz, *Decreeing Organizational Change: Judicial Supervision of Public Institutions*, 1983 Duke L J 1265; Robert Nagel, *How Useful Is Judicial Review in Free Speech Cases?* 69 Cornell L Rev 302 (1984). See also Neal Devins, *I Love You, Big Brother* (Book Review), 87 Calif L Rev 1283 (1999).

of courts as referees of tournaments to thinking of courts as the makers of decisions with important policy implications beyond the interests of the litigants before them. Such a step will enable courts to make policy more intelligently, but of course it is only a first step.

V. Conclusion: From Legitimacy to Institutional Competence

Debates about judicial power, in the United States and elsewhere, have been almost exclusively about legitimacy, and we still labor under the burden of the thinking that the "counter-majoritarian difficulty"[85] is the only productive way of addressing the allocation of powers in a multifaceted political system.[86] The assumption has always been that majority rule is the default position, and that judicial power, especially when exercised by nonelected judges in the federal and some state systems, is consequently in need of special justification and in equal need of limitations on its scope.

The question of legitimacy is not unimportant, but it is a mistake to think it the only question worth asking. Society through the various devices of democracy is not only a policy-maker but is also an institutional designer. And although the role and limits of majority rule and popular accountability are important issues of institutional design in any democracy, there are others as well. Chief among these others is a cluster of questions falling under the heading of institutional competence. Which kinds of institutions are better at making which kinds of decisions, independent of questions of majority rule? Which kinds of decisions require short-term popular accountability, and which are made better when they are removed from it? Which kinds of decisions are dependent on factual information, and how might they be acquired? Which decisions are ones in which there could be genuine expertise, and, for those decisions, should experts make the decisions,

---

[85] Alexander Bickel, *The Least Dangerous Branch* 16 (Yale, 2d ed 1986). For an example, see Matthew D. Adler, *Judicial Restraint in the Administrative State: Beyond the Countermajoritarian Difficulty*, 145 U Pa L Rev 759 (1997).

[86] For an intriguing look at the history of this pathology, see Laura Kalman, *The Strange Career of Liberal Legalism* (Yale, 1996).

and, if so, how should the experts be chosen and how should they make their decisions? Which interests should be heard before a policy is made, and which interests should have standing to object to a policy? How should decisions and policies be implemented, and what should be the relationship between the making of a policy and its implementation?

This series of questions merely scratches the surface. The question of institutional design is far more complex than a short series of big questions. But it is also far more complex than the majoritarian/countermajoritarian straitjacket into which far too many institutional design questions involving the judiciary have been strapped. Only when we recognize that the full range of questions of institutional design are as pertinent to the judiciary as they are to other societal decision-making institutions can we begin to make real progress.

Questions of judicial institutional design have been burdened not only by assuming that questions about majoritarianism are the only ones worth asking, but also by traditional and arguably erroneous views about the nature of judicial decision making. Despite a hundred or more years of legal realism in its various forms, we still believe that the kinds of skills that were taught in the first year of law school in 1956 are the kinds of skills that are most relevant to deciding most of the cases that wind up in our appellate courts. Yet cases like *PGA v Martin*, far more typical than it is exceptional, challenge that belief in the most direct of ways. As long as the judicial task involves questions like "What is golf?" as much as it involves questions like "Is there a remedy under the Securities Act of 1933 against the use of a misleading statement in the sale of an unregistered security?"[87] the judiciary and those of us who comment on its performance will be faced with the alternatives of suggesting, as Justice Scalia has suggested, that the judiciary should behave to minimize the necessity of answering questions like the former, or with suggesting, as Justice Breyer has suggested, that the judiciary should modify its methods so that it

---

[87] See *Gustafson v Alloyd Co.*, 115 S Ct 1061 (1995), criticized in Edmund W. Kitch, *Gustafson v Alloyd Co.: An Opinion That Did Not Write*, 1995 Supreme Court Review 99. I use this example only because it strikes me as one in which the skills required to answer the question are much more the skills of close reading and analysis of a highly complex statutory scheme than is the question whether walking is part of the fundamental nature of tournament golf.

can start to answer questions like the former with the same sophistication that is uses to answer questions like the latter.

Indeed, *PGA v Martin*, precisely because of and not in spite of the fact that it is about golf and not about securities regulation, and because of and not in spite of the fact that it was so widely followed in legal and nonlegal circles alike, may actually turn out to be especially important in molding future discussions of judicial expertise. That is, one of the incidental benefits of the case having been about golf is that the question of expertise was not quite on the surface initially in the way it is when the issue is science rather than sports. If the required expertise is about DNA testing, the causes of cancer, or the theory of relativity, it is usually obvious to judges and to other nonscientists confronting these topics that they are out of their depth and in need of assistance. When the question is golf, however, or is any of a large number of other policy issues that may appear somewhat less esoteric at first or even second glance, the temptation to assume that expertise is not relevant and that the knowledge of the curious generalist is sufficient will be much greater. The fact that junk science is about science often is sufficient to raise the proper degree of suspicion, but junk politics, junk sociology, junk policy analysis, or even junk golf can often sneak in undetected. Yet although the confidence of the curious generalist in her nonexpert knowledge of golf or the economics of industrial organization will be greater than her confidence in her nonexpert knowledge of the theory of relativity, this confidence may well be misplaced. It is no coincidence that almost all of the existing debate about judicial nonexpertise has been about science, but it is the great virtue of the debate in *PGA v Martin* that it demonstrates so well that the issues range far beyond science, and that the problems of judicial ignorance may be even more pressing when the technical modesty that science tends to engender is not present.

down a Missouri initiative amending the state constitution to require that the failure of candidates for U.S. Congress to support a particular term-limits amendment to the United States Constitution be noted on the ballot. In an opinion joined by seven Justices, the Court held that the Missouri law exceeded the scope of states' powers to regulate the "time, place and manner" of holding congressional elections.[2] Two other Justices concurred in the judgment but on the ground that the ballot-labeling requirement violated the First Amendment right of a political candidate "once lawfully on the ballot, to have his name appear unaccompanied by pejorative language required by the State."[3] The opinions are analyzed preliminarily in Part I.

Part II below suggests that even if there were no Elections Clause, or no First Amendment, the basic structure of the Constitution of the government of the United States would require the same result as that which the Court reached under those provisions. Paying attention to the structures and relationships of structures under the Constitution, as Charles Black urged,[4] one could say that a representative democracy—plainly contemplated by the Constitution's provisions for the federal legislature and federal elections—is dependent on the operation of elections unbiased by the existing government. Free choice in the selection of representatives is a foundational linchpin in representative democracies. Comparative constitutional experience in countries that lack obvious textual analogues to the First Amendment or the Elections Clause supports the result. Thus, even without those clauses, this case was, as Justice Kennedy suggested, not a close one for a constitutional court in a representative democracy.

Part III explores some reasons why the Court may have chosen to rely on particular constitutional text and to have crafted a narrow holding. First, there is the familiar attraction of text and precedent as bases for decision. Second, the shadow of *Bush v Gore*[5] may have made appeal to an explicit and discrete text more attractive. Third, anti-incumbency and ballot-labeling measures gener-

---

[2] *Cook v Gralike*, 121 S Ct 1029 (2001).

[3] Id at 1042 (Rehnquist, CJ, concurring in the judgment).

[4] See Charles L. Black, Jr., *Structure and Relationship in Constitutional Law* (LSU Press, 1969).

[5] 531 US 98 (2000).

ally pose difficult normative questions about what kind of democracy the Constitution commits us to, as well as difficult questions of the permissible range of government speech.[6] These substantial, lurking conceptual difficulties, and their relationship to the multiple functions of elections in checking, choosing, and legitimating representatives, may help account for the narrowness of the holding.

I. THE JUSTICES' OPINIONS

In contrast to the closely divided Court of *U.S. Term Limits, Inc. v Thornton*,[7] the nine Justices of the Court in *Cook v Gralike* were all agreed on the result.[8] The requirement at issue was that the ballot note failures by candidates for the office of U.S. Senator or Representative to support a particular proposed term-limits amendment to the U.S. Constitution, by including the words "DISREGARDED VOTERS' INSTRUCTION ON TERM LIMITS," or "DECLINED TO PLEDGE TO SUPPORT TERM LIMITS" next to their names on the ballot. Justice Stevens, writing for the Court, held this requirement to be unconstitutional, and in so doing, relied on two propositions.

Most centrally, the Court held that, regardless of whether states had some reserved powers to instruct their national representatives, the states' only powers to regulate or control elections to Congress were those given in Article I, Section 4, clause 1 of the Constitution to regulate the "Times, Places and Manner" of elections, powers that did not extend to the proposed ballot labels. The so-called Elections Clause, the Court held, was " 'a grant of authority to issue procedural regulations,' " not a "source of power to dictate electoral outcomes, to favor or disfavor a class of candi-

---

[6] See Mark G. Yudof, *When Government Speaks: Politics, Law and Government Expression in America* (U Cal, 1983); Steven Shiffrin, *Government Speech*, 27 UCLA L Rev 565 (1980); David Cole, *Beyond Unconstitutional Conditions: Charting Spheres of Neutrality in Government-Funded Speech*, 67 NYU L Rev 675 (1992); Robert C. Post, *Subsidized Speech*, 106 Yale L J 151 (1996); Martin Redish and Daryl Kessler, *Government Subsidies and Free Expression*, 80 Minn L Rev 543 (1996); Abner Greene, *Government of the Good*, 53 Vand L Rev 1 (2000) and *Government Speech on Unsettled Issues*, 69 Fordham L Rev 1667 (2001).

[7] 514 US 779 (1995).

[8] See 121 S Ct at 1041 (Kennedy, J, concurring) (noting that "[i]n today's case the question is not close").

dates. . . ."[9] The ballot-labeling requirement, the Court said, bore "no relation to the 'manner' of elections" in its " 'commonsense' " meaning "encompass[ing] matters like 'notices, registration, supervision of voting, protection of voters, prevention of fraud and corrupt practices, counting of votes, duties of inspectors and canvassers, and making and publication of election returns'."[10] The Missouri law was "plainly designed to favor candidates" willing to support the particular term limit amendment and disfavor others, by "attach[ing] a concrete consequence to noncompliance" with the voters' wishes—the " 'pejorative' " ballot label.[11] Further, the "adverse labels handicap candidates 'at the most crucial stage in the election process—the instant before the vote is cast'."[12] And by calling attention to only one issue, the label implies that that issue is the most important.[13]

Insisting that the states had no reserved powers to regulate federal elections but only those powers specified in the Constitution, the Court also rejected the argument that the state law in question, enacted by referendum as part of the Missouri constitution, should be upheld as part of the state's reserved power to give instructions to its representatives in the Congress. In Part III of the opinion— a portion joined by only five members of the Court[14] and qualified by Justice Kennedy's concurrence—Justice Stevens rejected the state's argument that its law was "a valid exercise of the State's reserved power to give binding instructions to its representatives . . . ."[15] Evaluating historical evidence, Justice Stevens's opinion stated that members of the First Congress concluded that "binding instructions would undermine an essential attribute of Congress by eviscerating the deliberative nature of that National Assembly."[16]

---

[9] Id at 1038, quoting U.S. Term Limits, Inc. v Thornton, 514 US 779, 833–34 (1995).

[10] Id at 1038 quoting Smiley v Holm, 285 US 355, 366 (1932).

[11] Id at 1038–39.

[12] Id at 1039, quoting Anderson v Martin, 375 US 399, 402 (1964).

[13] Id.

[14] Justice Thomas concurred in the judgment and in Parts I and IV of the Court's opinion; Chief Justice Rehnquist, joined by Justice O'Connor, concurred in the judgment but on First Amendment grounds; and the Court's opinion notes that Justice Souter does not join in Part III of the Court's opinion. Part IV of the opinion, joined by seven Justices, addresses the Elections Clause issue.

[15] 121 S Ct at 1036.

[16] Id at 1037.

Justice Kennedy, who joined Part III of the Court's opinion, also wrote separately, agreeing that the ballot label was unconstitutional because states cannot "interfere with the direct line of accountability between the National Legislature and the people who elect it," but emphasizing that states may engage in more hortatory conduct requesting the Congress "to pay heed to certain state concerns."[17] He sought, then, to distinguish ballot labels that seek to "interpose [the State] between the people and their National Government" from "nonbinding petitions or memorials by the State as an entity."[18] Chief Justice Rehnquist, with whom Justice O'Connor joined, would have held that Missouri's Article VIII violated the First Amendment right of a candidate once lawfully on the ballot to have his name appear unaccompanied by pejorative language required by the state.[19]

The majority decision, then, rested on the Elections Clause. The Elections Clause appears to be a relatively narrow basis for decision. To illustrate, consider whether the holding—that the Elections Clause does not authorize states to require ballot labels, such as that required here—would apply as well to the federal government's authority to regulate federal elections pursuant to the same clause. Would a national law, requiring identical labeling for candidates who oppose amending the constitution to provide for term limits, likewise be unconstitutional? Must the limitations of the Elections Clause apply in pari materia to federal as well as state laws regulating congressional elections? The Court's opinion strongly suggests but does not clearly require this result.

On the one hand, since the federal government's authority is likewise derived from the Constitution, and the congressional power to set forth such rules is also most obviously based on the Elections Clause, it would be reasonable to conclude that the same

---

[17] Id at 1041.

[18] Id at 1040, 1041. Justice Thomas concurred in only a portion of the Stevens opinion, noting his continued disagreement with the premise, derived from *Term Limits*, that states lack authority to regulate congressional elections other than that expressly given to them. Id at 1041–42. Justice Thomas wrote, however, that since the parties conceded the validity of that premise, he concurred in the judgment. None of the other *Term Limits* dissenters joined Thomas's separate opinion here. Logically, it would seem that Justice Thomas agreed with the Court's analysis of the scope of the Elections Clause's recognition of states' power to determine the time, place, or manner of elections, for had he thought this ballot-label law fairly encompassed in that grant of power he would presumably have dissented.

[19] Id at 1042.

limitations would apply—that is, that the federal government would lack power to make regulations that are other than procedural in character, that are designed to favor one class of candidates over another. On the other hand, *Gralike* is arguably distinguishable because the federal government may have greater powers over the scope of election regulations than do the state governments. The states, the Court's opinion was at pains to emphasize, can have no reserved powers with respect to the elections of a federal government, and "[n]o other constitutional provision gives the States authority over congressional elections."[20] Does the scope of Congress's enumerated powers leave room for an argument that other federal powers support a broader federal authority with respect to the conduct of congressional elections than that provided in Article I itself?[21] While there is a strong argument that it does not, in part because of the relatively specific provisions for shared state-federal authority over the conduct of national elections,[22] even this closely allied question is not thoroughly put to rest by the *Gralike* opinion.

[20] *Cook v Gralike*, 121 S Ct at 1038. This has been regularly asserted. See *U.S. Term Limits v Thornton*, 514 US at 805; see also *Newberry v United States*, 256 US 232, 280–81 (Pitney, J, concurring) (1921) (referring to Article I, Section 4 as "conferring" power on state legislatures subject to revision and modification by Congress and as being the only source of such authority, the states having no reserved powers over "a matter that had no previous existence"). But see Justice Thomas's dissent in *Term Limits*, 514 US at 846–52 & n 3. Note, too, that *Term Limits* relied in part on *Powell v McCormack*, 395 US 486 (1969), which held that the House of Representatives could not add to the qaulifications for office set forth in Art I § 2 in "judg[ing] . . . the Elections, Returns and Qualifications of its own Members" under Art I § 5; *Powell* did not address the scope of Congress's powers to enact laws concerning the time, place, or manner of holding elections under Art I § 4.

[21] Could Congress invoke its power over foreign commerce to enact a statute requiring that the ballots for congressional offices remind voters to consider the candidate's records on foreign affairs issues in deciding for whom to cast their vote? Evaluating such a statute would require going beyond the reasoning in *Gralike* to consider the relationship between Congress's Article I, Section 8 powers and the power granted Congress in Article I, Section 4 to otherwise direct the states as to the time, place or manner of holding elections. On the one hand, a "holistic" approach to constitutional interpretation might read the powers in these two sections together, cumulatively, or perhaps even synergistically, to support the claimed power. But see *Newberry v United States*, 256 US 232, 249 (1921) (rejecting argument that "because the offices were created by the Constitution, Congress has some indefinite, undefined power over elections for Senators and Representatives not derived from section 4"). On the other hand, as I will argue below, there is a more basic structural principle that underlies both the rule in *Gralike* and the correct resolution of the constitutionality of this hypothetical statute: that governments cannot, in their governmental capacity, try to influence voters' decisions in an election for or against particular candidates.

[22] On this point, see *Smiley v Holm*, 285 US 355, 367 (1932). The availability of other powers as a basis to regulate elections outside the confines of the Elections Clause is related to a more general question whether grants of power in the Constitution should be read

Moreover, to the extent that the Court's opinion rests on conceptions of the deliberative democracy contemplated for the federal government by the Constitution, there might be even more reason to think that a different standard would apply to elections for state offices, in light of the Court's refusal to find constitutional requirements for a deliberative rather than plebiscitary democracy at the state level in the context of lawmaking by referendum.[23] Consider a state law requiring, let us say, that candidates for public state office who oppose a term-limits provision for state office be so identified on the ballot—does *Cook v Gralike* speak to the constitutionality of such a requirement? The opinion by Justice Stevens for the Court certainly does not do so directly; the holding appears limited to state authority to regulate elections for federal office. For an answer to this question, though, the separate concurrence of Chief Justice Rehnquist, joined by Justice O'Connor, speaks quite clearly.

Rehnquist articulates a First Amendment violation: the right of a political candidate once lawfully on the ballot to have his name appear "unaccompanied by pejorative language."[24] Associating this right of a candidate with the right of a voter, the Chief Justice goes on to describe the nature of the evil in terms not that dissimilar, from a functional point of view, from the majority. Indeed, in the second paragraph of his opinion he links Article I, Section 4's authority to regulate the "Times, Places and Manner of holding Elections" to the scope of authority under First Amendment case

---

so as to avoid redundancy. Compare *Ex parte Yarbrough*, 110 US 651, 666–67 (1884) (upholding federal criminal statute relating to state officials' conduct of elections and asserting that "it is a waste of time to seek for specific sources of the power to pass these laws" because such a power is essential to sustaining a free and democratic republic and thus is well within the powers of the national government), with *Newberry v United States*, 256 US at 255–56 (quoting *Federalist Papers* to support a very limited concept of the authority of the federal government to regulate elections, pursuant only to the Elections Clause). For further discussion, see *United States v Lopez*, 514 US 549, 588–89 (1995) (Thomas, J, concurring) (arguing that enumerated powers should be construed to avoid redundancy); Paul J. Heald and Suzanna Sherry, *Implied Limits on the Legislative Power: The Intellectual Property Clause as an Absolute Constraint on Congress*, 2000 U Ill L Rev 1119 (arguing that intellectual property clause (for "Authors and Inventors") constrains powers in ways that circumvent the limitations of that clause); see also Mark Tushnet, *The Redundant Free Exercise Clause*, 33 Loyola U Chi L J 71 (2001); John Hart Ely, *Interclausal Immunity*, 87 Va L Rev 1185 (2001).

[23] See, e.g., *Pacific States Tel. & Tel. Co. v Oregon*, 223 US 118 (1912) (holding Guarantee Clause attack to be nonjusticiable with effect of sustaining validity of state laws enacted by initiative and referendum).

[24] 121 S Ct at 1042.

law to regulate the time, place, and manner of speech. Importing First Amendment standards of content and viewpoint neutrality into the regulation of elections, the Rehnquist opinion seems to suggest that the First Amendment and the Time, Place, and Manner Election Clause should in some sense be read in pari materia— as structurally related one to the other.[25] More concretely, for my purposes here, under the Rehnquist opinion there is little question that the first of the hypotheticals posed above—a federal law requiring similar ballot labeling for congressional elections—would be found unconstitutional, as would a state ballot labeling law for state office with a description deemed "pejorative."

But neither the majority opinion nor that of Chief Justice Rehnquist provides clear guidance on more general questions of ballot labeling. Consider a different kind of state ballot labeling law, one not so obviously designed to disadvantage candidates of one particular view—for example, by describing whether the candidate supported or opposed term limits for members of Congress (without language about "disregard[ing] voters" or "declin[ing] to pledge"),[26] or, to take another example, noting whether the candidate supported or opposed the death penalty. Would the majority consider such a label as an attempt to "favor or disfavor a class of candidates" and thus within the scope of its ruling? Would an evenhanded law requiring a ballot label for legislative candidates pass constitutional muster?[27]

To answer this question, one needs to decide the extent to which the majority opinion rests on the concern over the ballot identifying any one issue as of central importance. It is unclear whether the Court's conclusion that the Missouri ballot-labeling requirement was outside the scope of "Times, Places and Manner" regulations turned on the existence of *any* label on the ballot (at the

---

[25] For discussion of intratextual structural interpretation, see Akhil Reed Amar, *Intratextualism*, 112 Harv L Rev 747 (1999).

[26] It was widely noted that the language of the ballot label in the Missouri case was designed to invite voter dislike for the candidate based not only on the candidate's position on term limits but on questions of the character and responsibility of a candidate who "disregards" voters instructions or "declines to pledge" to support "voters' instruction." See, e.g., Elizabeth Garrett, *The Law and Economics of "Informed Voter" Ballot Notations*, 85 Va L Rev 1533, 1576–77 (1999).

[27] For a helpful discussion of the relationship between viewpoint, subject matter, and motive in First Amendment law, see Geoffrey R. Stone, *Restrictions of Speech Because of Its Content: The Peculiar Case of Subject-Matter Restrictions*, 46 U Chi L Rev 81 (1978).

moment before voting), on the presence of a label relating to *one particular issue*, or on the finding that the label is *"pejorative"* and thus clearly intended to influence voters one way in the election. It is likewise unclear to what extent Chief Justice Rehnquist's opinion turns on the derogatory implications of the required ballot label.[28] Rehnquist's invocation of *Anderson v Martin* might suggest that any effort on the ballot to include even "evenhanded" labeling as to particular issues would meet constitutional objection. *Anderson* found an equal protection violation from the state law requiring designation of a candidate's race on the ballot. Rehnquist suggested that *Anderson*, like *Gralike*, also presented a problem of the state choosing "one and only one issue to comment on the position of the candidates."[29] Yet *Anderson* did not involve a label as to the political views of the candidate, but rather as to the candidate's race. The designation of race could obviously be seen as an effort by the state to promote racism; in context, it had a high likelihood of being seen as "pejorative" and as fostering unconstitutional policies.[30] So it is not entirely clear that Rehnquist meant to hold objectionable the singling out of one and only one issue for evenhanded comment, in light of the fact that the *Anderson* precedent was one in which the "one" issue could predictably be expected to influence voters to disfavor black candidates.[31] On an issue like whether to retain the death penalty, which the Court has held to be within the range of choices for state legislatures, a stronger

---

[28] See 121 S Ct at 1042 (Rehnquist, CJ, concurring in the judgment) (describing violation of candidate's right to appear on ballot without a "pejorative" label).

[29] Id at 1042–43, discussing *Anderson v Martin*, 375 US 399 (1964). *Anderson* is also invoked by the Court. Id at 1039.

[30] See Laurence Tribe, *American Constitutional Law* 1481 n 9 (2d ed 1988) (suggesting that *Anderson* rested on the labeling provision's "inevitably discriminatory" effects in light of private prejudice).

[31] Instead, we might conclude, the Court and Justice Rehnquist would condemn only those ballot labels that are based on a constitutionally irrelevant or problematic basis—in *Anderson*, the race of the candidate, and in *Gralike*, the views and actions of a candidate with respect to a term-limits amendment. But the language of Rehnquist's opinion suggests that, at least in *Gralike*, it was not that the activity being commented on may have been independently constitutionally protected but rather the fact that the ballot comment was pejorative that was dispositive. See 121 S Ct at 1042 (describing "First Amendment right of a political candidate, once lawfully on the ballot, to have his name appear unaccompanied by pejorative language required by the State"). His language suggests that any pejorative language on the ballot about a candidate—whether it referred to the candidate's beliefs, partisan identity, or prior actions or job experience—would run afoul of his sense of the constitutional principles of fair elections at stake.

claim could perhaps be made that a ballot-label requirement was purely informational, rather than designed to help one side or the other.

But *Anderson* may be illustrative of a deeper proposition of "single issue" politics: it is difficult to envision the political dynamics by which a requirement of a statement on the ballot of a candidate's position on a certain issue could come to pass without one side in a contentious debate believing that it was more to its advantage than the other. It is the relatively rare situation in which "neutral" "good government" principles can attract sufficient consensus decision making to overcome the possibility that the reforms in questions are intended, or perceived by some, as a means to particular substantive ends. A "death penalty" label would come about, on this view, only because proponents or opponents believed that requiring such a designation would be more likely to benefit one or the other view. On this view, then, any posited distinction evaporates between labels that favor or disfavor a class of candidates and labels that are "neutral." While overtly "pejorative" labels may be identified, it is likely to be the case that an "evenhanded" label on a particular issue would have the purpose and effect of favoring or disfavoring a class of particular candidates.[32]

Thus, should the case arise in which there is a less obviously pejorative ballot-label requirement about candidates on particular issues, the questions the *Gralike* Court's opinion asked about the ballot-label rule would need to be addressed and might be difficult to answer. The Court in *Gralike* asked both whether the law was "designed to favor" or disfavor a class of candidates—that is, something akin to a "purpose" test[33]—and whether the ballot label

---

[32] For discussion of an analogous issue, see Stone, 46 U Chi L Rev at 110 (cited in note 27) (noting danger of apparently neutral, subject-matter-based restrictions on speech because, despite their facial neutrality, such "restrictions [or, by analogy, compelled disclosures of positions] will often disadvantage one 'side' of an issue more than the other, depending upon which 'side' is more likely to be affected by the restriction [or mandatory label]"); see also Elena Kagan, *The Changing Faces of First Amendment Neutrality: R.A.V. v St. Paul, Rust v Sullivan, and the Problem of Content-Based Underinclusion*, 1992 Supreme Court Review 29, 66–67, 68–70 (agreeing with Stone that viewpoint restrictions are more likely to arise from impermissible motives than subject-matter restrictions and exploring difficulty in determining whether distinctions on their face about "subject matter" should be treated as viewpoint regulations). See also note 34.

[33] 121 S Ct at 1038.

in fact "handicapped" those candidates on one side of the issue, that is, an "effects" test.[34] In the future, single-issue ballot-labeling requirements for candidates might well fall under the weight of *Gralike*, if the Court adopts a commitment to a thorough, substantive inquiry into purpose and effect.[35] Alternatively, a nonpejoratively phrased single ballot-labeling requirement might survive a more formal approach that seeks to determine purpose and effect only from the language of the ballot label itself: a more formal inquiry might conclude from the absence of overtly pejorative language in a ballot label that there was no pejorative purpose, and then either conclude that no particular adverse "effects" can be anticipated or conclude that in the absence of bad purpose, adverse effects are irrelevant.[36]

So, to recap: Both the majority opinion and the Chief Justice's concurrence were relatively narrow opinions, resting on a confluence of circumstances, with little to guide future courts on how to decide issues relating to nonpejorative labels, or to government speech about political candidates outside the ballot box. Both the Court's opinion and Rehnquist's concurrence turn on (1) a label with clearly pejorative language, (2) on a single issue, (3) appearing on the official ballot that voters see in the ballot booth. The majority's decision applies most clearly to elections for federal office, while Rehnquist's rationale would apply as well to elections for state or local office. With this major distinction, the reach of these opinions to other, more "evenhanded" ballot labels remains unclear, as do their implications for other forms of "government

---

[34] Id at 1039. At oral argument questions from the bench sought to address whether any singling out of an issue for a ballot label would be constitutional. See Transcript of Oral Argument, *Cook v Gralike*, No 99-929 (Nov 6, 2000), 2000 WL 1673928 *9–10 (Justice's question expressing concern for "hurt[ing] the First Amendment rights of all those who happen to think that term limits is not the most important issue in the election . . . [and would] prefer the election [to be] decided on the basis of other issues").

[35] Compare *McIntyre v Ohio Elections Commission*, 514 US 334, 345 n 8 (1995) (noting possibility that facially neutral ban on anonymous electioneering pamphlets "places a more significant burden on advocates of unpopular causes than on defenders of the status quo").

[36] The Court is often skeptical of the degree to which a constitutionally wrongful intent can be inferred from the existence of constitutionally suspect impact. See, e.g., *Washington v Davis*, 426 US 229 (1976), and *Employment Division v Smith*, 494 US 872 (1990). As Elena Kagan has argued, despite a formal emphasis on effects, much First Amendment law "has as its primary . . . object the discovery of improper governmental motives." Elena Kagan, *Private Speech, Public Purpose: The Role of Governmental Motive in First Amendment Law*, 63 U Chi L Rev 413, 414 (1996).

speech" related to elections, ballot propositions, or other public issues.[37]

II. An Alternative Approach: Structure and Relationship

Gralike relies on the *Term Limits* conclusion that the Elections Clause is only " 'a grant of authority to issue procedural regulations, and not [a] source of power to dictate electoral outcomes [or] to favor or disfavor a class of candidates . . . .' "[38] This conclusion—that the government bodies running elections cannot seek to dictate electoral outcomes—would follow even if there were no "Elections Clause" or First Amendment but only provisions specifying that members of Congress were to be chosen by elections. Coercion by force—voting at gunpoint for the powers that be—is obviously a more extreme form of undue influence than last minute government propaganda on behalf of one or another candidate in the ballot booth. Yet both forms of conduct pose risks that current officeholders will act so as to prevent the election from performing its most fundamental tasks in a democracy.[39]

---

[37] Justice Kennedy's separate concurrence emphasized the legitimacy of forms of government speech by states, with respect to federal constitutional amendments, that are "nonbinding." See 121 S Ct at 1041. For discussion, see note 122.

[38] *Gralike*, 121 S Ct at 1038, quoting *Term Limits*, 514 US at 833–34.

[39] The short opinion in *Gralike* relies in large part on *Term Limits*. *Term Limits* was, in a sense, an opinion based on constitutional structures of federalism and representative democracy. But federalism values, rather than democracy concerns, played the most important role in the *Term Limits* opinions. Despite invocation of the " 'fundamental principle of our representative democracy' " that " 'the people should choose whom they please to govern them' " as favoring open access to the ballot by a wide range of candidates, *Term Limits*, 514 US at 819, quoting *Powell v McCormack*, 395 US 486, 547 (1969), the Court's opinion does not treat term limits for state offices as unconstitutional. See *Term Limits*, 514 US at 837. Lower courts have generally treated *Term Limits* as applying only to federal congressional office and have upheld state term limits as against claims that they infringed the voters' right to choose. See, e.g., *Citizens for Legislative Choice v Miller*, 993 F Supp 1041, 1048 n 8 (ED Mich) (collecting cases upholding term limits for state offices), aff'd 144 F3d 916 (6th Cir 1998); *Bates v Jones*, 131 F3d 843 (9th Cir 1997) (en banc), cert denied, 523 US 102 (1998). See also Kathleen M. Sullivan, *Dueling Sovereignties: U.S. Term Limits, Inc. v. Thornton*, 109 Harv L Rev 78, 102 n 181 (1995) (noting use of language of citizen rights in *Term Limits* but concluding that the case turned on disagreement over structural questions of federalism, because "[o]ne cannot decide whose right is prior—that of the federal citizen to reelect a popular congressman in a given election, or that of the state citizen to tie his own and his fellows' hands against succumbing to such a representative in the future—without first deciding the structural question of which people, federal or state, ought to control this aspect of federal elections"). Moreover, the Court's commitment to free choice by the voters on the election ballot is surprisingly tempered across election issues: the Court has upheld substantial restrictions both on ballot access by candidates having small levels of popular support and free voting, most remarkably, in sustaining Hawaii's ban on write-in votes. See *Burdick v Takushi*, 504 US 428 (1992). See note 111

Commitments to free and fair elections are plainly entailed in the Constitution. Article I makes elections a central mechanism by which the Congress is constituted: it assumed elections for state legislatures and required elections for members of the House. By the 1880s, the Supreme Court had so interpreted Article I, describing the "right to vote for a member of Congress" as fundamental to the Constitution of the United States, and emphasizing that the government's duty to protect that right "does not arise solely from the interest of the party concerned, but from the necessity of the government itself . . . that the votes by which its members of Congress and its President are elected shall be the *free* votes of the electors, and the officers thus chosen the free and uncorrupted choice of those who have the right to take part in that choice."[40]

Even with no First Amendment, or no "time, place, and manner" Elections Clause, a constitution for a representative government should be interpreted to prevent undue influence by existing governments on voters' choices in the ballots in order to assure that the choice is "free and uncorrupted."[41] The centrality of commitments to a national government based on the people's frequently expressed and changing views led Charles Black to view the First Amendment itself as "only evidentiary of what would in

---

(discussing tension between free choice on ballot and free choice in designing structures of governance).

[40] *Ex parte Yarbrough*, 110 US 651, 662, 663–64 (1884); see also *Ex parte Siebold*, 100 US 371, 388 (1880) ("[t]he due and fair election of [congressional] representatives is of vital importance to the United States").

[41] See John Hart Ely, *Democracy and Distrust* 120 (Harvard, 1980) ("We cannot trust the ins to decide who stays out. . . ."). Determining what government influence is "undue" is enormously complex. See Part III. The "ins" inevitably have substantial access to the means to influence public opinion, even speaking only for themselves. Much of governing involves attempts to be responsive to voters, to influence them favorably in their regard for the officeholder, often with at least an eye on the next election. Judicial doctrine designed to constrain undue government influence must distinguish current holders of office speaking in their individual capacity from the "government" speaking in its magisterial voice on the ballot, both to protect the speakers' speech rights and the interests of citizenry in hearing from their public officials. See generally *Bd of Regents of Univ. of Wisconsin v Southworth*, 529 US 217, 229 (2000): "The government, as a general rule, may support valid programs and policies by taxes or other exactions binding on protesting parties. Within this broader principle it seems inevitable that funds raised by the government will be spent for speech and other expression to advocate and defend its own policies." Some scholars conclude that the factors that should be considered in distinguishing permissible from impermissible government speech are too varied to permit of any single approach, see Shiffrin, 27 UCLA L Rev at 605–22, 655 (cited in note 6) (complexity of interests in government speech require "eclectic" multicategory analysis), and in some respects too difficult for courts to manage other than by remanding to legislatures, see Yudof, *When Government Speaks* at 165–73, 259–306 (cited in note 6).

any case be reasonably obvious—that petition and assembly for the discussion of national governmental measures are rights founded on the very nature of a national government running on public opinion."[42] The provisions of Article I for a representative elected body, and the guarantee of a "republican" form of government, imply a government based on the periodically expressed choices of the people. Elections plainly were contemplated even in 1787 as the mechanism for constituting the federal House of Representatives; the Republican Form of Government Clause authorizes the national government to prevent states from having self-perpetuated or hereditary legislatures. Moreover, some form of state elections for parts of the state legislatures was plainly contemplated, because the qualifications for electors for federal office were linked to those for the state legislatures. This commitment to a representative democratic structure would of itself require the conclusion that elections must be free from undue influence by incumbents, fair in their processes, and open to a range of candidates to compete and offer choice to the voters. And were there any doubt as to the constitutional centrality of regular, free, and fair elections, they would be put to rest by the many amendments to the Constitution designed to expand the franchise. The centrality of voting to American citizenship and government—if uncertain in 1789—becomes only more clear when the original document is viewed through the lens of more recent amendments.[43]

To be meaningful in securing the legitimacy of government and in checking abuses by elected officeholders, elections generally

---

[42] Black, *Structure and Relationship* at 41 (cited in note 4). Indeed, he went on to argue that the voting and representation scheme of Article I and the Seventeenth Amendment— the "very structure of the relation between the national representative and his constituency"—itself gives rise to a "compelling inference of some national constitutional protection of free utterance, as against state infringement." Id at 42.

[43] See Ely, *Democracy and Distrust* at 123 (cited in note 41) (arguing that Fourteenth Amendment and later franchise-expanding amendments reflect "a strengthening constitutional commitment to the proposition that all qualified citizens are to play a role in the making of public decisions"); cf. Vicki C. Jackson, *Holistic Interpretation: Fitzpatrick v. Bitzer and Our Bifurcated Constitution*, 53 Stan L Rev 1259, 1284–95 (2001) (arguing that more recent franchise- and equality-expanding amendments should inform interpretation of earlier parts of the Constitution); but cf. David A. Strauss, *The Irrelevance of Constitutional Amendments*, 114 Harv L Rev 1457 (2001) (arguing that amendments themselves may have little effect). The right to vote is assumed in several amendments designed to prevent its being denied based on race, gender, inability to pay a poll tax, or age, and even the Twenty-Seventh Amendment might be understood to reflect the enhanced importance of elections as a check on representatives.

must be free, fair, competitive, and held at relatively frequent intervals. Regular intervals producing frequent elections help avoid reliance on the fiction that popular inertia is acquiescence. Competitive elections require that multiple people actually stand and offer a choice. Free and fair elections are those not tilted by government forces or private violence or monopoly toward any particular candidate. The need for constraint in the use of governmental authority or funds to influence elections is widely reflected in federal statutory law and has been inferred by both state courts in the United States and by constitutional courts of other nations as a basic implication from constitutional commitments to democracy.[44]

A constitutionally inspired infrastructure of statutory law at both state and federal levels prohibits the use of government monies or resources for the purpose of supporting a particular candidate for election or reelection.[45] Restrictions are also found on the use of government funds to engage in grassroots lobbying, though a distinction is sometimes drawn between such prohibited lobbying and the permissible provision of information.[46] Such statutes may be

---

[44] This is not to say that elections are themselves sufficient for constitutionally legitimate government, but that they are necessary. See Robert Dahl, *On Democracy* 37–38, 95–96 (Yale, 1998) (describing why democracy requires "free, fair and frequent elections"). On the importance of heightened judicial review of efforts by current governments to entrench themselves as against changing views (and demographics) of the people, see Ely, *Democracy and Distrust* at 109–25, 157–70 (cited in note 41); Michael J. Klarman, *Majoritarian Judicial Review: The Entrenchment Problem*, 85 Georgetown L J 491 (1997).

[45] See, e.g., Ala Code Ann § 17-1-7(b) & (c) (1995) (prohibiting use of official authority to influence votes or use of public money for political purposes); Alaska Stat Ann § 15.13.145 (2000) (prohibiting state bodies from spending public money to influence the outcome of the election of candidates to state or local office); Conn Gen Stat Ann § 9-333*l* (West 1989) (prohibiting any incumbent candidate in three months before election in which he is a candidate to use public funds to mail flyers intended to bring about his election); Fla Stat Ann § 106.15(2) (West 1992) (prohibiting candidate from using state-owned aircraft or motor vehicle solely for purpose of furthering candidacy); Iowa Code Ann § 56.12A (West 1999) (barring expenditure of public moneys for advocacy of election issues); N D Cent Code § 16.1-10-02 (1997) (prohibiting use of public funds, property, or services to support a candidate); SC Code Ann § 8-13-1346 (1986, Supp 2001) (prohibiting use of public funds or property to influence election outcome); Tex Election Code Ann § 255.003 (Vernon 1986, Supp 2002) (prohibiting use of public money for political advertising); Wash Rev Code Ann § 42.17.128-130 (West 2000) (prohibiting use of public funds or facilities for political campaigns). See also Yudof, *When Government Speaks* at 170–71, 186–87 (cited in note 6) (citing older New York and Texas laws). Compare 5 USC § 1501 et seq & 7321 et seq (1996) ("Hatch Act" restrictions on political activities of federal employees and on some state and local employees on federally financed activities).

[46] See, e.g., Ill Stat ch 10, § 5/9-25.1(b) (Smith-Hurd 1993, Supp 2001) ("No public funds shall be used to urge any elector to vote for or against any candidate or proposition. . . . This section shall not prohibit the use of public funds for dissemination of factual

thought of as a kind of "invisible constitution," reflecting, and supporting, constitutional values though not in their specific terms necessarily constitutionally required.[47] The Constitution does not require criminal sanctions for breach of such rules, but it does suggest that bans on electioneering uses of government money are consistent with basic constitutionalism commitments.[48] Of course, relying on the presence (or absence) of statutory commitments to prove a constitutional proposition is a tricky business.[49] Yet in at

information relative to any proposition appearing on an election ballot. . . ."); Iowa Code Ann § 56.12A (West 1999) (stating that ban on expenditure of public moneys for political purposes, expressly including advocacy on ballot issue, shall not be construed to prohibit state or political subdivision from expressing an opinion on a ballot issue through passage of a resolution or proclamation); La Const, Art 11, § 4 (West 1996) ("No public funds shall be used to urge any elector to vote for or against any candidate or proposition. . . . This provision shall not prohibit the use of public funds for dissemination of factual information relative to a proposition appearing on an election ballot"); Tex Election Code Ann § 255.003 (Vernon 1986, Supp 2002) (providing that "communication that factually describes the purpose of a measure" is not barred by prohibition on spending public funds for political advertising "if the communication does not advocate passage or defeat of the measure"); Utah Code Ann § 20A-11-1203 (1998) (exempting from prohibition of public expenditures to influence election the provision of "factual information about a ballot proposition. . . . so long as the information grants equal access to both the opponents and proponents of the ballot proposition").

[47] Compare Owen M. Fiss, *The Irony of Free Speech* 48 (Harvard, 1996) (suggesting that government subsidy programs, though perhaps not constitutionally obligatory, "may be more than merely permissible," and may be "constitutionally *favored*—an intermediate category lying between the permissible and the obligatory").

[48] It might be argued, however, that the widespread adoption of laws restricting the use of public funds for political, election-related purposes coexists with other laws, like the one at issue in *Gralike*, that could be understood to establish a competing tradition. See Brief of Amicus Curiae State of Nebraska in Support of Petitioner, in *Cook v Gralike*, No 99-929 (June 23 2000), 2000 WL 864210, at *3 (stating that following the *Term Limits* decision, ten states adopted similar ballot-label laws concerning term limits). Although this spate of term-limits ballot labels (and the earlier use by some states of arguably similar methods to encourage adoption of the Seventeenth Amendment) can be distinguished in scope and longevity from the kinds of statutes generally prohibiting political uses of public funds, their presence points out that identifying the content of any statutorily embodied constitutional principle is difficult and risks arbitrary distinctions between old and new that might improperly freeze development of constitutional understandings. I explore these ideas further in a work in progress, *The Invisible Constitution*.

[49] See note 48 supra. Statutes are sometimes invoked, though often over dissent, to establish that a constitutional power, or right, exists. See, e.g., *Dames & Moore v Regan*, 453 US 654 (1981) (power); *Coker v Georgia*, 433 US 584, 592 n 4 (1977) (right). Their absence has also been invoked to establish that a power, *Printz v United States*, 521 US 898 (1997) (commandeering), or right, *Stanford v Kentucky*, 492 US 361 (1989) (execution of minors), does not exist, again often over dissent. Some argue that "framework" statutes in particular may reflect constitutional understandings, often seeking to resolve tensions between different constitutional commitments. See, e.g., Geoffrey R. Stone, Louis M. Seidman, Cass R. Sunstein, and Mark V. Tushnet, *Constitutional Law* 390 (Little, Brown, 2d ed 1991) (citing works of Casper and Dam to consider whether the Impoundment Control Act, or War Powers Resolution, or Gramm-Rudman-Hollings are "framework statutes" of a quasi-constitutional nature). For related discussion of U.S. statutory law, see William N. Eskridge,

least one Western constitutional system, France, the Conseil Constitutionnel has relied on well-established statutory regimes as evidence of a "fundamental principle" of associational freedom sufficient to declare invalid a later-enacted statute,[50] and in Britain the constitution is embodied in a mix of practices and statutory provisions subject to change (at least until recently) by simple act of Parliament. As renewed interest in the constitution outside the courts reflects, constitutional meaning can at least sometimes be found in the work, and output, of legislative branches.[51]

State courts have been deeply skeptical of uses of government money to directly sway voters in elections.[52] Even where legisla-

---

Jr. and John Ferejohn, *Super-Statutes*, 50 Duke L J 1215, 1267–76 (2001) (defining super-statutes as those which "successfully penetrate public normative and institutional culture in a deep way" and discussing their value in allowing constitutional norms to evolve).

[50] See the descriptions of the French Associations Case (1971) in Alec Stone, *The Birth of Judicial Politics in France* 64–69, 257–60 (Oxford, 1992); John Bell, *French Constitutional Law* 272–73 (Oxford, 1992).

[51] See, e.g., David P. Currie, *The Constitution in Congress: The Jeffersonians, 1801–1829* (Chicago, 2001); *The Constitution in Congress: The Federalist Period, 1789–1801* (Chicago, 1997). Enthusiasm for crediting nonjudicial constitutional interpretation ranges widely and varies with context, cf., e.g., Mark Tushnet, *Taking the Constitution Away from the Court* (Princeton, 1999), with, e.g., Larry Alexander and Frederick Schauer, *On Extrajudicial Constitutional Interpretation*, 110 Harv L Rev 1359 (1997), but many scholars acknowledge some role for constitutional understandings reflected in the practice and output of other branches of government. For a recent challenge to judicial "sovereignty" over constitutional interpretation, see Larry D. Kramer, *Foreword: We the Court*, 115 Harv L Rev 4 (2001) (arguing for legitimate authority of political branches in constitutional interpretation in spirit of "popular constitutionalism").

[52] See, e.g., *Stanson v Mott*, 17 Cal 3d 206, 217 (1976) (referring to "uniform judicial reluctance to sanction the use of public funds for election campaigns"); *Anderson v Boston*, 380 NE2d 628 (Ma), stay granted, 439 US 1389 (1978), appeal dismissed, 439 US 1060 (1979); *Stern v Kramarsky*, 375 NYS 2d 235 (NY Sup Ct 1975); see also *Mountain States Legal Foundation v Denver School Dist.*, 459 F Supp 357 (D Colo 1978); *District of Columbia Common Cause v District of Columbia*, 858 F2d 1 (DC Cir 1988); *Carter v City of Las Cruces*, 915 P2d 336, 338–40 (NM App 1996); cf. Ark Op Atty Gen No 98-204, 1998 WL 709534 (Ark A G) (discussing permissible and impermissible uses of public funds and forms of government speech); but see *Alabama Libertarian Party v Birmingham*, 694 F Supp 814 (ND Ala 1988) (upholding city's promotional campaign to encourage passage of taxes and charges to improve public library and emergency 911 services). Note the possible evolution of Justice Brennan's views. In *Citizens to Protect Public Funds v Board of Education*, 98 A2d 673 (NJ 1953), sitting on the New Jersey Supreme Court, Justice Brennan held impermissible municipal expenditures for a pamphlet on an upcoming local referendum issue. Although the presentation of factual material in such a pamphlet was permissible, Brennan held, the pamphlet went too far in advocating a yes vote and in predicting dire consequences from voting no on the referendum issue. See also *Stanson v Mott*, 17 Cal 3d at 216–17 (approving distinction drawn in *Citizens to Protect* between permissible provision of information and impermissible advocacy of votes). Yet in *Boston v Anderson*, 439 US 1389 (1978), Justice Brennan as Circuit Justice issued a stay of a decision of the Massachusetts Supreme Judicial Court, which had held impermissible a municipality's expenditures of funds to advocate voter passage of a state-wide referendum. The Court had recently, in *First National Bank of Boston v Bellotti*, 435 US 765 (1978), invalidated another Massachusetts law restricting

tures have authorized government bodies in unmistakable terms to promote a view on controversial issues, courts have been reluctant to extend this authority to activity directed at the government unit's voters as to how they should vote in an election.[53] As the Supreme Court of Oregon wrote,

> It hardly seems necessary to rely on the First Amendment, at least when government resources are devoted to promoting one side in an election on which the legitimacy of the government itself rests. The principles of representative government enshrined in our constitutions would limit government intervention on behalf of its own candidates or against their opponents even if the First Amendment and its state equivalents had never been adopted.[54]

State courts have not only distinguished between informational and electioneering activities, but also between lobbying another governmental body at a different level of government and "lobbying" one's own voters,[55] between advocacy of policies and advocacy of particular candidates,[56] and between advocacy by govern-

---

corporate power to speak on a referendum issue in a decision to which Brennan dissented. Justice Brennan's opinion granting the stay referred to the *First National Bank of Boston* decision. See 439 US at 1390.

[53] See *Miller v California Commission on the Status of Women*, 198 Cal Rptr 877, 883 (1984) (upholding commission's activities, explicitly authorized by state law, to promote passage of Equal Rights Amendment, including lobbying the legislature, but distinguishing such activities from attempts to influence the voters in a matter "submitted to a vote of the people").

[54] *Burt v Blumenauer*, 699 P2d 168, 175 (Or 1985). The Court held that it was impermissible under state statutory law to expend public monies to persuade members of the public to vote for water fluoridation during an election period but also held that if the expenditures were for informational health purposes, rather than electioneering purposes, they would be permissible.

[55] See, e.g., *Burt*, 699 P2d at 176–77; *Mott*, 17 Cal3d at 218 (approving "clear distinction" drawn in state statutes between legislative lobbying activities and use of public funds to influence voters in election campaigns); cf. 44 Or Op Atty Gen 448, 1985 WL 200063, *7–8 (Or A G) (student fees cannot be used to fund organization that advocates positions on ballot measures before Oregon voters but may be used under some circumstances to fund groups that take positions on legislation before the state assembly and issues before state or federal courts).

[56] See, e.g., *Alabama Libertarian Party*, 694 F Supp at 817 (distinguishing between municipal support for "a particular candidate, doctrine or ideology" and municipal support for voter approval of tax increase and levy to improve existing public services). Although this court upheld municipal use of funds to influence voters to approve a tax increase, other courts in the United States and elsewhere have reached quite different conclusions on similar issues. See, e.g., *Burt v Blumenauer*, 699 P2d at 175–81; *Carter v City of Las Cruces*, 915 P2d at 338–39 (raising doubts about federal constitutionality of use of municipal funds to advocate for voter approval of utility acquisition); see text at notes 70–73.

ments themselves and advocacy by individual members of the government.[57] As the Oregon Supreme Court also said, "Certainly, at a minimum, governments must refrain from supporting a particular candidate for office."[58]

That this conclusion can be derived from basic structure even in the absence of more particularized text is suggested by constitutional decisions in several other countries, each of which has a history of reliance on regular elections and representative democracy, and in which propositions derived from general constitutional commitments to representative government were found to constrain legislative schemes deemed to favor or disfavor particular candidates in elections or particular viewpoints on public referendum.

Consider first *Bergman v Minister of Finance* (1969),[59] an early effort at judicial review of legislation by the Israeli Supreme Court. At this time, it was unclear whether Israel had an entrenched constitution that could be relied on by the court to invalidate statutes. As a result of the Harari settlement, Israel's legislative body, the Knesset, enacted a series of so-called Basic Laws that over time addressed different major subjects. The Knesset also enacts other laws, and until 1969 the High Court had not held that a Basic Law could be relied on to invalidate a subsequently enacted statute; indeed, in a system of parliamentary supremacy the ordinary rule would be that the later enactment trumps the earlier one. Bergman challenged a campaign finance law as discriminating against new political parties because it provided election-related funding only for political parties already represented in the Knesset. The Israeli Supreme Court interpreted an earlier-enacted Basic Law on the Knesset to require equal opportunity in the political process and thus to prohibit funding only those parties that had previously had electoral success,[60] and enforced the prior statute's requirement for

---

[57] See, e.g., *Anderson v Boston*, 380 NE2d at 641 (noting plaintiffs' agreement that mayor and others in policy-making positions of government may advocate for proposed amendment and stating that other individual city employees may also have rights to speak even during work hours).

[58] *Burt v Blumenauer*, 699 P2d at 176.

[59] For an English translation, see 8 *Selected Judgments of the Supreme Court of Israel* 13 (1992). I am in debt to Gary Jeffrey Jacobsohn, *Apple of Gold: Constitutionalism in Israel and the United States* (Princeton, 1993), especially at 124–32, for much of my understanding of this case.

[60] Section 4 of the Basic Law: The Knesset, provided: "The Knesset shall be elected by general, country-wide, direct, equal, secret and proportional elections, in accordance with

a special majority to overcome its provisions to invalidate the later-enacted campaign finance law. The Court did so, notwithstanding that Basic Laws are initially enacted by the same ordinary majority voting rule as other laws. It did so, moreover, even though, as the Court itself acknowledged, there was some ambiguity in the Basic Law and despite the Attorney General's argument that there was no written principle prohibiting the particular financing law.[61] In the face of statutory ambiguity, the Court held, it would choose an interpretation that advances a more general principle of equality.

The decision was notable in two respects: First, it treated the entrenching provisions of the Basic Law as trumping a later-enacted statute, thus taking a step toward the constitutionalization of (at least portions of) the Basic Laws and the institution of judicial review of the validity of laws in Israel; and second, it interpreted the Basic Law to provide an expansive equality principle used to invalidate incumbency-protecting legislation. Significantly, the first time the Israeli Supreme Court held an act of the Knesset invalid was one in which it acted to protect the integrity of the election campaign process.

Similarly, notwithstanding the absence of any clause guaranteeing freedom of speech or expression, the Australian Supreme Court invalidated a statute that made free television time available to incumbents and political parties already represented in the parliament but that did not automatically make funding available to most other challengers.[62] Chief Justice Mason's opinion described

---

the Knesset Elections Law; this section shall not be varied save by a majority of the members of the Knesset." See Jacobsohn (cited in note 59) at 126. It was the first part of this sentence that the Court interpreted as prohibiting a later law funding only those political parties already represented in the Knesset, as inconsistent with the commitment to equality. Although the Court's treatment of the second part of the sentence as validly "entrenching" this law as against the later-enacted Election Law was of considerable moment, for my purposes here I want to emphasize the Court's willingness to elaborate from this commitment to general, direct, equal elections a ban on funding only incumbent parties, notwithstanding the government's argument that the equality guaranteed by this clause meant only that each voter's vote should be of equal weight. See Jacobsohn, *Apple of Gold* at 126–27 (cited in note 59).

[61] See Jacobsohn, id at 127–28.

[62] *Australian Capital Television Pty, Ltd. v Australia*, 177 CLR 106 (High Court of Australia, 1992). The case involved a constitutional challenge to a campaign finance law that generally prohibited paid political advertising on television, but that also required broadcasters to make free time available to incumbent candidates and political parties "represented . . . in the [preceding] Parliament or legislature," id at 126, while other challengers had to seek free time from a government tribunal.

the statute, which allocated 90 percent of the total free time to incumbent candidates and parties, as "manifestly favour[ing] the status quo." Notwithstanding the absence of any textual analogue to the First Amendment, the Chief Justice's analysis rested on the implications of representative democracy for freedom of speech on political issues. He concluded that the Australian constitution contained an "implied guarantee of freedom of communication, at least in relation to public and political discussion," derived, he argued, as a matter of logic and practical necessity from the constitutional principle of responsible and representative government as an integral element of the constitution. The Australian constitution, he observed, embodied a fundamental decision not to "place fetters" on legislative action through a bill of rights. Rather it reflected the view that "the citizen's rights were best left to the protection of the common law in association with the doctrine of parliamentary supremacy." But, he concluded, freedom of expression in relation to public and political speech is "an essential concomitant of representative government,"[63] and thus necessarily implied in the prescription of that system, and required broader access to television time for political campaigning. Justice McHugh reasoned similarly, concluding that "in conferring the right to choose their representatives by voting at periodic elections, the Constitution intended to confer on the people of Australia[ ] more than the right to mark a ballot paper with a number . . . . The 'share in the government which the constitution ensures' would be but a pious aspiration unless [the provisions] carried with them more than the right to cast a vote. The guarantees . . . could not be satisfied by the Parliament requiring the people to select their representatives from a list of names drawn up by government officers." The words "directly chosen by the people" in the constitution, then, "interpreted against the background of the institutions of representative government and responsible government, are to be read, therefore, as referring to a process . . . [that] includes all those steps which are directed to the people electing their representatives—nominating, campaigning, advertising, debating, crit-

---

[63] For this and the preceding quotations from the Chief Justice's opinion, see id at 132, 133, 136, 138; see generally id at 136–42. For other opinions likewise finding the statute unconstitutional, see id at 174–75 (Deane, J, and Toohey, J); id at 208–17 (Gaudron, J). Note that the use of seriatim opinions is found in both Australia's and Ireland's high courts.

icizing and voting." From this it followed that "the people have a constitutional right to convey and receive opinions, arguments and information concerning matter intended or likely to affect voting in an election . . . ."[64] Even dissenting Justice Dawson agreed that although "the Australian Constitution, unlike the Constitution of the United States, does little to confer upon individuals by way of positive rights those basic freedoms which exist in a free and democratic society," nonetheless when the constitution provided for a parliament whose members were to be chosen by the people, in providing a choice, "that must mean a true choice."[65]

Finally, consider decisions of both the German Constitutional Court and the Irish Supreme Court on government "propaganda" designed to support a particular political party in an election and approval of a government-supported referendum, respectively. In a proceeding that might be difficult to bring in the United States because of standing rules,[66] officers of one political party chal-

---

[64] For the source of this and the preceding quotations from Justice McHugh's opinion, see id at 230–32. With McHugh's emphasis on the words "directly chosen by the people," compare US Const, Art I, § 2 (members of House to be "chosen every second Year by the People . . .").

[65] *Australian Capital Television*, 177 CLR at 182, 187 (Dawson, J). Whether the freedom to communicate information extends beyond the election period, he said, was something it need not decide, but emphasized the importance of ensuring that freedom of speech is not unduly restricted during an election period. Accepting that an act might intrude on such necessary freedom, Dawson concluded that the act was consistent with the demands of representative government. See id at 149–50, 157–62. (Justice Brennan also wrote separately, recognizing the principle of freedom for political speech, id at 149, but arguing that these provisions were, for the most part, constitutional as a reasonable and proportional effort to prevent the "covert influences [which] flow from financial dependence," id at 157–64.) For a later and more cautious treatment of implied constitutional rights in Australia, see *Lange v Australia Broadcasting Corp.*, 189 CLR 520 (High Court of Australia, 1997).

[66] Standing rules in Article III federal courts are at least episodically more restrictive than those found in some state courts and in some foreign jurisdictions. Unless a taxpayer challenges an expenditure of public funds as violating the Establishment Clause, standing to sue as a taxpayer over misuse of federal funds or property is likely to be denied. See, e.g., *United States v Richardson*, 418 US 166 (1974); see also *Valley Forge Christian College v Americans United for Separation of Church and State, Inc.*, 454 US 464 (1982). In addition, standing is sometimes withheld where a party claims injury from a government action where the injury is caused by effects on third parties, see *Allen v Wright*, 468 US 737 (1984), as would often be the case where government speech is claimed to impermissibly skew debate. See also Erwin Chemerinsky, *Protecting the Democratic Process: Voter Standing to Challenge Abuses of Incumbency*, 49 Ohio St L J 773, 774 (1988) (lamenting that "most courts have held that it is not the role of the federal judiciary to resolve challenges to improper actions by incumbents"); Thomas Emerson, *The System of Freedom of Expression* 708 (Vintage, 1971) ("it is plain that judicial restriction can hardly be . . . a viable device for . . . [protecting] private expression against abridgment by government expression"). By contrast, in many state and local jurisdictions taxpayers are authorized to sue public officials for unauthorized government expenditures. See, e.g., Oregon Rev Stat § 294.100(2) (authorizing taxpayer suits against public officials who expend public funds for purpose not authorized by law), relied on in *Burt*,

lenged expenditures during the 1976 election campaign made by the German Press and Information offices to buy advertisements in newspapers and magazines to identify the accomplishments of the incumbent administration.[67] Invoking Article 20 of the German Basic Law—which describes Germany as a "democratic" state— the Court held that "Elections can confer democratic legitimation in the sense of Article 20(2) only if they are free." This requires not only freedom in the casting of ballots but also freedom to form opinions freely. The organs of government, the Court concluded, "may not in their official capacity [try to] influence the formation of the popular will by employing additional special measures during elections in order to gain control over these organs. . . . the constitutional principle that limits the tenure of the [legislature and the government] does not permit the current federal government in its capacity as a constitutional organ to seek reelection, as it were, and to promote itself as the 'future government,'" although individual members of the federal government may campaign in a nonofficial capacity.[68] Notwithstanding the Basic Law's guarantees of freedom of thought (Art. 4) and expression (Art. 5), and of equality (Art. 3), according to Professor Donald Kommers the Court's decision invalidating the expenditures was based on their offending the idea of democracy under Article 20, the principle of equality among political parties found in Article 21, and the principle of free and equal elections found in Article 38.[69]

The Irish case arose out of a series of efforts to amend the Irish Constitution to permit divorce. Under Articles 46 and 47 of the

---

699 P2d at 169–70; *Stern v Kramarsky*, 375 NYS 2d at 240 (upholding standing of taxpayer to seek injunction against expenditure of public funds to urge voters to support a proposed state constitutional amendment); *Schulz v State*, 654 NE2d 1226 (NY Ct App 1995) (upholding taxpayer's right to challenge use of public funds to print "New York, New York brochure" that served private partisan interests of incumbent governor and his campaign committee).

[67] See Donald P. Kommers, *Constitutional Jurisprudence of the Federal Republic of Germany* 177–79 (Duke, 2d ed 1997) (describing and translating the *Official Propaganda Case*, 1977, 44 BverfGE 125). For historic examples in the United States, see Yudof, *When Government Speaks* at 8–9 (cited in note 6) (discussing franking privileges of incumbents); id at 123 (describing controversy over printing in 1943 by Office of War Information of pamphlet entitled "Roosevelt of America—President, Champion of Liberty, United States Leader in the War to Win Lasting and Worldwide Peace"). As Yudof notes, governments spend moneys on "advertising" campaigns designed to influence public opinion not only in electoral contexts, or about particular political leaders, but about a wide range of issues.

[68] For this and the preceding quotations from the case, see Kommers, *Constitutional Jurisprudence* at 178–79 (cited in note 67).

[69] Id at 178.

Irish Constitution, such a proposal, once passed by both houses of the national legislature, must go to the public for a vote in a referendum whether to make the proposed change to the constitution. Article 47 says that the referendum shall be conducted in accordance with a law, and the referendum law in question specifically provided that the legislature could provide a statement to accompany the referendum. A four to one majority held that it was impermissible for the government to expend public monies to campaign for ratification (with a suggestion that individual members of the government could speak in favor of it).[70] Stating that neither the Constitution nor the 1994 act was explicit on how the government was to carry out its duty to submit the referendum to the people, Justice Blayney was "satisfied that constitutional justice requires that the executive should act fairly in discharging it, not favouring any section of the people at the expense of any other section," and that the government here "has not held the scales equally between those who support and those who oppose the amendment."[71] Justice Denham identified three constitutional rights infringed by such expenditures of public funds: equality, freedom of expression, and right to democratic process in referenda. The Denham opinion explained, "Ireland is a democratic State. The citizen is entitled under the Constitution to a democratic process. The citizen is entitled to a democracy free from governmental intercession with the process no matter how well intentioned. No branch of the government is entitled to use taxpayers' monies . . . to intercede with the democratic process either as to the voting process or as to the campaign prior to the vote.

---

[70] See *In re Bunreacht na hÉireann, McKenna v An Taoiseach*, 1995 Nos 361 & 366, [1996] 1 ILRM 81 (Supreme Court, Ireland) (Nov 17, 1995). In addition to the opinions discussed in text, see id at 102 (Hamilton, CJ) ("Once the bill has been submitted for the decision of the people, the people were and are entitled to reach their decision in a free and democratic manner," and the government use of public funds for a campaign to influence the referendum is "an interference with the democratic process," and with the constitutional process of amendment and also "infringes the concept of equality which is fundamental to the democratic nature of the State"); id at 103 (O'Flaherty, J) (stating that while it was "unrealistic" that government remain neutral on a topic that its own initiative brought to the people, "the government must stop short of spending public money in favour of one side which has the consequence of being to the detriment of those opposed to the constitutional amendment" and describing this proposition as "bordering on the self-evident"; clarifying that the decision against use of public funds to prepare advertising materials urging a yes vote does not affect rights to speak as ministers to public media to put forward their point of view).

[71] See id at 109.

This is an implied right . . . in keeping with the democratic nature of [the Constitution]."[72]

These decisions are obviously interpretations of other constitutions, each of which differs in important respects from the American Constitution. Yet each reflects a resort to fundamental understandings of democracy, and popular sovereignty, as a basis to constrain the government from disfavoring particular candidates (in the case of Australia and Israel, candidates from nonincumbent parties) or from favoring an incumbent-party position or one side of a controversial matter up for a public vote. The structural method of reasoning from the basic relationships of a representative democracy is striking.[73] And the reasoning in each suggests how the Court might have come to the result it did in *Gralike* (given the plainly pejorative language about particular candidates on the state-sponsored ballot) in light of the constitutional provisions of Article I and Amendment 17 structuring relationships between voters and representatives by requiring popular election of members of Congress on a periodic basis.

The provisions that the Court does rely on are, of course, closely related to the fundamentality of elections. As Charles Black observed, there is a "close and perpetual interworking between the textual and the relational and structural modes of reasoning, for the structure and relations concerned are themselves created by the text, and inferences drawn from them must surely be controlled by the text."[74] He argues that being more clear about the structural bases for decisions is based on the proposition that "clarity about what we are doing . . . is both a good in itself, and a means to sounder decision."[75] Let me illustrate the possible benefits of more clearly identifying the Constitution's commitment to the structures of popular voting for representatives as fundamental to this decision by returning to Chief Justice Rehnquist's opinion.

Although Chief Justice Rehnquist relies on the First Amendment, there is a sense in which the opinion is even more centrally

---

[72] For the source of this and the preceding quotations from Justice Denham's opinion, see id at 111–12, 113.

[73] With respect to outcomes on particular issues (perhaps especially the Irish referendum case), arguments from such basic relationships might work in different directions. See text at note 123.

[74] Black, *Structure and Relationship* at 31 (cited in note 4).

[75] Id at 32.

concerned with elections than it is with free speech. First, like the Court, the Chief Justice relies on *Anderson*, a case involving not the First Amendment but the Equal Protection Clause in an election context. His reliance on *Anderson* suggests that the speech component of the *Gralike* label was perhaps less important than the place where the pejorative labeling occurred.[76] Consider also his assertion that the problem is not only content nonneutrality but "discriminat[ion] on the basis of viewpoint," with the "result . . . that the State injects itself into the election process at an absolutely critical point—the composition of the ballot, which is the last thing the voter sees before he makes his choice—and does so in a way that is not neutral as to issues or candidates."[77] In other words, Rehnquist seems to be saying, when governments regulate the conditions for elections, they are regulating a centrally important phenomenon consisting of the election (not speech)—an area in which concerns for equality, and for government "fairness" in the sense of impartiality, join with concerns arising directly from the character of the government as a representative democracy.[78]

---

[76] On the other hand, one could think of *Anderson* as a case about racial discrimination rather than as an election case. One could readily imagine a constitutional rule prohibiting the government from requiring disclosure of information about a person's race in any setting in which any individual or public benefit or detriment (including attracting votes vel non) turns on that designation. Thus, one could perhaps read both *Anderson* and *Gralike* as forbidding the government from requiring any form of labeling, whether in a ballot setting or not, that has the purpose or effect of penalizing a candidate or a citizen for a constitutionally protected, or constitutionally irrelevant, activity or status (one's speech or one's race)—a theory that does not crucially depend on the label being a condition for ballot access. As discussed below, I do not believe this was Rehnquist's theory in *Gralike*. See text at notes 77–86.

[77] *Gralike*, at 1042 (Rehnquist, CJ, concurring in the judgment). Note the possible ambiguity in meaning of the idea of "neutrality as to issues"—as between a "neutral" choice of issues on which to focus or neutrality as to the approved view of the particular issue.

[78] I do not mean to suggest that government-required labels for speakers, in contexts other than elections, would not raise First Amendment free speech concerns—clearly, they would. If, for example, a municipal government were to require those who wished to speak in parks, or other traditional public fora, to identify themselves, or to follow some state-specified formula for designating what kind of issues or views they were promoting (e.g., with respect to the bombing of Afghanistan), it is not difficult to imagine the Court holding such provisions unconstitutional. Compare *Buckley v American Constitutional Law Foundation, Inc.*, 525 US 182 (1999) (invalidating requirement that paid petition signature gatherers wear name-identification badge); *McIntyre v Ohio Elections Comm'n*, 514 US 334 (1995) (holding unconstitutional a ban on anonymous pamphleteering on election issues or candidates); *Talley v California*, 362 US 60 (1960) (finding unconstitutional a local law prohibiting all anonymous leafleting). Mandatory labeling of persons' views in any setting risks harm to First Amendment principles and warrants serious scrutiny. Yet the election context poses specialized concerns: it is one in which some mandatory labeling is permitted, for example, of political party affiliation, when comparable identification requirements on a driver's license would be plainly impermissible. Compare Post, 106 Yale L J at 186–87 (cited in

Reflection on Rehnquist's articulation of the kind of First Amendment issue here supports this conclusion.[79] Rehnquist identifies a "First Amendment" right not to be pejoratively identified on the ballot.[80] Under *Paul v Davis*,[81] there is no general constitutional right to be free from pejorative government description. *Paul v Davis* did not involve pejorative labeling based on First Amendment protected activities, and so it might be contended that where the label concerns a person's speech activities, the government is more constrained. Yet despite his invocation of the First Amendment, what Rehnquist finds objectionable seems to be more that the description is pejorative than that it is a pejorative characterization of speech. A comparison of this case with *Meese v Keene* suggests that the election context played a critical role in Rehnquist's willingness to see a constitutional violation.[82] *Keene* in-

---

note 6) (suggesting a distinction between specifically political conceptions of fairness and commitments to vigorous freedom of speech).

[79] Chief Justice Rehnquist explains that he disagrees with the lower court, which had found a problem of compelled speech. 121 S Ct at 1042 n *. Rehnquist argues persuasively that the ballot label is not likely to be thought of as issuing from the candidate. In so doing, however, he simply ignores the lower court's conclusion that the candidate's speech was compelled *prior* to the election by the specter of the negative ballot label; the lower court believed that in both senses the candidate's speech was being compelled. *Gralike v Cook*, 191 F3d 911, 917 (8th Cir 1999).

[80] Note that in some circles being a "democrat" or a "republican" or a "socialist" or a "liberal" would be seen as "pejorative." The kind of "pejorative" designation that concerns Rehnquist is evidently one not based on a voluntary association by the candidate with a party—one that is in some sense more a matter of what the government requires than what the candidate voluntarily associates himself or herself with in the course of seeking office. Compare *Burdick v Takushi*, 504 US 428 (1992), where Rehnquist joined the Court's opinion upholding a ban on write-in voting, a ban that arguably reinforced the significance of party-affiliated candidacies.

[81] See *Paul v Davis*, 424 US 693 (1976) (rejecting constitutional challenge to unwarranted posting of person's name as a shoplifter because reputation by itself was not a form of liberty constitutionally protected from government action by the Due Process Clause). The state had expressly relied on *Paul v Davis* in defending its statute, arguing that the ballot label should not be seen as impermissible coercion of speech merely from potential reputational effects. See Reply Brief for the Petitioner, in *Cook v Gralike*, No 99-929 (filed Sept 13, 2000), 2000 WL 1339202, *12, *13. *Paul v Davis* involved a procedural due process challenge to the allegedly false listing and identification of the plaintiff as a shoplifter. Its holding that such false identification was not constitutionally actionable absent a more concrete legal harm, such as loss of employment, suggests that the Court would not see the Constitution generally as constraining government speech that is pejorative about individuals, though it would not necessarily be inconsistent with *Paul v Davis* to argue that the Constitution nonetheless constrains pejorative government labels based on a person's speech or other constitutionally protected activities.

[82] 481 US 465 (1987) (concluding that although designation of film as "propaganda" created injury sufficient to establish plaintiff's standing to challenge labeling requirement, "propaganda" could be regarded as a "neutral" and not pejorative designation and thus did not offend the First Amendment). The label required for the film stated, in essence,

volved a claim that a government-required label and statutory designation of a film violated the First Amendment. Outside of the
election context, the *Keene* Court concluded that the designation
of a film as "political propaganda" was not pejorative and did not
offend the First Amendment. It is hard to credit what the Court
says in *Keene* about the term "propaganda" not being pejorative,
given the Court's concession that the phrase had pejorative meanings, and that 49 percent of the voters would be less inclined to
vote for a candidate who distributed a film so identified.[83] But if
the labeling and designation in *Keene* were not pejorative even
though they would adversely affect voters' views, it is a harder
question to see why Rehnquist believes the label in *Gralike* is
pejorative.

Although at a very formal level *Keene* is not inconsistent with
the claim that the First Amendment is violated by pejorative labeling,[84] the best way to understand these decisions is that the government has wider latitude to engage in pejorative labeling in settings
outside the ballot booth. The more restricted latitude of the government to engage in pejorative labeling within ballot booths is,
I would suggest, related to the far greater latitude the government
has to impose conditions on the ballot—including prohibiting
anonymous candidacies (even though anonymous speech is permitted in other settings) and discouraging independent candidates

---

that the material was circulated by an entity registered under the Foreign Agents Registration Act, which in turn described material required to be registered as "political propaganda." Id at 470–71 (citing 22 USC § 614). The Court reasoned that because the statutory
definition of "political propaganda" included not only misleading statements, as in the popular pejorative sense of the term, but also accurate material intended to influence foreign
policy, the Act's use of the term in connection with the mandatory labeling was a "neutral
and evenhanded" rule with "no pejorative connotation." Id at 484. But see Justice Black-
mun's dissent, id at 485–96 (criticizing majority for avoiding inquiry into actual history
and real effect of designation as political propaganda and asserting that "[i]t simply strains
credulity for the Court to assert that 'propaganda' is a neutral classification").

[83] See id at 473–74 & nn 7, 8 (describing survey data supporting claim of injury for
standing purposes); id at 484 (stating that predictions of adverse consequences are sufficient
for standing but "fall far short of proving" that public perceptions have had any adverse
impact on distribution of materials subject to scheme). The Court's decision in *Keene* is
better accounted for by its discussion of the label and designation as forms of government-
provided information and the opportunity for the film distributor to provide more information to dispel any negative effects of the government-required label. See id at 480–81.

[84] That is, because *Keene* found the designation "political propaganda" not to be pejorative
for First Amendment purposes (though sufficiently harmful and injurious to meet Article
III standing requirements), it is not inconsistent with a rule that the government cannot
require pejorative labels for First Amendment protected activities.

(even though independence of speech and thought is generally highly valued).[85] It is something about elections in particular, rather than freedom of speech, or government speech, in general, that explains *Gralike*.

What underlies Rehnquist's concern with the government speaking in a pejorative way about a person is that the person is a political candidate and the pejorative speech is a condition for appearing on the ballot.[86] This case is at least as centrally about the government's role in elections as it is about First Amendment free speech values. It is the ballot that constrains government from speaking pejoratively, not necessarily citizens' more general rights. While the discussion may be framed in terms of a candidate's "right," that right is a proxy for the public right to free and fair elections. The deeper concern here, I suggest, is with the permissible role of government speech in the context of an election. Opinions that make central the role of elections in a representative democracy would better capture this underlying intuition.

III. Some Speculations on Why the Court Wrote as It Did: Habit, Prudence, and Avoidance

Although a more structural opinion could well have been written in this case, there are a number of possible reasons why the Court did not do so. First, habit. As Charles Black noted long

---

[85] As to anonymity, virtually every state election code requires that the candidate's name appear on the ballot. See, e.g., Ala Code § 11-46-25 (1996) (requiring name of candidate together with title of office to which the candidate seeks election); Cal Elec Code § 13211 (West 1996) (requiring name of candidate to be printed on ballot in roman capital boldface type). In contrast, the First Amendment has been held to protect the right of political pamphleteers to circulate their political writings anonymously. *McIntyre v Ohio Elections Comm'n*, 514 US 334 (1995) (invalidating ban on anonymous pamphleteering). As to discouraging independent candidacies, see e.g., *Burdick v Takushi*, 504 US 428 (1992) (upholding state ban on write-in voting); *Storer v Brown*, 415 US 724 (1974) (upholding state limits on independent candidacies by those recently having been affiliated with a political party); *Jenness v Fortson*, 403 US 431 (1971) (upholding requirement that independent candidates, to appear on the ballot, gather signatures of 5 percent of total registered voters in last election). A hallmark of First Amendment law in other settings is to protect independent, even lonely voices.

[86] As noted above, *Paul v Davis* may be distinguished by the argument that there are core First Amendment interests in play where a pejorative label is determined by a candidate's speech. Yet Rehnquist's reliance on *Anderson*—where the "pejorative" information was not about the candidate's speech but the candidate's race—suggests that the "speech" component of what motivates the label may have been less important than *where* the pejorative labeling occurred. Cf. note 76 supra.

ago, "in dealing with questions of constitutional law, we have preferred the method of purported explication or exegesis of the particular textual passage considered as a directive of action, as opposed to the method of inference from the structures and relationships created by the constitution in all its parts or in some principal part."[87] Although the Court has been hospitable to structural reasoning in several federalism cases, in part this has been the result of apparent necessity: In *Printz*, there was simply no text that plausibly could be interpreted in any particularly specific level to preclude commandeering. In the area of sovereign immunity, the available text of the Eleventh Amendment could most plausibly be read to permit federal jurisdiction over states in a large class of cases (suits by citizens against their own state) that the Court believed was inconsistent with more basic constitutional postulates. So the style of the opinions in *Gralike* could be in part mere reversion to habit. It might also arise in part from the tradition of associating election law and voting cases to First Amendment rights (of both association and speech).[88]

Another possibility worth noting is the shadow of the most high profile "election" case of the Term—the litigation over the November 2000 presidential election. The unanimity of the Court in *Gralike* may be contrasted not only with its division in the federalism cases but also its division in *Bush v Gore*. Anchoring the *Gralike* decision firmly in a discrete portion of the oldest text of the Constitution may have been attractive to a Court whose legitimacy had come under attack. The substantial scholarly criticism of *Bush v Gore* might have made resting decision in *Gralike* on something more concrete—a portion of the Constitution text that feels more like a specific text (in contrast to structural arguments or the Due Process and Equal Protection Clauses) but with an available body of precedent with which the decision can be linked—attractive as

---

[87] Black, *Structure and Relationship* at 7 (cited in note 4). See also id at 8 (the "preference for the particular-text style has been a decided one, leading not only to the failure to develop a full-bodied case-law of inference from constitutional structure and relation but even to a preference, among texts, for those which are in form directive of official conduct, rather than for those that declare or create a relationship out of the existence of which inference could be drawn.").

[88] Reinforcing the role of habit is the relative dearth of federal case law on the nature of and limits on government speech in elections. For a possible explanation, see Chemerinsky, 49 Ohio St L J (cited in note 66) (describing obstacles to federal court resolution of challenges to incumbent-favoring legislation).

a prudential matter. Moreover, a Court whose quick remedial intuitions on a 5–4 vote (as to remedy) decided a close presidential
election might well seek to express other election decisions in the
most conventional, and narrow, terms possible.[89]

The sequence of decisions may also shed light on Chief Justice
Rehnquist's decision to rest on the First Amendment rather than
the Elections Clause in *Gralike*. Respondent Gralike argued, in
support of the judgment below, that the ballot-labeling law was
an invalid exercise of state authority under Article I, Section 4,
because the constitutional powers given to state legislatures could
not be exercised by popular referendum (at least absent authorization by Congress).[90] Article I, Section 4 (at issue in *Gralike*) and
Article II, Section 1 (at issue in *Bush v Gore*) both specifically refer
to the role of the state legislature in determining the conditions
for selecting, respectively, members of Congress and presidential
electors.[91] In his separate opinion in *Bush v Gore*,[92] the Chief Justice
argued that the state court's interpretations of Florida election laws
were inconsistent with the special constitutional role of the state
legislature contemplated by Article II's "exceptional" language by
"which the Constitution imposes a duty or confers a power on a
particular branch of a State's government."[93] This position, though
perhaps hospitable to the respondent's argument against the role
of popular initiative in the exercise of state powers under Article

---

[89] The Court's decision in *Bush v Gore* has already been the subject of fierce criticism.
See, e.g., Elizabeth Garrett, *Leaving the Decision to Congress*, in Cass R. Sunstein and Richard
A. Epstein, eds, *The Vote: Bush, Gore and the Supreme Court* 38 (2001); Pamela S. Karlan,
The Newest Equal Protection: Regressive Doctrine on a Changeable Court, in Sunstein and
Epstein, supra at 77; David A. Strauss, *Bush v Gore: What Were They Thinking*, id at 184;
Jack M. Balkin and Sanford Levinson, *Understanding the Constitutional Revolution*, 87 Va
L Rev 1045 (2001). Other academics have been more supportive. See, e.g., Richard A.
Epstein, *"In Such Manner as the Legislature Thereof May Direct": The Outcome in Bush v Gore
Defended*, in Sunstein and Epstein, supra at 13; Michael W. McConnell, *Two and a Half
Cheers for Bush v Gore*, id at 98.

[90] See Brief for Respondents in *Cook v Gralike*, No 99-929 (Aug 14, 2000), 2000 WL
1409741, at *12, n 8 (distinguishing *Ohio ex rel Davis v Hildebrandt*, 241 US 565 (1916),
involving use of a referendum in congressional redistricting, because Congress had by statute contemplated state use of referenda for those purposes).

[91] See Art I, § 4, cl 1 (the "Times, Places and Manner" of holding elections for Representatives "shall be prescribed in each State by the Legislature thereof . . ."); Art II, § 1, cl
2 ("Each State shall appoint, in such Manner as the Legislature thereof may direct . . ."
presidential electors).

[92] 531 US 98, 111 (2000) (Rehnquist, CJ, concurring).

[93] Id at 112.

I, Section 4, is in some tension with cases interpreting this clause to afford wide latitude to state constitutions in structuring the exercise of state power to regulate the manner of holding congressional elections.[94] Avoiding the Elections Clause ground in *Gralike* avoided the need to attempt to reconcile his *Bush v Gore* opinion with the role of the popular initiative in establishing the ballot label in light of those earlier cases on Article I, Section 4.[95]

Whatever may account for the form of the opinion, it is important to explain why I think it likely that a structural opinion would have been just as narrow as these opinions were. It might, however, have called for more of an effort to acknowledge the very real conceptual difficulties that lie just a short distance beyond the facts presented in this case. It is relatively simple, as Justice Kennedy indicated, to decide that overtly pejorative statements imposed under state law on the ballot offend the Constitution. But the structural principle, that no existing government can use the machinery

---

[94] For cases rejecting arguments that Article I, Section 4's reference to the state legislature limited states from authorizing other forms of lawmaking under state constitutions, see *Smiley v Holm*, 285 US 355, 367–68 (1932) (upholding authority of state to decide that governor participates through veto in state lawmaking and finding "no suggestion in the Federal constitutional provision of an attempt to endow the legislature of the State with power to enact laws in any manner other than that in which the constitution of the State has provided that laws shall be enacted"); *Davis v Hildebrandt*, 241 US 565 (rejecting challenge to reapportionment plan adopted by referendum and upholding state's power in its constitution to vest part of the legislative power in the people; describing the authority of the state to act by way of referendum in apportioning congressional seats as a question of state law not reviewable by the Supreme Court). Although *Davis* relied in part on the proposition that the challenge to lawmaking by referendum must rest in part on the Guarantee Clause, which was nonjusticiable, the challenge was described as specifically based on the idea that for purposes of Article I, Section 4, a referendum was not part of the "legislative authority" of the state required to act. Id at 567.

[95] It is possible that Chief Justice Rehnquist could have reconciled these cases to his views in *Bush v Gore* by arguing that the reference to legislatures implies a commitment to state lawmaking (whether understood to include the governor, or popular referendum) up to the moment of creating binding state law, but not to extend to the "judicial" task of interpreting the law once given. But compare *Kimble v Swackhammer*, 439 US 1385, 1387 (1978) (Rehnquist, as Circuit Justice, denying motions for interim relief), explaining that the objection there to citizen participation in the Article V role of state legislatures, through an advisory referendum on whether the state should ratify a proposed federal constitution amendment, was without substance "because of the nonbinding character of the referendum." In *Cook v Gralike*, the initiative by which the ballot-label requirement was enacted was apparently binding on the state officials charged with preparing the ballot. My point, though, is not that the cases are impossible to reconcile, but rather that, had he focused centrally on the role of elections under Article I, Section 4 in *Gralike*, he might have felt called on to harmonize his *Bush v Gore* position with an opinion addressing whether Missouri's ballot-label law, enacted through an initiative rather than by the state legislature, was consistent with the Elections Clause.

of government to influence an election in favor of incumbency or any particular party or position, though rhetorically appealing in its simplicity, requires considerable qualification, perhaps especially in the setting of proposed term limits.

As I discuss below, that general principle, if taken to its limits, would intrude on many areas of government speech that are plainly beneficial to electoral processes in democracies.[96] Moreover, evaluating whether ballot labels are consistent with the role of elections in a democracy is complex and requires more than rhetorical resort to first principles, because concerns for democracy point in conflicting directions—not so much for "pejorative" labels but for more evenhanded, or informational, labeling. Although ballot labels can pose a threat to the legitimating purpose of elections, they may enhance the "checking" functions of elections by providing information about whether incumbent representatives have been sufficiently responsive to their constituents.[97] Finally, preserving electoral choice by invalidating the results of a popular initiative might seem paradoxical: overcoming a "democratic" decision in the name of democratic principles poses dilemmas at the heart of the tensions between constitutionalism and democracy and among competing conceptions of democracy. Examining these concerns in related but harder cases may help explain both the attraction of specific texts and the narrowness of the Court's opinion and Chief Justice Rehnquist's concurrence.

Free and fair elections in a democracy serve at least three functions. First, as noted above, elections play a "checking function," acting as an accountability mechanism on current officeholders and

---

[96] For discussions of the difficult constitutional issues posed by government speech, see sources cited in note 6. Treating the *Gralike* ballot label as a form of government speech can be contested; why not treat the label as the voters' speech, not the government's? My intuition is that when a position is represented as that of "the voters," the position assumes the governmental quality of purporting to bind those who disagreed but were in the minority. In this sense, the act of placing a label expressing the "voters' instruction" is governmental, both from the perspective of those voters in the minority at the prior referendum and for purposes of evaluating the freeness of the choices made by the next set of voters who come to the ballot booth at a different election. If one were to look at the ballot label as posing a "state action" question, there could be little doubt that a label enacted into law, enforced by a state official, as a condition for appearing on the official state ballot, is a form of "state" action.

[97] For elaboration on different understandings of the role of a representative and, in particular, for an argument that a representative must be responsive to the represented, see Hanna Fenichel Pitkin, *The Concept of Representation* (U Cal, 1967).

their policies.[98] Second, elections have operative significance (beyond "expression") in that they *choose* who will hold office in, enact, and implement policies and conduct the government for some period of time into the future. Third, elections function to confer *legitimacy* on that choice as flowing from the voters' decisions, rather than from the existing government's. Although elections play other important roles (as occasions for expressive and associational activity of a high order), these three functions—checking, choosing, and legitimating elected government officials—are uniquely performed by public elections.[99]

Consider the implications of the decision in *Cook v Gralike* for a state law, enacted by initiative, requiring candidates for state legislative position to proffer their own 250-word statement on term limits for members of legislative bodies.[100] Although this proposal might eliminate the state's use of pejorative language to align itself

---

[98] See Ely, *Democracy and Distrust* at 78 (cited in note 41) (desire for reelection as "insurance policy" against unreasonable behavior by elected representatives); see also Rebecca L. Brown, *Accountability, Liberty and the Constitution*, 98 Colum L Rev 531, 565 (1998) (arguing that political accountability in the Constitution was not designed to maximize satisfaction of preferences but to minimize the risk of tyranny, and that elections "provide the people with an opportunity to punish those who have violated" people's trust). As Pitkin has noted, being a representative may entail both "descriptive" and "symbolic" purposes that do not necessarily fulfill the substantive aspects of political representation in the sense of acting for and responsively to the represented. In a political democracy, though, part of what people can choose to vote on are the descriptive, demographic, or symbolically "representational" characteristics of representatives. Whether over time the representative is found sufficiently responsive to constituents is one, but only one, factor determining whether people continue to vote for the representative at elections.

[99] In *Burdick*, the Court insisted that it could not treat elections as simply a form of expression without undermining the ability of states to hold effective elections. *Burdick v Takushi*, 504 US at 438 ("Attributing to elections a more generalized expressive function would undermine the ability of States to operate elections fairly and efficiently."); see also *Munro v Socialist Workers Party*, 479 US 189, 193 (1986) ("States may condition access to the general election ballot by a minor-party or independent candidate upon a showing of a modicum of support among the potential voters"). But cf. Adam Winkler, Note, *Expressive Voting*, 68 NYU L Rev 330 (1993) (distinguishing instrumental from expressive aspects of voting and criticizing the Court for focusing only on the former).

[100] This hypothetical is intended to (1) eliminate the major federalism concerns discussed in *Term Limits v Thornton* and relied on as well in *Gralike*, (2) remove the distorting effects of having a state official decide on a candidate's compliance with a particular term-limits proposal, and (3) avoid "pejorative" language on the ballot by allowing each candidate to explain his or her position in their own words. Obviously some of these difficulties cannot be overcome: in any plausible scheme such as this a state official of some sort would have to review the candidate statement for conformity to standards of both length and possibly accuracy, which might pose insuperable obstacles to such a scheme being constitutional on other grounds. The use of a candidate's own statement is one device suggested inter alia by Professor Garrett's very helpful analysis of the ballot-labeling requirement. See Garrett, 85 Va L Rev at 1584–85 (cited in note 26).

with a particular position, it does involve a single-issue ballot-label requirement. It will cause voters to focus on this issue, out of many others, and place pressure on candidates to say something so as not to have a blank near their names. Yet such a ballot label may be consistent with the checking functions of elections. As supporters of the Missouri term-limits labeling requirement noted, term-limits proposals are unlikely to emerge from representative bodies because current representatives are unlikely to act against their own interest in continuation in office.[101] Data show that in the period 1990–94, only one term-limits provision emerged from a state legislature, but over twenty emerged from initiative and referendum efforts.[102] One might think, then, that a concern for democracy[103] would support an "exception" to a general ban on ballot labeling for issues like term limits (and like the earlier effort to amend the Constitution to provide for direct election of senators) which would be so contrary to the immediate self-interest of representative bodies as to make it unlikely that they would be enacted.[104]

The Court did not analyze whether a less pejoratively phrased ballot label concerning the candidate's position on term limits might survive. No party argued for a principled distinction between term-limits ballot labeling and ballot labeling about any other single issue,[105] even though amici argued that the state had

---

[101] See Brief Amicus Curiae of USPIRG Education Fund in Support of Petitioner, *Cook v Gralike*, No 99-929 (filed June 23, 2000), 2000 WL 1852445, *20–21. Similar arguments have been discussed in scholarly comment. See, e.g., Garrett, 85 Va L Rev at 1539–40 (cited in note 26).

[102] See Klarman, 85 Geo L J at 510–13 (cited in note 44).

[103] By "democracy" here I mean a system that generally provides mechanisms by which the views of majorities of the people over some period of time can be effected into law (provided that they do not violate other democratic commitments, e.g., against invidious discrimination). I take no position here on whether, on the whole, term limits for members of Congress would be a good thing. For discussion of different kinds of arguments for term limits, compare, e.g., Einer Elhauge, *Are Term Limits Undemocratic?* 64 U Chi L Rev 83 (1997) (arguing that term limits for members of Congress would be pro-democratic by solving collective-action problem for voters who would prefer to elect challenger but hesitate to vote incumbent out because of loss of advantages of seniority under non-term-limits system), with Elizabeth Garrett, *Term Limitations and the Myth of the Citizen-Legislator*, 81 Cornell L Rev 623 (1996) (disputing claim that term limits will produce "citizen legislators").

[104] See generally Klarman, 85 Geo L J (cited in note 44) (arguing that courts should not strike down term-limits laws because of their fundamentally anti-entrenching character).

[105] Compare Sullivan, 109 Harv L Rev at 99–100 (cited in note 39) (noting possible argument that term limits are consistent with the anti-entrenchment, equality-enhancing purposes the majority in *Term Limits* attributed to the Qualifications Clauses and should thus

a compelling interest in the ballot label because of the corrupting effect of long congressional terms on incumbents.[106] Even had such an argument been made, however, there are reasons why the Court might have rejected it (apart from the presence of pejorative language in the ballot label implicitly going to the candidate's trustworthiness).

First, support for term limits might be regarded as a partisan issue that, even if neutrally presented, would discernibly tend to favor a class of candidates associated not only with that issue but with a host of other issues that begin to look a good deal like the platform of one of the two major political parties in terms of retrenching on the powers of the national government. Data suggest that of the several groups most likely to support term limits, one of the two major national political parties was well represented and the other was not.[107] Term limits, then, is an issue, like many, with partisan freight.[108]

Second, it is not clear that no threat to the "checking" function is posed because of the uniquely anti-incumbency effect of a term-limits proposal. Representatives are required to address a range of issues in their elected offices, and thus are often evaluated on fac-

---

be upheld despite their formal inconsistency with prior interpretations of the Qualifications Clauses).

[106] See Brief of Amicus Curiae The Initiative and Referendum Institute in Support of Petitioner, in *Cook v Gralike*, No 99-929 (June 23, 2000), 2000 WL 864205, *24. At oral argument, counsel for the state agreed, in response to a question from the Court, that there was no distinction between the ballot label concerning a term-limits amendment and a ballot label concerning abortion "or any other hot button issue." See Transcript of Oral Argument, *Cook v Gralike*, No 99-929 (Nov 6, 2000), 2000 WL 1673928, **15–16.

[107] See, e.g., Robert Kurfirst, *Term-Limit Logic: Paradigms and Paradoxes*, 29 Polity 118, 135–36 (1996).

[108] On possible reasons for government to refrain from speech on (or funding for private speech on) "controversial" issues, see, e.g., Cass Sunstein, *Democracy and the Problem of Free Speech* 229–31 (Free Press, 1993) (suggesting that viewpoint discrimination may be permissible in funding arts if done in a tightly limited context "not involv[ing] taking sides in a currently contested political debate," in light of likelihood that shared, nonpartisan values support the prohibition); Kagan, 1992 Supreme Court Review at 75 (cited in note 32) (suggesting that government funding of speech on one side of issue is permissible where debate has answers subject to verification, harm on other side of debate is great, and society has reached consensus on the issue); Post, 106 Yale L J at 186–87 (cited in note 6) (distinguishing funding limitations based on "shared values," e.g., decency, from funding limitations of a partisan nature); but see Greene, 69 Fordham L Rev (cited in note 6) (arguing that government should be free to participate in social debate so long as it is one voice among many and not establishing or proscribing ideas); Greene, 53 Vand L Rev (cited in note 6) (arguing that government may advocate a particular vision of the good so long as government does not have monopoly power over debate, engage in coercion, or mask the governmental source of messages through "ventriloquism").

tors beyond any single issue.[109] Having the ballot label on the ballot might "crowd out" other checking functions of the election for representatives.[110]

Third, an "evenhanded" term-limits ballot label may still threaten the legitimation function of elections. Regardless of the procedure by which such labels appear on the ballot, the labels would address issues that some persons or collective entity at some prior point in time found important. An election serves a legitimating role only if it is perceived to reflect the views of the voters *in that election*—freely formed, uncorrupted by fear of violence, and not subject to undue influence from any source. On this standard, it must be acknowledged that many of our elections are a long way from this ideal. Parties and candidates with more money have many more means to influence voters prior to the actual vote. And voters' choices on election day itself are not entirely free and unconstrained: the Court has concluded that states have legitimate interests in fostering a two-party system (i.e., in encouraging the voters on election day to choose between only two candidates for each office), and has upheld state laws that exclude write-in votes from the ballot.[111]

In the face of the rather substantial legal and economic constraints on voters' choices as they enter the ballot booth, preserving the integrity of the ballot itself from efforts to influence the already highly constrained choices voters have—whether by state legislative messages or by messages generated by initiative pro-

---

[109] See Sherman J. Clark, *A Populist Critique of Direct Democracy*, 112 Harv L Rev 434 (1998).

[110] But cf. Klarman, 85 Geo L J at 530–31 (cited in note 44) (criticizing *Term Limits* decision, though concluding that reasonable people could disagree on merits of term limitations).

[111] See *Timmons v Twin Cities Area New Party*, 520 US 351, 367 (1997) ("The Constitution permits the Minnesota Legislature to decide that political stability is best served through a healthy two-party system."); *Burdick v Takushi*, 504 US 428 (1992). Part of the complexity of analysis is that democratic values of self-governance may also be served by enforcing a polity's decision by majority vote to prescribe qualifications for elected public office. Cf. *Gregory v Ashcroft*, 501 US 452, 463 (1991), quoting *Bernal v Fainter*, 467 US 216, 221 (1984) (stating that "authority of the people of the states to determine the qualifications of their" government officials "lies at 'the heart of representative government'") (internal citation omitted). Democracy over time, then, is in tension with democracy at the moment of particular electoral decisions. Somewhat paradoxically, then, while statutes regulating elections may be necessary to permit the democratic process to go forward (and may be the product of previously elected legislators), to the extent that they unduly constrain choices of later electorates, they might be understood to impair the capacity of elections to choose legitimately.

cesses—may help preserve the legitimating effects of elections.[112] Allowing ballot labels can be seen to provide further opportunities for those who already hold public or private power to influence the most fundamental public act of the citizenry. Yet they can also be seen as helpful devices to educate voters, enhancing the "essential" "ability of the citizenry to make informed choices among candidates for office."[113] The question of characterization here is surely a difficult one, from normative, symbolic, and empirical standpoints.[114] For the effect of a ballot label necessarily gives pri-

---

[112] Notwithstanding the many cases upholding ballot access restrictions—that is, on who is legally allowed to appear on the ballot—once a candidate is legally entitled to appear on the ballot there is substantial support in the lower courts to invalidate laws that favor incumbents, or nominees of preferred parties, by allocating them preferred places on a ballot. See, e.g., *Gould v Grubb*, 536 P2d 1337 (Cal 1975) (invalidating automatic top-ballot placement for incumbent seeking reelection); *Sangmeister v Woodard*, 565 F2d 460, 465–67 (7th Cir 1977) (invalidating practice of election officials of placing their own political party in top position on the ballot); *McLain v Meier*, 637 F2d 1159, 1167 (8th Cir 1980) (invalidating "incumbent first" rule for ballot placement); *Graves v McElderry*, 946 F Supp 1569, 1573, 1579–82 (WD Okla 1996) (invalidating state law requiring that "'[f]or each ballot for which there are partisan candidates, the candidates of the Democratic party shall be printed in the first position . . . .'"). For a contrary view, see, e.g., *Clough v Guzzi*, 416 F Supp 1057 (D Mass 1976) (upholding state laws requiring "incumbent first" ballot placement and labeling incumbents as such on the ballot).

[113] *Buckley v Valeo*, 424 US 1, 14–15 (1976) quoted with approval, *McIntyre*, 514 US at 346–47.

[114] For an excellent argument in favor of educative ballot labels, see Garrett, 85 Va L Rev at 1540–55, 1576–77 (cited in note 26) (exploring capacity of ballot notations to increase voter competence). At oral argument, at least one member of the Court drew a distinction between the state's expressing a pejorative judgment, as in *Gralike*, and simply providing information to the voters. See Transcript, 2000 WL 1673928 *7 ("the voters are being given something more than information"). Although there may well be room for the government to provide evenhanded and impartial information about matters on the ballot, see, e.g., Cal Govt Code §§ 88001–02 (West 1993) (requiring ballot pamphlets that voters receive before the election to contain, inter alia, "arguments and rebuttals for and against each state measure" and "the official summary prepared by the Attorney General"), greater concerns would exist about government efforts to "educate" the people in the "moment of choice" setting of election day—when there is neither room nor time for other voices. See Shiffrin, 27 UCLA L Rev at 637–40 (cited in note 6) (arguing that California Legislative Analyst's "impartial statement" concerning the economic impact of each California ballot proposition and which appears on the ballot itself is an unconstitutional form of government speech because it singles out a particular feature for comment, but supporting the constitutionality of informational summaries of ballot measures appearing on the actual ballot, and of sample ballots including arguments pro and con ballot propositions). Cf. Cole, 67 NYU L Rev at 716, 736–38 (cited in note 6) (describing features of institutional settings that require government neutrality, which include that the institutions play an "important role in public debate or in the formation of individual opinion"). In *McIntyre* the Court was unwilling to accept the state's argument that its informational interest in providing to prospective voters information on the identity of those publishing pamphlets was sufficient "to support the constitutionality of its disclosure requirement." *McIntyre*, 514 US at 348–49. See also *Buckley v American Constitutional Law Foundation, Inc.*, 525 US 182 (1999) (invalidating Colorado requirement that ballot initiative circulators wear name-identification badge

ority to a particular issue, no matter how "impartial" and fair the descriptive labels are. In this sense, the educational function of ballot labeling would at the same time serve an agenda-setting role as well.

Now let me focus on the derivation of the ballot label from a popular initiative to amend the state constitution. Again, assuming we were not to deal with a term-limits pledge for federal but for state office, does representative democracy provide us an answer to whether the label is permissible? Does the fact of the initiative suggest that concerns about the availability of voting as the people's check on the government are not in play? The proposition that they are not at issue depends on an opposition between the vote of the people in the prior initiative and the current government. In other words, one could see the ballot label, not as an act of the "government" that challenges the checking or legitimation functions, but rather as an act of sovereignty of the people.[115] However, even if so characterized, there remain problems of democratic checking and legitimation. The vote of the people in the prior initiative was an act of governance, rather than simply election, in the sense that it was an effort to constrain future elections, not simply to fill a seat for a particular term. Not everyone agreed with the vote on the initiative, and even among those who did, two years later a different balance of opinion on that issue—or on

---

or that information about their names and how much they were paid be provided to the state notwithstanding state's argument that such measures helped inform voters).

[115] See note 96; cf. *West Virginia State Board of Education v Barnette*, 319 US 624, 641 (1943) (in striking down compelled flag salute: "We set up government by consent of the governed, and the Bill of Rights denies those in power any legal opportunity to coerce that consent. Authority here is to be controlled by public opinion, not public opinion by authority"). Query whether the required ballot labels in Missouri are an expression of "public opinion" or of "authority" seeking to control public opinion. For skepticism that "direct democracy" is less subject to the control of special interests, see Elizabeth Garrett, *Who Directs Direct Democracy*, 4 U Chi L School Roundtable 17 (1997) (identifying the role of money and organization in initiative and referendum campaigns); Julian N. Eule, *Judicial Review of Direct Democracy*, 99 Yale L J 1503, 1517 (1990) (noting "innovation in obfuscation" by some proponents of ballot propositions). For other objections to direct democracy, see Derrick A. Bell, Jr., *The Referendum: Democracy's Barrier to Racial Equality*, 54 Wash L Rev 1 (1978); Hans Linde, *When Initiative Lawmaking Is Not "Republican Government": The Campaign Against Homosexuality*, 72 Or L Rev 19 (1993); cf. David Magleby, *Governing by Initiative*, 66 U Colo L Rev 13 (1995) (describing the role of "initiative industry" and arguing that voting on ballot propositions "amplifies the social class bias" in voting generally, and that the "issue agenda of direct legislation" rarely reflects those issues most important to voters); Clark, 112 Harv L Rev (cited in note 109) (arguing that even when fairly conducted, initiatives do not allow people to make as effective use of political power across an array of issues and different intensities of preference as does voting for representatives).

the importance of that issue as a basis for decision—may be present.[116] Reification of the prior vote in the new election, then, in setting a one-issue agenda for the future might pose some threat to both checking and legitimation functions.[117]

And yet, the same could be said more generally about constitutions: the U.S. Constitution, for example, prohibits a twenty-four-year-old from serving in the House of Representatives, even though current voters might prefer this; New York City's charter prevented Rudolph Giuliani from running for another term despite overwhelming public regard. If the people of a state (or city) could enact term limits for their own legislatures, governors, councils, or mayors, why could they not decide to bind themselves to think hard about imposing such a term limit rule by requiring candidates for state office to provide information on the ballot about their views? To move to familiar federal constitutional issues, if we allow people to bind themselves to the two-senators-per-state rule, why should we not allow them to bind themselves to term limits—as the Twenty-Second Amendment does for the office of president? And if we are prepared to concede that a good democratic constitution might include term limits, then does the "greater" power to constitutionalize the rule imply a "lesser" power to include information about candidates' positions with the

---

[116] Professor Garrett has proposed that using a governmentally sponsored public opinion poll (the poll perhaps consisting of questions identified by groups petitioning with requisite signatures) to identify the several major issues of concern for voters that would then appear as ballot labels might avoid some of the distorting effects of campaigns for initiatives drafted by private groups seeking requirements for single-issue ballot labels. See Garrett, 85 Va L Rev at 1581–84 (cited in note 26). There is much to commend Garrett's proposal, perhaps as a new means to identify issues that could be the subject of ballot propositions with informational pamphlets prepared by government bodies. But one might still stop short of permitting ballot labels for candidates in a polling place, where there is no opportunity for other voices to be considered within the same forum. Cf. Post, 106 Yale L J at 164–65 (cited in note 6) (distinguishing managerial domains in which government speech is subject to less scrutiny from domains of public discourse); Cole, 67 NYU L Rev at 704–12 (cited in note 6) (arguing for focus on whether government function requires neutrality and relying importantly on whether government has a monopoly or domination over information and captive audience and the need to avoid risks of government propaganda and indoctrination).

[117] Compare Robert Post, *Meiklejohn's Mistake: Individual Autonomy and the Reform of Public Discourse*, 64 U Colo L Rev 1109 (1993) (arguing that agenda control by government, to improve quality of democratic self-government, is inconsistent with serious commitment to self-governance), with Fiss, *The Irony of Free Speech* at 23–24 (cited in note 47) (arguing that the power of determining substantive agenda must be placed "in agencies that are removed from the political fray"); id at 55 (noting that much of First Amendment law involves "protecting democracy from itself").

intent to encourage adoption of such a rule?[118] Why not allow the people to make some lesser form of "precommitment" to an issue, as part of a multi-stage, multi-election process of reconstituting their basic laws?[119]

If there is a fundamental objection here, it may come from some pre- or meta-constitutional idea of the autonomy of voting in an election. One might say that an essential characteristic of a fair election is that if something is to be voted on, the vote itself must not be skewed. In this sense, there may be an intuition like that behind the idea of unconstitutional conditions: one may not need to hold an election on term limits, but if one does put the question on the ballot, it should be done in a "fair" way.[120] Pejorative lan-

---

[118] One possibly important kind of difference is suggested by Bruce Ackerman's distinctions between ordinary and constitutional politics. See Bruce Ackerman, *We The People: Foundations* (Harvard, 1991). On this view, most people are—perhaps healthily—not that engaged in or attentive to public issues most of the time. They show up for elections in small numbers, and with ignorance of major issues. Elections held during such times are necessary to keep government going and to maintain political accountability, but cannot be relied on to provide evidence of the kind of public thinking to constitute binding commitments for a future beyond the time for the next election. In other words, given the instability of preferences over time, ordinary politics should not be allowed to bind the electorate for more than one election. This view, however, constitutes a major challenge to the use of initiative and referendum to amend state constitutions, which has a long history in many parts of the United States but which might equally be viewed as a form of "ordinary politics," especially to the extent that they do not require special majorities or authorization in consecutive elections or by special bodies to be approved. Whatever one might conclude about the legitimacy of amending constitutions by ordinary voting, one's answer may be influenced if the result of an amendment by way of initiative or referenda can be undone through the same mechanism. To the extent that a ballot label, enacted by initiative, were seen as an attempt to forestall future elections from acting as a check to undo the prior results (e.g., by privileging an issue, like term limits, in the different context of an election for representatives), it may pose special legitimacy concerns not present with respect to other forms of initiatives.

[119] For thoughtful argument in favor of using serial referenda in different elections as a mechanism for constitutional amendment that may, inter alia, overcome the deficiencies in one-time referenda lawmaking, see Bruce Ackerman, *The New Separation of Powers*, 113 Harv L Rev 633, 664–68 (2000); Bruce Ackerman, *We The People: Transformations* 403–14 (Harvard, 1998).

[120] In part this insight may assume that ballot labels might disguise a "decision under the influence" from one that is in some sense freer—at least of organized last-minute inputs. See Yudof's excellent discussion over concern for government speech creating a manufactured or "falsified" consent. Yudof, *When Government Speaks* at 174–99 (cited in note 6); Cole, 67 NYU L Rev (cited in note 6) (noting danger of indoctrination through government speech). And I do not mean to minimize the other possible objections to identifying a body and a process that can be trusted to provide accurate and "fair" information on all sides of a controversial issue. One would need to have trust in some body to fairly do or supervise the labeling. Cf. Magleby, 66 U Colo L Rev at 24–25 & n 47 (cited in note 115) (noting that official summaries of initiatives, prepared by government bodies, are often challenged in court).

guage interferes with the fairness of the vote and hence with the legitimacy of the result.

But what about a nonpejorative label of a candidate's position on an issue? Even assuming that it were possible to write a description that most people agreed was "neutral" and not pejorative, there is a second objection that may be made to affixing such a label to a candidate for office. To the extent that the selection of candidates is for a general function legislative body,[121] even a nonpejorative ballot label on a particular issue arguably skews the checking and choosing functions with respect to other aspects of what representatives do. If one is thoroughly committed to a deliberative conception of representation in a democracy, such a result is particularly troublesome. Even if one believes in a more "instructional" concept of representation (in which the representative is to reflect the views of constituents), in a general legislative body representatives reflect views on a range of issues that may require compromise or inconsistent treatment in order for the legislature to actually reach decisions; pointing electors to a single issue in the selection of a member of a general legislative body risks diverting voters from considering that broad range of functions at the moment of decision.[122] Whether these concerns are sufficient to condemn as unconstitutional even neutral ballot labels for candidates is a hard question.

For the government to mandate (and pay for) a ballot label designed to influence public decisions on candidates in an election, then, is arguably—but only arguably—inconsistent with the check-

---

[121] Query whether there is a difference in principle, or only in degree, between instructions to delegates to a single-issue assembly (e.g., whether to ratify a proposed amendment, or whom to select as President) and instructions on a particular issue to a member of a general legislative body. Statutory provisions for apparently binding instructions of members of single-issue bodies are not uncommon. See, e.g., Cal Elec Code § 6906 (Deering 2000) (presidential electors); Ariz Rev Stat Ann § 16-705 (West 1996) (delegates to ratifying convention on proposed amendment).

[122] The expression of voters' views on a specific issue—unattached to a candidate—could be a source of important expressive information, provided in a way that poses smaller risks to the political process. This function may lie behind the distinction emphasized in Justice Kennedy's opinion between "nonbinding petitions or memorials by the State as an entity" and the ballot labels required by the Missouri law at issue. See 121 S Ct at 1041 (Kennedy, J, concurring). Cf. Brief for the United States as Amicus Curiae Supporting Affirmance in *Crosby v National Foreign Trade Council*, 530 US 363 (2000), No 99-474, at 28 (Feb 2000) (noting permissibility of States petitioning Congress or enacting resolutions of disapproval of foreign government while arguing against permissibility of legal sanctions amounting to regulaiton of foreign commerce).

ing, choosing, and legitimation functions of elections. Whatever role there may be for government use of funds to provide information (or even take positions) on issues in pamphlets prepared prior to an election, the polling place and ballot box itself are fora in which the government arguably ought to be highly constrained in the way in which it presents choices to the voters, with elections for candidates held distinct from votes on ballot propositions, or on expressions of opinion on resolutions, and the like.[123] This position does not necessarily preclude "instruction"; it does not take a position on deliberative or instructive democracy; but rather it claims that voting for candidates for ongoing government posts is sufficiently distinctive in a complex democracy that the choice—in each election—of what matters most must be one that voters make, generally, on a slate as clean from government support as possible.

Although Rehnquist anchored his opinion in the First Amendment, he did not frame the issue as involving questions of government speech.[124] Government speech poses genuinely difficult problems. Frequently it is motivated by efforts to influence elections and to retain the power of incumbents—but it is often a good idea for government to be responsive to those it represents, at least most of the time on most issues. Moreover, as many have noted, citizens have "an interest in knowing the government's point of view," and there are legitimate interests in using speech to advance government programs and policies.[125] Yet to allow unrestricted use

---

[123] Ballot labeling for referendum and initiative, in the sense of information providing, poses distinctive issues for constitutional analysis of what forms of government speech or influence are undue. Although the choice presented on a ballot initiative is typically binary, it is possible to explore some of the nuances of concern in competing ballot statements. And the lower courts have been more divided on the permissibility of government advocacy for referenda than government advocacy for particular candidates. See note 56 supra.

Ballot labeling by candidates themselves, in the form of a short candidate statement, would also require further separate analysis. See Garrett, 85 Va L Rev at 1584–86 (cited in note 26) discussing this proposal. Such self-labeling has the advantage of allowing the candidate herself to decide what issues or values to focus on in providing "last minute" information to voters; in this sense it is not "government speech" and does not bear the risks of allowing a government in power to control the agenda or information flow to voters on the ballot unduly. Such self-labeling, however, retains the potential for having an undue impact on voters in the absence of response time, a concern mediated somewhat by the presence of statements of competing candidate; it also presents concerns about the accuracy of the descriptions and state processes for judging accuracy.

[124] See note 96 for brief discussion of whether the ballot label should be regarded as government speech.

[125] Cole, 67 NYU L Rev at 681 (cited in note 6).

of government speech resources to influence elections could threaten the legitimacy of elections and lead to authoritarian (or worse) governments. Thus, as David Cole writes, government speech "is both necessary to and potentially subversive of democratic values."[126]

Had the issue in *Gralike* been framed as one of permissible government speech, I think the answer would be the same: that the one-sided ballot label in this case was impermissible. The ballot is a government-monopolized forum in no sense involving "managerial" domains but rather a public discourse and decision forum in which government neutrality is central.[127] What does our knowledge of "government speech" tell us about our hypothetical evenhanded ballot label? I think that humility should make us skeptical of even evenhanded ballot labels in this setting. The monopoly over speech in the ballot marks this arena as one very different from arts funding, the subsidized provision of medical services, or legal services.[128] It makes it different from many other settings in which government speech occurs (including statutory preambles, congressional reports, speeches from executive branch officials or individual members of Congress, official task force reports, judicial opinions or dissents) when the government itself frequently speaks with fragmented voices—the "official report" being subject to disagreement by minority members of Congress, or by sources in the executive branch.[129] No other voice can enter the ballot other than by being printed on it. Yet cacophonous and seriously multivoiced ballot labeling would defeat any effort at clarity on the ballot for

---

[126] Id.

[127] See Post, 106 Yale L J (cited in note 6); see also Cole, 67 NYU L Rev 675, 680–82, 702–17 (cited in note 6) (noting dangers not only of government coercion but of the "indoctrinating effect of a monopolized marketplace of ideas" and arguing for a "spheres of neutrality" approach that would require "public institutions central to a system of free expression" (or, presumably, democracy) to maintain independence from government views and neutrality as among views).

[128] See Emerson, *The System of Freedom of Expression* at 697–99 (cited in note 66) (emphasizing the value of government speech in democracy, but not where government holds monopoly or near-monopoly on expression).

[129] On the value of decentralization and fragmentation of "governmental" power to speak, see Yudof, *When Government Speaks* at 179–88 (cited in note 6) (noting decentralization of congressional speech as helping to avoid risks of government propaganda to "falsify" majority consent), 216 (noting that "fragmentation of responsibility for education among governments reduces the potential danger of a thoroughgoing indoctrination," as does the autonomy of classroom teachers).

voters.[130] While government speech in other settings may plausibly be understood to increase expressive activities, without suppressing critique or difference, inside the ballot or polling booth the absence of other voices, and the absence of "response" time,[131] caution against reliance on information-providing as a justification for ballot labeling of candidates. Yet there are many jurisdictions that provide far greater information in connection with the ballot than that proposed in my hypothetical,[132] and thus it may to some extent be an empirical question whether on particular issues on particular ballots the provision of "evenhanded" information would enhance the reliability of the vote or instead de-legitimate election results or interfere with the checking function of elections.

A more basic difficulty in approaching the issue as one of government speech is that the judicial doctrine lacks any coherent theory of a positive role for the government in the protection of freedom of speech. The Constitution generally has been interpreted not to require affirmative government action but rather to impose limits or conditions on the government when it does act. Without some constitutional framework for determining what the purpose of affirmative government action should be, it is easy to criticize as unsatisfactory and ad hoc efforts to distinguish permissible from impermissible government speech.[133] And yet the intuition that one

---

[130] For a vivid description of the California ballot pamphlet, see Eule, 99 Yale L J at 1508–09 (cited in note 115).

[131] On the importance of response time in evaluating, under the First Amendment, government speech or government restrictions on speech, see *McIntyre*, 514 US at 352 n 16 (distinguishing *Burson v Freeman*, 504 US 191 (1992) because the state's interest in preventing voter intimidation and election fraud was "enhanced by the need to prevent last minute misinformation to which there is no time to respond"); see also *Buckley v American Constitutional Law Foundation, Inc.*, 525 US 182, 198–99 (1999) (agreeing with the 10th Circuit's concern that requiring paid initiative circulators to wear name badges operates when reaction to the message is most intense, emotional, and unreasoned, exposes them to unpleasantness, and diminishes their willingness to circulate possibly unpopular positions). Information on the ballot, though generally made public before the voting, is probably read by voters (if at all) at the last minute with no response time. Cf. Magleby, 66 U Colo L Rev at 38 (cited in note 115) (reporting that most voters face "informational vacuum" on noncontroversial ballot measures and that "most voters make snap judgments on the measure in the voting place"); but cf. Jane S. Schacter, *The Pursuit of "Popular Intent": Interpretive Dilemmas in Direct Democracy*, 105 Yale L J 107, 117–24, 130–44 (1995) (describing studies showing that mass media reporting and political advertising were the most important influences on voters' understanding of initiatives on ballot, in contrast to the materials courts relied on to interpret voters' intent in enacting those initiatives, including statutory language and official ballot material).

[132] See note 130 supra.

[133] See, e.g., why a leading scholar on government speech approves of the Court's rejection in *Wickard v Filburn*, 317 US 111, 117–18 (1942), of an effort to invalidate wheat

can draw such a line is reflected in lower court rulings, for example, distinguishing providing information on ballot issues from engaging in advocacy, or in the distinctions between government officials speaking for themselves or speaking for the whole government,[134] or in the possible constitutional significance of whether the government is speaking on "controversial" or noncontroversial areas.[135]

The larger point here is that once one gets past the pejorative language of this particular term-limits provision, resolving how, on representative democracy grounds, one should think of a ballot label designed to focus attention on term limits and itself enacted by popular initiative is a difficult one—whether one reasons from basic structural principles of representative government, from the Elections Clause, or from the First Amendment's commitment to the protection of expressive activities.

So if a structural approach was likely to yield a holding not that different in scope from the approach taken either by the Court or by Rehnquist, why does the form of reasoning matter? First, it matters because the core of the argument here is deeply structural, and to treat the issue as if it turned on the particularities of the Elections Clause, and of whether the ballot-labeling law can be shoehorned into the word "Manner," is to miss the point of repre-

---

production quotas because the referendum that adopted the quota was the subject of an assertedly inaccurate and misleading speech by the Secretary of Agriculture. "Drawing the line in terms of what is 'good' or 'bad' executive advocacy; of what distorts judgment and what is public leadership; and of government versus private speech by a public official is so difficult that it is preferable to rely upon the pluralistic character of the system of freedom of expression." Yudof, *When Government Speaks* at 292 (cited in note 6). Yudof argues that if the secretary's speech was inaccurate, those opposed should engage in more, or counterspeech, and, more generally, that the problems of government speech should be redressed by legislatures and not courts. A number of scholars have sought to develop a more affirmative framework for defining the work of the government in light of the First Amendment, which in turn may provide a basis for developing more complete understandings of government-funded private speech and of the many forms of more direct "government" speech. See, e.g., Sunstein, *Democracy and the Problem of Free Speech* 81–92 (cited in note 108) (arguing for active government intervention in, e.g., media regulation in order to foster a more deliberative democracy); Fiss, *The Irony of Free Speech* at 44 (cited in note 47) (arguing for active government subsidy for unorthodox ideas); Greene, 53 Vand L Rev (cited in note 6) (arguing for permissibility of governmental advocacy of concepts of the good in many settings).

[134] See notes 41, 57.

[135] See note 108; Fiss, *The Irony of Free Speech* at 44 (cited in note 47) (suggesting that the least-known unorthodox ideas may have best claim to public funding).

sentative democracy.[136] Basic principles bear repeating. The Court has not been loath to do so in the area of federalism, and with respect to contested versions of those first principles. The Court should be no more loath (and possibly more willing) to do so where the basic significance of elections in a democracy is at stake.[137]

Second, it matters as a matter of intellectual clarity. As I hope to have shown above, both the majority and the Rehnquist opinions are driven more by assumptions about elections than by more generalized assumptions about government speech, or individual rights to be free from adverse labeling. Rehnquist's assumptions about the injury caused by pejorative government speech are centrally defined and limited by the electoral ballot context.

Third, it matters because an approach grounded in the constitutional commitment to representative democracy would engage our Court in a transnational discourse with other constitutional courts around the world that, with respect to some matters, is finding much basic agreement on foundational principles. It is not the case that we "happen" to have an Elections Clause, or a First Amendment, that just "happens" to yield results similar in principle to those reached by constitutional courts operating in other representative democracies, sometimes interpreting specific language but oftentimes not. Recognizing the deep structural source of the decision in *Gralike*—the constitutional commitment to representative democracy—would place our Court's decision in the same conversational domain as the robustly developing comparative constitutional discourse among the great constitutional courts of the world, positioning the United States better to influence and be influenced in the future by the reasoned decisions of other representative democracies.[138]

---

[136] Justice Stevens's argument about the meaning of the term "Manner" is ultimately unpersuasive. See 121 S Ct at 1038, quoted in text at note 10 supra. The term "manner" is sufficiently open-ended to embrace almost any form of regulation of the ballot. The term alone does not distinguish the common requirement to list party affiliations on the ballot from the novel requirement to list candidates' positions on particular issues.

[137] For a foundational work on the importance of elections and opposition ("public contestation"), see Robert Dahl, *Polyarchy, Participation and Opposition* (Yale, 1971).

[138] For further discussion of comparative constitutional understandings, see Vicki C. Jackson, *Narratives of Federalism: Of Continuities and Comparative Constitutional Experience*, 51 Duke L J 223 (2001).

GEORGE RUTHERGLEN

INTERNATIONAL SHOE AND THE
LEGACY OF LEGAL REALISM

The modern law of personal jurisdiction owes its existence, and most of its structure and detail, to Chief Justice Stone's magisterial opinion in *International Shoe v Washington*.[1] It does not, however, owe its legal rules to this opinion, because Chief Justice Stone set out systematically to discredit most of the rules that had previously restricted the exercise of personal jurisdiction. In this effort, he succeeded beyond his wildest dreams—or, perhaps more accurately, his worst nightmares. The law of personal jurisdiction, and of such related fields as venue and choice of law, has been swept clear of nearly all rules, at least those that can be applied in a more or less determinate fashion, yielding all-or-nothing results. Rules in this sense have been in a steady retreat since the decision in *International Shoe*, and not just with respect to the constitutional issues addressed in that case. State statutes on the exercise of personal jurisdiction have generally been interpreted to reach to the constitutional limits, or at least to approach them. Venue rules often are so generous in identifying a proper forum that they provide only a preliminary to the case-by-case application of transfer statutes and the judge-made doctrine of forum non conveniens.

George Rutherglen is O. M. Vicars Professor of Law and Earle K. Shawe Professor of Employment Law, University of Virginia.

AUTHOR'S NOTE: I would like to thank Curtis Bradley, Barry Cushman, Earl Dudley, Jack Goldsmith, Daryl Levinson, Graham Lilly, Liz Magill, Caleb Nelson, Chris Sanchirico, Bob Scott, Paul Stephan, Larry Walker, Ted White, Ann Woolhandler, and my colleagues who attended a workshop on this article. I am also grateful to the editors of the *Supreme Court Review* for their suggestions and to Amy Voorhees for her work as a research assistant.

[1] 326 US 310 (1945).

And choice of law, at least at the constitutional level and in states that have abandoned the first Restatement of Conflict of Laws, has abandoned all but the most lenient restrictions on a state's ability to choose its own law to govern a case.

Not all of these developments followed *International Shoe*. Some preceded it, such as the decisions on conflict of laws. But none are so well known or so clearly changed our understanding of the limits on state power over civil litigation. Before *International Shoe*, the law of personal jurisdiction was governed by the venerable decision in *Pennoyer v Neff*,[2] which established as constitutional doctrine the theory of territorial sovereignty articulated by Justice Story in his treatise on the *Conflict of Laws*.[3] The decision takes as its premise the principle "that every State possesses exclusive jurisdiction and sovereignty over persons and property within its territory."[4] Accordingly, the location of the defendant or the defendant's property within the forum state at the time of service of process became crucial to the exercise of personal jurisdiction. This principle was subject to several exceptions, whose scope and importance increased over the decades of the late nineteenth and early twentieth centuries. Yet these exceptions remain confined within the strict territorial theory of *Pennoyer v Neff*, until *International Shoe* replaced this network of detailed exceptions with a single overriding principle: that a state court can exercise personal jurisdiction over a defendant if he has "certain minimum contacts with it such that the maintenance of the suit does not offend 'traditional notions of fair play and substantial justice.' "[5] This principle eventually displaced the entire conceptual structure of the strict territorial theory, and with it, most of the legal rules derived from that theory.

Some may deplore these consequences of *International Shoe*, while others may applaud them. Few deny that they have occurred. The only dispute, as a descriptive matter, is over how many remnants are left of the old formal territorial theory, such as the rule that service on an individual inside the forum state is always suffi-

---

[2] 95 US 714 (1877).

[3] See id at 722 (citing Joseph Story, *Commentaries on the Conflict of Laws* (Little, Brown, 2d ed 1841)).

[4] *Pennoyer*, 95 US at 722.

[5] 326 US at 316.

cient to confer personal jurisdiction.[6] These exceptions stand like isolated ruins, revealing how completely the old rules have been devastated and how little reconstruction has occurred. This consequence should come as no surprise. The opinion in *International Shoe* is one of the enduring monuments of Legal Realism and this is, we are told, "a negative philosophy fit to do negative work."[7] Only the Uniform Commercial Code has a comparable pedigree as a product of Legal Realism and a comparable influence on existing law. Its provisions in Article 2 are derived directly from the realist teachings of Karl Llewellyn and these, too, have had a destructive influence on legal rules, but not nearly so apparent and so complete as *International Shoe.*

What is surprising is that both of these contributions of Legal Realism have been attributed to the constructive rather than the skeptical branch of this movement in legal thought. The constructive phase of Legal Realism inclined toward empirical studies of law and reformist projects, like the Uniform Commercial Code, designed to bring the "law on the books" into closer harmony with the "law in action."[8] In its skeptical aspects, Legal Realism has been identified as the predecessor of Critical Legal Studies: as a thoroughgoing conceptual critique of the foundations of all legal rules.[9] Yet it is difficult, in all the controversy that Legal Realism generated when it came on the scene, to find a more effective and more thorough job of "trashing" legal rules than has been accomplished by *International Shoe.* What's more, this triumph of deconstruction was initiated by a pillar of the establishment, Harlan Fiske Stone, a former dean of the Columbia University School of Law, former Attorney General, Justice, and then Chief Justice of the Supreme Court. Moreover, the scholars who recognized the critical implications of the opinion, to be sure some decades later,

---

[6] *Burnham v Superior Court,* 495 US 604 (1990).

[7] Ronald Dworkin, *Dissent on Douglas,* New York Review of Books at 6 (Feb 19, 1981).

[8] The realists' agenda for empirical studies quickly split off from their agenda for reform and never fulfilled their ambitious goals for an empirical form of legal science. See Henry Schlegel, *American Legal Realism and Empirical Social Science* 8–11 (North Carolina, 1995). Perhaps for this reason, another great reformist project, the Federal Rules of Civil Procedure, has never been regarded as a product of Legal Realism. The principal drafter of the rules, Charles H. Clark, was a realist, but his work on the rules began just as his empirical studies of procedure abruptly left off. Id at 113–14.

[9] Morton J. Horwitz, *The Transformation of American Law 1870–1960: The Crisis of Legal Orthodoxy* 208–10, 269–71 (Oxford, 1992).

were hardly precursors of CLS: Philip Kurland and Geoffrey Hazard, both at the University of Chicago Law School at the time of publication of their articles,[10] and Arthur T. von Mehren and Donald T. Trautman, both of the Harvard Law School.[11] None of these authors sought to deconstruct the law of personal jurisdiction. On the contrary, they sought to build a general theory on the foundations of *International Shoe*. But what they built was not a theory of rules. At most, it was a call for particularized rules to be developed either through legislation[12] or through case law.[13] Neither of these developments has come to fruition.

This article offers one reason why not: Legal Realism made the criticism of legal rules far easier than the task of formulating and defending them, resulting in a systematic bias of modern jurisdictional analysis toward open-ended standards applied on the facts of each case. This conceptual bias has then been exploited by in-state interest groups—not the least of which has been the plaintiff's bar—to expand the reach of state long-arm statutes so that virtually no restraints remain on the exercise of personal jurisdiction. Experience has now shown the need for some such restraints, and although the nature of these restraints remains a matter of dispute, the form that they take should not be slanted against legal rules. The roots of this bias lie in the realist origins of *International Shoe*.

I. REALIST ORIGINS

In the intellectual world from which *International Shoe* emerged, personal jurisdiction was not an issue that fell plainly within the boundaries of civil procedure, which was a narrower subject than we now understand it to be. Civil procedure gave far more prominence to pleading, the forms of action, and the separation of law and equity than is done today, leaving personal jurisdic-

---

[10] Philip B. Kurland, *The Supreme Court, the Due Process Clause and the In Personam Jurisdiction of State Courts: From Pennoyer to Denckla: A Review*, 25 U Chi L Rev 569 (1958); Geoffrey C. Hazard, Jr., *A General Theory of State-Court Jurisdiction*, 1965 Supreme Court Review 241.

[11] Arthur T. von Mehren and Donald T. Trautman, *Jurisdiction to Adjudicate: A Suggested Analysis*, 79 Harv L Rev 1121 (1966).

[12] Hazard, 1965 Supreme Court Review at 283 (cited in note 10).

[13] Von Mehren and Trautman, 79 Harv L Rev at 1175–76 (cited in note 11).

tion as an optional subject, covered in some casebooks[14] and not others.[15] A revealing, if atypical, compromise between these two approaches is found in a casebook published three years after *International Shoe*, which confined the treatment of the case to a single short note on service of process on corporations, concluding with this disclaimer: "These matters are left for development in such courses as Business Associations, Constitutional Law, and Conflicts of Laws."[16] As this example illustrates, the treatment of personal jurisdiction could be assimilated to the issue of service of process, which more closely resembled the narrow and technical issues common to courses in civil procedure.

The tendency to leave *International Shoe* for more specialized treatment survived the introduction of the modern civil procedure casebook with the publication of the first edition of Field and Kaplan in 1953.[17] That pathbreaking casebook placed the decision in a section on "Jurisdiction over Corporations,"[18] an aspect of the case that continues to be emphasized to this day.[19] And indeed, the opinion itself invited this treatment, since the only two secondary sources that it cited were concerned specifically with this issue.[20] This issue, however, touched a nerve in the field of conflict of laws, where the intellectual roots of the decision are most clearly apparent.

Fictions of corporate consent and presence came under attack early in the twentieth century in choice-of-law theory. Criticism of these fictions was so widespread that it was accepted even by

---

[14] Roswell Magill and James H. Chadbourn, *Cases on Civil Procedure* 599–678 (Foundation, 3d ed 1939); Austin Wakeman Scott and Sidney Post Simpson, *Cases and Other Materials on Judicial Remedies: From the Forms of Action and the Classical Equity Practice to the Federal Rules of Civil Procedure* 519–50 (Harvard Law School, 1938).

[15] James P. McBaine, *Introduction to Civil Procedure: Common Law Actions and Pleading* (West, 1950); Paul R. Hays, *Cases and Materials on Civil Procedure* (Foundation, 1947).

[16] Thomas E. Atkinson and James H. Chadbourn, *Cases and Other Materials on Civil Procedure* 168 (Foundation, 1948).

[17] Richard H. Field and Benjamin Kaplan, *Materials for a Basic Course on Civil Procedure* (Foundation, 1953). The "temporary edition" of this casebook was published in 1952. Id at viii.

[18] Id at 795–817.

[19] E.g., Stephen C. Yeazell, *Civil Procedure* 104 (Aspen, 5th ed 2000).

[20] Gerard Carl Henderson, *The Position of Foreign Corporations in American Constitutional Law: A Contribution to the History and Theory of Juristic Persons in Anglo-American Law* 94–95 (Harvard, 1918); Note, *What Constitutes Doing Business by a Foreign Corporation for Purposes of Jurisdiction*, 29 Colum L Rev 187 (1929).

the First Restatement in its analysis of personal jurisdiction over corporations.[21] Consent under the First Restatement had to be "a real consent, not a fictitious one."[22] And instead of relying upon the fiction of corporate presence, the First Restatement relied upon incorporation in the forum state or "doing business" in the forum state as the crucial determinant of jurisdiction.[23] In the latter circumstance, jurisdiction was limited to claims arising out of the corporation's business inside the state. These positions, not surprisingly, were entirely in accord with those expressed by the reporter of the First Restatement, Joseph Beale, who published his *Treatise on the Conflict of Laws*[24] a year after the First Restatement appeared. In this comprehensive three-volume treatise, he took pains to reject the fiction of presumed consent: "It is surely unfortunate to deal with a question of jurisdiction on the basis of a fiction."[25] The concept of "doing business within the state" was his substitute for this fiction, as well as for the fiction of corporate presence.[26]

Despite such cautious disclaimers, Beale's work in the First Restatement and his treatise became a favorite target of the Legal Realists and, in particular, of Walter Wheeler Cook, who devoted an entire book, *The Logical and Legal Bases of the Conflict of Laws*, to the criticism of what he called "current dogma in the Conflict of Laws." The tone of Cook's critique is best captured by his tongue-in-cheek apology for not offering affirmative proposals, quoting an author who said that "often in our carefully cultivated garden of thought some rank weed grows with such vigor as to stunt the growth of the neighboring useful vegetables."[27] The "useful vegetables" presumably include the doctrine of personal jurisdiction that we have today. Yet for all his invective, Cook

---

[21] Restatement of the Law of Conflict of Laws §§ 87–93, 167 (1934).

[22] Id § 90, Comment a. Consent could be "by acts as well as words," id, and also encompassed appointment of an agent for service of process. Id § 91, Comment a.

[23] Id §§ 87, 89, 92–93. Jurisdiction could also be asserted over a corporation, to the same extent as over a natural person, if the corporation entered a general appearance in a case or filed a claim as a plaintiff. Id §§ 82, 83, 88.

[24] Joseph H. Beale, *A Treatise on the Conflict of Laws* 382–90 (Baker, Voorhis, 1935).

[25] Id at 388.

[26] Id at 388–89.

[27] Walter Wheeler Cook, *The Logical and Legal Bases of the Conflict of Laws* ix (Harvard, 1942) (quoting Gilbert Lewis).

barely touches on Beale's treatment of personal jurisdiction over corporations, commenting only on Beale's insistence that a corporation, like an individual, must have a domicile in the state of its incorporation.[28] Given Beale's own admonitions against the fictions of corporate consent and presence, there was little on these narrower issues for him to criticize.

Instead, Cook left this task to Felix Cohen, whose article "Transcendental Nonsense and the Functional Approach"[29] was cited in the course of Cook's discussion of corporate domicile.[30] Beale did not come in for specific criticism, or even citation, by Cohen, but it is plain enough that he fell under the general indictment of "classical jurists" whose age had passed. As Cohen said, "The 'Restatement of Law' of the American Law Institute is the last long-drawn-out gasp of a dying tradition."[31] In a passing comment, Cohen also indicated that he found the concept of "doing business" fully as objectionable as the concept of corporate presence. Discussing an opinion by Justice Brandeis that equated corporate presence with "doing business," he conceded that "it would be captious to criticize courts for delivering their opinions in the language of transcendental nonsense."[32] It was precisely such criticism that Chief Justice Stone embraced in *International Shoe*, or at least sought to escape in fashioning his own standards for the exercise of personal jurisdiction over corporations.

Stone did so by scrupulously avoiding any use of "doing business" in his opinion. This omission is all the more striking because the phrase appeared in both parties' briefs and in the opinions of the lower courts.[33] Stone substituted instead the standard of "minimum contacts" for which the opinion in *International Shoe* is known. In an elliptical reference to the concept of "doing business" he said, "The test is not merely, as has sometimes been suggested, whether the activity, which the corporation has seen fit to

---

[28] Id at 207–08. For a similarly muted criticism of the sections on jurisdiction, despite overall hostility to the Restatement as a whole, see Ernest G. Lorenzen and Raymond J. Heilman, *The Restatement of the Conflict of Laws*, 83 U Pa L Rev 555, 566–68 (1935).

[29] 35 Colum L Rev 809, 809–12 (1935).

[30] Cook at 209 n 30 (cited in note 27).

[31] Id at 833.

[32] Id at 812.

[33] See 326 US at 312, 314; Brief of the Appellant at 14–20; Brief of the Appellee at 32–41.

procure through its agents in another state, is a little more or a little less."[34] The suggestions disavowed in this sentence were contained in two decisions of the Supreme Court, cited at the end of the quoted sentence, which relied on the concept of "doing business" to determine the existence of jurisdiction over corporations.[35] This was the same as the approach taken in the First Restatement, which devoted a separate section to defining the concept of "doing business."[36] The examples of what does, and what does not, constitute "doing business" that followed this section cannot be reconciled with the result in *International Shoe*. For instance, the First Restatement excluded from the definition of "doing business" activities such as manufacturing automobiles in one state and supplying them to an independent franchise in the forum state, and more surprisingly, entering into (but not performing) a construction contract in the forum state.[37]

Stone himself was hardly a dogmatic Legal Realist, let alone an adherent of the provocative arguments of realists like Cook and Cohen. He is better characterized as a legal progressive from an earlier generation.[38] By the same token, however, Stone was no friend of the First Restatement and its formal territorial approach to choice of law and personal jurisdiction. In two famous opinions concerned with constitutional limitations on state choice of law, he rejected the entire approach represented by Beale and the First Restatement.[39] This should have led the parties in *International Shoe* to search for other sources of support for their views, but the lawyers for International Shoe unwisely cited Beale's treatise in support of their arguments that jurisdiction was lacking.[40] Stone

---

[34] Id at 319.

[35] *St. Louis S.W. Ry. v Alexander*, 227 US 218, 228 (1913) (finding personal jurisdiction based on "transaction of business"); *International Harvester v Kentucky*, 234 US 576, 587 (1914) (finding personal jurisdiction based on "doing business" that was "something more than mere solicitation"). The argument in the briefs in *International Shoe* closely followed these precedents. See note 32.

[36] Restatement of the Conflict of Laws § 167; see also id § 92 (applying this concept to corporations).

[37] Id § 167, Illustrations 3, 4, 5.

[38] Horwitz, *The Transformation of American Law* at 182 (cited in note 9).

[39] *Alaska Packers Ass'n v Industrial Accident Comm'n*, 294 US 532 (1935); *Pacific Employers Ins. Co. v Industrial Accident Comm'n*, 306 US 493 (1939). For this assessment of these decisions, see Brainerd Currie, *The Constitution and the Choice of Law: Governmental Interests and the Judicial Function*, in his *Selected Essays on the Conflict of Laws* 201–14 (Duke, 1963).

[40] Brief of Appellants at 18–19, 26.

conspicuously failed to cite it himself in his opinion, apparently not wanting to dignify the authority that he rejected.

Of course, Stone did not cite any Legal Realists in his opinion either. Yet he was certainly aware of Cook's writings on the conflict of laws and he shared with Cook close associations with Columbia Law School. Indeed, while he was dean at Columbia, Stone had arranged for Cook's appointment to the faculty in 1919, and then somewhat to his chagrin, undertook to mediate the conflicts that Cook instigated, along with the other Legal Realists on the faculty, over issues of appointments and curriculum.[41] Stone went so far, in a letter of recommendation written after his deanship, to commend Cook as "almost, if not quite a genius," although one who "threw away the golden opportunity" presented by his appointment at Columbia.[42] Both aspects of this observation are confirmed by Stone's decision, as dean, to make Cook the highest paid law professor in America.[43] He was, to all appearances, a faculty member whose brilliance justified the dean in defending him and whose personality made it necessary. Cook began his work on conflicts of laws just after he and Stone both left Columbia: Cook to become a faculty member at Yale and Stone to enter private practice briefly before becoming Attorney General.[44]

Stone remained in regular correspondence with Cook during his tenure on the Supreme Court, until Cook's death in 1943, two years before the decision in *International Shoe*. In a eulogy to his former colleague, Stone singled out for particular praise Cook's contributions to the conflict of laws. Stone found these "so fundamental that they form the basis for the cleavage between what might be called two schools of thought in conflicts, one of which follows the late Professor Beale; the other Professor Cook."[45] Only a few months earlier, Cook had sent Stone a copy of his recently

---

[41] Alpheus Mason, *Harlan Fiske Stone: Pillar of the Law* 128–30 (Viking, 1956). The disputes were tied up with Stone's own disagreement with the president of Columbia, Nicholas Murray Butler. Id at 131–35; Schlegel, *American Legal Realism* at 15–16 (cited in note 8).

[42] Id at 129–30, quoting a letter to Charles P. Howland (Dec 9, 1927).

[43] John A. Garraty and Mark C. Carnes, eds, *American National Biography* 389 (Oxford, 1999).

[44] Cook at x (cited in note 27). Cook started writing his articles on conflicts of laws in 1923. Id.

[45] Papers of Harlan Fiske Stone, Library of Congress, Box 10, General Correspondence, Folder on Cook, Walter Wheeler 1928–43.

published book, *The Logical and Legal Bases of the Conflict of Laws*, and Stone had responded, "I have already dipped into it and found much in it which will be profitable to me in the solution of conflict of laws cases."[46] Two months later, he again thanked Cook for his book and added, "You have made a real contribution in leading us away, more than I would have supposed possible, from the artificial sort of reasoning which seems to have enveloped the conflict of laws."[47] These exchanges were entirely typical of their correspondence, concerned as much with decisions of the Supreme Court as with academic developments.[48] And in one case, early in Stone's career on the Court, he explicitly asked Cook for advice about how it should be decided. The case, *Second Russian Insurance Co. v Miller*,[49] concerned the effect of Russian law on a German corporation doing business in the United States and resulted in an opinion by Stone, for a unanimous Court. Cook's response to Stone's letter came too late to affect the decision, but it is consistent with the approach taken in Stone's opinion, refusing to give extraterritorial effect to Russian law.[50] Be that as it may, this exchange of letters reveals the deference that Stone was willing to give to Cook's views.

Like Cook, Cohen also had ties to Columbia, although these all developed after Stone's tenure as dean. Cohen received a fellowship to study at the Columbia Law School while he finished his doctoral dissertation in philosophy at Harvard and then went on to attend law school there, graduating in 1931.[51] Cohen's "Transcendental Nonsense" was published in the *Columbia Law Review*, where he had also served as a student editor. Stone naturally preserved his own ties to Columbia after his deanship, selecting his

---

[46] Id letter from Stone to Cook, March 16, 1943.

[47] Id letter from Stone to Cook, June 28, 1943.

[48] E.g., id letter from Stone to Cook, Feb 2, 1933 (on *Bradford v Elec. Light Co. v Clapper*, 286 US 145 (1932)); letter from Stone to Cook, March 16, 1934 (on *Yarborough v Yarborough*, 290 US 202 (1933)).

[49] 268 US 552 (1925).

[50] Papers of Harlan Fiske Stone, Letter from Stone to Cook, May 27, 1925; letter from Cook to Stone, June 1, 1925 (cited in note 45). The decision in *Second Russian Insurance* was handed down also on June 1.

[51] John A. Garraty, ed, *Dictionary of American Biography* 119 (Charles Scribner's Sons, Supp V 1977).

law clerks from among students recommended by his successor as dean and another member of the faculty.[52] He also served as a trustee of the law review, and in the nature of the process of selecting law clerks, generally chose editors-in-chief of the law review as his clerks, some of whom undoubtedly knew of Cohen or his article.[53] The article itself was widely cited in the law review literature and even created something of a controversy, eliciting criticism that Cohen himself felt bound to reply to personally.[54] It is also apparent that either Stone, or his law clerks, kept up with pieces in the *Columbia Law Review*, since the only law review literature cited in the opinion in *International Shoe* (but not in the briefs) is a student note from that journal.[55]

None of this evidence establishes that Stone actually referred to the work of Cook and Cohen in preparing his opinion in *International Shoe*. In fact, the file in Stone's papers on *International Shoe* shows only an exchange with Justice Black on the use of the phrase "traditional notions of fair play and substantial justice," which was subsequently made famous by the opinion. In his concurring opinion, Black criticized the use of this phrase as an indefensible return to "natural justice" as a restriction on state power under the Due Process Clause, part of his campaign to purge any vestige of natural law from interpretation of the Constitution.[56] In response, Stone altered the original draft of his opinion by explicitly attributing the phrase to the opinion in *Milliken v Meyer*,[57] decided only five years earlier, and to the views of Justice Holmes.[58] Justice

---

[52] Mason, *Harlan Fiske Stone* at 646 (cited in note 41).

[53] For instance, Herbert Wechsler, who was a contemporary of Cohen's at Columbia, and Harold Levanthal, the editor-in-chief of the Columbia Law Review when *Transcendental Nonsense* was published.

[54] For a discussion of the controversy, neglect, and subsequent revival of the article, see Jeremy Waldron, *"Transcendental Nonsense" and System in the Law*, 100 Colum L Rev 16, 17–18 n 13 (2000). For the central role of this article in defining Legal Realism, see Laura Kalman, *Legal Realism at Yale 1927–1960* 3–5 (North Carolina, 1986).

[55] Note, 29 Colum L Rev at 187–95 (cited in note 20).

[56] 326 US at 323–25 (opinion of Black, J); see Dennis J. Hutchinson, *Decisionmaking in the Supreme Court, 1948–1958*, 68 Georgetown L J 1, 48 (1979).

[57] 311 US 457, 463 (1940).

[58] "See Holmes, J." was added in the final version of the opinion to the citation of *McDonald v Mabee*, 243 US 90 (1917). Papers of Harlan Fiske Stone, Box 72, 1945 Term, *International Shoe Co. v State of Washington*, No. 107, Memorandum for the Court by Chief Justice Stone, Nov 27, 1945 (cited in note 45); Draft opinion of Nov 24, 1945, p. 5. Stone also deleted a "compare" citation to *Pennoyer v Neff*, 95 US 714 (1877). Id.

Black responded, in turn, by adding a few sentences to his opinion seeking to distinguish these sources of authority.[59]

Stone's reluctance to retreat from "traditional notions of fair play and substantial justice" has proved to be prophetic. Just as much as "minimum contacts," it is the phrase for which his opinion is best known. It also reveals his sympathy with the Legal Realists and with their critique of the formal territorial theories of Beale and the First Restatement. It was, however, a selective sympathy, one that only heightens the uncertainty created by his opinion, which is in many ways a synthesis, preserving the results in as many earlier cases as possible.[60] Yet it is at the same time a deconstruction, rejecting the formal territorial theory that was invoked in many of the prior decisions themselves. Both of these tasks could simultaneously be conducted only at a very high level of abstraction, which explains the tendency of the opinion to reply upon phrases like "traditional notions of fair play and substantial justice." Only language that is this open-ended could allow realist criticism to be disguised as a magisterial summary of existing law. Nevertheless in writing an opinion that tried to satisfy everyone, Stone offered guidance to no one.[61] The reception and consequences of *International Shoe* bear this out.

II. THE RECEPTION OF INTERNATIONAL SHOE

The immediate reaction to *International Shoe* was surprisingly subdued. It was regarded, as noted earlier, as a case concerned almost exclusively with the exercise of personal jurisdiction

---

[59] Papers of Harlan Fiske Stone, Box 72, 1945 Term, *International Shoe Co. v State of Washington*, No. 107, Memorandum of Justice Black to the Members of the Conference, Nov 28, 1945 (cited in note 45); *International Shoe*, 326 US at 324 (opinion of Black, J).

[60] Even *Pennoyer v Neff*, 95 US 714 (1877), is distinguished, with the bland statement that there is no jurisdiction over a defendant "with which the state has no contacts, ties, or relations." 326 US at 319. This statement is followed by a "cf." citation to *Pennoyer* and to case holding that a corporation was not doing business in the forum state, despite advertising and solicitation there. *Minnesota Commercial Men's Ass'n v Benn*, 261 US 140 (1923). Neither case, of course, fits the description of one in which the defendant had "no contacts, ties, or relations" with the forum state.

[61] Nor did he not succeed in satisfying Justice Black, who filed a separate opinion making public his objections to the standard of "traditional notions of fair play and substantial justice" and expressing his willingness to dismiss the appeal as insubstantial. 326 US at 322–26. See note 56. In a deconstructive vein himself, Justice Black offered no alternative justification for this conclusion.

over corporations. Casebooks and treatises on conflicts of laws discussed the case under this heading,[62] as did the law review literature.[63] In only a few of these sources, and mainly in the writings of Herbert Goodrich, then a judge on the Third Circuit, were the general implications of the case first discerned.[64] Perhaps Goodrich was especially attuned to the way in which *International Shoe* undermined the First Restatement because he was an advisor and co-reporter (on one chapter) along with Beale. His premonitions were soon vindicated by the younger generation of scholars who wrote the articles that made the case the foundation for the modern law of personal jurisdiction.

These authors—Kurland, Hazard, and von Mehren and Trautman—correctly saw that *International Shoe* called for the replacement of the old formal territorial theory of jurisdiction, although they did not themselves offer much in the way of a replacement. The most promising alternatives were offered by von Mehren and Trautman, who drew the distinction between general and specific jurisdiction: between cases in which the defendant's contacts with the forum are so substantial that they support jurisdiction over any claim against the defendant, whether or not it arose in the forum, and cases in which the defendant's contacts permit jurisdiction only over claims related to those contacts themselves. In this latter category, they also distinguished between cases in which an out-of-state defendant initiated interstate activity resulting in contacts in the forum and cases in which an in-state plaintiff did so; only interstate activity initiated by the defendant was sufficient for jurisdiction.[65] These authors also argued for the development of still

---

[62] Fowler V. Harper, Charles W. Taintor II, Charles Wendell Carnahan, and Ralph S. Brown, Jr., *Conflict of Laws: Cases and Materials* 687–718 (Bobbs-Merrill, 1950); Elliott E. Cheatham, Herbert F. Goodrich, Erwin N. Griswold, and Willis L. M. Reese, *Cases and Materials on Conflict of Laws* 118–32 (Foundation, 3d ed 1951); Herbert F. Goodrich, *Handbook of the Conflict of Laws* 215–16 (West, 3d ed 1949). The last two sources strike a slightly adventurous note by assimilating minimum contacts of corporations to acts of an individual inside the state sufficient for jurisdiction.

[63] E.g., J. P. McBaine, *Jurisdiction Over Foreign Corporations: Actions Arising Out of Acts Done Within the Forum*, 34 Cal L Rev 331, 340–43 (1946); Note, *The Growth of the International Shoe Doctrine*, 16 U Chi L Rev 523 (1949); Comment, *Foreign Corporations—State Boundaries for National Business*, 59 Yale L J 737 (1950).

[64] Herbert F. Goodrich, *Yielding Place to New: Rest versus Motion in the Conflict of Laws*, 50 Colum L Rev 881, 886–89 (1950). See note 62.

[65] Von Mehren and Trautman, 79 Harv L Rev at 1136–63, 1168 (cited in note 11). The comparative perspective was more fully developed in their casebook. Arthur Taylor von

more concrete rules of personal jurisdiction, relying in part on a comparative analysis of rules from other legal systems.[66] Yet almost two decades later, von Mehren could not go any further than offering five broadly framed factors for determining personal jurisdiction,[67] and more recently, he has recognized the continued uneasiness evoked by the realist revolution in American choice of law, with its parochial refusal to consider the approaches of other legal systems.[68]

As the influence of *International Shoe* has grown, eventually to embrace all assertions of personal jurisdiction, interpretation of the decision has become at once more abstract and more doctrinaire. Two divergent strands in the opinion, in particular, have come to dominate academic analysis of its consequences. The first is the invocation of "traditional notions of fair play and substantial justice" as the test for jurisdiction under the Due Process Clause. Those who emphasize this strand in the opinion usually criticize any decision that invokes territorial reasons as a ground for denying jurisdiction. The major targets for such criticism are *Hanson v Denckla*[69] and *World-Wide Volkswagen v Woodson*,[70] both decisions denying personal jurisdiction because the defendant had not "purposefully avail[ed] itself of the privilege of conducting activities within the forum State, thus invoking the benefits and protections of its laws."[71] In both of these cases, as von Mehren and Trautman had foreseen, it was the plaintiff (or someone other than the defendant) who initiated the interstate activity that created contacts with the forum state. Critics of these decisions argue, instead, that any examination of the defendant's contacts with the forum state must be subordinated to an overall inquiry into the fairness of continu-

---

Mehren and Donald Theodore Trautman, *The Law of Multistate Problems* 587–747 (Little, Brown, 1965).

[66] Id at 1175–76.

[67] Arthur Taylor von Mehren, *Adjudicatory Jurisdiction: General Theories Compared and Evaluated*, 63 BU L Rev 279, 311–13 (1983).

[68] Arthur Taylor von Mehren, *American Conflicts Law at the Dawn of the 21st Century*, 37 Williamette L Rev 133 (2001).

[69] 357 US 235 (1958).

[70] 444 US 286 (1980).

[71] *Hanson*, 357 US at 253; *World-Wide Volkswagen*, 444 US at 297. For these critics, it only added insult to injury to find *International Shoe* cited to support the quoted phrase.

ing the litigation there.[72] This approach, similar to the doctrine of forum non conveniens in the law of venue, abandons any pretense of devising concrete rules of personal jurisdiction. It substitutes instead a case-by-case examination of fairness, achieving a degree of uniformity in decisions only by imposing a heavy burden on the defendant to demonstrate the unfairness of proceeding in the forum chosen by the plaintiff.[73]

The Supreme Court has come closest to adopting this approach in *Asahi Metal Industry Co. v Superior Court*,[74] but paradoxically only because the Justices could not agree on the extent of the defendant's contacts with the forum state. In opinions that otherwise did not command a majority, eight Justices reached agreement only on the issue of unfairness, holding that a Japanese corporation could not be required to defend an indemnity claim brought by a Taiwanese corporation in a California court.[75] Ironically for the fairness approach, this decision did not expand jurisdiction but contracted it, leading one advocate of the fairness approach to condemn the Court's narrow view of convenience in litigation.[76] This criticism, although understandable, has a self-defeating quality to it. Having invited a "chancellor's foot" analysis in terms of overall fairness, advocates of such an approach can hardly complain that chancellor's shoe is too small.

The second strand of interpretation, unlike the first, takes the standard of "minimum contacts" at face value, emphasizing territorial limitations on state power. This approach relies precisely on those cases that the fairness approach finds most problematic. Thus, it emphasizes the passages in *Hanson v Denckla* and *World-*

---

[72] E.g., Russell J. Weintraub, *Due Process Limitations on the Personal Jurisdiction of State Courts: Time for Change*, 63 Or L Rev 485, 522–27 (1984); Martin H. Redish, *Due Process, Federalism, and Personal Jurisdiction: A Theoretical Evaluation*, 1981 Nw U L Rev 1112, 1137–42; Hazard, *Interstate Venue*, 74 Nw U L Rev 711 (1979); Albert Ehrenzweig, *The Transient Rule of Personal Jurisdiction*, 65 Yale L J 289, 311–13 (1956). While acknowledging the force of both strands of interpretation, von Mehren seems to be partial to this one. Von Mehren, 63 BU L Rev at 337–40 (cited in note 67).

[73] Weintraub, 63 Or L Rev at 523 (cited in note 72); Redish, 1981 Nw U L Rev at 1138 (cited in note 72).

[74] 480 US 102 (1987).

[75] Id at 116.

[76] Russell J. Weintraub, *Asahi Sends Personal Jurisdiction Down the Tubes*, 23 Tex Intl L J 55 (1988).

Wide Volkswagen that appeal to the territorial allocation of power among the states. The restrictions on personal jurisdiction, the Court said, "are more than a guarantee of immunity from inconvenient or distant litigation. They are a consequence of territorial limitations on the power of the respective States."[77] This approach, however, has trouble explaining how these territorial limitations are connected to the Due Process Clause, which the Court invokes to restrain state power. Unlike the fairness approach, which is closely connected to the right to be heard in litigation, the territorial approach has no obvious basis in constitutional requirements for adequate procedures. This dilemma has proved to be so severe that it led Justice White to take inconsistent positions on behalf of the Court, both asserting and denying that there is a relationship between the individual rights protected by the Due Process Clause and the principles of interstate federalism that allocate power among the states.[78]

Whether or not this dilemma can be avoided by looking to other parts of the Constitution, such as the Full Faith and Credit Clause, it leaves advocates of the territorial approach with a still further question: What precisely constitutes a "contact" with the forum state? This term, which invokes the metaphor of "touching," does not constitute an obvious improvement over the fiction of corporate presence.[79] The usual solution to this problem ties the relevant contacts to the nature of the plaintiff's claim on the merits. But this solution just displaces the problem of determining appropriate contacts to the issue of choice of law. Plaintiffs often seek a particular forum in order to obtain the benefit of that forum's law, a tendency that is especially strong in tort cases that arise overseas.[80]

---

[77] *Hanson*, 357 US at 251. For a similar passage in *World-Wide Volkswagen*, see 444 US at 293.

[78] *World-Wide Volkswagen*, 444 US at 293 ("The sovereignty of each State, in turn, implied a limitation on the sovereignty of all of its sister States—a limitation express or implicit in both the original scheme of the Constitution and the Fourteenth Amendment."); *Insurance Corp. of Ireland, Ltd. v Compagnie des Bauxites de Guinee*, 456 US 694, 702 (1982) ("The personal jurisdiction requirement recognizes and protects an individual liberty interest. It represents a restriction on judicial power not as a matter of sovereignty, but as a matter of individual liberty."). A footnote following the latter quotation seeks to reconcile it with the former. Id n 10.

[79] Lea Brilmayer, *How Contacts Count: Due Process Limitations on State Court Jurisdiction*, 1980 Supreme Court Review 77; Allan R. Stein, *Styles of Argument and Interstate Federalism in the Law of Personal Jurisdiction*, 65 Tex L Rev 689, 733–65 (1987).

[80] E.g., *Piper Aircraft v Reyno*, 454 US 235 (1981); see Peter Hay, *The Interrelation of Jurisdiction and Choice-of-Law in United States Conflicts Law*, 28 Intl & Comp L Q 161 (1979);

The power of the forum state to apply its own law, however, depends upon defendant's contacts, as well as the plaintiff's contacts and other aspects of the case, with the forum state.[81] This renewed appeal to contacts is all the more problematic because the standards for choice of law are, if anything, even more indeterminate than the standards for personal jurisdiction. Invoking choice of law to resolve questions of personal jurisdiction amounts to jumping from the frying pan into the fire.

Nevertheless, the territorial approach to interpreting *International Shoe*, like the fairness approach, does have something to be said for it. The decision rejected the formal territorial theory of jurisdiction found in the First Restatement. Where the fairness interpretation emphasizes the rejection of a territorial theory—one based on presence inside the forum state—the territorial approach emphasizes the rejection of a formal theory—one based on more or less definite rules. *International Shoe* rejected both features of the First Restatement, and so any interpretation that rejects one of them can claim some support from the decision.

The Restatement (Second) of Conflict of Laws took this eclectic approach one step further. In an obvious compromise, the Second Restatement accepted the grounds of jurisdiction already recognized in the First Restatement and added "relationships to the state which make the exercise of judicial jurisdiction reasonable" as a further ground of jurisdiction.[82] This compromise, like the opinion in *International Shoe* itself, preserved most of the decisions under the formal territorial theory, but added the flexibility of an open-ended standard of reasonableness. As a descriptive matter, it might have accurately reflected the role of minimum contacts in adding to the jurisdiction of state courts. Yet even this minimal descriptive role became outmoded when *Shaffer v Heitner*[83] made "traditional notions of fair play and substantial justice" a test that "can be as readily offended by the perpetuation of ancient forms that are not longer justified as by the adoption of new procedures that are inconsistent with the basic values of our constitutional her-

---

Earl Maltz, *Visions of Fairness—the Relationship Between Jurisdiction and Choice-of-Law*, 30 Ariz L Rev 751 (1988).

[81] E.g., *Phillips Petroleum Co. v Shutts*, 472 US 797, 821–22 (1985).

[82] Restatement (Second) of the Conflict of Laws § 27(k) (1970).

[83] 433 US 186, 207 (1977).

itage."[84] Old rules, it seems, can be just as inconsistent with tradition as new ones. As a conceptual matter, however, the Second Restatement failed to resolve any of the inconsistencies between the old theory and the new.

In this respect, as in choice of law generally, the Second Restatement sought to submerge disagreement in an overall balancing test that embraced all the factors that might conceivably bear on the choice of one state over another, either as the forum for litigating a case or as the source of the law to be applied.[85] Disagreement over this entire range of issues was fueled by the same realist arguments that animated the attack on the formal territorial theory of jurisdiction. Indeed, all of the attacks on Beale and the First Restatement were inseparable parts of the same intellectual movement, resulting in surprisingly similar results both in choice of law and in personal jurisdiction. The power of state courts, and the states themselves, over these issues was increased, with a corresponding erosion in the constitutional restrictions on state power. The standards used to resolve these issues became increasingly abstract and increasingly depended on all the facts of each case. And any consensus over what to put in place of the old strict territorial theory entirely disappeared, or more precisely, never materialized.[86] All the theorists could agree on was what they rejected.

If these intellectual developments are clear enough, so is the mechanism by which they influenced the law. In the aftermath of *International Shoe*, several states enacted "long-arm statutes" that took advantage of the expanded jurisdiction recently made available to their courts. Illinois was the first to enact a comprehensive statute expanding personal jurisdiction over all defendants, both corporate and individual, and other states rapidly followed suit.[87] Most of these statutes have sought to extend personal jurisdiction to the constitutional limits or, at least, close to them. This result is usually achieved by judicial interpretation, but the long-arm stat-

---

[84] Id at 212.

[85] Restatement (Second) of the Conflict of Laws § 6 (1970).

[86] For a candid, if deliberately overstated, description, see Perry Dane, *Conflict of Laws*, in Dennis Patterson, ed, *A Companion to Philosophy of Law and Legal Theory* (Blackwell, 1996) ("choice of law has sometimes resembled the law's psychiatric ward").

[87] David P. Currie, *The Growth of the Long Arm: Eight Years of Extended Jurisdiction in Illinois*, 1963 U Ill L F 533, 537.

utes in a number of states, following the example of Rhode Island, explicitly provide that they reach to the constitutional limits.[88]

The explanation for these developments also is apparent: long-arm statutes work to the benefit of in-state plaintiffs at the expense of out-of-state defendants. A state legislature systematically, if not exclusively, favors the interests of resident individuals and firms. On most issues, out-of-state litigants have nowhere near the same influence over its deliberations as in-state interests. And, of course, in-state attorneys benefit from litigation inside the state, regardless of which party they represent. What can be said of state legislatures is likely also to apply to state courts. If a long-arm statute does not already explicitly reach to the constitutional limits, a state court is likely to interpret it to do so in light of the legislature's purpose of expanding jurisdiction. It is especially likely to do so if the case is brought by an in-state plaintiff, who would otherwise be forced to litigate in a distant forum against an out-of-state defendant. Nor are these difficulties reduced if the plaintiff chooses to sue in federal court, whose rules generally follow the standards for personal jurisdiction of the state in which it sits, or failing that, applies even broader standards of jurisdiction that depend upon the defendant's contacts with the entire United States.[89]

The same dynamics in the legislative and judicial process also explain the continued erosion of venue rules as a limitation on the plaintiff's choice of forum. Many venue statutes provide that the plaintiff's residence is a permissible venue and others list a multiplicity of factors, any one of which the plaintiff can invoke to find a permissible venue.[90] The general federal venue statute is representative of the decline of venue as a significant restriction upon the plaintiff's choice of forum, allowing venue in any district "in which a substantial part of the events or omissions giving rise to the claim occurred," and for a corporate defendant, in any district "in which it is subject to personal jurisdiction at the time the action is commenced."[91] And even these provisions do not exhaust the range of

---

[88] See Anthony L. Ryan, *Principles of Forum Selection*, 103 W Va L Rev 167, 172 (2000); Jack H. Friedenthal, Mary Kay Kane, and Arthur R. Miller, *Civil Procedure* 141–44 (West, 3d ed 1999).

[89] FRCP 4(k).

[90] Friedenthal, Kane, and Miller, *Civil Procedure* at 80 (cited in note 88).

[91] 28 USC § 1391(a)–(c) (1994).

permissible venues, either in the general venue statute or in a multitude of special venue statutes. As a consequence, venue now has become, like personal jurisdiction, less a matter of rules than of case-by-case determinations made on motions to transfer or to dismiss for forum non conveniens.[92] These latter devices, moreover, are used preferentially against out-of-state plaintiffs, precisely the parties with the least influence on the state legislative and judicial process.[93]

The Legal Realists, for all their realism about the effects of legal rules, seem to have been surprisingly naive about the interest groups that would have the greatest influence on state legislatures and courts. Or, perhaps they were resigned to it. In that other great achievement of Legal Realism, the Uniform Commercial Code, the drafters were acutely aware of the compromises that they had to make in order to get their proposals enacted. As Grant Gilmore, the principal draftsman of Article 9, has candidly acknowledged, Karl Llewellyn got his way with Article 2 only because the New York banks got their way with Article 9, and with most of the rest of the UCC.[94] In exchange, Llewellyn embedded the standard of "commercial reasonableness" deeply throughout Article 2.[95]

The standard of "commercial reasonableness" in the UCC bears a surprising resemblance to the standard of "traditional notions of fair play and substantial justice" in *International Shoe*. Both are framed in the most abstract terms; both make a reference to existing practices, either in commerce or in litigation; and both have failed to fulfill their promise of generating more concrete legal rules. Although the dynamics of legislative enactment of the UCC and of long-arm statutes are different, the underlying appeal of abstract standards of reasonableness is the same. As Bob Scott has pointed out, the abstract standards in Article 2 command wide-

---

[92] 28 USC § 1404(a) (1994). See, e.g., *Piper Aircraft Co. v Reyno*, 454 US 235 (1981).

[93] See id at 252.

[94] Grant Gilmore, *The Good Faith Purchase Idea and the Uniform Commercial Code: Confessions of a Repentant Draftsman*, 15 Ga L Rev 605, 625–28 (1981). Another chapter in this story appears in Grant Gilmore and Charles L. Black, Jr., *The Law of Admiralty* 114–20 (Foundation, 2d ed 1975).

[95] Robert E. Scott, *The Uniformity Norm in Commercial Law: A Comparative Analysis of Common Law and Code Methodologies*, in Jody Kraus and Steven D. Walt, eds, *Jurisprudential Foundations of Corporate and Commercial Law* 149, 166, and 185 n 65 (Cambridge, 2000).

spread agreement among the academics who draft and revise the UCC, but they do not generate criticism from particular interest groups that would be harmed by more specific rules and that have, in any event, obtained the rules they need elsewhere in the code.[96] Long-arm statutes also satisfy both the academics and in-state interest groups, but by the more radical step of dispensing with rules in their entirety. All of this has been more easily accomplished because it has been done under the imprimatur of the Supreme Court in *International Shoe*.

III. THE FUTURE OF PERSONAL JURISDICTION

Legal Realism has been rightly criticized for its "rule skepticism," in the sense of a denial of the existence of legal rules. Such criticism can easily be extended to the conceptual skepticism of Cohen's arguments in "Transcendental Nonsense."[97] If concepts such as "corporate presence" and "doing business" can be attacked as metaphors, so can the terms, such as "minimum contacts," in which general legal standards are framed. Taken to its logical conclusion, no law would be left standing. Yet even without going so far, Legal Realism has engendered "rule skepticism" in a more prosaic sense, evident in the field of personal jurisdiction. It slanted the development of the law against legal rules that can be applied in a more or less determinate fashion.

Having absorbed the lessons of Legal Realism, it is now time to recognize their limitations, as the growing uneasiness over *International Shoe* reveals. This opinion was a fine first step in the reexamination of jurisdictional theories, but it was never intended to be the last step. What it provided as a constitutional ceiling on state power now has become the floor as well, determining how that power is actually exercised.[98] The standard of "traditional notions of fair play and substantial justice" makes far more sense as

---

[96] Id at 170–74.

[97] H. L. A. Hart, *The Concept of Law* 136–41 (Oxford, 2d ed 1994); Waldron, 100 Colum L Rev 16 (cited in note 54).

[98] Stephen B. Burbank, *Jurisdiction to Adjudicate: End of the Century or Beginning of the Millennium*, 7 Tulane J Intl & Comp L 111, 113–14 (1999); Kevin M. Clermont, *Jurisdictional Salvation and the Hague Treaty*, 85 Cornell L Rev 89, 107–08 (1999). For a general sense of the unease surrounding the status quo, see Symposium, *Fifty Years of International Shoe: The Past and Future of Personal Jurisdiction*, 28 UC Davis L Rev 513 (1995).

a second-order principle, governing the formulation of more concrete rules, than it does as a first-order rule of decision itself. In the
latter form, it imposes all of the costs of case-by-case adjudication
without conferring any benefits in the form of predictable outcomes. The "rule skepticism" of Legal Realism has caused these
defects to be ignored, in the apparent hope of having judges strike
exactly the right balance of fairness between plaintiffs and defendants in every case.

Three ways out of the current impasse are possible. First, we
can return to a regime of rules that, at least in some respects, re-
sembles the First Restatement. Second, we can go in the opposite
direction and extend *International Shoe* to abandon all restrictions
on the plaintiff's choice of forum. Or third, we can seek to devise
a system of rules intermediate in generality between the First Restatement and *International Shoe*. It is this last alternative that has
been explored most thoroughly by scholars of conflicts of laws,
drawing on two complementary sources that have not, so far, informed the law of personal jurisdiction: an analysis of the reciproc-
ity between sovereigns in restraining the exercise of jurisdiction
by their courts and a comparative analysis of the standards for exercising jurisdiction in different legal systems. There is no guarantee that this alternative will work out, but if it proves to be feasible,
it will only be because it leaves the legacy of Legal Realism behind.

The first of these alternatives, a return to rules like those of the
First Restatement, has been foreclosed by both legal and nonlegal
developments. The criticism of the Legal Realists and conflicts
scholars who followed in their wake has thoroughly discredited the
First Restatement. As Brainerd Currie observed, "Walter Wheeler
Cook discredited the vested-rights theory as thoroughly as the in-
tellect of one man can ever discredit the intellectual product of
another."[99] In choice of law, the First Restatement has only slightly
more authority than *Lochner v New York* in constitutional law. To
the extent that judges, lawyers, and academics rely upon it, they
try not to admit that they have done so. The negative arguments
of Legal Realism, skeptical though they were, were most effective
against the narrow, and seemingly arbitrary, concepts that underlie
the First Restatement. Thus, as noted earlier, the concept of "do-

---

[99] Brainerd Currie, *On the Displacement of the Law of the Forum*, in *Selected Essays* at 6
(cited in note 39).

ing business" under the First Restatement allowed personal jurisdiction over corporations based on performance of contracts in the forum state, but not based on formation of contracts. The rationale for this distinction no doubt had its roots deep in the old limits on state power to regulate foreign corporations engaged in interstate commerce. States could, on the one hand, exclude foreign corporations from engaging in purely intrastate business, but they could not prevent them from engaging in interstate commerce within the forum state. Doing business within the forum state sufficient for personal jurisdiction fell between these extremes.[100]

The doctrinal pedigree of such narrow concepts was impeccable, but they were outmoded almost as soon as the First Restatement was formulated. The increase in the volume and variety of interstate commerce had, even before *International Shoe*, led to decisions extending jurisdiction based on fictitious consent, by individuals as well as corporations.[101] And after *International Shoe*, the Supreme Court has repeatedly noted these developments and the resulting increase in interstate litigation and an attendant decrease in the cost of travel and communication necessary to defend against it.[102] All of these observations are still more forceful today, as more commerce is done internationally and by electronic means such as the Internet. The artificial concepts of the First Restatement, shaped for a world that was even then past or passing, would not fit the patterns to come in commerce and litigation. Nor would they fit the expanded power of government to regulate such activities, both at the national level and at the state level. The New Deal accomplished this expansion by freeing government regulation at both levels from constitutional restrictions,[103] a legal development evident in *International Shoe* itself, in its holding that Washington could impose an unemployment tax based on the activities of corporate salesmen inside the state. Going back on these changes in the economy and in the legal system would require an upheaval

---

[100] See, e.g., *International Harvester v Kentucky*, 234 US 579, 588 (1914).

[101] E.g., *Hess v Pawloski*, 274 US 352, 357 (1927).

[102] *McGee v International Life Ins. Co.*, 355 US 220, 222–23 (1957); *Hanson v Denckla*, 357 US 235, 250–51 (1958); *World-Wide Volkswagen Corp. v Woodson*, 444 US 286, 292–93 (1980).

[103] Stephen Gardbaum, *New Deal Constitutionalism and the Unshackling of the States*, 64 U Chi L Rev 483, 485–91 (1997).

fully as profound and sweeping—and far more improbable—than the New Deal.

The second alternative to *International Shoe* would be to abandon all restraints on personal jurisdiction. This was Justice Black's position expressed in his separate opinion criticizing the majority's reliance upon "traditional notions of fair play and substantial justice." This position has the virtue of simplicity, at least at the level of constitutional law. It eliminates the need for an extended inquiry on the facts of each case into the defendant's contacts with the forum. It does not accomplish much, however, if it just displaces this inquiry to a nonconstitutional level of analysis, as in the doctrine of forum non conveniens. The latter doctrine preserves, and in some respects limits, the amount of judicial discretion in determining the proper forum. But conversely, if the doctrine of forum non conveniens were also abolished, hardly any restraints would remain on the plaintiff's choice of forum.

Achieving doctrinal simplification by these means would come at too great a price. In fact, it would repeat the mistake that plagued the reception of *International Shoe* in state long-arm statutes: It would neglect the inherent political advantage of in-state plaintiffs, and particularly in-state lawyers, in expanding jurisdiction at the expense of out-of-state defendants. Even the doctrine of forum non conveniens, although it requires a case-by-case analysis of the fairness of conducting litigation in the forum, seldom is invoked to deprive an in-state plaintiff of the forum where she has chosen to litigate.[104] Strategic manipulation by plaintiffs and their attorneys in choosing the forum for litigation cannot just be neglected. It has to be restrained by some means, and as the experience with state long-arm statutes reveals, it is not likely to be addressed at the state level. The need for federal law is apparent, and in default of action by Congress, rules developed under the Due Process Clause are the only likely means of restraint.

The third alternative raises the question of precisely what those rules should be. If a return to the First Restatement is impossible and if some rules still are necessary, then the crucial question is the shape that those rules should take. The most promising candidates are rules of intermediate generality: not as rigid as those of

---

[104] Margaret Stewart, *Forum Non Conveniens: A Doctrine in Search of a Role*, 74 Cal L Rev 1259, 1321 (1986).

the First Restatement and not as open-ended as the abstract standards of *International Shoe*. Such rules, moreover, would correspond to the widespread sense that the decisions applying the test of minimum contacts are all broadly consistent with another. If so, it should be possible to state more specifically the form that such consistency takes. Few authors have tried to do so. This effort, it should be emphasized, would be entirely consistent with the structure and ambitions of *International Shoe* itself. As the scholars who first recognized the significance of the decision observed, it promised to foster the development of other, more concrete rules of decision. Recent developments, both theoretical and practical, provide reason to believe that such rules might still be formulated.

In the scholarship on choice of law, a turn toward game theory has suggested that solutions can be found to the competition between states and nations to apply their own law to a controversy. This question, of course, is closely related to the question of personal jurisdiction, since a court is more likely to apply its own law than the law of any competing sovereign. Choice of forum often determines choice of law. Instead of insisting upon a competition that no state can consistently win, and in which all may lose, presumptive rules can be devised to allocate cases in a way that fosters interjurisdictional cooperation.[105] Just to take one example that has given rise to recurrent problems, a personal injury plaintiff who sues the manufacturer of a defective product (and has a completely adequate remedy against this defendant) often asserts claims against manufacturers of components, distributors, or retailers from outside the forum state, or if the plaintiff does not sue them, the manufacturer of the product does.[106] A solution to this recurrent problem, whether to deny jurisdiction as the American decisions indicate or to assert jurisdiction as the European decisions allow,[107] should be devised by a rule, not by a redetermination of minimum contacts, fairness, and convenience in each case.

---

[105] Lea Brilmayer, *Conflict of Laws: Foundations and Future Directions* 155–75 (Little, Brown, 1991); Larry Kramer, *Rethinking Choice of Law*, 90 Colum L Rev 277, 319–44 (1990).

[106] These are the facts, respectively, of *Asahi Metal Industry Co. v Superior Court*, 480 US 102, 114 (1987), and *World-Wide Volkswagen Corp. v Woodson*, 444 US 286, 299 (1980).

[107] Clermont, 85 Cornell L Rev at 96 (cited in note 98); Linda J. Silberman and Andreas F. Lowenfeld, *A Different Challenge for the ALI: Herein of Foreign Country Judgments, an International Treaty, and an American Statute*, 75 Ind L J 635, 640–41 (2000).

The need for a cooperative approach to personal jurisdiction has become all the more pressing because of the expansion of international commerce and litigation. Just as these developments at the national level justified the abandonment of the First Restatement, at the international level they justify a reexamination of the need for concrete rules that foster international cooperation. Choosing between national legal systems creates greater risks of forum shopping purely for favorable law or to impose costs upon the defendant than choosing among American states with relatively homogeneous laws and legal cultures. As an English judge has said, "As a moth is drawn to the light, so is a litigant drawn to the United States. If he can only get his case into their courts, he stands to win a fortune."[108]

The immediate prospects for achieving international agreement upon multilateral treaties are not great, as evidenced by the disputes surrounding the proposed Hague Convention on Jurisdiction and Foreign Judgments in Civil and Commercial Matters.[109] This proposed convention is modeled on the Brussels Convention on Jurisdiction and the Enforcement of Judgments in Civil and Commercial Matters,[110] which applies among members of the European Union. In its current draft, the proposed convention identifies three separate categories of cases: those in which jurisdiction is permitted and the resulting judgment is entitled to recognition in all signatory states; those in which jurisdiction is prohibited and the resulting judgment is void in all signatory states; and a middle category of cases in which jurisdiction is permitted but recognition of the resulting judgment is not required outside the forum state.[111] In the first category are familiar forms of jurisdiction, as in tort cases, in the country where a tort or injury occurs, or in contract cases, where goods or services are provided or supplied.[112] It is the

---

[108] Denning, J, Master of the Rolls, in *Smith, Kline and French Laboratories Ltd v Bloch*, 1980 S No 6514 (CA May 13, 1982).

[109] Hague Conference on Private International Law, Preliminary Draft Convention on Jurisdiction and Foreign Judgments in Civil and Commercial Matters (Oct 30, 1999).

[110] Sept 27, 1968, 1990 O J (C 189) 2 (consolidated). The convention applies to the twelve states that were members of the European Community (now the European Union) before January 1, 1995.

[111] Silberman and Lowenfeld, 75 Ind L J at 638–41 (cited in note 107).

[112] Preliminary Draft, arts 6, 10 (cited in note 109).

second and third categories that have given rise to most of the disputes over drafting and agreement to the convention.

These disputes have embraced a variety of issues, some of them curiously reminiscent of the conceptual scheme rejected in *International Shoe*. Thus, "doing business" as a basis for general jurisdiction on claims unrelated to the defendant's activities in the forum state has been relegated to the second, prohibited category;[113] and "tag jurisdiction" for human rights claims under international law has been placed in the third, optional category. Some of these disputes might be attributed to the European preference for rules of personal jurisdiction and choice of law, although in the particular disputes just mentioned, the United States seems to have taken the side favored by the concepts of the First Restatement. Even if disputes such as these have forestalled agreement for the moment, it does not follow that attempts at international coordination by this means, or by others, should be given up. These efforts would inevitably require a departure from *International Shoe*, which has not been imitated in other countries. European nations, in particular, have been unsympathetic to abstract standards for personal jurisdiction (and for choice of law as well), although the concrete rules that they have adopted have not always narrowed the jurisdiction of their courts.[114]

The compromises inherent in achieving greater international uniformity would also facilitate the acceptance of those inherent in devising concrete legal rules. If they were accepted and proved to be workable in international cases, they would provide a comparative model for interstate cases as well. All such rules must necessarily be too broad in some cases and too narrow in others. Unlike an abstract standard of justice, they do not hold out the promise of exact application in every case, only to cause disappointment when they are actually applied. A look at foreign sources might remind us of the wisdom of the observation of Justice Holmes, speaking of a specific legal rule, "If it is right as to the run of cases a possible exception here and there would not make the law bad."[115]

---

[113] Clermont, 85 Cornell L Rev at 111–14 (cited in note 98); Burbank, 7 Tulane J Intl L at 116–19 (cited in note 98).

[114] Clermont, 85 Cornell L Rev at 91–95 (cited in note 98).

[115] *Louisville Gas and Elec. Co. v Coleman*, 277 US 32, 41–42 (1928) (Holmes, J, dissenting).

IV. Conclusion

The opinion in *International Shoe* deserves praise in sweeping away the formal territorial theory of the First Restatement. As a first step in devising new standards for personal jurisdiction, it is one of the great achievements of Legal Realism. As a last step, or so I have argued, it has been a great disappointment. The force of the realist critique of the rules of the First Restatement has blinded us to the desirability of rules in general, leaving the analysis of personal jurisdiction at a sterile level of abstraction. Rules precisely tailored to solve all the problems of personal litigation may be impossible to formulate. But even if it is too much to hope that law in this field can be reduced to rules, it is too little to expect that it must remain subject only to the most abstract standards. Over fifty years after *International Shoe*, it is time to move beyond "traditional notions of fair play and substantial justice" and to articulate more concrete legal rules for personal jurisdiction. Even if these rules prove not to be wholly satisfactory—and what legal rules are?—it is time to discard the skepticism that the Legal Realists cast upon this enterprise.

WILLIAM M. WIECEK

THE LEGAL FOUNDATIONS OF DOMESTIC ANTICOMMUNISM: THE BACKGROUND OF DENNIS v UNITED STATES

Treatments of *Dennis v United States* (1951)[1] and other Cold War decisions by the U.S. Supreme Court of the 1950–56 era[2] generally do not explore the background of anticommunism[3] in depth. In part this is because legal historians of an earlier day, as near-contemporaries, could assume that their readers knew that politico-cultural background, having themselves lived through it. But since

William M. Wiecek is Congdon Professor of Public Law in the College of Law and Professor of History in the Maxwell School, Syracuse University.

AUTHOR'S NOTE: I thank William C. Banks and Karen Bruner for valuable critiques and suggestions. This article is a fragmentary out-take from a work in progress on the history of the U.S. Supreme Court from 1941 to 1953 that I am preparing for the Holmes Devise History of the Supreme Court of the United States.

[1] 341 US 494 (1951).

[2] Marc Rohr provides a useful review and critique of these cases in *Communists and the First Amendment: The Shaping of Freedom of Advocacy in the Cold War Era*, 28 San Diego L Rev 1 (1991).

[3] In this article, I avoid the term "McCarthyism" as irrelevant and misleading, though at the cost of using the more cumbersome phrase "domestic anticommunism." Joe McCarthy came on the scene after the anticommunist apparatus was in place and had done most of its work. He opportunistically surfed its wave, but he was not the wave itself. To label the phenomenon after him is to suggest that had he not existed, the second Red Scare might not have occurred. That is false. McCarthy was its most spectacular manifestation, but he was not necessary to it, nor was he responsible for most of the issues discussed in this chapter. Stanley I. Kutler once noted that if we must name the era after some individual, we should call it McCarranism, while Ellen Schrecker has suggested Hooverism. These would be only a slight improvement, but they do suggest the irrelevance of McCarthy to the subject of this article.

the collapse of the Soviet Union, anticommunism must be approached as a historical artifact.

Accounts of the Cold War cases that slight their background anticommunism ignore the social and political matrix from which legal decisions and doctrine emerge. Michael Klarman has recently demonstrated how important it is to contextualize major cases or lines of decisions,[4] and we would do well to apply his example to Cold War First Amendment cases. Law emerges from a matrix that blends ideology, social structures, economic relationships, and policy responses to problems both foreign and domestic. It cannot sensibly be understood abstracted from that social and ideological environment, existing as it were in a state of conceptual autarky.

With that in mind, it would be useful to recount the development and impulse of anticommunism from its nineteenth-century origins to its legal culmination around 1950. Only in that way can we fully understand and explain the U.S. Supreme Court's reaction to the perceived menace of Communism, and the consequences of that response for our constitutional order.

When we look at the Court's Cold War decisions of 1950–56 in situ, as it were, they appear anomalous, seen against the broad sweep of the First Amendment's development in the twentieth century. From 1919 (*Schenck v United States*) to 1927 (*Fiske v Kansas*) or 1931 (*Stromberg v California*),[5] the First Amendment languished in a mean estate, from a libertarian perspective, enervated by the bad-tendency interpretation. The amendment began its speech-protective career in the decade of the Hughes Court, partially stalled out during World War II due to the abnormal strains of wartime, momentarily resumed its libertarian trajectory in 1945–46, and then plunged toward pre-1930 levels in *American Communications Association v Douds*[6] and *Dennis* in 1950–51. It began to recover from its swoon in 1957[7] and resumed its ascent

---

[4] Michael J. Klarman, *The Plessy Era*, 1998 Supreme Court Review 1; Klarman, *Race and the Court in the Progressive Era*, 51 Vand L Rev 881, 886–917 (1998).

[5] *Schenck v United States*, 249 US 47 (1919); *Fiske v Kansas*, 274 US 380 (1927); *Stromberg v California*, 283 US 359 (1931).

[6] 339 US 382 (1950).

[7] *Yates v United States*, 354 US 298 (1957); *Scales v United States*, 367 US 203 (1961); *Noto v United States*, 367 US 290 (1961). On these cases, see Arthur J. Sabin, *In Calmer Times: The Supreme Court and Red Monday* (1999).

(with some backing-and-filling in 1957–59) toward the pinnacle of near-absolute freedom for political speech in *Brandenburg v Ohio*.[8]

In the 1927–47 period, and then again a decade later, the Court's speech decisions consistently expanded freedom to communicate and correlatively restricted governments' power to suppress that communication. The 1950–56 decisions interrupted that trend. In those years, the Court regressed to the spirit of the 1919–27 era, where First Amendment thinking was confined again in the straitjacket of bad-tendency interpretations of clear and present danger.

Most explanations for this Cold War period of declension note the socially conservative outlook of a majority of the Vinson Court Justices. They were inclined to support governmental power and were ideologically predisposed to judicial restraint in cases implicating national security. But such assumptions, though valid in a general way, are circular and beg the question. The real issue challenging us is: Why did the Court as a collective decision-making body reverse the momentum of the previous two decades?

The answer, which is the thesis of this article, is that the Court imposed on Communists a special and diminished status under the Constitution. Confined in this status, Communists' liberties were constricted as compared with those of other Americans. Congress enjoyed greater power to suppress their freedoms. Justice Goldberg noted retrospectively in 1963 that "the Communist Party is not an ordinary or legitimate political party, as known in this country, and . . . because of its particular nature, membership therein is itself a permissible subject of regulation and legislative scrutiny."[9] Earlier, the second Justice Harlan asserted that the power of the federal government to investigate subversive activities "rests on the right of self-preservation, 'the ultimate value of any society,' [quoting *Dennis*]. Justification for its exercise in turn rests on the long and widely accepted view that the tenets of the Communist Party include the ultimate overthrow of the Government of the United States by force and violence. . . ."[10]

---

[8] 395 US 444 (1969). Conventional liberal accounts of this development include Paul L. Murphy, *The Constitution in Crisis Times, 1918–1969* (1972), and William F. Swindler, *Court and Constitution in the Twentieth Century: The New Legality, 1932–1968* 157–211 (1970).

[9] *Gibson v Florida Legislative Investigation Committee*, 372 US 539, 547 (1963).

[10] *Barenblatt v United States*, 360 US 109, 128 (1959).

An insight drawn from the nearly contemporary legal history of another society illuminates the process whereby judges come to accept the idea that members of a population can have diminished status within a liberal legal system. Richard Weisberg's compelling study of the Vichy regime's enforcement of the religious laws of 1940 (*Le Statut*[11] *des Juifs*) describes the process that sent some 75,000 French Jews, nearly all of them citizens, to the death camps in the east.[12] The French Holocaust was peculiarly legalistic. Liberal Catholic lawyers read their fundamental laws dating back to the Revolution through a Catholic hermeneutic that made Jews into something less than full citizens. Jews did not "have French soil in their sandals," in a phrase of the time. Vichy lawyers thus read Jews out of the French constitution: they were not really French. Thus excluded, French Jews could not appeal to the foundational principles of *liberté* and *égalité* available to authentic citizens. They stood outside the constitution and could not claim its protections.

This reading of the fundamental law was accompanied by a strict, positivist reading of statutes like the religious laws, which prohibited lawyers and judges from injecting their own moral principles into their interpretation or enforcement. The result was what Weisberg calls "a flexible statecraft that masks persecution under the felt needs of the political moment." Something disturbingly similar occurred a decade later in America.

The question for us then becomes: What accounts for the Court's willingness to accord a special status to Communists? The answer is found in the dominant outlook and anxieties of contemporary anticommunism. This outlook produced an image of Communists that depicted them as unscrupulous traitors controlled by Moscow, committed to subverting American freedom. Because Communists posed a fearsome threat to liberties enshrined in the Constitution, it seemed reasonable to restrict those very liberties when claimed by Communists, so that the Constitution would not be employed to destroy itself.[13]

---

[11] *Statut* may be read, significantly, as meaning both "statute" and "status," though in this context the former is the proper reading.

[12] Richard Weisberg, *Vichy Law and the Holocaust in France* 386–429, quotation at 424–25 (1996).

[13] Carl A. Auerbach, *The Communist Control Act of 1954: A Proposed Legal-Political Theory of Free Speech*, 23 U Chi L Rev 173 (1956); Robert H. Bork, *Neutral Principles and Some First Amendment Problems*, 47 Ind L J 1, 29–35 (1971).

This image of Communists was an artifact of the preceding eighty years of anticommunism. To understand the image and its force, we must therefore understand anticommunism and the course of its development. The Justices of the Supreme Court were not exempt from the fears and beliefs of other Americans. If anything, they were more forward than others in cultivating those beliefs and enforcing their consequences. It was natural for the Justices to employ the anticommunist image as a kind of general template to make sense of legal issues coming before them in cases implicating the liberties of Communists. Thus, to understand the Cold War cases, we must understand anticommunism, in order to account for its persuasive explanatory force to the Justices of the Supreme Court.

I. The Origins of Anticommunism

Fear of communism predated the appearance of Communism itself in America.[14] The specter that Marx heralded haunted America as well as Europe. Early nineteenth-century fears of Fourierite socialism and what was then called "agrarianism" (land redistribution) evolved after the Civil War into denunciations of "communism," as America's middle classes gave voice to their anxieties about the social turmoil that accompanied labor organizing.[15] As Chief Justice Oliver Wendell Holmes of the Massachusetts Supreme Judicial Court noted in his influential 1897 address, "The Path of the Law," "when socialism first began to be talked about, the comfortable classes of the community were a good deal frightened."[16] Indeed they were.

Chief Judge Thomas Durfee of the Rhode Island Supreme

---

[14] In this article, the words "Communist" or "Communism" will be capitalized when they refer to confirmed members of the Communist Party of the United States (CPUSA) or its predecessors, and to the political philosophy or program that that Party promoted, commonly referred to in the period covered by this article as Marxism-Leninism. Lowercase usage denotes programs or persons not so affiliated. In quotations, however, I will preserve whatever the original usage was.

[15] I review these anxieties and their causes at greater length in Wiecek, *The Lost World of Classical Legal Thought: Law and Ideology in America, 1886–1937* at 64–79 (1998), and merely summarize those conclusions here.

[16] Holmes, *The Path of the Law* (1897), reprinted in Sheldon Novick, ed, 3 *The Collected Works of Justice Holmes: Complete Public Writings and Selected Judicial Opinions* . . . . at 398 (1995).

Court announced in 1877 that "the spirit of communism is abroad."[17] The next year a New York financial paper denounced Granger laws and the Democrats' silver program as "merely phases of Communism in America."[18] The economist David Wells detected "organized communism" in proposals for income taxation.[19] Law professor Christopher Tiedeman's 1886 *Treatise on the Limitations of Police Power* alerted lawyers to the fact that "Socialism, Communism, and Anarchism are rampant throughout the world."[20] Judge Rufus Peckham of the New York Court of Appeals denounced rate regulation in 1889 as "communistic in its tendency."[21] In an influential address to the New York State Bar Association in 1893, Justice David Brewer advised his lawyer audience that "the black flag of anarchism [and] the red flag of socialism invit[e] a redistribution of property. . . ."[22] The eminent Wall Street lawyer Joseph Choate, arguing the *Income Tax Cases* in 1894, agreed: the federal income tax was "communistic in its purposes and tendencies . . . defended here upon principles as communistic, socialistic . . . as ever have been addressed to any political assembly in the world."[23] (It is amusing to reflect that the lawyers whose arguments he was condemning as communistic were Richard Olney and James C. Carter, two of the most prominent and conservative Supreme Court practitioners of their day.)

In a chilling preview of the later Red Scares, the normally sensible, level-headed Justice Samuel F. Miller advised an 1888 graduating class at the University of Iowa that European socialists and other varieties of leftists "come here and form clubs and associations; they meet at night and in secluded places; they get together large quantities of deadly weapons; they drill and prepare them-

---

[17] Thomas Durfee, *Oration Delivered at the Dedication of the Providence County Courthouse* at 34 (1879).

[18] Quoted in Joseph Dorfman, *The Economic Mind in American Civilization, 1865–1918* at 48 (1949).

[19] David A. Wells, *The Communism of a Discriminating Income Tax*, 130 North Am Rev 236 (1880).

[20] P vi.

[21] *People v Budd*, 117 NY 1, 68–71 (1889).

[22] David J. Brewer, *The Nation's Safeguard*, 47 Proceedings NY State Bar Assn 38–41 (1893).

[23] Choate's argument is reprinted in Joseph H. Choate, *Arguments and Addresses of Joseph Hodges Choate* 419, 422 (1926).

selves for organized warfare; they stimulate riots and invasions of the public peace; they glory in strikes."[24] He could as easily have been speaking in 1949.

This judicial mentality persisted well into the twentieth century. In 1927, a time of peace, prosperity, and muted social unrest in the United States, the Chief Justice of the United States, William Howard Taft, condemned Professor Felix Frankfurter's involvement in the Sacco-Vanzetti case. "He seems to be closely in touch with every Bolshevistic communist movement in this country," Taft complained to the president of Yale University. The Harvard law teacher utilized "the world wide conspiracy of communism to spread [his radicalism] to many many countries. Our law schools lent themselves to the vicious propaganda," he added to a Boston judge.[25]

What accounts for these seemingly groundless fears, reminiscent of Poland's peculiar postwar phenomenon of anti-Semitism without Jews? Why do anticommunism or its ideological predecessors seem to have been endemic in American society after the Jacksonian era?[26] Since the early nineteenth century, Americans have nurtured a consistent fear that alien ideologies, as well as the foreigners who were thought to be their vectors, were invading the pristine American republic. During periods of heightened social tension, such as in the 1712 New York "Negro Plot," the time of the Alien and Sedition Acts of 1798, the nationwide railroad strikes of 1877, the "Great Upheaval" of 1886, the labor violence of 1893–95, the Great War, and post–World War II America, this latent anxiety became linked to the image of an internal enemy, invariably The Other as defined by racial, ethnic, or religious characteristics, which was allied to hostile alien external forces. The external threat may be a hostile power or an "un-American" belief system: France, Spain, and Catholicism in 1712; the USSR and Communism in 1949. The Red Scares of the twentieth century were as virulent as they were because the alien was both.

---

[24] Miller, *The Conflict in This Country Between Socialism and Organized Society* (1888), reprinted in Charles N. Gregory, *Samuel Freeman Miller* at 168 (1907).

[25] William Howard Taft to James R. Angell, May 1, 1927, reel 291, and Taft to Robert Grant, Nov 4, 1927, reel 296, William Howard Taft Papers, Library of Congress, Manuscripts Division (hereafter "LCMss").

[26] Two valuable comprehensive surveys of antiradicalism are Robert J. Goldstein's *Political Repression in Modern America: From 1870 to the Present* (1978) and Richard M. Fried's *Nightmare in Red: The McCarthy Era in Perspective* (1990).

Modern anticommunism dates from the horrified reactions of America's middle classes to the Paris Commune of 1870–71. The Commune provided them with a lurid image of the sort of society and government that was to be expected when revolutionaries came to power with a collectivist, antireligious program. Perversely blaming the sufferings of Paris on the Communards and not on the Prussian siege, Americans drew their earliest lessons on what communism in action might entail. After that, Americans turned to the bogey of radicalism to account for many of the evils that beset their society. Four years after the great Chicago fire of 1871, Samuel Medill exclaimed in the *Chicago Tribune* that "every lamppost in Chicago will be decorated with a communistic carcass if necessary to prevent wholesale incendiarism."[27]

In the late nineteenth century, class conflict allied with nativism produced the earliest political effects of antiradicalism: the first wave of criminal anarchy statutes enacted in response to the Haymarket Massacre and the Great Upheaval of 1886, followed by a successor wave after the assassination of President William McKinley in 1902. New York's measure was typical: "Criminal anarchy is the doctrine that organized government should be overthrown by force or violence, or by assassination of the executive head or of any of the executive officials of government, or by any unlawful means. The advocacy of such doctrine either by word of mouth or writing is a felony."[28] These criminal anarchy laws originated the core statutory formula, "overthrow of government by force or violence."

But to their repeated dismay, patriots have found that such legislative responses never proved adequate for an effective crusade against the internal menace. Common-law conspiracy prosecutions might occasionally be of some value, as would be prosecutions for riot and affray where there was an outbreak of violence, but more was needed if law was to provide an effective supplement to vigilantism, Pinkertons, and the militia. The post-Haymarket criminal anarchy statutes were of more symbolic than practical value, criminalizing ideas but not jailing that many radicals.[29]

---

[27] Quoted in Goldstein, *Political Repression* at 25 (cited in note 26).

[28] NY Penal Law 1902, § 160, derived from NY Penal Code 1881, § 468-a. On the impact of anarchism generally, see Barbara Tuchman, *The Proud Tower: A Portrait of the World Before the War, 1890–1914* 63–113 (1966).

[29] For one such conviction, see *People v Most*, 171 NY 423, 64 NE 175 (1902).

In 1903, Congress emplaced a federal statute in the anticommunist edifice for the first time. Reacting to the assassination of President William McKinley by an anarchist in 1901, Congress in the Immigration Act of 1903[30] barred anarchists entry into the United States, permitted deportation of those illegally here, and prohibited naturalization of those legally present. The act adapted state statutory definitions of anarchists as "persons who believe in or advocate the overthrow by force or violence of the government of the United States or of all government or of all forms of law, or the assassination of public officials" and as

> a person who disbelieves in, or who is opposed to, all organized government, or who is a member of, or affiliated with, any organization entertaining and teaching such disbelief in, or opposition to, all organized government, or who advocates or teaches the duty, necessity, or propriety of the unlawful assaulting or killing of any officer or officers, either of specific individuals or of officers generally, of the government of the United States or of any other organized government.

The statute thus was both an advocacy and a membership measure, penalizing belief as well as action. It repeated the formula that became ritualistic, "overthrow by force or violence." It was the ancestor of all later federal antisubversive legislation. The Supreme Court readily upheld it in 1904 against a First Amendment challenge.[31] Before World War I, the First Amendment would provide little protection for the liberties of suspect minorities.[32]

The rise of the International Workers of the World (the Wobblies), with their militantly socialist/syndicalist program,[33] alarmed antiradical forces once again. The states responded with a spate of criminal syndicalism statutes, as well as laws prohibiting display of the red flag as a symbol of resistance to government. California's 1919 act, typical of the lot, prohibited "advocating . . . [criminal acts,] sabotage . . . or unlawful acts of force and violence or unlaw-

---

[30] Act of March 3, 1903, ch 1012, §§ 2, 38, 32 Stat 1213.

[31] *Turner v United States*, 194 US 279 (1904).

[32] David M. Rabban, *Free Speech in Its Forgotten Years* (1997); Michael K. Curtis, *Free Speech, the People's Darling Privilege: Struggles for Freedom of Expression in American History* (2000); Curtis, *Teaching Free Speech from an Incomplete Fossil Record*, 34 Akron L Rev 231 (2000).

[33] On whom, see Melvyn Dubofsky, *We Shall Be All: A History of the International Workers of the World* (2d ed 1988).

ful methods of terrorism as a means of accomplishing a change in industrial ownership or control, or effecting any political change."[34] Though aimed at the Wobblies, criminal syndicalism laws were part of a larger open-shop drive by western employers hoping to smash all unionization.[35] Such linkages between antiradicalism on one hand and interest- or ethnic-group agendas on the other were recurrent in all episodes of panicky response to social upheaval. In periods of antiradicalism, labor and reform groups have been targets of patriotic and nativist hostility. Racial, ethnic, or religious hostility also drove anticommunism and its antecedents. After 1948, partisan rivalry joined that list. This enduring characteristic accounts for much of anticommunism's destructive power in the post–World War II period.

II. World War I

American entry into World War I sacralized antiradicalism.[36] President Woodrow Wilson's patriotic rhetoric stimulated anticommunist sentiment. With his blessing, various federal agencies, most notably George Creel's Committee on Public Information, tried to enforce conformity of thought and support for the war.[37] Symptomatic of this were provisions of the Trading with the Enemy Act of 1917[38] that required all foreign-language newspapers to submit English translations of any articles concerning the American or foreign governments or the war to the Post Office for review. But despite the energetic efforts of Postmaster-General Albert S. Burleson and Attorney General Thomas W. Gregory, such federal capabilities for thought control proved to be limited. The only effective weapon in the federal arsenal was control of

---

[34] Cal Stats 1919, quoted in Stephen E. Rohde, *Criminal Syndicalism: The Repression of Radical Political Speech in California*, 3 W Legal Hist 309 (1990).

[35] Etheridge Dowell, *A History of Criminal Syndicalism Legislation in the United States* 143 (1939).

[36] On the place of the war in the development of anticommunism, see Paul Murphy, *World War I and the Origin of Civil Liberties in the United States* (1979); William Preston, *Aliens and Dissenters: Federal Suppression of Radicals, 1903–1933* (1963); Harry N. Scheiber, *The Wilson Administration and Civil Liberties, 1912–1921* (1960); and Robert K. Murray, *Red Scare: A Study in National Hysteria, 1919–1920* (1955).

[37] David M. Kennedy, *Over Here: The First World War and American Society* 45–92 (1980).

[38] Ch 106, 40 Stat 411.

immigration, and the Immigration Act of 1917[39] reenacted the anarchist-exclusion and -deportation provisions of the 1903 act. An ambitious young lawyer-bureaucrat named J. Edgar Hoover in the Justice Department's Alien Enemy Bureau was overwhelmed by the task of vetting the political beliefs of socialists and Wobblies, and the several hundred investigators of the department's Bureau of Investigation could hardly cope with widespread resistance to the war.

To this dilemma, government officials including Hoover found a solution of enduring significance: they turned to private auxiliaries. Government, civic, business, labor, and religious groups leagued themselves in a crusade to stamp out radicalism as they variously defined it. There was no dearth of patriotic organizations: the American Protective League with its quarter-million cryptovigilante members; the American Defense Society; the National Security League, which diverted its interests from military policy to alien control; even the old National Civic Federation, which did something similar. Business groups, notably the National Association of Manufacturers and the Chamber of Commerce at the national level, opportunistically climbed aboard the bandwagon of patriotism, where they joined Samuel Gompers's American Federation of Labor in bashing radical labor groups like the IWW. Seeing their opportunity, all those hoping to shore up the status quo made the most of it, using patriotism as a cover for their differing agendas of control and suppression.

Federal surveillance was not an innovation of the World War I era. Ever since independence, presidents have conducted intelligence-gathering and surveillance activities, with Congress's ready acquiescence.[40] This early experience accustomed Americans to viewing the world in terms of internal enemies leagued with threatening foreign powers, of expanded executive power to root out such spies, of loyalty and betrayal.

Aliens, not surprisingly, were a favorite target of the self-appointed patriotic forces. "100 percent Americanism" became more than a slogan justifying the Americanization efforts of previous decades that had tried to bleach native cultures and religions

---

[39] Immigration Act of 1917, ch 29, § 3, 39 Stat 874.

[40] William C. Banks and M. E. Bowman, *Executive Authority for National Security Surveillance*, 50 Am U L Rev 1–19 (2000).

out of immigrants. It now became a shibboleth that tested the loyalty of anyone whom patriots suspected of harboring radical ideas like socialism or support for industrial unions. Latent xenophobia, cultivated by the Wilson administration's support-the-war program, flourished and confirmed ideological antiradicalism.

Acting in unorchestrated concert, government and private vigilantes used law and extralegal violence to silence dissenters. The Bisbee deportations of 1917 that so exercised Felix Frankfurter, a few lynchings like that of poor Robert Prager (hanged for no other reason than that he was born in Germany) or of the Wobbly organizer Frank Little, and rituals of public humiliation, where socialists were made to kneel in the street and kiss the flag, were private supplements to the federal and state governments' systematic efforts to eradicate anticapitalist thinking.

Commenting on the lynching of Wobblies, the *New York Times* piously intoned that "I.W.W agitators are in effect, and perhaps in fact, agents of Germany. The Federal authorities should make short work of these treasonable conspirators against the United States."[41] Congress gladly complied, enacting first the Espionage Act in 1917 and then its precocious offspring, the Sedition Act, the next year.

In addition to criminalizing verbal sabotage (making "false statements" to interfere with military operations), interference with military recruitment, and encouraging insubordination in the armed services, the Espionage Act[42] contained a postal censorship provision permitting the Postmaster-General (the avid Burleson) to exclude from the mails anything "advocating or urging treason, insurrection, or forcible resistance to any law of the United States." The statute's amendment the next year in the Sedition Act went much further, criminalizing "any disloyal, profane, scurrilous, or abusive language about the form of Government of the United States, or the Constitution of the United States" or the armed forces or their uniforms, or anything intended to bring any of them or the flag "into contempt, scorn, contumely, or disrepute" (the common-law formula for libelous utterance), or anything that would "support or favor the cause" of an enemy in war-

---

[41] New York Times (Aug 4, 1917), p 6.

[42] Act of June 15, 1917, ch 30, 40 Stat 217, discussed below in greater detail.

time or "oppose the cause of the United States."[43] The Wilson administration deployed these new weapons with a vengeance, indicting prominent socialists like Eugene Debs and Congressman Victor Berger. The Supreme Court sustained the statutes and prosecutions under them in the *Schenck, Frohwerk, Debs, Abrams,* and *Pierce* cases of 1918–20.[44] These Espionage and Sedition Act trials during the first Red Scare anticipated later Cold War persecutions: the prosecution had no evidence that the defendants had actually committed any acts that might remotely be considered seditious (aside from their dissentient utterances), so it had to rely on party teachings. Professional informers provided their contribution. Judges relaxed protections for speech to enable convictions on flimsy evidence. All this was justified in the name of national security.[45]

Federal, state, and private suppression of dissent took on a greater sense of urgency after the success of the Bolshevik revolution in November 1917. Now, in addition to fighting a patriotic war against a demonized but conventional enemy (the Central Powers), America found itself confronting conservatives' worst nightmare: a large, potentially powerful nation governed by Communists, committed to an ideological position hostile to bedrock American values like democracy, Christianity, and capitalism. Because a few persons within the United States enthusiastically supported this new regime, the old pattern, fear of an ideologically alien foreign power leagued with a subversive domestic movement, suddenly seemed grounded in reality. Worse yet, the end of the war signaled Red uprisings all over Europe: at one time or another in 1918–20, Communist governments functioned in Bavaria, Hungary, and several northern German cities.

Responding to the Bolshevik success and the withdrawal of Russia from the war, the United States joined with other Allied powers in an invasion of the Soviet Union. President Wilson's half-hearted and vacillating policy limited the role of American troops to preventing war materiel from falling into German hands, and

---

[43] Sedition Act of 1918, ch 75, 40 Stat 553.

[44] *Schenck v United States*, 249 US 47 (1919); *Frohwerk v United States*, 249 US 204 (1919); *Debs v United States*, 249 US 211 (1919); *Abrams v United States*, 250 US 616 (1919); *Pierce v United States*, 252 US 239 (1920).

[45] Ellen Schrecker, *Many Are the Crimes: McCarthyism in America* 54 (1998).

he did what little he could to restrain the more bellicose French, who wanted to use the expedition to help overthrow the Bolsheviks. Three battalions of American infantry plus some engineering companies landed at the Arctic ports of Archangel and Murmansk, while a smaller American contingent debarked at Vladivostok in eastern Siberia. The United States was now, however stealthily, a quasi-belligerent involved in a de facto invasion of the Communist state aborning.[46]

For the first time, antiradicalism had a distinct and realistic anticommunist focus. Previously, "communism" had been a shadowy, indistinct, rhetorical figment. Now, real Communists governed a massive industrializing nation pursuing policies inimical to the interests of the United States, and they were being cheered on by individuals in the United States already suspect for their opposition to the war. The stage was set, the actors in place, for the first effective anticommunist offensive.

1919 seemed to be the year of the Red Dawn, abroad and at home. While Communist governments arose in the postwar turmoil of Europe, American society seemed vulnerable to the same menaces. The Left Wing, as it was called, of the Socialist Party hived out to form the Communist Labor Party and the Communist Party of the United States.[47] The USSR organized the Communist International (the Comintern), comprising Communist parties all over the world, including the American affiliates. Whatever its operational impact, the very existence of the Comintern convinced Americans that the Party was controlled by Moscow. Strikes shook the nation. In that year, a fifth of all American workers walked off the job, and some of these strikes were spectacular, especially the Seattle general strike. In Boston, a police strike evoked a new national figure, the governor of Massachusetts, Calvin Coolidge, who proclaimed that "there is no right to strike against the public safety by anybody, anywhere, any time," a maxim that eventually swept him to the White House. Anarchist bombings threatened to blow away figures like Attorney General A. Mitchell Palmer.

---

[46] David S. Foglesong, *America's Secret War Against Bolshevism: United States Intervention in the Russian Civil War, 1917–1920* (1995); Lloyd C. Gardner, *Safe for Democracy: The Anglo-American Response to Revolution, 1913–1923* 176–202 (1987).

[47] On this period of the Party's history, see Theodore Draper, *The Roots of American Communism* (1957).

America's antiradical forces responded to this social unrest ener-getically.[48] Conservative patriots who had been in the Allied Expe-ditionary Force organized the American Legion, "the largest mass-based organization within the countersubversive world and the one that most single-mindedly and continuously pushed an anticom-munist agenda."[49] Its Americanism Committee dedicated itself al-most exclusively to rooting out communist and alien elements in American life. The New York General Assembly expelled five of its members for no reason other than that they were members of the Socialist Party, and then re-expelled them when their constit-uents reelected them. Twenty-six states enacted red flag laws in 1919 alone.

In the federal Department of Justice, Palmer formed the Gen-eral Intelligence Division, better known as the Radical Division, and placed the rising J. Edgar Hoover in charge of it.[50] There Hoover made the most of his opportunity. He drew up the first of his rosters of radicals, with some sixty thousand names on it, and began accumulating files on some of them. He undertook an intensive study of communist literature, steeping himself in the rhetoric of revolution, thereby imprinting on his consciousness an indelible picture of communism as a violent, dangerous, and sub-versive force dedicated to the overthrow of democratic government in the United States. "Civilization faces its most terrible menace of danger since the barbarian hordes overran West Europe and opened the Dark Ages," he concluded with a bit of simplistic pop history.[51]

Hoover actively propagandized his vision, writing latter-day ver-sions of the *Malleus Maleficarum*.[52] He composed a screed that de-

[48] The most useful studies of the first Red Scare are Richard Gid Powers, *Not Without Honor: The History of American Anticommunism* 1–42 (1995); Preston, *Aliens and Dissenters* (cited in note 36); Murphy, *World War I and the Origins of Civil Liberties* (cited in note 36); Harold M. Hyman, *To Try Men's Souls: Loyalty Tests in American History* 267–324 (1959); and Murray, *Red Scare* (cited in note 36).

[49] Schrecker, *Many Are the Crimes* at 61 (cited in note 45).

[50] On Hoover, see Richard Gid Powers, *Secrecy and Power: The Life of J. Edgar Hoover* (1987); Athan G. Theoharis and John S. Cox, *The Boss: J. Edgar Hoover and the Great American Inquisition* (1988); and Curt Gentry, *J. Edgar Hoover: The Man and the Secrets* (1991).

[51] Quoted in Powers, *Not Without Honor* at 29 (cited in note 48).

[52] The aptness of this comparison can be seen from *Western European Magic and Folklore*, in Joseph R. Strayer, ed, 8 *Dictionary of the Middle Ages* 30b (1987).

manded the deportation of aliens,[53] brought out a newsletter, the *General Intelligence Bulletin*, and published a little book, *The Revolution in Action*. In these publications, he painted a picture of a unified, monolithic "radical" movement directed by Communists but including a broad penumbra of non-Left, nonradical libertarians and assorted critics of government policy. These included the likes of Walter Lippmann, Roger Baldwin, Rev. John A. Ryan, and others he designated "parlor pinks." He seemed particularly concerned about "certain wealthy women who are giving financial aid to various radical publications."[54] (The countersubversive movement always had an antifeminist caste to it, as well as its more obvious racial and ethnic slants, due to the prominence of women's peace groups like the Women's International League for Peace and Freedom, an enduring target of Right suspicions.)

Meanwhile, with President Wilson *dehors* the action because of his disabling stroke, Attorney General Palmer launched a massive deportation drive to rid the nation of alien radicals. Led by the Bureau of Investigation, assisted by private auxiliaries like the vigilante forces of the American Protective League, seconded by state red-squad activities, Palmer and Hoover led raids on centers of alien radical activity, rounded up and jailed some six thousand foreign-born Reds, anarchists, Socialists, and other undesirables, and managed to ship off several hundred of them to the Soviet Union aboard the *Red Ark*.

Such vigorous government activity provoked resistance. Civil libertarians like Baldwin and Zechariah Chafee formed the American Civil Liberties Union to protect First Amendment liberties.[55] They scored a stunning victory in 1920 with publication of the *Report Upon the Illegal Practices of the United States Department of Justice*, popularly known as the *Lawyers' Report*, which excoriated the Justice Department, Palmer, and Hoover for the Red raids and the department's propagandizing. The contributors were a remarkable group that included Roscoe Pound, Felix Frankfurter (an involvement that helped cement his early reputation for radical-

---

[53] Reprinted as *J. Edgar Hoover's Brief on the Communist Party*, in James D. Bales, ed, *J. Edgar Hoover Speaks Concerning Communism* 266–88 (1970).

[54] Quoted in Powers, *Not Without Honor* at 28 (cited in note 48).

[55] Samuel Walker, *In Defense of American Liberties; A History of the ACLU* 11–71 (2d ed 1999).

parties fused into a single group, the Communist Party of the United States, in 1923. (I will henceforth refer to this united body as "the Party," or CPUSA.) It was prominent in efforts to save Sacco and Vanzetti (1927). Communists were conspicuous in the Gastonia textile strike of 1929. They played a crucial role in saving the Scottsboro Boys in 1931. The trial and appeal of black Communist Angelo Herndon in 1937 set a milestone in First Amendment speech and association law.[66] Communists benefited so much from the Depression, the rise of fascism and Hitler, FDR's recognition of the Soviet Union in 1933, and their influence in the CIO that one prominent anticommunist could reasonably label the era "the Red Decade."[67] Above all, the Party benefited from the creation of the antifascist Popular Front in 1935. The alliances thus formed proved invaluable in tiding the Party over the embarrassment of the Stalinist terror and the show trials of 1934–37. But if the Popular Front was a blessing to the Party, it became a curse to fellow-travelers and non-Party front members during the second Red Scare.[68] Despite these gains, though, the Party's secretive nature and manipulative maneuvering alienated many Ameri-

---

Decline of American Communism: A History of the Communist Party of the United States since 1945 (1959), were part of that series. See also the ideologically kindred Irving Howe and Lewis Coser, *The American Communist Party: A Critical History* 319–437 (1962; rpt ed 1974). This view is commonly called "traditionalist," even by its modern exponents. The more recent works of Harvey Klehr and John Earl Haynes, including *The American Communist Movement: Storming Heaven Itself* (1992); Klehr, *Heyday of American Communism*; Klehr, Haynes, and Fridrikh Firsov, *The Secret World of American Communism* (1995) (a documentary collection); Klehr, Haynes, and Kyrill Anderson, *The Soviet World of American Communism* (1998) (a successor documentary collection), reaffirm that early approach, with depth and sophistication, reflecting the vastly expanded archival opportunities that the earlier authors could only dream of.

A more recent approach, commonly labeled "revisionist," stresses the humanity and agency of Party members, as well as the indigenous aspects of the CPUSA's evolution. Exemplars include Maurice Isserman, *Which Side Were You On? The American Communist Party During the Second World War* (1982) (see especially his historiographic orientation, pp vii–xiii); Joseph R. Starobin, *American Communism in Crisis, 1943–1957* 20–47 (1972); and Fraser M. Ottanelli, *The Communist Party of the United States: From the Depression to World War II* (1991). Where traditionalists wrote about Commun*ism*, revisionists were concerned with Commun*ists*.

John Earl Haynes provides an excellent historiographic review of the subject in *The Cold War Debate Continues: A Traditionalist View of Historical Writing on Domestic Communism and Anti-Communism*, 2 J Cold War Studies 76 (2000).

[66] *Herndon v Lowry*, 301 US 242 (1937).

[67] Eugene Lyons, *The Red Decade: The Stalinist Penetration of America* (1941).

[68] On these groups and their fate in the Cold War, see David Caute, *The Fellow-Travellers: A Postscript to the Enlightenment* 303–43 (1973).

cans. It established an ineradicable reputation for clandestine operations.[69]

Partly in reaction to Communism's gains, President Franklin D. Roosevelt took the fateful step of ordering Hoover, now head of the organization that had been renamed the Federal Bureau of Investigation, to collect intelligence, first on Nazi groups in the United States in 1934, and then on Communists in 1936. (In 1924, Attorney General Harlan Fiske Stone had limited Bureau of Investigations activities to violations of federal laws, expressly prohibiting political inquiries.) Coincidentally, at the same time the NKVD (the predecessor of the Soviet KGB) began cultivating a small coterie of native-born American Communists and others who began small-time espionage: sending reports on federal government activities or policies, filching an occasional minor document, passing along information. Their activities were clandestine and not very significant. Before 1941, the United States was an unimportant backwater as far as the NKVD was concerned.[70]

Meanwhile, in the larger society various groups began to develop a spontaneous anticommunist front not tied to former business and nativist activism. Labor leaders, especially in the AFL, grew uneasy about the influence of Communists in their ranks. The Roman Catholic Church, never favorably disposed toward an atheistic philosophy, was outraged at persecution of its communicants in the Mexican Revolution, in the USSR, and then by Loyalist forces in the Spanish Civil War. People on the Left end of the political spectrum, Socialists and the New York intellectuals above all,[71] came to despise the tactics and then the beliefs of Communism, producing an impressive yield of anticommunist intellectuals like Sidney Hook and Richard Wright. Defections from the Party produced professional anticommunists like J. B. Matthews (formerly one of the most important of the fellow-travelers in front organizations), Jay Lovestone, who became the labor movement's foremost anticommunist, and even Founding Father (of the Party) Benjamin Gitlow. At the other end of the spectrum, the Christian

---

[69] Guenter Lewy, *The Cause That Failed: Communism in American Political Life* 39 (1990).

[70] Maurice Isserman, *Disloyalty as a Principle: Why Communists Spied*, 77 Foreign Service J 29 (2000), offers a brief review of the origins of Soviet espionage in the 1930s.

[71] Allan W. Wald, *The New York Intellectuals: The Rise and Decline of the Anti-Stalinist Left from the 1930s to the 1980s* (1987).

Right contributed a stock of attitudes that influenced not only Protestant fundamentalists but also many persons not in the orbit of that religious element.

The Liberty League, formed in 1935 by businessmen and conservative Democrats disaffected with the New Deal, played an especially important role in the emerging anticommunist movement. By combining anticommunist appeals with assaults on FDR, the New Deal, and the federal government generally, Liberty Leaguers nudged the movement away from its partially discredited associations with anti-union and nativist groups, in a new direction. Anticommunism became a tactic in ordinary partisan competition, with Republicans recurrently attacking Democrats for harboring Communists or being "soft on Communism." The Democrats weakly attempted to repel the canard, adopting a me-too or more-anticommunist-than-thou stance that was not very convincing. This both diminished the Democratic Party as a source of libertarian impulses, and enlisted it in the anticommunist crusade.

Thus, for the first time, the anticommunist impulse became directed against the federal government itself. Anticommunists came to regard the federal government both as a shelter for subversives who burrowed from within, and as their puppet in its dealings with the USSR. Communists aside, the new alphabet-soup bureaucracy and the collectivist mentality attributed to New Dealers made the New Deal seem a betrayal of traditional American individualism and of the localist Jeffersonian model of American society. As Al Smith put it in 1936, the new "government by bureaucracy" forced a choice on Americans between "the pure air of America [and] the foul breath of communistic Russia."[72] In 1945, the House Un-American Activities Committee (hereafter: HUAC) became the permanent institutional vehicle for attacks of this sort.

This shift in targets provided business conservatives an opportunity to smear the New Deal's regulatory, tax, and welfare innovations with the taint of un-Americanism and communism. Enlisting popular support for this crusade called up a sorcerer's apprentice, though that was hardly a cause for concern in America's boardrooms. But the movement was not confined to businessmen. The diversity and wide-ranging appeal of the anticommunist movement

---

[72] Quoted in Heale, *American Anticommunism* at 112 (cited in note 58).

accounted for its power and influence in American life. As with diversity in ecological systems, the varied class, ethnic, religious, occupational, governmental/bureaucratic, and ideological loci of the movement carried it through dry spells, protected it from embarrassments like Dilling or Fish, and assured that any segment of the movement could find fellows in disparate places.

The Spanish civil war made its own distinctive contribution to the growing influence of anticommunism: a metaphor. As Falangist forces approached the Loyalist stronghold of Madrid in four columns of troops, Franco announced that fascists inside the city constituted a "fifth column," ready to rise up in insurrection to assist the external besiegers. The primal American linkage of foreign enemy to internal subversion now found its name and image, and that, in turn, introduced a kind of mental template into political rhetoric, a catchphrase that connoted liberal and reform groups' ties to subversion.[73]

IV. World War II

The years 1938–41, the threshold of World War II, constituted a time of what one scholar calls "the little red scare."[74] In 1938, the House of Representatives created its Special Committee on Un-American Activities (later HUAC), which was the launchpad for Rep. Martin Dies's gaudy wartime career of attacking the New Deal by purportedly rooting out subversives.[75] HUAC's predecessors had not augured well for its future. Hamilton Fish's 1930 investigative committee wrapped up its work amid derisive laughter when Fish was conned. Samuel Dickstein's 1934 committee, originally formed to investigate Nazi influence, did a little better, but was temporary. By an irony almost too delicious to be believable, Dickstein seems to have functioned for two years while a congressman as a Soviet agent![76] The House originally authorized

---

[73] On the power of this metaphor, see Francis MacDonnell, *Insidious Foes: The Axis Fifth Column and the American Home Front* (1995).

[74] Heale, *American Anticommunism* at 123–29 (cited in note 58).

[75] See generally Walter Goodman, *The Committee: The Extraordinary Career of the House Committee on Un-American Activities* (1968) (a thorough and hostile account).

[76] Allen Weinstein and Alexander Vassiliev, *The Haunted Wood: Soviet Espionage in America—the Stalin Era* 140–50 (1999). The Weinstein/Vassiliev conclusions throughout this book must be regarded as provisional, however, because of the problematic nature of the primary sources upon which they relied, as well as their limited and aborted access to those sources. See Weinstein's discussion, pp xv–xix.

HUAC as a temporary committee in 1938, and made it a standing committee in 1945. HUAC's charge was to investigate "1) the extent, character and objects of un-American propaganda activities in the United States, 2) the diffusion within the United States of subversive and un-American propaganda that is instigated from foreign countries or of a domestic origin and attacks the principle of the form of government as guaranteed by the Constitution. . . ."[77] For the first time, one of the houses of Congress committed itself to investigating political thought and speech among American citizens. Previously it had purported to direct its attention to aliens, and to their actions, not their words. HUAC was dominated by the conservative congressional anti–New Deal coalition, leavened with a few token liberals.

HUAC's seemingly evenhanded investigation of "un-American activities," lumping together Nazis and Communists, was a valuable move in legitimizing the anticommunist crusade. After the war, when the full extent of Naziism's atrocities became known, it proved useful to Red-hunters to have established the Nazi-Communist equation. If the one was as morally loathsome as the other, and if the "Good War" had consecrated the struggle against Nazis, then the Cold War might take on the same aura of legitimacy for its struggle against Reds. After the war, this linkage was cemented by the concept of "totalitarianism." While influential intellectuals like Arthur M. Schlesinger and Hannah Arendt popularized the moral equivalence of Naziism and Communism, linking the two by the umbrella concept of totalitarianism,[78] President Truman made them the centerpiece of, first, the Truman Doctrine, and then the Marshall Plan, defining Communist movements as "totalitarian." "The totalitarian idea—that the Communists were the successors of the Nazis and closely connected to them—was the most powerful political idea of the late 1940s,"[79] in the view of the leading authority on the subject. For over half a century after that, professional anticommunists applauded their own efforts as the moral equivalent of the struggle against Naziism. The small and impotent groupings of the far Right thus provided a conve-

---

[77] 83 Cong Rec 7568, 7586 (1938).

[78] Arthur M. Schlesinger, *The Vital Center: The Politics of Freedom* (1949); Hannah Arendt, *The Origins of Totalitarianism* (1951).

[79] Abbott Gleason, *Totalitarianism: The Inner History of the Cold War* 74 (1995).

nient cover for a suppressive crusade that was single-mindedly concerned with Communists and others of the Left. This also shielded Hoover et al. from charges of ideological bias: they could claim that they pursued the Right with as much vigor as they dedicated to the Left.

During the war, the anticommunist movement developed into something much more important than what it had earlier been, when it was little more than a vehicle for business' union-busting ambitions and nativists' animosity toward newer Americans. Noninvolved observers might have taken a more distanced view of the anti-Red drive in its earlier phases, seeing it for what it was, a disguised, class-based antipathy to unions and hyphenated Americans. But during the war it became a crusade for protecting America's national security. After the war, though, the nation's very survival seemed to be bound up with the anti-Red struggle, and indifference or detachment became impossible for most people. The Justices of the Supreme Court had already demonstrated that they could be stampeded by domestic-security anxieties in the 1918–27 political-speech cases; they could hardly be expected to do otherwise in the supercharged Cold War atmosphere.

HUAC quickly hooked a big fish on its line: Leon Trotsky, from his Mexican exile, agreed to testify before it. His assassination at the hands of one of Stalin's agents deprived the world of what would have been a fascinating interview. But there was plenty of other grain to winnow, albeit not as spectacular. J. B. Matthews, disillusioned former Red-fronter, and ex-Communist Benjamin Mandel became HUAC's principal investigators. Their scenarios of Communist penetration of the CIO and New Deal executive agencies made headlines, and the publicity thus generated provided the press with a supporting role in the anticommunist campaign.[80] Inadvertently or not, the media broadcast their anticommunist propaganda as news, giving it an air of authenticity.

Congress busied itself in other ways. In 1938, it enacted the Foreign Agents Registration Act, which required "agents of foreign principals" to submit semiannual reports of their activities.[81] The next year it passed the Hatch Act, which banned federal employees from "membership in any political party or organization

---

[80] Schrecker, *Many Are the Crimes* at 91 (cited in note 45).

[81] Foreign Agents Registration Act of 1938, ch 327, 52 Stat 631.

which advocates the overthrow of *our* constitutional form of government in the United States."[82] (The possessive pronoun added a gratuitous exclusionary and xenophobic frisson to the measure.) In that same year, it began a routine practice of attaching riders to appropriation bills forbidding disbursement of federal funds "to any person who advocates, or who is a member of an organization that advocates the overthrow of the government of the United States through force or violence."[83]

The executive branch also did its part, with FDR's tacit blessing and sometimes his active connivance. Hoover and the FBI began investigations into subversion in 1938. He recommended that such investigations be conducted "with the utmost secrecy in order to avoid criticism or objections which might be raised to such an expansion by ill-informed persons or individuals having some ulterior motive."[84] The next year, Hoover instructed FBI agents to investigate both aliens and citizens "on whom there is information available to indicate that their presence at liberty in this country in time of war or national emergency would be dangerous to the public peace and the safety of the United States government."[85] The FBI vigilantly carried out its countersubversive mandate throughout the war years, compiling dossiers that lived on after the war and hounding leftist emigrés.[86]

In an event of momentous consequence but completely unnoticed at the time (it took place the day after Germany invaded Poland), another disillusioned ex-Communist, Whittaker Chambers, approached Adolph Berle, then an Assistant Secretary of State, with revelations about Communist infiltration of the State, Agriculture, and Treasury Departments, as well as the SEC, the NLRB, and army weapons labs. Berle dutifully reported these to FDR, who dismissed the charges. The episode would return to bedevil a later administration.

In 1939, Hitler and Stalin signed their notorious nonaggression

---

[82] Act to Prevent Pernicious Political Activities (1939), ch 410, §§ 9, 9A, 53 Stat 1147 (ital added).

[83] E.g., Act of 28 Oct 1941, ch 460, § 301, 55 Stat 745.

[84] Quoted in Goldstein, *Political Repression* at 247 (cited in note 26).

[85] Hoover directive, dated Dec 6, 1939, reprinted in US Senate Select Committee to Study Governmental Operations with Respect to Intelligence Activities, *Hearings on the Federal Bureau of Investigation*, 94th Cong, 1st Sess 409.

[86] Alexander Stephan, *"Communazis": FBI Surveillance of German Emigré Writers* (2000).

pact. This had repercussions on the Party and its adversaries in the United States. While a mass exodus probably did not occur, the Party lost many prominent intellectuals and fellow-travelers, disgusted by its abrupt 180-degree turn and its obvious subservience to Moscow.[87] A powerful reaction set in against the Party and its fronts, while nonfront groups like the ACLU and the National Lawyers Guild expelled their Communist members, such as Elizabeth Gurley Flynn.

As tensions increased after outbreak of the European war in September 1939, the federal and state governments expanded their repertoire of antisubversive powers. In 1940, Congress reenacted the 1917 Espionage Act.[88] By a 382–4 margin in the House and a voice vote in the Senate, it then passed the Smith Act, formally titled the Alien Registration Act, the first peacetime federal sedition act in American history, realizing Hoover's dream of two decades earlier.[89] In the so-called Voorhis Act of 1940,[90] Congress required registration of organizations advocating such overthrow. (The sponsor of this measure, Rep. Jerry Voorhis, a liberal California Democrat, was Richard Nixon's first political quarry. There is some irony in the fact that his political career was terminated by Nixon's allegations that he was soft on Communism.)

After outbreak of the war, the FDR administration began a selective and ill-advised prosecution of assorted figures from the Left and Right. Even so liberal a public figure as Attorney General Frank Murphy boasted in a cabinet meeting that "every possible effort is being made to indict any Communist who has violated the criminal laws in any respect."[91] Under this program, CPUSA head Earl Browder was sentenced to four years imprisonment for a false passport statement. The Justice Department also prosecuted Minneapolis Trotskyites. It began its long and futile campaign against various "native fascists" for conspiracy under the Espionage and Smith Acts. These were an odd lot: David Dudley Pelley, leader of the Silver Shirts; Gerald Winrod, anti-Semitic ranter; Elizabeth Dilling, the earnest and indefatigable right-wing oddball;

---

[87] Isserman, *Which Side Were You On?* at 37 (cited in note 65).

[88] Act of March 28, 1940, ch 72, 54 Stat 79.

[89] Act of June 28, 1940, ch 439, 54 Stat 670, discussed below.

[90] Act of Oct 17, 1940, ch 897, 54 Stat 1201.

[91] Harold Ickes quoting Murphy, in *The Secret Diary of Harold Ickes* 97 (1953).

Bund Führer William Kunze; Nazi propagandist Sylvester Viereck, inter al. This effort culminated in a mistrial in 1944 and dismissal of a subsequent prosecution in 1946.[92]

The aborted trial, *United States v McWilliams*, provided several lessons for the coming repressive era.[93] The "Brown Scare" (persecution of fascists and the far Right during World War II) proved to be a dress rehearsal for the ensuing Red Scare. It recalled the maxim, "he who would sup with the devil must have a long spoon." Individuals were suspect on the basis of their group's ideology or, worse, the ideas of groups to which they had only tenuous connections, or none at all. Guilt by association, the use of informers and apostates, coordination between congressional investigating committees and prosecutors, and mobilization against a tiny, harmless fringe because of their ideas, all characterized both scares. Liberals split on the wisdom and justice of the prosecution, with many applauding suppression of the political speech of right-wingers. By a kind of karmic inevitability, this opportunistic stance would soon return to haunt them.

By way of contrast, the wartime Grand Alliance temporarily abated antisubversive activity aimed at leftists. The political climate returned to what it had been in the palmy days of the Popular Front.[94] The CPUSA flourished: its membership soared to over sixty thousand; it ran candidates in municipal elections, and sometimes won; it established a network of schools; its papers were freely distributed on the East and West Coasts. When Stalin dissolved the Comintern in 1943 as a gesture to his allies, Browder followed suit by disbanding the CPUSA and sheep-dipping it as the Communist Political Association. Numerous CIO affiliates, perhaps as many as a quarter, were dominated or at least infiltrated by Communists. The period marked the nadir of anticommunism, though that was to be only temporary.

But the anticommunist crusade had only receded; it did not disappear. At the state and local level, municipal police Red squads investigated and harassed leftists and labor organizers, while state legislative committees conducted investigations into the political

---

[92] Leo P. Ribuffo, *United States v McWilliams: The Roosevelt Administration and the Far Right*, in Michal R. Belknap, ed, *American Political Trials* 179 (rev'd ed 1994).

[93] On this case, see Ribuffo, *Old Christian Right* at 181–215 (cited in note 63).

[94] Isserman, *Which Side Were You On?* (cited in note 65).

views of suspect individuals. The most notorious of these was New York's 1940 Rapp-Coudert investigation of leftist tendencies in New York City public schools.

In 1941, HUAC's chairman Martin Dies sent the Justice Department a list of 1,121 names of potentially disloyal federal employees, the ancestor of many more lists to come that smeared innocent persons with a Red taint. A later avatar, the Attorney General's list, became "a bureaucratic device designed to routinize the process of identifying undesirable employees by designating certain organizations as 'subversive'."[95] Throughout the war, Dies probed the CIO, the WPA, the NLRB, fingering individuals with leftist or liberal sentiments. He perfected the technique of guilt by association, a poisoned legacy to those who would come after him.

V. The False Dawn of Civil Liberties: 1945–46

In the balmy climate of the immediate postwar period (1945–46), civil liberties seemed to be carried forward on the momentum that had been established since the Supreme Court's first speech-protective decision two decades earlier, *Fiske v Kansas*.[96] Supreme Court precedents dealing specifically with actual Communists exemplified the general pattern of that emergent protection for Communists' First Amendment liberties. The cases of the earliest period, 1919–27, sustained all prosecutions of Communists under state antisubversive legislation.[97] In dramatic contrast, all comparable cases of the Hughes era and later overturned Communists' convictions.[98]

Two decisions in 1945 and 1946 seemed to continue the Hughes-era pattern. The Court first stymied anticommunists' efforts to deport the leftist labor leader Harry Bridges, then overturned a congressional mandate that three federal employees be

---

[95] Schrecker, *Many Are the Crimes* at 113 (cited in note 45).

[96] 274 US 380 (1927).

[97] *Gitlow v New York*, 268 US 652 (1925); *Whitney v California*, 274 US 357 (1927). Anita Whitney was not a Communist, but she was prosecuted under the California criminal syndicalism statute for participating in the formation of the California branch of the Communist Labor Party.

[98] *Stromberg v California*, 283 US 359 (1931); *De Jonge v Oregon*, 299 US 353 (1937); *Herndon v Lowry*, 301 US 242 (1937); *Schneiderman v United States*, 320 US 118 (1943).

fired, holding it to be a bill of attainder. In the seemingly untroubled year after V-J Day, these decisions augured well for civil liberties, tendering a false promise that the Supreme Court would extend its vigilance to protect the speech rights of those hounded for their radical views.

Harry Bridges was a flamboyantly radical West Coast labor organizer, leader of the strategically sensitive longshoremen's unions, probably a Communist, certainly someone with extensive leftist affiliations and beliefs. Naturally, West Coast shippers and other conservatives had been trying to silence the Australian-born radical since the late 1930s. They were frustrated by *Bridges v California*,[99] an important decision upholding his speech and press freedoms through a stringent application of the clear-and-present-danger test. Returning to the project throughout the war, Bridges's numerous enemies sought to deport him under the 1917 Immigration Act and the 1940 Smith Act. The Court again thwarted these efforts in *Bridges v Wixon*,[100] holding that the government had not proved the requisite degree of "affiliation" with the Party that might have sustained deportation efforts. Mere "cooperation with Communist groups for attainment of wholly lawful objectives" was protected by the First Amendment.

A year later, the Court again disappointed legislators who had hoped to cleanse the nation of dissentient attitudes. *United States v Lovett* was the first of the Cold War cases, and the only one in the 1946–56 period that had a speech-protective outcome. The problem traced back to Diess' and Hoover's lists of "members of subversive organizations." Relying on one of these, a congressional committee in 1943 slipped a rider in an appropriations bill prohibiting salary payments to three specified State Department officers whom it suspected of being left-leaning in their views, stating that their "views and philosophies . . . constitute subversive activity."[101] The Court struck down this clumsy attempt as a bill of attainder in violation of Article I, Section 9's ban on such legislative punishments.[102]

---

[99] 314 US 252 (1941).

[100] 326 US 135, 145 (1945).

[101] "Report on Fitness for Continuance in Government Employment of Goodwin B. Watson . . . ," HR Rep No 448, 78 Cong, 1st Sess 6 (1943).

[102] 328 US 303 (1946).

VI. The Second Red Scare: Seedtime

The first and second Red Scares were not discrete, discon-nected events. Rather, they were phases on a continuum. Whether the libertarian momentum of the Court's First Amendment cases could have been sustained consistently throughout the postwar pe-riod must remain speculative. *Bridges* and *Lovett* suggest that the potential was there. But the growth of domestic anticommunism, developing in response to the deterioration in American-Soviet re-lations, strangled any such possibility. The second Red Scare ri-valed its predecessor in the damage it visited on First Amendment liberties of speech, press, and association. The Court again acqui-esced, though its compliant stance lasted less than a decade.

This collapse of the Court's libertarian impulse occurred be-cause the Justices differed little from other Americans in their atti-tudes toward Communism. They shared in the nation's mounting anxiety over international crises and believed in the emerging im-age of domestic Communists. A majority of the Justices regarded Communists and their Party as *sui generis*, different from other radical groups like the Klan, uniquely threatening to America's na-tional security. The Court therefore assigned Communists a spe-cial status under the Constitution, with diminished protections for their speech, press, and associational liberties. They saw this con-tracted and distinctive status as necessary if federal, state, and local governments were to ensure their own survival.

The constitutional world of the Vinson Court was different from ours, and to understand its work, we must see the world as they saw it. At the onset of the Cold War, the American idea of freedom underwent another of its many permutations.[103] During World War II, the struggle against Naziism and other tyrannies led many Americans to regard the preservation of civil liberties as an essential component of their idea of freedom, and this sense lingered on after the war. Similarly, as the extent of the Nazi Ho-locaust became known, those same Americans came to see the pro-tection of minority groups' civil rights as another component of the idea of freedom. The Allied powers condemned "enslave-ment"—including forced labor, treatment of prisoners of war, oc-

---

[103] Eric Foner, *The Story of American Freedom* 221–75 (1998).

The Powers polarity is too simple, but it is a useful heuristic device that helps account for the Cold War cases of the 1950–56 period. It suggests how underlying perceptions of domestic Communists, which the Justices shared with their fellow Americans, might have been compatible with concerns for speech, press, and associational liberties. Given the commitment of two members of the Court, Felix Frankfurter and Robert H. Jackson, to judicial self-restraint, if three other members of the Court could be persuaded of the validity of the liberal image of Communists, the Court would retreat from the First Amendment momentum that it had achieved since 1927, at least as to Communists.

In a perverse way, the appeal of liberal anticommunist values to all members of the Court conditioned them for a decade, 1949–59, to accept or at least tolerate policies derived from the harsher Right image of communism. Understanding the values of liberal anticommunism helps explain how and why the Court left the mainstream of its First Amendment jurisprudence in those years and drifted to *Dennis*.

C. THE POLITICO-IDEOLOGICAL CLIMATE

After World War II, the American politico-ideological climate was being reconfigured.[113] The conservative congressional coalition that had regularly flexed its muscles since 1937 was more powerful than ever, and was to score a stunning triumph in 1946, when Congress went Republican. Anticommunist institutions and interest groups throve in such a benign climate.[114] Outside government, the American Legion and other veterans' groups promoted their versions of "Americanism," which invariably contained a militantly antiradical emphasis. Business groups such as the Chamber of Commerce and the National Association of Manufacturers were determined to roll back labor's post-1936 gains, and more broadly to impose a free-enterprise ideology on American society, displacing New Deal "collectivism."[115] To that end, they tirelessly red-

---

[113] See generally the invaluable essays collected in Robert Griffith and Athan Theoharis, eds, *The Specter: Original Essays on the Cold War and the Origins of McCarthyism* (1974).

[114] David H. Bennett, *The Party of Fear: From Nativist Movements to the New Right in American History* 273–315 (2d ed 1995).

[115] Fones-Wolf, *Selling Free Enterprise* (cited in note 104).

baited the leftist unions in the CIO.[116] The wave of strikes in 1945–46 produced much popular support for that position. Even the AFL sometimes cooperated, seeking to undermine its rival federation. Religious groups, above all the Roman Catholic Church, intensified in their hostility to the Left's secularizing and atheistic tendencies, especially when Communist governments tried to suppress the churches of eastern Europe. The white South, sensing an imminent threat to segregation, imputed civil rights and labor movements to communist initiatives. (This view was not irrational. Memories of Scottsboro and Gastonia were still fresh; the Left-led Mine, Mill, and Smelter Workers Union was the most racially integrated labor organization in the nation.[117]) The right-wing press, which included the large Hearst and Scripps-Howard chains as well as important nonaffiliated papers like the *Chicago Tribune* and the *Los Angeles Times*, attributed much that it disliked to communist machinations.

While these groups marshaled, a decisive rightward shift was taking place in American political coalitions. As the wartime Grand Alliance gave way to bipolar global rivalry in 1945, its domestic counterpart, a neo-Popular Front alliance of liberals, labor, and the Left, was coming undone. The CPUSA itself was riven with faction. At the Kremlin's bidding, relayed through a letter published in the French Communist press by Jacques Duclos, Party regulars deposed their wartime leader Earl Browder on charges of reformist and revisionist policies—Browder had promoted cooperation with other noncommunist political forces—and replaced him with the more hardline Stalinist William Z. Foster.[118]

The 1948 presidential elections finally disrupted the liberal-Left alliance. Some liberal veterans of the Popular Front, deploring the Cold War and yearning for a continuation of the wartime USA-USSR cooperation, joined hands with fellow-travelers and a few Communists to form the Progressive Citizens of America and support the presidential candidacy of Henry Wallace, hoping to un-

---

[116] George Lipsitz, *Class and Culture in Cold-War America: "A Rainbow at Midnight"* 37–172 (1981).

[117] See generally Robin D. G. Kelley, *Hammer and Hoe: Alabama Communists During the Great Depression* (1990). See also Mark Naison, *Communists in Harlem During the Depression* (1983).

[118] On the Party's travails, see Starobin, *American Communism in Crisis* 51–214 (cited in note 65).

seat Truman and thus reverse the "imperialist" course of American foreign policy. This drove anticommunist liberals to form Americans for Democratic Action, which combined resistance to Communism at home and abroad with a revised New Deal agenda. Their vision of the New Deal was consumer-oriented, content to accept the permanence of capitalism, disinclined to pursue confrontational policies with corporate America, less enamored of planning and reformist programs, preferring instead fiscal management and compensatory welfare policies.[119] They held their noses and backed Truman, without enthusiasm.

Liberal anticommunists were blessed by the presence of nonpareil publicists in their ranks, most notably the historian Arthur Schlesinger, Jr., the theologian Reinhold Niebuhr, and the philosopher Sidney Hook. Schlesinger's book *The Vital Center* (1949)[120] quickly became the most persuasive apologia of those who wished to combat Communism yet preserve American liberties while doing so. Schlesinger portrayed domestic Communists as subversives who posed a real danger of espionage. He contended that the Communist Party was different from other political groups in that its mission was "to run interference for Soviet foreign policy." Endorsing containment abroad and "identification and exposure" of Communists at home, Schlesinger nevertheless condemned the excesses of HUAC. His tract articulated the mindset of those who would suppress Communists and fellow-travelers while believing that they remained faithful to constitutional liberties.

Hook's contribution, aside from his tireless pamphleteering, lay in his organizing left-of-center intellectuals in the Congress for Cultural Freedom (CCF). This haven for anticommunist intellectuals did much to legitimize anticommunist thought among educated Americans, including lawyers and judges. Revelations of its CIA funding came much later; at the time it seemed to be an independent entity. The CCF encouraged former Communists of the "god that failed" school—Arthur Koestler, Ignazio Silone, George Orwell, and James Burnham among them—to expose the moral shortcomings of Communism, lending an aura of respectability to less thoughtful assaults on the Left emanating from other quarters.

---

[119] Alan Brinkley, *The End of Reform: New Deal Liberalism in Recession and War* 265–72 (1995).

[120] Schlesinger, *The Vital Center: The Politics of Freedom* at 101, 210 (cited in note 78).

Ironically, the triumph of anticommunist politics in 1948–52 can be credited largely to Truman's unexpected 1948 victory and the return of Democrats to control of both houses of Congress in that election. (As always, though, nominal Democratic control was less significant than the dominance of the bipartisan conservative coalition.) Smarting from their losses, stung by the knowledge that they had snatched defeat from the jaws of victory, Republicans determined to regain control of national politics, and seized on anticommunism as their best opportunity for doing so. This provided them their political salvation. They were doomed to permanent minority status if they could offer the American electorate nothing better than the negative demand to roll back the New Deal. They needed something distinctly their own; anticommunism provided it. It gave them an impeccably American platform from which to belabor Democrats as tainted with a foreign collectivism.[121]

In this enterprise, they were joined by an invaluable ally, the nation's foremost anticommunist, J. Edgar Hoover. Hoover, the consummate bureaucratic empire-builder, burnished the "FBI in Peace and War" image,[122] making strategic alliances with congressional conservatives that would serve both well. Hoover was a tireless propagandizer, beginning as early as 1920. His literary efforts culminated in his *Masters of Deceit: The Story of Communism in America and How to Fight It* (1958) and *J. Edgar Hoover on Communism* (1969). Hoover's hatred of Communism had never abated, and the postwar chill in U.S.-Soviet relations spurred him to revive or intensify three cherished projects: the "custodial detention program" (a scheme for interning the politically suspect in concentration camps), the Security Index (the roster of those so suspect), and a propaganda initiative dubbed the Mass Media Program that glorified the FBI and warned of the dangers of Communist infiltration.

His frustrating experiences in the first Red Scare cautioned Hoover that he would require the unstinting backing of political allies, lest he again find himself unsupported in the face of the inevitable liberal criticism. He considered Truman's loyalty program half-hearted and inadequate. Deciding that the time had

---

[121] Lucas Powe, *The Warren Court and American Politics* 76 (2000).

[122] Richard Gid Powers, *G-Men: Hoover's FBI in American Popular Culture* (1983). The quoted phrase is the title of a 1943 book on the Bureau by Frederick L. Collins.

come to make a strategic switch in political alliances, Hoover appeared before HUAC in March 1947 to warn of the Communist menace, to encourage HUAC in its investigative activities, and to hint obliquely that the Truman administration had not done enough to purge Communists from its ranks.[123] Hoover there crossed a political Rubicon: the powerful *apparat* of his FBI was now leagued with conservative congressional Republicans against the beleaguered Truman. (By a coincidence, another prominent anticommunist also appeared before HUAC as a friendly witness in the fateful year of 1947. The president of the Screen Actors Guild, Ronald Reagan, a popular star of B-movies, was eagerly cooperative.) The national security state had begun to spawn its domestic counterpart, a "domestic intelligence state."[124]

Moreover, the emergence of the national security state occurred in the highly charged political atmosphere of the postwar years. This had the effect of intensifying the domestic reverberations of foreign policy crises. The national security ideology embodied in NSC-68 blurred the line between civilian and military, war and peace. Internationalist commitments regimented the American people and economy. American freedom became inseparably linked to the global anticommunist crusade. Yet traditional American values did not disappear: frugality, self-sufficiency, isolationism, dedication to balanced budgets, antimilitarism, and antistatism expressing itself in nostalgia for a weaker federal government. Anxious traditionalists warned of an impending garrison state. The contest was for nothing less than the soul of the American people. In contrast to the complacent mood of normalcy that followed the previous war, Americans in 1945 lived through a period of heightened tensions and challenges to the nation's self-image.[125]

Republicans smelled blood in the water. Regrouping after their electoral disappointments of 1948, they determined to exploit the Communism issue by using it for partisan advantage. At this critical juncture, the gods showered them with golden opportunities. First came Alger Hiss. Star witnesses Whittaker Chambers and

---

[123] Menace of Communism: Statement of J. Edgar Hoover . . . Before Committee on Un-American Activities . . . , S Doc No 26, 80th Cong, 1st sess 1 (1947).

[124] William W. Keller, *The Liberals and J. Edgar Hoover: Rise and Fall of a Domestic Intelligence State* (1989).

[125] Michael J. Hogan, *A Cross of Iron: Harry S. Truman and the Origins of the National Security State, 1945–1954* 1–22, 463–82 (1998).

Elizabeth Bentley ("the beautiful blonde spy queen," the nation's press glamorized that dowdy witness) appeared before HUAC to finger Hiss as a Communist who had been a member of a Red cell in the New Deal Agriculture Department and had passed documents to Communist contacts. Since Hiss had participated in the organization of the United Nations and had accompanied FDR to the Yalta conference, he was the ideal candidate for the decade-long Republican effort to identify treason in Democratic administrations. Hiss denied the charges, Chambers and Nixon staged the drama of the Pumpkin Papers, Hiss was indicted for perjury, and was eventually convicted. The Republicans seemingly had judicial confirmation in a full and open trial (two, actually, the first having resulted in a hung jury) of their New Deal treason charges.[126] The next year, Judith Coplon was arrested and convicted of espionage after having clearly passed classified material to a Soviet agent. (Her convictions were later reversed because the FBI obtained evidence against her by illegal wiretapping and had destroyed evidence.) In 1950, the British government announced the arrest of Klaus Fuchs on atomic-spying charges. His arrest unearthed a trail of evidence that soon led to Julius and Ethel Rosenberg.[127]

The anticommunists certainly had their work cut out for them in the postwar era. The years 1945 through 1950 were marked by an appalling progression of international crises and mounting tensions.[128] Just to enumerate them conveys the sense of imminent apocalypse that contemporary Americans felt, and that crested around the time of *Dennis:* the Yalta Conference (which anticommunists interpreted as FDR's perfidious abandonment of gallant Poland to a Stalinist fate); Truman's clumsy and unsuccessful attempts at nuclear blackmail; Stalin's 1946 prediction of an inevitable conflict between communism and capitalism, promptly followed by Winston Churchill's declaration of the Cold War in his Iron Curtain speech; Soviet pressures in Iran, Turkey, and Greece;

---

[126] See generally Allen Weinstein, *Perjury: The Hiss-Chambers Case* (1978). Hiss presented his side in *In the Court of Public Opinion* (1957) and in *Recollections of a Life* 149–60 (1988). Chambers offered his in *Witness* (1952). Chambers has been well served by Sam Tanenhaus, *Whittaker Chambers: A Biography* (1997).

[127] Lisle A. Rose presents a snapshot of the nation at this high-water mark of domestic anticommunism in *The Cold War Comes to Main Street: America in 1950* (1999).

[128] On the historiographic reconsideration of the Cold War in its international aspects, see John L. Gaddis, *We Now Know: Rethinking Cold War History* (1997).

the administration's responses, the Truman Doctrine and the Marshall Plan; Stalin's eradication of Polish, Czech, Hungarian, Romanian, and Balkan independence; the formation of NATO, followed by the counterresponse of the Warsaw Pact. What Americans called "the free world" was now ranked in hostile array confronting the superior land forces of the Red Army and the bloc nations. By 1948, American policy-makers concluded that the nation's strategic and economic interests were imperiled by Soviet expansionist impulses. The resulting sense of vulnerability drove them to protect security abroad and at home by any means possible. The crucial issue for them was maintaining a favorable balance of power on the Eurasian land mass, and on that question, the portents looked dismal.[129]

A recently propounded strategic theory helps us understand the emotional fervor that drove Cold War anticommunism. Norman Friedman has suggested that the half-century that followed World War II was not merely a string of relatively low-level crises amounting to little more than obstacles in the path of American foreign policy.[130] Rather, he proposes, the period of 1945 through 1990 was in reality a slow-motion hot war, conducted on the periphery of rival empires, sometimes by the principals themselves, sometimes by their proxies. It threatened to escalate to nuclear conflict at any time. That experience was, in reality, the World War III that contemporaries feared, fought at a subnuclear level. Seeing the period of the Cold War as actually a slow-paced, intermittent military engagement, a nightmare from which we could not disengage and that threatened our annihilation at any moment, helps us understand the fears and reactions of another time.

Nineteen forty-nine was a year of unprecedented challenges and disasters: the Berlin Blockade and Airlift; the Soviet atomic bomb; the fall of China. To alarmed Americans, Communist governments now controlled most of the Eurasian land mass, and western Europe seemed a besieged outpost of more-or-less democratic governments in danger of Red aggression from the East in league with

---

[129] Melvin Leffler, *The American Conception of National Security and the Beginnings of the Cold War, 1945–1948*, 89 Am Hist Rev 346 (1984).

[130] Norman Friedman, *The Fifty-Year War: Conflict and Strategy in the Cold War* (1999). Richard Crockatt advances a similar theme for the diplomatic history of the era: *The Fifty Years War: The United States and the Soviet Union in World Politics, 1941–1991* (1995).

subversion from within France and Italy, where the Communist Party functioned openly as a legitimate political party, something inconceivable to the American imagination. In the next year, the Cold War turned hot, with the North Korean invasion of the South. Nuclear armageddon seemed to loom.

The Truman administration responded to these challenges vigorously.[131] The foremost official exposition of its liberal anticommunist riposte was presented in a remarkable 1950 state paper known as NSC-68. This document constituted the fullest expression of the Truman administration's worldview, out of which its anticommunist policies flowed. Popular and judicial attitudes mirrored this official ideology. The "design" of Soviet Communist leaders, NSC-68 proclaimed, "calls for the complete subversion or forcible destruction of the machinery of government and structure of society in the countries of the non-Soviet world and their replacement by an apparatus and structure subservient to and controlled from the Kremlin."[132] To achieve this end, "the Kremlin seeks to bring the free world under its domination by the methods of the cold war. The preferred technique is to subvert by infiltration and intimidation [of] labor unions, civic enterprises, schools, churches, and all media for influencing opinion." The apocalyptic thinking of NSC-68 incubated a complementary approach toward domestic radicalism, which in turn quickly found legal expression.

A familiar pattern repeated itself in this period. International tensions made the situation of domestic radicals more parlous, as atavistic fears of foreign-menace-abetted-by domestic-betrayal reasserted themselves. Frustrated by being unable to eliminate the foreign threat, patriots had to content themselves with bashing the internal enemy. In part this was a strategy of kicking the master by kicking the dog; in part it was an attempt to control the domestic reverberations of alien and threatening forces. Homer Capehart, a Republican senator from Indiana, expressed patriots' dismay and alarm: "How much more are we going to have to take? Fuchs and Acheson and Hiss and hydrogen bombs threatening outside and

---

[131] Richard N. Freeland, *The Truman Doctrine and the Origins of McCarthyism: Foreign Policy, Domestic Politics, and Internal Security, 1946–1948* 115–50, 201–45 (1972).

[132] The document, which should be read in full by anyone seeking to understand the thinking of America's leadership in the Cold War, is reprinted in Ernest May, *American Cold War Strategy: Interpreting NSC-68* 23–83, quotation at 26–27 (1993).

New Dealism eating away the vitals of the nation. In the name of heaven, is this the best America can do?"[133]

D. "SOFT ON COMMUNISM"

Developments in domestic anticommunism moved in lockstep with the recurrent and escalating crises in U.S.-Soviet relations. First came the *Amerasia* incident in 1945, when the FBI discovered classified documents in the offices of that journal, which was critical of the Kuomintang and sympathetic to the Chinese Communists.[134] In the next year, the defection of the Soviet code clerk Igor Gouzenko enabled the Canadian government to expose a Soviet spy ring that had ties to sensitive American sources. One of the espionage agents disclosed in the affair was Alan Nunn May, a physicist who had ties to the Manhattan Project. But this early appearance of an "atomic spy" was premature: four years would elapse before atomic espionage came to dominate the anticommunist agenda.

In the public arena, Republicans and the Chamber of Commerce inflated these incidents, claiming they proved widespread Communist penetration of the most sensitive American interests. In response, behind the scenes Truman authorized the FBI to investigate possible espionage in the federal government. Attorney General Tom Clark urged an investigation into the loyalty of federal employees and resumed wiretapping of suspected subversives. The president concurred: he took the fateful step of approving a Temporary Commission on Employee Loyalty in 1946. Though Truman was only trying to preempt Republicans on the issue, his action entered the administration and the Democratic Party in a race that they could not win, an effort to be more anticommunist than the GOP.[135] This also introduced a separation-of-powers rivalry into presidential-congressional relations, with each branch trying to control the turf of antisubversive activity.

---

[133] Quoted in Joel Kovel, *Red-Hunting in the Promised Land: Anticommunism and the Making of America* 119 (1994).

[134] Harvey Klehr and Ronald Radosh, *The Amerasia Spy Case: Prelude to McCarthyism* (1996).

[135] On the Truman program, see Eleanor Bontecou, *The Federal Loyalty-Security Program* (1953), an exceptionally thorough and fair-minded appraisal, and Alan D. Harper, *The Politics of Loyalty: The White House and the Communist Issue, 1946–1952* (1969).

Truman's vigorous anticommunist approach to foreign and domestic matters proved unavailing in the face of the Republican partisan onslaught. Their simplistic charges that the Truman administration was "soft on communism," that it harbored Communists
within its ranks, that it was indifferent (or worse) to Soviet power,
that it abetted domestic subversion and treason, were opportunistic
ploys to repudiate the New Deal and its proposed Fair Deal successor. But such charges resonated with widespread popular dissat-
isfaction with Truman's conduct of foreign affairs and domestic
policy. They prodded Truman to ever more strenuous measures
creating the national-security and domestic-security state, though
that earned him no gratitude from his partisan foes or much credit
from the American people. Truman's innumerable enemies shifted
the focus of debate from the realities of Soviet power in Europe
to subversion within. They accounted for all the frustrations of
American policy not by external forces but by treason and espionage in the federal government. That Truman was hoisted by his
own anticommunist petard in this matter may have been poetic
justice, but it neither strengthened American security nor enhanced the freedoms that that security was to safeguard.[136]

The separation-of-powers struggle intensified when Congress
went Republican in 1946, forcing Truman to up the ante, which
he did by converting the temporary loyalty program to a permanent basis in 1947 in what one scholar calls the "domestic Truman
Doctrine."[137] The president might have been deterred by the
Lovett case of 1946, which seemed to proscribe firings on mere
suspicions of disloyalty. But *Lovett* was a bar to legislative firings,
and its bill-of-attainder rationale masked a separation-of-powers
conflict. When loyalty investigations were conducted entirely
within the executive branch, a different configuration of constitutional issues was presented, and *Lovett* became irrelevant.

Under Executive Order 9835,[138] federal employees could be fired
when "reasonable doubts exist for belief that the person involved
is disloyal to the United States." The chief criterion for disloyalty
was membership in any organization on the Attorney General's

---

[136] Athan Theoharis, *Seeds of Repression: Harry S. Truman and the Origins of McCarthyism* (1971).

[137] Freeland, *Truman Doctrine* at 113 (cited in note 131).

[138] 12 Fed Reg 1935, 1938.

List. (Executive Order 9835 was in fact the official origin of the Attorney General's List, and the linkage between the list and all subsequent employee-loyalty programs was crucial.[139]) An employee so fingered could request a hearing before a loyalty review board, and could present evidence and have the assistance of counsel. But the employee could not examine the evidence against him (principally material in FBI files), and could not force disclosure of the identity of those who provided the unfriendly evidence. The employee could appeal an adverse finding to a national Loyalty Review Board, whose review would be final.

Truman modified the original program in 1951 by Executive Order 10241,[140] which upgraded the loyalty standard to "reasonable doubt as to the loyalty of the person involved." Under this looser criterion, government now need only demonstrate a "reasonable doubt," whereas under the earlier program it had to affirmatively demonstrate some degree of disloyalty. Even this did not satisfy the Republicans, however, and when one of their own took over the White House, he promulgated Executive Order 10450,[141] which provided the loosest criterion imaginable: an employee could be fired if continued employment might not be "clearly consistent with the interests of national security." (Ex-President Truman was appalled at the Eisenhower extension, calling it "Ike's terrible gestapo ex. order.!"[142]) Going beyond the Attorney General's List, the Eisenhower order identified seven categories of disqualification: treason, sabotage, leaking of classified information, drug addiction, sexual immorality or "perversion," conspiracy, and refusal to testify before any government body on grounds of possible self-incrimination. Under this succession of executive orders, some federal employees had to undergo one or more subsequent loyalty reviews after having been cleared under an earlier one.

Under the Truman orders, nearly half a million federal employees were vetted, but the program produced only 560 who were

---

[139] Alan Harper provides a detailed review of the political/bureaucratic evolution of the program in *Politics of Loyalty* at 20–59 (cited in note 135).

[140] 16 Fed Reg 3690.

[141] 18 Fed Reg 2489, 2491.

[142] Truman handwritten note on ms. interview with Philip Perlman ca. 1954, in Post-Presidential Name File, Memoirs File, Interviews, Philip Perlman, box 642, Harry S. Truman Presidential Library, Independence, Mo.

fired or denied employment. (The looser Eisenhower program added another 315.) Critics insisted that the loyalty programs denied their victims procedural due process; that people were fired or put under suspicion for attitudes, innocent associations, and activities clearly lawful; that firing under the loyalty program was a bill of attainder condemned by *Lovett;* and that reliance on faceless informers was odious.[143] Truman's defenders relied on the right-privilege distinction, insisted that the administrative hearings provided adequate process, pointed out that no criminal consequences were involved, and that the FBI had to protect the confidentiality of its informants.[144]

A contemporary critic, Alan Barth, described the character of these loyalty hearings: "police were authorized to search out the private lives of law-abiding citizens, . . . a government official was authorized to proscribe lawful associations, . . . administrative tribunals were authorized to condemn individuals by star-chamber proceedings on the basis of anonymous testimony, for beliefs and associations entailing no criminal conduct."[145]

In 1947, Truman also authorized the Attorney General's List of Subversive Organizations, an offshoot of the loyalty program. When Clark publicized the list, membership in one of its organizations became a marker of disloyalty if not subversion. The listed organizations had no hearing or other opportunity to challenge their nomination. Clark conceded that the purpose of the list was "to isolate subversive movements in this country from effective interference with the body politic" and stanch their "propaganda activity of a subversive nature."[146] Truman, concerned about growing popular resistance to his 1947 international initiatives, used the list, as well as his subsequent red-baiting of Henry Wallace and the Progressive Party in the 1948 campaign, to rebuff Republican charges that his administration was "soft on communism" and that it was riddled with Communists bent on subversion and espionage,

---

[143] Clifford J. Durr offered a contemporary critique of the system in *The Loyalty Order's Challenge to the Constitution,* 16 U Chi L Rev 298 (1949).

[144] For a defense of the employee loyalty program by the man who was head of the Loyalty Review Board and the named respondent in the principal test case, *Bailey v Richardson,* 341 US 918 (1951), see Seth W. Richardson, *The Federal Employee Loyalty Program,* 51 Colum L Rev 546 (1951).

[145] Alan Barth, *The Loyalty of Free Men* 139 (1951).

[146] Quoted in Freeland, *Truman Doctrine* at 212 (cited in note 131).

to whose treasonous machinations he was supposedly indifferent. He also tried to use anticommunism to rally an indifferent or resistant American public to his foreign policies and the huge financial outlays they would entail. Containment, the Marshall Plan, nuclear weapons and their delivery systems would not come cheap, and the American taxpayer was going to foot the bill. As Senator Arthur Vandenburg had counseled in 1947, the president was going to have to "scare the hell out of" the American people to sell his foreign-policy initiatives. What cheaper way than by exposing and attacking the internal fifth column of Reds and fellow-travelers?

Congress and state legislatures trumped the president. They erected a formidable array of legislation to suppress Communists, the CPUSA and related organizations, fellow-travelers, and those leftists who were particularly vulnerable to legislative reprisal: government employees, aliens, and naturalized citizens. State and local activity, including statutes, ordinances, and legislative investigations, provided an inseparable part of the background of Cold War restrictions on speech and association.[147] In general, state legislation fell into the following often-overlapping or redundant categories: (1) sedition acts; (2) criminal syndicalism statutes; (3) criminal anarchy statutes; (4) red flag statutes; (5) laws concerning the loyalty of public employees (including oath requirements); (6) a miscellanea of statutes dealing with conspiracy, treason, labor relations, incitement, and so on.

E. THE FEDERAL LEGISLATIVE RESPONSE

The image of American Communists was bolstered at first somewhat inadvertently, then later deliberately, by a federal statutory complex that ratified its premises. The content and structure of this anticommunist legislation comprised the most important nets that enmeshed those people who were politically left-of-center. This array consisted of four major statutes:

---

[147] See generally Walter Gellhorn, ed, *The States and Subversion* (1952; rpt ed 1976); M. J. Heale, *McCarthy's Americans: Red Scare Politics in State and Nation, 1935–1965* (1998); Legislative Reference Service, comp, *Internal Security and Subversion: Principal State Laws and Cases* (1965) (report prepared for US Senate Committee on the Judiciary); and for a specialized state study, Philip Jenkins, *The Cold War at Home: The Red Scare in Pennsylvania, 1945–1960* (1999).

1. The Espionage Act of 1917,[148] as amended in 1940,[149] criminalized conventional espionage (the transfer of militarily sensitive information), incitement to disloyalty or insubordination, obstruction of military recruitment, and making false statements with an intent to interfere with military operations. Postal censorship provisions declared matter that advocated "treason, insurrection, or forcible resistance to any law of the Untied States" to be "nonmailable."

2. The Smith Act, technically the Alien Registration Act of 1940,[150] was the first federal peacetime sedition statute. Replicating earlier state criminal anarchy statutes at the federal level, it criminalized advocacy of overthrow of government by force and violence, organization of groups to advocate such overthrow, membership in such groups, and conspiracy to do any of the forbidden acts. It amended the Immigration Act of 1917 to bar and deport aliens holding the proscribed views. The Nationality Act of 1940[151] provided for denaturalization of naturalized citizens who had been Communists and prohibited naturalization of anyone who belonged to an organization advocating overthrow of the government by force and violence.

3. The anticommunist oath provision of the Taft-Hartley Act of 1947[152] was a narrowly-applicable statute, limited not merely to union officials but only to those who wished to call on the services of the NLRB. Nevertheless, within its constricted ambit, it was draconian.

4. The Internal Security Act of 1950, popularly known as the McCarran Act,[153] was the legislative centerpiece of legal anticommunism. It consisted of two titles:

---

[148] Act of June 15, 1917, ch 30, 40 Stat 217.

[149] Act of March 28, 1940, ch 72, 54 Stat 79.

[150] Act of June 28, 1940, ch 439, 54 Stat 670.

[151] Act of Oct 14, 1940, ch 876, § 305, 54 Stat 1137. Congress later supplemented this with the McCarran-Walter Act, more properly the Immigration and Nationality Act of 1952, ch 477, § 241, 66 Stat 163, which permitted deportation of aliens affiliated with the CPUSA and those who advocate "doctrines of world communism."

[152] Act of June 23, 1947, ch 120, § 9, 61 Stat 136.

[153] Act of Sept 23, 1950, ch 1024, 64 Stat 987. President Truman vetoed the measure on civil liberties grounds. Congress repassed it over his veto by margins of 57–10 in the Senate and 248–48 in the House.

Arthur E. Sutherland provided a contemporary review, defense, and partial critique of the measure in *Freedom and Internal Security*, 64 Harv L Rev 383 (1951). This article is valuable as a thoughtful liberal balancing of the need for containing risks to the nation's

Title I, known as the Subversive Activities Control Act, provided a lengthy legislative predicate in its Section 2 that constituted the authoritative statement of the threat to the United States posed by international and domestic Communism. This 1,200-word screed is too lengthy to quote *in toto* or even *in extenso* here, but it is essential to a full understanding of the mindset that produced the Cold War cases. Every member of the *Dennis* Court shared its assumptions and outlook; only Justices Black and Douglas were able to distance their beliefs about Communism from their understanding of the First Amendment. The other seven read the amendment to be confined by the McCarran Act weltanschauung.

Section 2 posited a "world Communist movement" that operated by "treachery, deceit, infiltration . . . , espionage, sabotage, [and] terrorism." It sought to impose a "totalitarian dictatorship" everywhere. The "direction and control" of the worldwide Communist movement and of all the fraternal parties (as they were then known), including the CPUSA, was in the hands of "the Communist dictatorship" of the USSR. All fraternal parties "are controlled, directed, and subject to the discipline of" Moscow. The CPUSA and its ilk "are in fact constituent elements of the worldwide Communist movement." The Party is "organized on a secret, conspiratorial basis" and operates extensively through "Communist fronts." "The Communist network in the United States is inspired and controlled in large part by foreign agents" who operate by "clever and ruthless espionage and sabotage tactics." Individual Party members are "rigidly and ruthlessly disciplined." Persons who participate in Communist activities "repudiate their allegiance to the United States."

Section 2 concluded with this apocalyptic vision:

> Awaiting and seeking to advance a moment when the United States may be so far extended by foreign engagements, so far divided in counsel, or so far in industrial or financial straits, that overthrow of the Government of the United States by force and violence may seem possible of achievement, it seeks converts far and wide by an extensive system of schooling and indoctrination.

Given that nightmare scenario, the statute declared the Commu-

---

national security against the need to protect First Amendment liberties. As such, it portrays the climate of opinion in which the Dennis cases were tried and argued.

nist movement to present "a clear and present danger to the security of the United States and to the existence of free American institutions." Under the doctrine of *Gitlow v United States*,[154] when a legislative body makes such a finding, no court may apply the clear-and-present-danger test, being precluded by the legislative declaration itself. (*Dennis*, however, ignored that doctrine, in part because it implicitly overruled *Gitlow*.)

Later sections of the statute prohibited conspiracies to do anything that "would substantially contribute" to the creation of a "totalitarian dictatorship" in the United States; required registration, lists of officers, sources of funding, and membership lists of "communist-action organizations" and "communist front organizations" (the latter exempted from the membership-list requirement); created a Subversive Activities Control Board having power to require such registration; prohibited members of Communist organizations from working for the federal government or in defense industries, and from applying for passports; required Communist organizations to label their publications as emanating from a "Communist organization"; barred from entry those aliens who were members of or "affiliated with" Communist parties or who advocated "totalitarianism"; similarly barred aliens engaged in "activities prejudicial to the public interest" or that would endanger the "welfare, safety or security" of the nation; and permitted denaturalization of persons joining such organizations.

Title II was captioned the "Emergency Detention Act of 1950."[155] It authorized the president to declare an "internal security emergency" in times of war, invasion, or insurrection. The Attorney General was then empowered to detain all people who there was "reasonable ground" to believe "probably will engage in, or conspire with others to engage in, acts of espionage or sabotage." The section authorized administrative hearings but not judicial trials, and did not permit confrontation of hostile witnesses. This shift to a reliance on administrative procedures avoided a model of Communist control based on traditional criminal sanc-

---

[154] 268 US 652 (1925).

[155] By an irony that now seems perverse, the emergency detention section was the offspring of Senate Democratic liberals like Paul Douglas, Herbert Lehman, and Hubert Humphrey. On their motives, see Keller, *The Liberals and J. Edgar Hoover* 28–72 (cited in note 124). Title II of the 1950 Act, the Emergency Detention provision, was repealed by Act of Sept 25, 1971, PL 92-128, § 2, 85 Stat 347.

tions, which came encumbered with the nuisance of respecting defendants' procedural rights. The new administrative model was superior because of its informality, its looser procedures, its greater range of ex post facto penalties, its speed and efficiency. In administrative proceedings, the government did not have to prove that the accused had committed an illegal act, or even that he might do so in the future. Rather, the burden of proof shifted to the individual to demonstrate his loyalty and fitness. The new administrative model endowed government with greater power to punish individuals for their political beliefs or associations because of the greater reach of the administrative state.[156]

The McCarran Act attempted to make it impossible for the targeted organizations to function, though they might nominally exist. It permitted drastic inroads into personal liberty based on nothing more than a surmise that the suspect individuals "probably" would commit certain acts, in effect authorizing imprisonment before an act was committed. Congress authorized and funded six detention centers for suspected subversives in Arizona, California (the Tule Lake site that had been used for Japanese internment), Florida, Oklahoma, and Pennsylvania. The centers were mothballed but available for service when needed.[157]

The FBI's Security Index, J. Edgar Hoover's list of persons suspected of entertaining radical notions, contemplated even looser restraints on the government's detention powers, permitting it to round up "dangerous" persons, prohibiting judicial review of their detention, and authorizing suspension of habeas corpus. By 1955, the Security Index had swollen to 26,000 persons. Forced to pare this list of potential detainees, the bureau created a Reserve Index of the discards who would be subject to "priority consideration for action," whatever that meant, if they "were in a position to influence others against the national interest" or contribute funds "to subversive elements due to their subversive associations and ideology."[158]

---

[156] Daniel L. Levin, *The Communist Party Cases and the Origins of the Due Process Revolution*, unpublished paper delivered at meeting of Southwestern Political Science Association, 1997.

[157] Richard Longaker, *Emergency Detention: The Generation Gap, 1950–1971*, 27 W Pol Q 395–408 (1974); William Hedgepeth, *America's Concentration Camps: The Rumors and the Realities*, Look 32 (May 28, 1968), pp 85–91.

[158] US Senate Select Committee to Study Governmental Operations with Respect to Intelligence Activities, *Hearings on the Federal Bureau of Investigation*, 94th Cong, 1st sess 659–

Supplementing this statutory apparatus was the vast institutional structure of anticommunism, the formidable network of federal, state, and municipal legislative and law enforcement bodies, plus private and volunteer anticommunist crusaders who flourished in the miasma of fear and suspicion that hung over the nation like an invisible smog in 1950.[159] HUAC conducted investigations into Communist influence in Hollywood's movie industry, which led to contempt citations and prison sentences for the "Hollywood Ten," a group of Communist or leftist screen writers and directors.[160] State and municipal governments conducted their own loyalty probes, firing suspected leftist public employees, and enforcing loyalty oaths. Outside government, private groups, battening on leaked FBI information, began publishing lists of groups and individuals they considered fronts or subversive. The most influential of these was *Red Channels*, a blacklist of the entertainment industry. The CIO, the ACLU, the NAACP, CORE, and the National Education Association all purged their ranks of Communist members.

Finally, the age was about to call forth its eponymous hero, who boldly seized the moment in his February 1950 Wheeling speech: "I have in my hand fifty-seven cases of individuals. . . ."[161]

VII. Judicial Perceptions of the Red Menace: Harvest

The antiradical crusade after World War II finally succeeded in imprinting the image of Communists on the public mind that it had been purveying for more than half a century. This image demonized Communists, endowing them with extraordinary powers and malignity, making them both covert and ubiquitous.[162] Servants of an alien, hostile power, Communists became The

---

62, at 659, 416–27; US Senate, *Final Report of the Select Committee . . . : Book II: Intelligence Activities and the Rights of Americans*, 94th Cong, 2d sess 55–56.

[159] Two studies detail the operations of this network and its interconnections: Schrecker, *Many Are the Crimes* (cited in note 45), and David Caute, *The Great Fear: The Anti-Communist Purge Under Truman and Eisenhower* (1978).

[160] Victor S. Navasky, *Naming Names* (1980).

[161] Joe McCarthy's Wheeling speech is reprinted in Ellen Schrecker, ed, *Age of McCarthyism* 211 (1994).

[162] Valuable studies of demonization include John Higham's classic *Strangers in the Land: Patterns of American Nativism, 1860–1925* (1955); Michael P. Rogin, *Ronald Reagan, The Movie and Other Episodes in Political Demonology* 68–75, 236–71 (1987); Kovel, *Red-Hunting in the Promised Land* (cited in note 133).

Other. Popular culture, in movies like *On the Waterfront*, *My Son John*, and *Invasion of the Body Snatchers*, effectively delivered this image to a mass audience.

In this transformation of ordinary human beings into something superhuman both in power and in malice, those in power presented themselves as victims, even as they were using that power to harass and imprison their enemies. Demonizing Reds made it legitimate to diminish their rights. In this sense, Communists were different from other fringe or radical groups like the Jehovah's Witnesses or the Klansmen of the 1940s. Annoying or obnoxious as such groups may have been to their contemporaries, they retained their human nature. But the manufactured image of the domestic Communist, cultivated and propagated by Hoover, the Catholic Church, the American Legion, and political opportunists, made of Communists something less than full humans, full citizens, fully rights-endowed. Even sophisticated jurists like Learned Hand, Felix Frankfurter, and Robert Jackson were captives of that image, anesthetizing their sensitivity to deprivation of rights. To resist the ideological and emotional pressures of the Cold War era would have required superhuman wisdom and equanimity. Whatever else might be said of the Justices of the *Dennis* Court, the majority of them did not have those qualities.

Four judges exemplify both the judicial mindset of the Cold War and its increasingly extremist bent. Three of them were individuals of extraordinary sophistication and repute, being among the most influential judges of the twentieth century. If they could succumb to what Justice Black in *Dennis* referred to as "present pressures, passions and fears,"[163] how much more susceptible must have been more ordinary judges to the blandishments of anticommunism. The attitudes of one of those ordinary judges, Irving Kaufman, are presented last.

In 1942, Felix Frankfurter expressed a qualified, restrained image of the Party and its members that marked the early phase of the judiciary's conversion to an anticommunist worldview. He dissented in *Schneiderman v United States*,[164] a case that overturned the denaturalization of an American Communist who had been born in Russia. Frankfurter would have permitted the United

---

[163] *Dennis v United States*, 341 US at 581 (Black dissenting).
[164] 320 US 118 (1943).

States to expel William Schneiderman solely for his activities in the Party. He wrote a disgruntled note to Justice Frank Murphy, author of the majority opinion, explaining why membership in the Party was qualitatively different from protected political activity:

> the Soviet Government, after the last war, expected a Bolshevist Revolution throughout the world. . . . after a little while, the Soviet Government fashioned the Comintern—the Third International—as the instrument of the political export business of the Soviet and the Communist Party. In each country there was a branch office of this international export business of the Soviet Government. And those who were running the branch business in the various countries were, in fact, political instruments of the Soviet regime. Of course, many, many people who became Communists in the United States were perfectly devoted and loyal Americans, but found in Communism a practical expression of their hopes for a better society. But the active managers of the Communist Party [like Schneiderman, who had run for governor of Minnesota on the Communist Party ticket in 1932] were knowing and eager instruments of their foreign masters, the Comintern, and the Comintern was, as I have said, the instrument of the Soviet Government.[165]

In conference debates on the same case, Chief Justice Harlan Fiske Stone, one of the most level-headed jurists of the era, joined Frankfurter in supporting revocation of Schneiderman's citizenship. From his reading of Communist scripture, Stone reached these conclusions about the Party and all its members:

> These documents are so contrary to Const. that one who advocates them wants lack of attachment to Constitution. . . . These documents do teach systematic conduct that is violent, illegal & includes breaking up the army. 3rd point is ultimate dictatorship of proletariat. There is no Bill of Rights, no minorities. The government, judiciary, executive & legislature is [sic] not to be allowed[,] only dictatorship of proletariat. . . . These people advocate dictatorship that excludes Constitution. *What they advocate is entire antithesis of constitutional government.*[166]

---

[165] Frankfurter to Murphy, [Dec 1942], captioned "No. 2. Schneiderman v United States," in box 26, Robert H. Jackson Papers, LCMss.

[166] Frank Murphy conference notes, conference of Dec 5, 1942, reel 127, Frank Murphy Papers, Bentley Historical Library, University of Michigan (hereafter "UMich"); italics in original.

Further conference debates only solidified his views. Four months later, he reaffirmed them. Communists

> wanted to do away with representative government, destroy private property, & set up a dictatorial form of government. . . . No Bill of Rights. Abolition of all existing form [*sic*] of government. . . . Within meaning of statute this naturalization was unlawfully acquired, for by his conduct he showed he was not attached to constitution of U.S.[167]

If a judge like Stone could entertain such an image of the Party, without even Frankfurter's concession to ambivalence, what could be expected of lesser judges who did not enjoy his access to information?

Frankfurter at least recognized the possibility of two different views of Party members. As the Cold War intensified, however, that ambivalence became less tenable, and the Party assumed the proportions of a superhuman menace. When the Communist Party leaders appealed their convictions to the U.S. Court of Appeals for the Second Circuit, Chief Judge Learned Hand affirmed in 1950, largely on the basis of his vision of the CPUSA:

> The American Communist Party . . . is a highly articulated, well contrived, far spread organization, numbering thousands of adherents, rigidly and ruthlessly disciplined, many of whom are infused with a passionate Utopian faith that is to redeem mankind. It has its Founder, its apostles, its sacred texts—perhaps even its martyrs. It seeks converts far and wide by an extensive system of schooling, demanding of all an inflexible doctrinal orthodoxy. The violent capture of all existing governments is one article of the creed of that faith, which abjures the possibility of success by lawful means.

Hand conceded that the American Party disclaimed violence, but dismissed such protestations because its real objectives were "covered by an innocent terminology, designed to prevent [their] disclosure."

Having affirmed the Party's true nature, Hand then went on to locate its relationship to the United States in a global context in 1948, when the *Dennis* indictments were first brought:

---

[167] Frank Murphy conference notes, conference of April 22, 1943(?), reel 125, Frank Murphy Papers, U Mich.

By far the most powerful of all the European nations had been a convert to Communism for over thirty years; its leaders were the most devoted and potent proponents of the faith; no such movement in Europe of East to West had arisen since Islam. Moreover in most of West Europe there were important political Communist factions, always agitating to increase their power; and the defendants were acting in close concert with the movement. [The United States] had become the object of invective upon invective; . . . we had been singled out as the chief enemy of the faith; we were the eventually doomed, but the still formidable, protagonist of that decadent system which it was to supplant. Any border fray, any diplomatic incident, any difference in construction of the modus vivendi—such as the Berlin blockade we have just mentioned—might prove a spark in the tinder-box, and lead to war. We do not understand how one could ask for a more probable danger, unless we must wait till the actual eve of hostilities.

From this anxious scenario, Hand drew the urgent lesson: "our democracy . . . must meet that faith and that creed on the merits, or it will perish; and we must not flinch at the challenge."[168] His language, more appropriate to HUAC or Hoover, suggests how deeply committed American judges were to the ideological construct of Communism.

Two years later, a judge no less sophisticated than Hand, but one with far more experience in the executive branch and in international affairs, Justice Robert H. Jackson, repeated Hand's worldview. In a draft of what eventually became the majority opinion in *Harisiades v Shaughnessy* (1952),[169] Jackson wrote in a passage later excised:

With Muscovite Marxism as a cohesive force, [the USSR] has achieved a Communist hegemony consisting of a number of client states and of strong revolutionary factions in other states. . . . That this combination of Communist governments seeks to undermine, weaken, embroil, and ultimately overthrow our Republic is something Congress could be forgiven for believing.

He then affirmed the anticommunist view of linkages between foreign enemy and domestic Other: "that this hostile confederation could coordinate formidable military forces with domestic vio-

---

[168] *United States v Dennis*, 183 F2d 201, 212, 213 (1950).

[169] 342 US 580 (1952).

lence caused by the Communist party, can hardly be doubted, whatever view one may take as to its chance of success."[170]

When U.S. District Court Judge Irving Kaufman sentenced Julius and Ethel Rosenberg to death for atomic espionage in 1951, he delivered himself of a homily on the evils of Communism. Addressing the couple as "the arch criminals in this nefarious scheme," he advised them that "this country is engaged in a life and death struggle with a completely different system. . . . never at any time in our history were we ever confronted to the same degree that we are today with such a challenge to our very existence. [The Rosenbergs] made a choice of devoting themselves to the Russian ideology of denial of God, denial of the sanctity of the individual, and aggression against free men everywhere instead of serving the cause of liberty and freedom."

Kaufman then uttered a *cri du coeur* that captures the judicial outlook of the Cold War and accounts for the distortions of law attained in that era:

> I consider your crime worse than murder. . . . In committing the act of murder, the criminal kills only his victim. . . . But in your case, I believe your conduct in putting into the hands of the Russians the A-bomb years before our best scientists predicted Russia would perfect the bomb has already caused, in my opinion, the Communist aggression in Korea, with the resultant casualties exceeding 50,000 and who knows but that millions more of innocent people may pay the price of your treason. Indeed, by your betrayal you undoubtedly have altered the course of history to the disadvantage of our country. . . . I feel that I must pass such sentence [of death] upon the principals in this diabolical conspiracy to destroy a God-fearing nation, which will demonstrate . . . that traffic in military secrets, whether promoted by slavish devotion to a foreign ideology or by a desire for monetary gains must cease.[171]

* * *

Beset by the same anxieties that gripped other Americans at the time, most of the Justices of the Vinson Court acknowledged anticommunism as a legitimate expression of democratic politics, validating not only the national security state erected by NSC-68 but the domestic security state as well, with the FBI and legislative

---

[170] Jackson draft opinion in Harisiades, box A15, Tom Clark Papers, Rare Books & Special Collections, Tarlton Law Library, University of Texas at Austin.

[171] *Rosenberg v United States*, 195 F2d 583, 605–06 n 29 (1952).

investigating committees functioning as the core of a state-security apparatus. From 1950 through 1953, the Court upheld the elaborate and drastic statutory net meant to ensnare Reds. It abetted the anticommunists' determination to suppress the CPUSA and harry its adherents.

Stampeded by the frightening sequence of international setbacks to American foreign policy from 1946 through 1950, facing a genuinely brutal and repressive totalitarian regime in a world increasingly bipolar and dangerous, most of the Justices gave free rein to executive, legislative, and popular determination to destroy the domestic arm of the international Communist movement.

In *Dennis* and other Communist cases between 1950 and 1956, the Supreme Court overcame the problem of facts not supporting the results it was determined to reach by accepting a generic "proof" of Communism's seditious nature. Disregarding all evidence of both the Party's and individual members' renunciation of violence, the Court substituted literary evidence from outdated classics of Marxism-Leninism, most written by Europeans of an earlier era, and then refused to consider whether the living people before them actually subscribed to those doctrines. It was enough to impute the thoughts of the Red fathers to their grandchildren. In doing so, the Court adopted the formalist approach of classical legal thought in order to ignore the realities of what was happening to individuals who posed no credible threat to the nation's safety. The judges substituted bloodless abstractions or legal fictions in place of the real live human beings before them, shutting their eyes to the real-world consequences of antiradical persecution.